DANTE LIGHTS THE WAY

Dante

LIGHTS THE WAY

This way he goes who goes in quest of peace.
Purgatorio XXIV:141

RUTH MARY FOX

THE BRUCE PUBLISHING COMPANY
MILWAUKEE

Library of Congress Catalog Card Number: 58–11657

© 1958 BY RUTH MARY FOX
MADE IN THE UNITED STATES OF AMERICA

To
MY DANTE STUDENTS OF THIRTY YEARS

CONTENTS

PART THREE

THE ROAD TO PEACE

A NOTE ON TRANSLATIONS AND RELATED MATTERS

henever a whole terza rima from the *Divine Comedy* is quoted, either the Longfellow or Huse text* is used unless some other translation is specified. Shorter quotations are my own or possibly short phrases that have stuck in my mind from one of the numerous translations I have used across the years. Quotations from the *Banquet* and the *Dedicatory Epistle to Can Grande Della Scala* are taken from the translation of Katharine Hillard; those from the *New Life* are from the text of Dante Gabriel Rossetti. For the *Monarchy*, the *De Vulgari Eloquentia*, the *Eclogues*, the *Quaestio de Aqua et Terra*, and most of the *Epistles*, I have used *Dante's Latin Works* in the Temple Classics, though for the *Monarchy* and *Epistles V, VI,* and *VII* I have occasionally used the translation of Mr. Donald Nicholl in the Noonday Press edition of 1954. For the lyrical poems of Dante, other than those of the *New Life* and the *Banquet*, I have quoted from the translations of Charles Lyell, published in London in 1845. All scriptural references are to the Douay version; all references to the *Summa Theologica*, to the *First Complete American Edition in Three Volumes Literally Translated by the Fathers of the English Dominican Province* (New York: Benziger Brothers, 1947).

All references to actual works of Dante appear in the text and are enclosed in parentheses, as are references to the *Summa Theologica*, Sacred Scripture, and an occasional other source on which Dante leans at a given point. The casual reader may skip them; the serious student will find them convenient for immediate reference. Supplementary information and specific references to authorities are put in notes at the end of each chapter.

Quotations from various sources divide the chapters into sections. They serve as headings: their function is to indicate structure, to interpret or forecast material, or to establish the mood. I have appended no bibliography. "Anyone," says Mr. Eliot, "can easily dis-

---

* Copyright, 1954, by H. R. Huse. Published by Rinehart & Company.

cover more Dante bibliography than anyone can use." I owe a great debt to many writers on Dante whom I have read across the years; where I have found any writer particularly helpful at any specific point, I have tried to indicate my indebtedness in the context or in the Notes at the end of the chapter.

ACKNOWLEDGMENTS

My debts are many and varied. Since a good place to begin anything is at the beginning, I wish to acknowledge first my deep debt of gratitude to Dr. Frank E. Baker, president of the Wisconsin State College in Milwaukee (now called the University of Wisconsin — Milwaukee) from 1923 to 1946, under whose stimulating leadership I taught during his whole term of office. Except for his interest in developing a broad educational program, I should not have had the joy of working so constructively with students from all divisions of the college and this book might never have been conceived.

To many of the Dominican Fathers of the American Province of Saint Albert the Great my debt is boundless, particularly to Very Reverend Timothy M. Sparks, O.P., S.T.M., Ph.D., one of the founders of The Thomist Association, and to all the other scholarly Dominican Fathers who have taught its courses in philosophy and theology for the past twenty years. My knowledge of the *Summa Theologica,* developed through these courses, has greatly deepened my appreciation and understanding of the *Divine Comedy.*

No words are adequate to express my appreciation of the help given me by the Reverend Dominic Hughes, O.P., S.T.D., of Saint Joseph's Province, who, when I was in Florence in 1954, was a professor of theology at the Angelicum, the international ferences both in Rome and in Florence. Since his return to this country I have had, too, the constant generosity of his help. Nor Dominican studium in Rome, and with whom I had many concan I ever thank adequately Signorina Emma Detti, dean of women and professor of Italian Literature at Institute Pius XII and of courses for foreigners at the University of Florence. A native Florentine, she gave me warmly the benefit of her intimate and scholarly knowledge of Florence, its environs, and its people. She knows Dante well and the Dante country and helped me to re-create its thirteenth-century atmosphere.

To several other friends I am indebted for special helps. I am grateful to the Very Reverend Francis Roth, O.S.A., provincial of the Augustinian Fathers of Our Lady of Consolation, New York City, for his suggestions after a critical reading of the historical and liturgical chapters; to the Reverend John Murphy, of Saint Francis Major Seminary, Milwaukee, specialist in Mariology, who helped me find the material which Dante borrows from Saint Bernard and Saint Bonaventure; to Corinna del Greco Loebner for her help from time to time as interpreter in my several conferences in Florence with Professor Arrigo Levasti, when the philosophical and scientific discussion went beyond the bounds of my Italian vocabulary. I am indebted especially to Professor John W. Nash, Ph.D., chairman of the Department of History of the University of Wisconsin — Milwaukee, with whom for many years I co-operated in the teaching of the Humanities. From the inception of this work he has given me the help of his scholarship and expert judgment. To him, to Dr. Rachel Salisbury, formerly director of freshmen English at Milwaukee; and to Dr. Virginia Burke of the Department of English I am indebted for their critical reading of the manuscript and for their continued encouragement.

In a number of indescribable ways I am deeply obligated to my lifelong friend and classmate of undergraduate days, Sister Mary Aquinas Devlin, O.P., Ph.D., professor of English at Rosary College. She was one of the ten freshmen introduced to Dante when I was, and from the beginning she has taken a deep personal interest in the progress of the writing. For her help in the revision of parts of the manuscript and her assistance in preparing it for the printer, I give her devoted thanks. To her colleague in the department, Sister Mary Jeremy, O.P., Ph.D., who with her read the manuscript and gave helpful suggestions, I am deeply grateful.

I am mindful, too, of the many friends and former students who have encouraged me to write, who in and out of the classroom have stimulated me to learn more about Dante and who have given me spiritual help of various kinds. In particular, I wish to thank Marcella O'Leary who has twice companioned me in part of my sojourn in Florence and who has assisted me in innumerable ways. I am indebted, too, to Sister Mary Eunice, O.P., first director of Institute Pius XII whose insistence in the summer of 1953 prodded me into asking for a leave of absence from the college that I might begin, and who died shortly after my return from Italy.

Last, but perhaps first in importance, I must acknowledge my debt to my friend of many years, the late Frank M. Bruce, of the Bruce Publishing Company, who ten years ago invited me to write this book.

PROLOGUE

> It is useful that many books, diverse in style not different
> in faith, should be produced by many, even concerning the
> same question, so that the matter itself may reach many,
> some in one way, others in another.
>
> — Saint Augustine, *On the Trinity*

f books on Dante and his *Divine Comedy* there will be
no end, for there will be no end of reading him and
of noting the challenge of the man and his book for
each succeeding generation. That men of each century
find a challenge, the vast Dante literature of the past six hundred
years bears abundant witness. That contemporary English readers
want to know him is attested by the fact that in 1954 alone there
were three new translations of the *Divine Comedy* published in
paperback editions. In America the publishers of paperbacks are
inclined to provide what the public wants. Dante's political work
De Monarchia (*Concerning Government*) has been issued twice
in English in the past five years. It is not generally known that this
political treatise and the Constitution of the United States of
America were the chief documents used in drawing up the constitution of the United Nations.[1] In 1957 his *De Vulgari Eloquentia*
(*Concerning Vernacular Eloquence*) also appeared in a paperback.

My introduction to Dante came when I was a college freshman.
A member of the music department just returned from a three-year
sojourn in Florence, eager to share her discovery of the great poet,
gathered a group of ten girls and read the *Divine Comedy* with them.
When one is introduced to the *Divine Comedy*, one of two things
happens: one catches fire or one does not. I caught fire. From that
time until the present, I have read Dante assiduously and have
talked with Dante scholars in America and Italy. The *Divine
Comedy* has become one of the books by which I live. Like Mr.

T. S. Eliot, I believe that it is one of the few books which one can only just grow up to at the end of life.

For many years I have lectured on Dante and taught the *Divine Comedy* to college students, to whom Dante speaks on a variety of levels. Art and music majors have been delighted with his use of the materials of their special interest: art students have found him as pregnant with suggestions as have artists from the time of Giotto, Fra Angelico, and Signorelli to twentieth-century Galezzi; music students intrigued by the way in which he weaves music through all the episodes of the last two thirds of the poem, enjoy singing the secular music he suggests in many cantos, as well as his thirteenth-century chant; science majors have studied with amazement his knowledge of the physics of light; and those interested in philosophy and psychology have been challenged by his Aristotelianism and his consistent point of view in ethics. It has not been unusual for the Dantists to meet behaviorists and pragmatists in debate. All of these young people are alike in their idealism, and the values set forth in the *Divine Comedy* help them in their search for security.

The reaction of the more mature students has been most exhilarating. Veterans who deluged the classes in 1945 and for almost a decade after — disillusioned with force, Machiavellian diplomacy, and science as saviors of the freedom of men — discussed thoughtfully Dante's presentation of the ways that lead to justice and love and peace, here and hereafter. These men — and women — are intensely aware of the derangement in our modern world and of what has seemed a futile search for integration. They are aware that again and again, on both the speculative and practical level, philosophers and statesmen and poets of their own time fail. Dante who is all of these, a philosopher, a statesman, and a poet, helps them to analyze the failure; he helps them, too, by giving them a positive approach to freedom, peace, and happiness.

It is, of course, not only students who have this awareness. The average citizen craves help in his search for peace, not only peace in the world but peace in his own soul. Possibly because of the interest in Dante's solution to these problems which somehow I have quickened in students, I have been asked to give hundreds of off-campus lectures on Dante to widely diversified groups, among them library groups and great books groups; Knights of Columbus and Serra Clubs; vocational school faculties met in convention and faculties interested in the humanities; high school literature classes, young business girls at the Y.W.C.A., and college alumni.

Year after year, class after class, audience after audience, when we have climbed the mountain of purgation and made our lightsome journey from star to star and reached the magnificent climax of Dante's poem — the vision of the unity of men in the unity of the Trinity — and have contemplated the meaning of the Incarnation, groups of whatever composition have sat motionless, stirred into deep silence by this glimpse of Infinite Truth and Infinite Love.

It is only natural that one who lives deeply with a man's thought should desire to learn as much as possible about his life and times. The *Divine Comedy*, it is true, is every man's book, but it is peculiarly Dante's book. That I might become better acquainted with Dante — after studying all his works and the literary, philosophical, and theological works which shaped his thought — I tried through travel to reconstruct his life and the material and spiritual world in which he lived and wrote: I visited places where scholars agree that he went and where tradition claims he went. Of me, as of the sons of Christian in *Pilgrim's Progress*, it may be said that I "covet to tread in his steps; yea that if I do see any print of his foot, it ministereth joy to me and I covet to tread in the same." During the summer of 1924, I spent several days in Florence; in 1950, I followed Dante in Florence and in other parts of Italy, notably Ravenna; in 1954, I set up my residence in Florence for a six-month period and "followed the imprints of the beloved feet" (*Inf.* XXIII:148) there and in other places in Italy associated closely or remotely with Dante and his *Commedia*.

Several chapters of the book were written in Villa Schifanoia on the Via Boccaccio just outside "the great town on the fair River Arno where Dante was born and grew up" (*Inf.* XXIII:94–95). In Dante's day, Schifanoia was a part of the countryside, a vast stretch probably forming one single estate. According to an old tradition the villa to which Boccaccio led his ten characters from Santa Maria Novella in Florence on that May day in 1348 when they decided to leave the plague-stricken town, is the Villa Palmieri, the fruitful acres of which are today separated from those of Villa Schifanoia by the Via Boccaccio. Bordering Schifanoia or contiguous to it was another section, Camerata, an old name still used.[2] The country house of Dante Alighieri was in Camerata. Schifanoia and Camerata lie halfway between Florence and Fiesole.

In all of my ventures I was greatly helped by the Italian people, to whose hearts Dante still speaks in their own tongue. In 1950, in an audience with His Holiness, Pope Pius XII, I said, "I am doing some research for a book on Dante and I ask your blessing on the book and on all my Dante students, past and future." He smiled upon me benignly and pronounced the blessing, not alone as the Holy Father who blesses his children but as a gifted Italian scholar who loves Dante. Everywhere in 1954 the simple sentence, "Sto scrivendo un libro su Dante," was fraught with magic. To one who was writing a book about Dante and knew what she wanted to see, the learned and the lowly of Italy were unfailingly courteous and generous, even at the cost of personal inconvenience. They opened their villas, their houses, their public offices, their libraries. They took out their keys and let me handle ancient documents or walk in ancient hallways where Dante had set his shoe. They gave generously of their time and their energy, of their learning and their culture.

Through their interest and courtesy, I held in my hands in the Archives of State the *Book of the Nail,* so called because of the daggerlike nail affixed to the cover, and read the notation made in 1302, our reckoning, of the decree of banishment of Dante and fourteen others. In the bright reading room of the Laurentian Library I poured over the early manuscripts: the unbelievably beautiful text of Dante's son Jacopo, the commentary of Imola, and the texts of Buti and the Ottimo and Boccaccio. Always when I was there, Signorina Theresa Lodi, the head librarian, came to see that I had everything I wanted.

One bright July morning Dr. Piero Bargellini, procurator of education and of all artistic and cultural works in Tuscany, whom I met that day quite by chance in the Palazzo Vecchio, offered spontaneously to take me through the most ancient parts of the old palace, explaining, as we went, the changes that had taken place through the six and a half centuries since its construction and showing me just what rooms were occupied by Dante Alighieri and the Priors of 1300, who were the first to use them.

Paolo, a cab driver much in demand at Schifanoia, in whose car I made most of my excursions in the environs of Florence, was born at Poppi and knew every inch of the Casentino Valley. His devoted interest took me many places there that I might otherwise have missed. At Dante's tomb at Ravenna in 1950 an old guide, when pressed with definite questions, opened his treasure trove; and then when we were leaving, called after us and hobbled toward us carrying a little branch from a large bush overhanging the tomb saying, "For the lady that loves Dante."

My sojourn in Italy did not greatly increase my information about either Dante or the *Divine Comedy;* scholars of many decades had sifted the facts and set them down and I had read them. It did, however, aid me greatly in interpreting the facts, in evaluating them: many which had not seemed important became so; all became more vital. Cities, countrysides, buildings, commented on in the *Divine Comedy,* glowed in a new light; many incidents sharpened in a now vivid setting; historical personages came to life in their own environment. Properties of the dramatic action, for example, the gates, gained the significance which to an Italian they must always have had — massive gates set in massive walls which close in and close out whole segments of the world, gates behind which lie mystery. A study of the art with which Dante was familiar: the sculpture, the stained glass, the frescoes, the illuminated manuscripts helped me to visualize in their majesty and vigor the angels, the Madonnas, the saints, and the demons which throng the cantos. But most rewarding of all was the opportunity to exchange ideas with such Dante scholars as Professor Arrigo Levasti and Professor P. Rebora.

This book is not an exegesis of the text of the *Divine Comedy.* It is not an attempt to deal with Dante's poem primarily as poetry, though many of his poetic images will be discussed. It is planned as a general handbook for those who are not familiar with Dante as a man or with his times or with his mental climate. It is an effort to clear away a few of the difficulties — philosophical, theological, and liturgical — which have interposed for many readers between his time and ours. Though the *Divine Comedy* is timeless, it is rooted in the deep religious faith of thirteenth-century Catholicism, and I thought it might be helpful to draw together into chapters Dante's treatment of major Catholic doctrines and liturgical practices which are of the very warp and woof of his thought. It attempts, too, to show how apropos Dante's program is for us today.

The book follows Dante's own triad structure. The first section, comprising four chapters, aims to acquaint the uninitiated reader with necessary historical, personal, and structural background: Chapter I with some notion of what Dante's thirteenth-century world was like; Chapter II with some of the major facts of his life; Chapter III with the figure of Beatrice, for whom the poem was written; and Chapter IV with a schematic view of the thought and structure of the *Divine Comedy* as a whole and of its major parts.

As Mr. T. S. Eliot points out in his admirable essay on Dante, it is not at all essential to an appreciation of Dante that one assent to his religious beliefs, but it is essential that one understand them. The second section, therefore, attempts to familiarize the contemporary reader with the beliefs to which Dante adhered with simplicity and firmness but which in part are foreign to the belief of many today. The chapters of this section deal with the angels and devils in their relation to God and man, and with the Virgin Mary and the Deity. The first chapter endeavors to make clear where Dante got his theological concepts of angels, discusses the functions of angels in the *Divine Comedy*, and points out that there is a parallel in Sacred Scripture for every function which an angel, fallen or faithful, performs there. The second chapter clarifies the position of the Virgin Mary in the teaching of the Church and therefore in Dante and presents relevant data from the theologians upon whom he leans in his Mariology. The third and fourth chapters deal with the Deity: the third with the unity and trinity of God; the fourth with the Incarnation and Redemption. The third aims to make clear that the attributes of God and the theology of the Trinity as discussed by Saint Thomas are a significant part of Dante's thought in the *Commedia* and form the background of some of his most splendid images; the fourth, that the theology of the Incarnation and Redemption is at the very heart of the poem and supplies the blood for all its arteries.

The chapters of the third section present Dante's analysis of the means by which man can attain that "in-Godding" made possible by the Incarnation and Redemption and enjoy here and hereafter that peace which is man's goal: first, the setting of love in order by discipline and purgation and penance; second, liturgical prayer in which men raise, as it were, one voice to God. It was my original intent to combine the chapters which deal with the Deity and add here a third chapter on the seven Sacraments, all but one of which are explicit or implicit in the *Commedia*; but the book got out of bounds and I included some discussion of the Sacraments in the two chapters of this third section, particularly the first. The chapters number ten, Dante's symbol of unity.

NOTES

1. In a lecture which he gave on May 24, 1949, at the Milwaukee State Teachers College, Dr. G. A. Borgese, Professor of Humanities at the University of Chicago, made this statement: "The two basic sources I used in the drafting of *The Preliminary Draft of a World Constitution* were the American Constitution and Dante's political treatise, *De Monarchia*." At the time Professor Borgese was secretary of the Committee to Frame a World Constitution; Robert M. Hutchins was chairman.

2. Emma Detti, *Villa Schifanoia from the Time of Decameron to Institute Pius XII* (Firenze: Sansoni, 1953).

PART ONE

An Introduction to Dante
and the Divine Comedy

CHAPTER I

THE TIMES AND THE BOOK

The twelfth and thirteenth centuries were a period
when men were at their strongest; never before
nor since have they shown equal energy in such
varied directions or such intelligence in the direction of their energy.

— Henry Adams
Mont-Saint Michel and Chartres

he life of Dante Alighieri began in 1265 in Florence,
"the great town on the fair river Arno" (*Inf.* XXIII:
94–95), that ardent, turbulent, creative city which he
loved with all the devotion of his passionate nature, but
which was to prove a harsh mother to him who was destined to be
her greatest son. Dante wrote his *Divine Comedy* in exile, and
Florence honored neither him nor it until more than a generation
after his death in Ravenna in 1321.

The century before Dante's birth and the period covered by his
life was one of restlessness and amazing activity in every area of
human endeavor. It was an age of striking contrasts, of titanic leaders, of extraordinary movement. It was the age of Frederick II and
his cousin Saint Thomas Aquinas, both intellectual giants — one
a skeptic and absolutist always at variance with the Church, and
though greatly admired by Dante for some of his achievements,
damned by him as a heretic (*Inf.* X:119); the other perhaps the
greater fighter — "a cool, scientific, deadly warrior," whose *Summa
Theologica* Dante follows as the definitive work in dogmatic theology.

3

It was the age of Saint Francis and Saint Dominic and their begging friars, and of unworthy churchmen who amassed untold wealth in ill-gotten benefices. It was the age when Hohenstaufen armies struggled over the Alps to Italy and from Italy back again to Germany to establish and maintain an imperial domain, and when a new doctrine of national sovereignty was sweeping Europe. It was the age of troubadours and minstrels on their way from castle to castle, of knights clad in mail spurring to tournaments, of robber barons and robber counts and their maurading armies, of thousands of the dispossessed seeking refuge, of caravans of merchants moving by land and by sea.

The exuberance of the age carried over into every field of human endeavor. The universities were full of intellectual vitality and disputation, fruitful in sifting truth. In this age schoolmen dared to apply the rationalism of Aristotle to the elucidation of articles of faith; in this age pagan philosophy and Christian theology came to terms, and eminent theologians established the principle that there is no quarrel between faith and reason. In this age intellectual giants fought with razorlike logic to subdue their adversaries before a university public numbering thousands. In this age every art flourished to an astounding degree. We have from this period a vast, vigorous, anonymous literature: the *Nibelungenlied, Aucassin and Nicolette, Reynard the Fox,* the *Fioretti* — to give only a sampling.

Religious exuberance was at its height, too. Ascetics, hermits, flagellants, and missionaries flourished. In all areas of society, there were holy men and women, who though brilliantly engaged in temporal affairs had their eyes fixed on eternal verities: Bonaventure and Thomas in their university classrooms; Louis of France and Elizabeth of Hungary in their courts; James of Genoa and Albertus Magnus in their bishoprics; to say nothing of the holy ones like Zita of Lucca in her kitchen; and Mechtilde of Magdeburg and Clare of Assisi, who lived lives of prayer and penance in the cloisters which flowered in all the countries of Europe. The religion of Dante's time at its best was robust, ready to do all, ready to give all.

It is true that the vigorous questing life of the era was filled with discords, political intrigues, crimes, and cruelties — under some of which Dante himself suffered. Nevertheless, as all of its works testify, it was an age more strongly united than any subsequent age has been. Though politics tore it asunder, faith made it one. All men worshiped at the same altar and held the same code of morals. Though ecclesiastics and princes might be struggling for power, everyone knew in his inmost soul that he should be struggling for sanctity; and hundreds of worldly men and women at the end of their lives fled to monasteries and convents to do penance for the sins of their earlier years.

This tumultuous age of diversity yet essential unity is the age which Dante portrays in the *Divine Comedy*. He presents it with such distinction that the poem has in a superlative degree the four qualities which characterize a classic: the penetrating treatment of universal problems, a vivid picture of a people and a period, the stamp of a distinctive personality, and form and words of enduring beauty. There are no matters of human concern, intellectual, religious, moral, political, or personal, with which the *Commedia* does not deal; it gives so complete a picture of the people, the institutions, the learning and culture — in fact, of the whole life of the Middle Ages — that Taylor in his two-volume study *The Medieval Mind* calls Dante the full-grown medieval man and entitles his final chapter "The Medieval Synthesis: Dante"; it shows these through the lens of a personality distinguished by width and depth of emotional range, vehement loves and hates, and extraordinary symbolic imagination; it presents all these in form and words of singular beauty. For what makes the *Divine Comedy* unique is Dante's capacity to put into language which is peculiarly his own his reasoned assimilation of all that he had read and thought, all that he had experienced in his boundless contacts with men of all classes and conditions, all his minute observations of everything in nature and art. The fusion of these four qualities: the universal, the historical, the personal, the aesthetic into a perfect unity marks Dante as a master.

No period in the world's history has been so characterized by intellectuality as the scholastic period. Its subtleties have been a

*byword, its brilliant distinctions and rigid
logic rarely if ever equalled; and yet these
intellectuals of the intellectuals come out
at the point of declaring that the sum and
essence and ultimate goal of all science is
the love of God and man.*

— Ernest Cushing Richardson
Materials for a Life of Jacopo da Varagine

To understand Dante and the *Divine Comedy* it is necessary to
bring into focus certain aspects of the intellectual, artistic, and political life of the thirteenth century. The intellectual activity of the
period is astounding. From the time of Saint Benedict there had
been fine monastic schools, and from the time of Charlemagne
cathedral schools of distinction; in the twelfth century grammar
schools flourished; and many of the great universities — among them
Paris, Oxford, and Bologna — had been founded. But in the thirteenth
century there was a tremendous upsurge of education among laymen.
Kings and emperors established centers of learning throughout their
domains; in Italy particularly, the communes inaugurated and supported universities. Laymen and ecclesiastics traveled eagerly all
over Europe in quest of knowledge; in university towns so large
was this fluid population that there was a special body of legislation
for it. The mobility, not only of men but of ideas, is one of the
amazing things about education in the Middle Ages.

Neither professors nor students were limited by racial or national
boundaries or hampered by language difficulties. The language of
all universities was Latin; the scheme of instruction and the requirements in subject matter were essentially the same. Therefore a man
was at home in whatever lecture room he found himself. Particular
universities eventually became distinguished for learning in special
fields: for example, Paris for theology and philosophy; Salerno and
Padua for medicine; Bologna for law. This does not mean that a
general education was not to be had in every school. Every uni-

versity conferred the B.A. and M.A. degrees. It does mean that men studying a profession, persons often of wealth and position — perhaps even holding important ecclesiastical or civil office — went to the university where the greatest teachers were to be found.[1]

Both Boccaccio and Villani claim that during his exile Dante studied at the University of Paris, though neither says at what time;[2] Boccaccio claims also that he held a degree from Bologna. Certainly he has thorough knowledge of philosophy and theology and law. Though there is no certitude of his having received a university degree, there is no question of his knowing well what the oral examinations at the universities were like. In the *Paradiso*, Cantos XXIV, XXV, XXVI, he is given such an examination in the theological virtues by an examining board made up of Saints Peter, James, and John. While Beatrice is presenting him to Saint Peter, the first examiner, Dante says (*Par.* XXIV:46–52):

> As baccalaureate arms himself, and speaks not
> Until the master doth propose the question,
> To argue it, and not to terminate it,

> So did I arm myself with every reason,
> While she was speaking, that I might be ready
> For such a questioner and such profession.

Dante's answers are given in true scholastic fashion from reason, and from truth revealed in Sacred Scripture.[3]

There are many aspects of university life which one might study in relation to Dante but none more pertinent than that which centers about Aristotle and his great champion, Saint Thomas Aquinas: for Dante is an Aristotelian and a Thomist. To understand what that meant in the thirteenth and early fourteenth centuries is to get into the thick of an important controversy which merits brief review here. To gain the proper perspective, however, one needs to step back for a moment into the twelfth century.

In the early days of the universities, the contributions of the Arabs were extremely important. In the second quarter of the twelfth century, Raymond, first Archbishop of Toledo, which in 1085 had been reconquered from the Moslems by Alfonso VI of Castile, had set up a school of translators from Mohammedan writers, which spread Latin versions of the work of Arabian scholars through Western Christendom.[4] Through Toledo and other doors as well, Arabian works in various fields entered such academic centers as Chartres and Paris, enormously widening the intellectual horizons of the schools. Into them came mathematical and medical treatises, writings on astronomy and astrology (the *Elementa Astronomica* of Alfraganas was well known to Dante);[5] and, most important of all, the works of Aristotle, which in the thirteenth century changed the whole temper of the intellectual life.

The coming of Aristotle into the University of Paris created a furor difficult to understand in an age like ours when most teachers hold whatever opinion they will and teach it. That was an age when men who had sharpened their instruments of thought with the study of dialectic challenged every principle. Saint Albert the Great (known in the Middle Ages as Albertus Magnus), who with the Franciscan Alexander of Hales brought many of the works of Aristotle into the university, studied assiduously the treatises of the Greek master on ethics, natural science, physics, and metaphysics, pointed out what was acceptable and what was opposed to the Christian faith, commented on the works and supplemented them, introducing Aristotle to his students, among whom was the brilliant youth from Aquino. By the middle of the century all the important works had been translated into Latin from the Arabic; however, in 1263 Saint Thomas, recognizing the inadequacies of these translations, directed the work of a group of Dominican scholars who translated Aristotle directly from the Greek.[6] It was upon these translations that he based his *Commentaries*. All of these works of Aristotle, and probably the commentaries of both Albert and Aquinas, seem to have been familiar to Dante, who quotes from them frequently and who (*Inf.* IV:131) calls Aristotle "the master of those who know."

In the same group in Limbo in which he places Aristotle, he places the two Arabian philosophers through whom Aristotle first came into the schools of the Middle Ages, Avicenna (*Inf.* IV:143) and Averroës (144), giving special honor to the latter for his "great commentary." The quarrels between the friars and the seculars, clergy and laymen at the University of Paris, where the contention was hottest, centered to a considerable extent about the use and abuse of the philosophy of Aristotle as it appeared in the works of these two Arab scholars, who themselves had translated the Stagirite from a Syriac translation of the original Greek. Because of the Oriental influences which had filtered into the work of Aristotle and because he was a pagan and his translators Moslems, the old-school theologians at Paris looked askance at him and were inclined to label as heretics those who applied Aristotelian methods to theological problems. Chief among the theologians who so used Aristotle was Saint Thomas Aquinas.

Saint Thomas and Saint Albert, both of whom held chairs of theology at Paris, though not at the same time, applied Aristotelian methods and principles to revealed doctrine, thereby giving the world the scholastic system which embodies the reconciliation of reason and orthodox faith. Saint Thomas taught that *there can be no quarrel between philosophy and theology, that truth is one.* To insistence on this idea he dedicated his vast talent, his extraordinary intellectual powers. His conviction brought him back to Paris in 1268 to re-enter the intellectual arena there, after more than a decade spent in teaching, preaching, and writing, chiefly in Naples and Rome. Some say that he was sent back to Paris with the definite mission of refuting the errors in Averroism.

The controversy on Aristotle split the university two ways. In the Faculty of Theology there were those Masters who still held that mixing reason and faith was dangerous business. Generally speaking, the Franciscans were in this camp, the combined groups calling themselves the Augustinians. There was also friction between the Faculty of Arts and the Faculty of Theology. Some of the Masters in the school of arts saw no difficulty in presenting as philosophically true what would not square with divine revelation and must, therefore, be theologically false. Most of these masters were younger men, some of them nonclerics, whose interest lay in philosophy. In both the *New Life* and the *Divine Comedy,* as we shall see in following chapters, Dante tackles the problem of so-called "double truth." This he does after the manner of a literary artist and moral theologian, holding staunchly to the point of view held by Saint Thomas. These young Masters held another point of view, one taken by many intellectuals today, that the business of the professor is merely to clarify the text without pointing out where it deviates from truth, leaving students to come to their own conclusions. With neither of these groups was Thomas in agreement. To him truth was one: what was true in philosophy could not be false in theology; the chief business of the teacher was to lead his students in the way of truth, which to his mind included commenting on a text to show what was not in accord with Christian teaching.

Among the Masters in the Faculty of Arts was one very gifted, a priest, Siger of Brabant, whom Saint Thomas challenged to public debate but who did not appear to meet the challenge. He was, however, worsted as a result of Thomas' treatise *De Unitate Intellectus Contra Averroistas,* and in 1270 a decree was issued which forbade any Master of Arts to dispute any theological question. In the year 1277 Siger's *Quaestiones in Libros Aristotelis De Anima* was condemned. In these Questions, says Etienne Gilson in *Dante the Philosopher,*[1] Siger professes to discuss and solve the problems with which he deals from the standpoint of reason alone. M. Gilson points out that since Pierre Mandonnet published his two-volume work, *Siger of Brabant,* the figure emerges clearly for modern readers, showing that when the conclusions to which Siger is led by the philosophy of Aristotle contradict the teaching of faith, Siger contents himself with propounding them *qua* the conclusions of philosophy, but maintains at the same time that the teachings of faith are the true ones. However, M. Gilson points out, philosophers or theologians whose rational conclusions were in harmony with the teachings of faith could not but disapprove of his attitude, Saint Thomas among them.

Strangely enough the same old-school theologians who condemned Siger's *De Anima* in 1277, in that same year, three years after the death of Saint Thomas, spearheaded an attack on Saint Thomas also and the Aristotelian doctrine he taught, charging him with heresy. These men, who had never liked the Dominicans, whom they considered as interlopers at the university, were backed by Stephen Tempier, a former chancellor, now bishop of Paris. In the minds of the diehard theologians and of Stephen Tempier himself, Siger and Thomas were linked, for both had looked upon philosophy as a matter of reason, and theology as a matter of faith. Moreover, Aristotle was for both the philosopher *par excellence.* To the defense of Thomas rose Albert, at that time bishop of Cologne, who came on foot to Paris, as was his wont, to take up the cudgels for his former student.

For the moment, the cause of Aristotle seemed lost. The Dominicans in general chapter at Milan in 1278 adopted a resolution to defend the works of Thomas; the Franciscans in general chapter in 1282 placed his *Summa* on their list of forbidden books. However, in 1323 all controversy was silenced, for Pope John XXII raised Thomas Aquinas to the altars, declaring that he alone had illumined the Church more than all the other doctors together. The cause of Aristotle was secure in Catholic thought.

Without an understanding of this heated controversy concerning Aristotle and his Arabian commentators, one misses the drama in the Heaven of the Sun (*Par.* X–XIV), where Dante represents the reconciliation and exchange between the two great traditions in theology, the dogmatic and the mystical, and brings into action several figures prominent in the contention. Here Saint Thomas leads one circle, that of the Dominicans; and Saint Bonaventure the other, that of the Franciscans, each eulogizing the founder of the other order. Dante's selection of leaders is, on many counts, a good one; for beyond the reason that each was the leading theologian of his order, there is the additional reason that they testify to the possibility of a fast friendship among those who hold opposing points of view, for the friendship of Thomas and Bonaventure was well known. All of truth is not in the possession of any one man. As a matter of fact in several sections of the *Divine Comedy* Dante follows Saint Bonaventure rather than Saint Thomas.

But even more dramatic is the position of Saint Thomas in the circle which he leads, his right hand clasping that of Saint Albert who introduced him to the study of Aristotle, his left in that of Siger of Brabant whom he had worsted in 1270. No situation in the *Divine Comedy* has aroused more controversy. Whole volumes have been written about it. Among the solutions proposed, that of M. Gilson seems to have most merit because it is in keeping with Dante's use of symbolic characters throughout the *Paradiso* and is so completely in harmony with his thought. Some time between

1270 and 1277, possibly in 1275, Siger had abjured Averroism and cannot be considered a heretic; a consideration which is important, though recent scholarship would claim that he had never taught the so-called "double-truth" of the Averroists. In the *Paradiso* (X:133–138) Dante says that Siger had taught or *"syllogized truths* which brought him hatred."* He taught *truths based on reasoning,* that is, *philosophical truth.* M. Gilson argues that Siger in the circle of the learned in the Heaven of the Sun represents philosophy and philosophic truth, that he here stands in apposition to Saint Thomas, whom Dante uses to represent theology at its best, but who maintained a clear distinction between philosophy and theology. Dante, who was both a philosopher and a theologian, was profoundly interested in the distinction.

That Dante had the opportunity as an adult to study the works of Saint Thomas under Fra Remigio Girolami (1235–1319), who had been at the University of Paris during the stirring years when Saint Thomas expounded there the works of Aristotle, is attested by many Florentine scholars. This former student of Saint Thomas was a man of deep learning and versatile talent, who came to Florence from Paris to lecture on theology some time before 1290 and who was prior at Santa Maria Novella in 1294 and again in 1313. At the studium there, probably during his first priorship, a group of laymen — among them Dante Alighieri — gathered to hear him expound what he had learned from the lips of the great Aquinas.[8]

That Dante should have been drawn to Saint Thomas is not strange. The two men have the same incisiveness of mind, the same fearless realism in facing men and issues and — what may seem paradoxical to some — the same tendency toward mysticism. What is interesting, if one follows the dates carefully, is that Dante should have adhered to Saint Thomas when in some intellectual circles he was under a cloud. Saint Thomas died in 1274; the Franciscans made the *Summa* a forbidden book in 1282. Dante is said to have studied at the Franciscan studium at Santa Croce in Florence before 1290, and his work reveals considerable Franciscan influence.[9] But when later he was brought face to face with Aristotle and Saint Thomas, they became his intellectual masters. He finished the *Divine Comedy* shortly before his death in 1321. In it he had canonized

Saint Thomas before Pope John XXII spoke in 1323.[10]

Books have been written about the vigorous intellectual life at the universities in areas other than philosophy and theology as well as about the contributions in these fields. Sometimes the reader of the twentieth century is surprised to find how much was being done, for instance, in the field of science by men like Saint Albert and his gifted Franciscan pupil, Roger Bacon. Saint Albert laid down the principle that *experiment is the only safe guide in investigation.* Using experiment as a basis he produced writings in the field of chemistry, botany, physical geography, astronomy, and physics. He has been overshadowed in this field, however, by Roger Bacon, whose scientific experiments are for his time most extraordinary. His work in optics, evidently stimulated by Saint Albert who knew much about the physics of light and the refraction of the solar ray, probably came into the possession of Dante, whose knowledge of light throughout the *Divine Comedy* amazes every contemporary physics student.[11]

Though neither Saint Dominic nor Saint Francis had founded his order for the ministry of teaching, the friars became in the thirteenth century the university professors *par excellence.* Among the Franciscans are Alexander of Hales, Saint Bonaventure, whose influence on Dante is considerable (see Chapter VI), and Duns Scotus. Together, Dominicans and Franciscans were responsible for the greater part of the intellectual productivity of the century, and it is their achievement in this and every other area of the life of the period which makes Dante represent them in the Earthly Paradise as the two wheels by which the chariot of the Church moves forward (*Purg.* XXIX:107). He develops the matter further in *Paradiso* XII.

Art is the grandchild of God.
— *Inferno* XI:105

If the thirteenth century was one of great intellectual endeavor, it also evidenced a ferment of endeavor in the arts. In Sicily, Monreale and the Palatine chapel with their fusion of the Byzantine, Saracenic, and Norman cultures — the mosaics of which were wrought with such skill that they are still perfect — were already built by the Normans, as was Saint Michael by the Sea in northernmost France. But the thirteenth is the century when the best of the mosaics are set in Saint Mark's in Venice, when the matchless *graffiti* are engraved in the pavement of the cathedral in Siena, when Amiens and Cologne fling out their flying buttresses and rear their great towers, when the exquisite beauty of La Sainte Chapelle comes into being, and when the austere Bargello and Palazzo della Signoria rise in Florence.

All the world today bows before the engineering skill of the builders of these architectural marvels. It bows, too, before the skill of the legions of craftsmen of all sorts who worked in stone, metal, wood, and glass to give beauty of form and color to enhance the architecture. The perfection of the craftsmanship indicates highly specialized training, education of a vocational kind. These skilled workmen received their training through the guilds, which were trade unions of a sort with their own rigid requirements for membership and their own international affiliations. The mobility of those being trained in the arts and crafts paralleled that of university students, and the examination which gave evidence of accomplishment was quite as exacting. A study of the achievements of the guildsmen gives some idea of the intellectual capacity of the thirteenth-century workman. One understands better why Dante could write his poem in the vernacular so that the "people" might come to know it.[12]

The art of Dante and that of his contemporaries have much in common. The *Divine Comedy* is often likened to a cathedral: the most familiar comparison is perhaps Longfellow's sonnet sequence entitled *La Divina Commedia*. Like the cathedrals the poem is an architectural marvel, built on the basic concept of *three in one* as a profession of belief in the Blessed Trinity, all its multitudinous details brought into an amazing harmony. Like the cathedrals it is full of symbols, often the same symbols that appear in the sculptured portals, the stained-glass windows and the fresco-covered walls.[13] Like the cathedrals it is filled with figures of men and beasts, each in his own place; like the cathedrals it has its Madonnas and its clouds of angelic witnesses. And as everything in the cathedral moves toward the altar with its unquenched lights where in the Mass the redemptive act is renewed, so in the *Divine Comedy* everything moves to that vision of the Incarnation, the Second Person of the Trinity become man, the circle in Dante's final vision in which the human figure is conformed to the divine circle — Dante's attempt to present pictorially the central doctrine of the Christian Faith. The *Divine Comedy* is not only the summation of the learning of the thirteenth century; it is, like the cathedrals, a treasury of the visual arts.

> *Play is necessary to human society.*
> — Saint Thomas Aquinas
> *Summa* II, II, 168, a. 2

> *Let every lover who loves the Lord come*
> *to the dance singing of love.*
> — Jacopone da Todi

A study of Dante reveals, too, his familiarity with the social arts: drama, lyric poetry, music with its accompaniment song, and the dance, all of which made a tremendous impact upon the medieval man and were integrated into his life pattern. Except in Greece in the fifth century before Christ or in Elizabethan England or possibly the Rome of the Caesars, there has never been a time when people were so fond of theatricals and all manner of popular entertainment as in the thirteenth century. Through most of the Romanesque era and in the early Gothic centuries there had been drama in court and cloister: the beginnings of liturgical drama in abbeys and cathedrals had marked the important feasts from the tenth century; there were singular instances of plays based on classical models like those of the nun Roswitha in her convent at Gandersheim. Acrobats, jugglers, and minstrels were found in the courts of princes and in the market place. But in the thirteenth century, especially in Italy, theatricals of all kinds came into popular control; in cities like Florence, Pisa, Siena, Perugia they were the exuberant expression of the vigorous life of the people.

Italy had her own characteristic folk festivals, known as Palio and Ponte,[14] with their processions, triumph cars, commemorative mimic battles, elaborate symbolic pageants, and races — all of them highly dramatic, all of them intimately associated with religion. Some, like the Palio in Siena, took place (one is tempted to say "were staged") on the feasts of the Virgin; some, like that in Florence, on the feast of the patron saint of the commune; some, like the Ponte of Pisa — presented in gratitude for a long-ago victory — on an anniversary of the event or on a date fixed by custom. The influence of all of these is found in the *Divine Comedy* in the masques, processions, pageants, and tableaux of the Earthly Paradise and the Starry Heaven. Even in the *Inferno* (XXI) there is an episode suggested by a morality play given in Florence in 1304. Dante, brought up in these colorful times, again and again proves himself a brilliant dramatist, his transforming imagination spiritualizing what more often than not had lost much of its religious character.

Any understanding of the thirteenth century is incomplete without some vivid realization of the spread of popular religious song and dance. Ecclesiastics complained frequently that the popular minstrel songs, the lyrics and the dances were far from moral, that the performers were outcasts of earth and heaven, some of the clergy inveighing against all popular entertainments without exception. The Franciscans and Dominicans, however, fought fire with fire; they substituted sacred amusements for secular amusements; they fought the spirit of the world with its own weapons. Two of the most dynamic of these were Saint Francis of Assisi in Umbria and Blessed Jacopo da Varagine in the north of Italy. As is well known, the impetus for popular sacred drama came from Saint Francis, who in 1225 in the wood at Greccio, had dramatized the Christmas story; he was the first, too, to set minstrel against minstrel.

It will be remembered that in his youth Saint Francis composed songs in the manner of the troubadours; he understood the spirit of the minstrel and the craving of the people for entertainment. To counteract the ill effects of the popular minstrelsy, he later wrote and sang popular songs in the vernacular, organized his "minstrels of the Lord," trained them in their songs, and sent them out to sing throughout Umbria.[15] The flower of these Franciscan minstrels, Blessed Jacopone da Todi, a Doctor of Laws from Bologna, who, before becoming a Franciscan, had been a distinguished jurist, wrote popular hymns and went about the country singing them. Many of them have come down to us; some, like the *Stabat Mater Dolorosa,* have retained their popularity through the centuries.[16] At precisely the time that Jacopone da Todi was tramping the hillsides of Umbria, the Dominican Jacopo da Varagine was organizing his company of minstrels in Milan.

To one who has not caught the spirit of the thirteenth century, to find Jacopo, the Dominican provincial of the whole north of Italy (including such major cities as Milan and Genoa), deeply interested in minstrelsy may come as a surprise. But it should not. He believed in minstrelsy as the good man of today believes in television. These things are a part of the civilization in which one finds himself; they are in the air. Jacopo and Dante absorbed at every breath minstrelsy and all that went with it. They, like the twentieth-century reformer, were interested in having the entertainment clean. It is true that Jacopo was distinguished for his erudition, his ability as a teacher, writer, preacher, administrator, and peacemaker — he was made Archbishop of Genoa because of his remarkable ability in adjusting differences; he was the first to translate Scripture, both Testaments, into Italian; he was the author of a scholarly chronicle of Genoa. But he was also the author of the *Golden Legend,* that collection of all the popular stories of the saints, known to the learned and the unlearned, the most popular book of the century. He was in as close touch with the hearts of the people as was Francis; he shared the Franciscan's dramatic impulse.

Those who deem it incongruous to find a man of the stature of Jacopo interested in organizing a band of minstrels will find it even more incongruous to see him recruiting his performers from the many novices of Saint Eustorgio in Milan, Varagine's official residence as provincial. It says something about the spirit of the age that he found among the novices able performers in all the areas in which his troupe became so skilled that they could compete successfully with the secular troupes and draw the crowds.[17]

The performances of Jacopo's Dominican minstrels included songs of the deeds of princes and saints (the author of the *Golden Legend* and the chronicle of Genoa would see to that); musicians who accompanied these stories with song; ballini whose dances ranged from accompaniment to the songs of troubadours down to comic dancing; and the humblest kinds of entertainers — buffoons, acrobats, jugglers, jesters, and ventriloquists. Songs to the Virgin replaced the love songs of the troubadours. Jacopo's troupe were dressed in the style of the secular ministrels of the day — in loose ivory-colored short cloaks and flat shoes. Like his friend Saint Thomas, Jacopo held that play is necessary to human society. It is no wonder that Dante makes Saint Thomas, Saint Albert, and other scholars dance in the Heaven of the Sun.

Those accustomed to thinking of Franciscans and Dominicans as great hymn writers, associating with them such masterpieces of Latin hymnody as the *Dies Irae*, the *Stabat Mater*, and the *Pange Lingua*, may not be aware that they were carol makers too — a carol strictly speaking, being a ring dance accompanied by song. Often these poets took old tunes and supplied religious words, writing the stanzas in the vernacular, though sometimes inserting an occasional familiar Latin phrase; often the carols have a Latin refrain taken from some part of the liturgy. An example of such a macaronic carol dating from the thirteenth century is the well-known "Angels we have heard on high" with its Latin refrain *Gloria, Gloria in excelsis Deo*. All manner of carols have come down to us, not all of them by any means associated with Christmas, not all of them religious. Caroling was a popular pastime in every area of life in the Middle Ages. Every courtier and every peasant knew the steps; everyone knew the words and the melodies of dozens of these circular song-dances.[18]

Certainly Dante knew the steps. Nor had he any doubt that they were known by Saint Thomas, Saint Albert, Saint Bonaventure, and the other scholars of his time. There is no more delightful episode in the whole *Divine Comedy* than that in the Heaven of the Sun where Dante presents twenty-four men in the university of the eternities, among them all the eminent doctors of the rival schools, singing and dancing a carol in honor of the Blessed Trinity. It is particularly delightful to see Saint Thomas (known for his great stature and obesity) pause — poised on one foot, ready to make the turn when the music changes — to name for Dante all those in his circle. Rejoicing that the music waits until he is through, with Dante the reader watches "the glorious wheel move on, voice answering voice" (*Par.* X:145–147) until each light has returned to the point where it had been at first and stands, the carol finished — "like a candle in a candlestick" (*Par.* XI:15) while Saint Thomas eulogizes Saint Francis. As soon as he has said the final word, the circle moves again; but before it has turned a full round, a second ring of carolers encircles it as a rainbow encircles a rainbow, making a double crown about Dante and his guide. The music of the one answers the music of the other as flashing light answers flashing light. The first circle is, as we know, made up of Dominicans; the second, of Franciscans. So does Dante pay tacit tribute to the minstrels of the Lord, the ballini, the makers of carols!

If one is intrigued by the picture of Saint Thomas Aquinas and the other profound theologians singing and dancing a carol, he is even more intrigued by the caroling of Saints Peter, James, and John before and after they examine Dante. It would seem that one should approach even a difficult oral examination with a merry heart. But why be surprised! Throughout the *Paradiso* saints have left their caroling to come to speak to Dante, though some like Justinian and his companions (VII:4–9) continue to carol as they come; the angels carol in the Primum Mobile (*Par.* XXVIII) about the Point of Light, which represents God. Even in the highest heaven there is caroling. The carol in the *Divine Comedy* is the symbol of great joy.

Since everybody sang in the thirteenth century — crusaders on the march, students in the universities, princes and troubadours in the castles, friars and the populace in the market place, flagellants in the city streets, lovers to those who were also makers of love lyrics, and everybody in the abbeys and cathedrals — it is not surprising that Dante's great poem, which so well reflects the spirit of the age, is full of singing. All through the *Purgatorio* and *Paradiso* there is music: the chanting of psalms and antiphons, the singing of hymns.

On the cornice of the avaricious in the *Purgatorio* when the angels intone the *Gloria* (*Purg.* XX:136), Dante probably has in mind not only the *Gloria* as it is sung in the Mass but also the joyous Christmas carol built on it, for the scene he evokes is that of Bethlehem. Repeatedly, chiefly in the *Purgatorio,* he pays tribute to some troubadour or other lyric poet of the Italy of his day. And at the very moment when the souls in the Ante-Purgatory are entering into the penance which will lead them to eternal joy, he has Casella entertain them by singing one of the lyrics from the *Banquet* (*Purg.* II:112; *Banq.* III).

> *For the name of each he has prepared a grateful place.*
> — Purgatorio XXVI:137–138

That Dante knew well all the popular French and Italian art poetry of his day is also evident from numerous references in his writings. In his *De Vulgari Eloquentia* (*Concerning Vernacular Eloquence*), his critical comments show that he was familiar with Provençal art-poetry covering about a century: he cites many examples to illustrate the ability of the troubadours in the use of meter, in the choice and arrangement of words, and in stanzaic structure. That he himself could write excellent French verse is apparent from his felicitous use of the language (*Purg.* XXVI:140–147), where he meets Arnaut Daniel (flourished 1180–1200) and pays him the tribute of putting into his mouth splendid verses in his native Provençal. He quotes also from the Italian poets of Sicily, the Bolognese school, and his own native Tuscany.

To all of these schools Dante acknowledges his indebtedness. In the *Eloquence* (II, ii) after declaring that there are three fit subjects for song: safety (arms, politics), love, and virtue, he selects troubadour poets who have distinguished themselves in each of these areas and from whom he had learned techniques; in the *Divine Comedy* he again singles them out for special attention.[19]

The cantos of the *Divine Comedy* sing of all three themes; it is difficult to say sometimes which is dominant.

To the poets of the Sicilian school Dante owes an even greater debt, for they were in a certain sense the creators of what may be called literary Italian. Dante points out in the *Eloquence* (I, xii) that the graces and intellectuality of the court of Frederick II and his son Manfred (*Purg.* III:103–145) furnished the proper atmosphere for the burgeoning of the work of the best *Italians* (Italian poets). The poets who flourished at this court were an educated folk assembled from all of Italy, chiefly officials of the emperor: notaries, secretaries, officers, counselors. Their conversation was a fusion of Sicilian with dialects from all over Italy, a courtly speech which resembled the Tuscan dialect. Frederick and Manfred were both poets, Frederick's chancellor and friend, Pier delle Vigne (*Inf.* XIII:55–78), is credited with originating the sonnet form used so felicitously by Dante, Guido Cavalcanti, and his many friends in Tuscany, brought to perfection in the next generation by Petrarch, and used by major poets through all succeeding centuries.

The third group of art poets to influence Dante was the group from Bologna, chief among them being Guido Guinizelli (*Purg.* XXVI:16–132). To the University of Bologna came students from all over Italy because of its famous work in law. Frederick II was interested in it; consequently to it came various representatives of the Sicilian school of poets. Bologna in the middle of the thirteenth century had a joyous, as well as a keen intellectual air and the best of the poets fused the two. The love poetry of this group differed from that of the troubadours: these poets did not sing of sensuous love filled with carnal desire. These are poems in the *dolci stil nuovo*, the sweet new style, in which the lady of the poet's song is a lofty figure whose love ennobles the passionate heart of the lover; the lover is face to face with an ideal love. Of the lyrics of Guinizelli, Dante says when he meets him that they make precious the very ink in which they are written (*Purg.* XXVI:112–114).

In the *Divine Comedy*, Dante acknowledges all his indebtedness. He pays tribute to all who taught him his science and his art: Virgil, whom he calls his master, and the other ancients; the writers of the Scriptures; Brunetto Latini; the Provençal tellers of tales of great deeds and singers of romantic love; the poets of Sicily who helped him discover and shape his own literary Tuscan vocabulary; the poets of the sweet new style; the Dominicans and Franciscans who taught him philosophy and theology, whose high minstrelsy helped him to free himself from didacticism and cast essentially religious thought into lyric vernacular; Saint Bernard and the other mystics; and all those contemporaries and near contemporaries who in any way contributed to his work.

By needful "discernment," by "strenuous effort," "constant practice," and the "habit (arduous study) of the sciences (physical science and metaphysics, moral science or ethics, and divine science or theology)" Dante made himself ready to "sing of the highest subjects in the highest style" and like the "eagle to soar to the stars" (*Eloquence* II, iv); he disciplined himself and his art, making himself "lean for many years" that he might write "the sacred poem to which heaven and earth lent a hand" (*Par.* XXV:1–3). As a result he gave the world a love poem the like of which no man has written, a political poem than which there is no greater, a poem of virtue and righteousness which transcends all other poems dealing with man's capacity for goodness.

> *Rome, that reformed the world, accustomed was*
> *Two suns to have, which one road and the other,*
> *Of God and of the world, made manifest.*
>
> *One has the other quenched, and to the crosier*
> *The sword is joined, and ill beseemeth it*
> *That by main force one with the other go,*
> *Because, being joined, one feareth not the other.*
>   — *Purgatorio* XVI:106–112

The thirteenth century was one of great political turmoil. To understand Dante one must have some understanding of the conflicts between the Papacy and the emperors, and among the political powers themselves — many of them Italian communes striving for commercial and political supremacy in that restless age. The cities of Dante's Italy were sovereign states, several of them with the status of world powers. The history of the struggle between the popes and the emperors runs through all the history of the early and high Middle Ages. Dante in his *Monarchy* (III, X) and in the *Divine Comedy* (*Inf.* XIX:115–117) dates the problem back to the days of the Roman Empire, to Constantine, who turned his back on Rome and the West, moved his seat of empire from Rome to Byzantium (under the name Constantinople) and made — so it was thought in Dante's time — to Pope Sylvester a gift of Italy and the West, though the West was still administered by the emperors, first from Rome and then in 408, just before the sack of Rome by Alaric in 410, from Ravenna. From Constantine's donation, so Dante believed, came the papal concern with political affairs which led to the corruption of his time.

The history of the centuries between 410 and the crowning of Charlemagne in Rome on Christmas Day in the year 800 is a long story of the struggle of both the Eastern and the Western empires with various tribes who succeeded in founding kingdoms in the West throughout the former Western Roman empire; and in the East, in the later part of the period, with Arabs and other Mohammedans who took over the eastern and southern parts and the southwestern peninsula of Spain. For the protection of its interests in the West the Church had looked to the German emperors. In the Middle Ages she became aware that she had raised up strong rulers who contested her supremacy in a number of situations where ecclesiastical and political interests came into conflict. The Church was the greatest landholder; kings and princes endeavored to keep some control over these lands by what is known in history as lay investiture. The years are marked by the entrance into Church positions of many unworthy men as abbots and bishops and by the abuses of simony and nepotism, all of which Dante denounces vehemently in the *Commedia*. There are many recorded instances of conflicts between popes and emperors relative to these abuses, the most famous of which is the quarrel in 1077 between Pope Gregory VII and Henry IV on the matter of lay investiture.

But long before this came to pass, the Arabs — who were Mohammedans — were held at bay in the West in 732 by Charles Martel,
the grandfather of Charlemagne, who had gained control of all
the Frankish kingdoms, and whose son Pepin III followed his father's
example of acting as though he were king and who then had his
kingship sanctioned by being anointed king by Saint Boniface.
This anointing gave to the royal office a sacred character, which it
was to retain. (In our own day the Western world witnessed such an
anointing at the coronation ceremonies of Elizabeth II of England).
A little later Pope Stephen II pronounced an anathema against
anyone who should try to fight against hereditary succession in Pepin's
family. All these acts were to establish a precedent mighty in its
effects in subsequent centuries when later popes claimed the right
to depose as well as to appoint monarchs.

Just before Dante's day the struggle was particularly bitter because, among other things, of the union in one person, that of
Frederick II, grandson of Frederick Barbarossa, of the crown of the
kingdom of the two Sicilies, which he inherited through his mother,
and of the imperial title which came to him through his father.
The cause of the popes was to keep the Emperor out of Italy, to
create a barrier of powerful cities against him south of the Alps.
Gregory IX had maintained (1236) in his conflict with Frederick
that Constantine had given temporal power to the popes and that
emperors and kings were only his auxiliaries, bound to use the
material sword at his direction; Boniface VIII in his struggle with
Philip the Fair at the end of the thirteenth century was to make the
same assertion. In his great bull *Unam Sanctam* promulgated in
1302 he says, "There are two swords [i.e., powers], the spiritual and
the temporal; the first borne by the Church, the second for the
Church; the first by the hand of the priest, the second by that of
the king, but under the direction of the priest."[20] It is with these
problems that Dante deals in the *Monarchy* and the *Divine Comedy*.

The shadow of Frederick II is over much of the *Divine Comedy*.
Born in Sicily, bred in a semi-Oriental atmosphere, he was feared
in Rome, both as a political antagonist and as a freethinking enemy.
In 1245, at the Council of Lyons, he was declared by Innocent IV
deposed both from his empire in Germany and his kingdom in

Sicily. Though he held his own until his death in 1250, rival forces which the Popes called in ultimately brought death and destruction to all of his descendants, and all his possessions passed into other hands. In Italy the chief agent of the Papacy was the French. Though in Dante's early boyhood they wiped out the last of Frederick's line, their power in Italy did not remain uncontested. In 1282, when Dante was seventeen, there took place that massacre of the French known in history as the Sicilian Vespers; in the early part of the fourteenth century the contest between the Papacy and the French proved to be as bitter as that between the Church and Frederick. After the death of Frederick, never again until modern times — though Dante hoped all his life it would come to pass — was that section of the world involving Italy in the hands of a strong ruler (*Banq.* IV, iii, 3; *Par.* III:118–120). He calls Frederick the last emperor of the Romans.

In Dante's day all of Italy was lined up as supporting either the political claims of the Papacy or those of the Emperor. Frederick Barbarossa, the grandfather of Frederick II, had been handicapped in his Italian policy by troubles at home in Germany with the rival house of Welf, Dukes of Saxony and Bavaria. The strife of Welfs and the Hohenstaufen family gave rise to two words which are very important in the Italy of Dante's time. The Welf leader, having built up great Welf possessions in Germany, refused to aid Barbarossa in his Italian campaigns; his party became known in Italy as the *Guelphs,* the party against the Emperor. The Emperor's party became associated in Italy with the struggle between the emperors and the Papacy and became known there as the *Ghibelline* party, the word Ghibelline being an Italian corruption of Waiblingen, a German estate of the Hohenstaufen family. Hence the Pope's party became known as the Guelph and the Emperor's party as the Ghibelline.

It must be borne in mind that the terms were political terms: both Guelphs and Ghibellines acknowledged the spiritual supremacy of the Pope and were loyal adherents of the Papacy in all matters of faith and morals. But the Guelphs did not believe in a strongly centralized government in imperial hands; the Ghibellines did. The Guelphs were the party of the middle class, commercial interests, a capitalistic economy: their cry was liberty. The Ghibellines had the pride of blood, magnificence, largeness of mind represented by the house of Swabia. Dante began his political career as a Guelph; in his later years he believed strongly that the only hope for peace was a world unified politically under the emperor as it was united spiritually under the pope. His *Monarchy* is his profession of faith in that point of view, one which did not originate with Dante. As early as the fifth century Pope Gelasius I (492–496) in his famous letter to Emperor Anastasius developed the theory of the two powers essentially as we find it in the *Monarchy*.

> Two things there are by which the world is ruled, the sacred authority of the pope and the royal power. Christ has ordered different dignities and duties to the office of each power . . . so that the Christian emperors need the pontiffs for the things that pertain to everlasting life, while these need the imperial dispositions for the course of things temporal.[21]

Here as in Dante's *Monarchy* the spiritual religious sphere is assigned to the Church, the temporal secular sphere, to the State.

Those who accuse Dante of Caesarism, that is, of placing the Church under the jurisdiction of the Empire, find in the *Monarchy* the justification for their point of view. The *Monarchy* is not, however, Dante's final word on the subject. At least by the time that he wrote the last cantos of the *Purgatorio* and the whole of the *Paradiso*, Dante was neither Guelph nor Ghibelline: he saw clearly the true mission of Rome to be the mission not of the Empire but of the Church by which alone could come peace, temporal and eternal.[22]

For many years, the people of Florence were neither Guelphs nor Ghibellines. But in 1215 as a result of a blood feud between two powerful Florentine families, the Buondelmonti and the Amidei, Florence was split into two rival factions (*Par.* XVI:136–141) which allied themselves with the two political parties in Italy. The conflict in Florence raged for many years, now one side, now the other being in the ascendancy. In 1248 with the help of Frederick II the Ghibellines expelled the Guelphs from Florence and razed their houses. When Frederick died in 1250 the Guelphs returned. A study of Dante's family shows their participation in the struggle at this point. Of the subsequent return of the Ghibellines under Farinata degli Uberti, Dante writes in the *Commedia* (*Inf.* X:22–114), and of their later eclipse at Campaldino we know from historical records. A number of Tuscan cities had leagued together to declare war against Arezzo, which had become a powerful Ghibelline stronghold; on June 11, 1289, they defeated the Arentines on a plain in the Casentino Valley called Campaldino. In the front rank of the cavalry from Florence rode young Dante Alighieri.[23]

NOTES

1. In the imposing Aula Magna of the University of Padua, the walls are covered with the coats of arms of masters and undergraduates from the great houses of Europe, who, across the centuries, have taught or studied there. The guide assigned by the rector points to many of these with evident pride.
2. A contemporary Italian scholar, Francesco Filippini, in his *Dante Scolare e Maestro* (Geneva, 1929), holds that Dante studied at Bologna first in 1287, matriculating in the College of Law and that it was then that he fell under the influence of Guido Guinizelli, the chief exponent of the Bolognese school of lyric poetry (see pp. 4–16). He holds also that Dante again studied at Bologna from 1291 to 1294, enrolling this time in the College of Natural Philosophy, pursuing courses in medicine, but that he became so interested in metaphysics (p. 27 seq.) that his attention was diverted and he did not come up for his degree. It is well known that in 1295, so that he might enter public life in Florence, he joined the Guild of Physicians and Apothecaries. Some time between 1290 and 1300 (see note 8) he studied at Santa Maria Novella in Florence.

   Signor Filippini sets out to prove the thesis that Dante received a degree from Paris, perhaps as late as 1314 (p. 146), his immense interest in theology attracting him to that university. He makes the point that Dante must have had a degree or he could not have been invited by Giovanni del Virgilio at the instance of the university authorities to accept a chair at Bologna (pp. 195–197), one of the leading universities of the time, nor could he have been offered the laurel wreath (p. 182) since the prerequisite for such an honor was a university degree, nor could he have had a chair in letters in Ravenna, as Boccaccio says he did. The invitations from Bologna came to Dante during his sojourn in Ravenna.

   If Signor Filippini is correct in the conclusions he draws from evidence in Dante's works as well as other records, we have symptoms of the intellectual unrest between 1287 and 1300 which brought Dante into the "dark wood" of *Inferno* I.
3. Boccaccio cites an instance of Dante's ability in disputation:
   "Indeed, when he was at Paris, in a disputation *de quolibet* held there in the schools of theology, wherein fourteen different theses were being maintained by various able men on diverse subjects, Dante without a break gathered all the theses together in their sequence, with the arguments *pro* and *con* that were advanced by their opponents, and then, following the same order, recited them, subtly solved them, and refuted the counter-arguments – a feat that was reputed all but a miracle by them that stood by."

James Robinson Smith, *The Earliest Lives of Dante*, trans. from the Italian of Giovanni Boccaccio and Lionardo Bruni Aretino, Yale Studies in English, No. X (New York, 1901), p. 45.
4. See *Avicenna: Scientist and Philosopher, A Millenary Symposium*, ed. G. M. Wickens (London, 1952), A. C. Crombie, "Avicenna's Influence on the Medieval Scientific Tradition," pp. 84–108.
5. See Paget Toynbee, *Dante Studies and Researches* (London, 1902), "Dante's Obligations to the *Elementa Astronomica* of Alfraganas," pp. 56–77.
6. "The capture of Constantinople by the Crusaders in 1204 enlarged the opportunity of Western scholars to study the Greek language and philosophy." Henry Osborn Taylor, *The Medieval Mind* (Cambridge, 1949), II, p. 421.
7. Etienne Gilson, *Dante the Philosopher*, trans. David Moore (New York, 1949), pp. 257–281.
8. The following is a translation of a certified statement made on January 3, 1956, by P. Angelico Paolo Alori, O.P., pastor of Santa Maria Novella. A photostatic copy of the original and a photograph of the plaque are included in the Appendix, p. 355.

    "Text of the inscription engraved in marble, on the left side of the arch at the entrance of the Chapel of St. Dominic in the Basilica of Santa Maria Novella in Florence. It was written by Father Giuseppe Manni of the Pius Schools, and was inaugurated in 1922, during the cycle of the celebration commemorative of the VII Centenary of the death of St. Dominic after a commemorative conference on Fr. Remigio de' Girolami, held by Father Maestro Reginaldo Fei, O.P.

    " *'Seven centuries having passed since the death of St. Dominic and six since that of Alighieri, the sons of the saintly Spaniard joyfully remember the Florentine Dominican Remigio de' Girolami, philosopher, orator, a poet unusually illustrious in his city, teacher, educator and an affectionate father of Dante during his years of exile. Dante in the school of the adjoining convent, which was then a public school, learned that science which later he adapted in the Sacred Poem as the integrating factor of his conception of oneness in the universe and made of it a monument of contemporary thought and the Catholic faith, as eternal as the Summa of Thomas Aquinas.' "*

The following item and footnote also throw light on the matter. They are taken from the Italian of P. Stephano Orlandi, O.P., *Necrologio di Santa Maria Novella 1235–1504* (Florence, 1955).

    "It seems that prior to this for some time it had been the concern of Fr. Remigio and the Fathers of Santa Maria Novella to maintain at the Convent a school for the laity.

    "Florence had not as yet a public university. It seems that Fr. Remigio had promoted the school at the Convent and that there also Dante Alighieri, in his youth, had been able to study the doctrine of St. Thomas of which in his *Divine Comedy* he shows such excellent knowledge.

    "*Footnote:* That Alighieri had been a scholar of Fr. Remigio at Santa Maria Novella is affirmed by Salvadori, G., *On the Youth of Dante*, p. 109 seq. Cf. also Papini, G., *The Living Dante*, p. 115 seq. This is denied, however, by Father Mandonnet, *Dante the Theologian*, pp. 129–130 who believes it is more probable that the Maestro (teacher) of Dante at Santa Maria Novella was Fr. Nicola Brunacci, who in 1294 was made General Master of Studies."

9. For the Franciscan influence in Dante see Chapter VI, "Dante and the Virgin Mary."

10. For an account of how Pope Pius XI on the occasion of the sixth centenary of the canonization of Saint Thomas honored Dante see Chapter VII, "Dante and the Deity," Note 2.

11. Some of Roger Bacon's statements sound like prophecies. He made a serious study of gunpowder, which had come to Europe from the Arabs, and prophesied that *one might cause to burst forth from bronze, thunderbolts that will destroy a city or an army.* He concludes that some high explosives can be used constructively, that art can construct instruments of navigation such that *the largest vessels, governed by a single man will traverse rivers and seas more rapidly than if they were filled with oarsmen. One may also make carriages which without the aid of any animal will run with remarkable swiftness.* Frederick Ozanam, *Dante and Catholic Philosophy in the Thirteenth Century,* trans. Lucia D. Pychowska, 2 ed. (New York: The Cathedral Library Association, 1913), p. 85.

   These schoolmen were not alone in their scientific interest. Dr. James J. Walsh, himself a physician, in his *The Thirteenth the Greatest of Centuries* discusses at some length experiments carried on in the field of medicine.

   One is surprised to find that the Emperor Frederick II performed all manner of scientific experiments; some of them in physiology and anatomy were exceedingly cruel, but they manifest, nevertheless, the questing mind of the man. He produced a remarkable work on ornithology, based on firsthand knowledge of the habits and anatomical structure of birds, which his son Manfred completed after his death in 1250. For many reasons Dante is greatly interested in these rulers.

12. As a rule the craftsmen associated with the erection of the cathedrals were supplied by the towns themselves, often very small towns, though architects, painters, and sculptors were sometimes brought in. A young man who in his own town showed interest and promise in some area worked as an apprentice to some guildsman at home for four or five years and then became a journeyman for at least three more years, studying in these craft-wanderings the work of skilled craftsmen in other cities, perhaps in other lands. He then presented to the officials of the guild a piece of work which gave evidence of his skill, and if it was found acceptable was enrolled as a master. The work in precious metals and jewels, shown in the treasuries of the cathedrals, including chalices and other sacred vessels, was often done by these nameless craftsmen, as were the splendid sculptured figures in stone and wood.

13. Perhaps the best book from which to get an understanding of thirteenth-century symbolism is the *Rationale Divinorum Officiorum* of William Durandus (1221–1296). Bishop Durandus filled many important ecclesiastical posts, among them Auditor of the Sacred Palace and Captain of the Papal Forces. He was Bishop of Mendes in France in 1286. Part of the *Rationale* is available in English. It was translated by Rev. John Mason Neale and Rev. Benjamin Webb, under the title *The Symbolism of Churches and Church Ornaments* (London: Gibbings & Company, 1906).

14. The Palio of Siena, the most dramatic of these medieval celebrations to survive, has the colorful procession, the triumph car, and other features which Dante includes in the pageant of the Church in the Earthly Paradise. For a detailed discussion of these palii, the most famous of which in the thirteenth century was that of Saint John the Baptist in Florence (*Par.* XVI:40–42), see William Heywood, *Palio and Ponte* (London, 1904).

15. St. Francis of Assisi, *The Legends and Lauds*, ed., selected, and annotated by Otto Karrer, trans. N. Wyderbruck (New York, 1948).
16. Frederick Ozanam in his *The Franciscan Poets in Italy of the Thirteenth Century* gives a colorful picture of Jacopone da Todi. Frederick Ozanam, *The Franciscan Poets of the Thirteenth Century*, trans. and ed. A. E. Nellen and N. C. Craig (London, 1914).
17. Excellent material on the social work of Jacopo da Varagine and other Dominicans is to be found in Ernest Cushing Richardson, *Materials for a Life of Jacopo da Varagine* (New York, 1935), from which these facts were drawn.
18. Richard Leighton Greene, *The Early English Carols* (Oxford, 1935), discusses at some length the origin and development of carols and the work of the friars, especially the Franciscans, in using them as a means of entertainment and reform.
19. The poets Dante names in this connection are Arnaut Daniel (*Purg.* XXVI: 136–148), the poet of love *par excellence*, from whom he had learned the use of verse and prose in the way in which he has used it in the *New Life*; Bertran de Born (*Inf.* XXVIII:118–142) and Sordello (*Purg.* VI, VII, VIII) for their political songs; and Folquet de Marseille (*Par.* IX:67–142) for songs of righteousness. For a detailed discussion of Dante's indebtedness to Provençal, Sicilian, and Bolognese poets, consult Karl Vossler, *Medieval Culture, An Introduction to Dante and His Times*, trans. William Cranston Lawton (New York, 1929), Vol. II, Section IV.
20. Thomas Oestreich, "Boniface VIII," *The Catholic Encyclopedia*, Vol. II, Knights of Columbus special ed., p. 667.
21. Heinrich A. Rommen, *The State in Catholic Thought* (Saint Louis, 1945), 523.
22. For a good presentation of the ultimate point of view held by Dante and expressed in the *Divine Comedy* read A. P. d'Entréves, *Dante as a Political Thinker* (Oxford, 1952), Section III, "Ecclesia."
23. Today at Campaldino, a distance of thirty-seven miles from Florence, a column by the roadside erected in 1921 commemorates this event. The column has a rectangular block at the top, in size about eighteen by twenty-four inches, which resembles an open book, bearing on either side the coats of arms of Arezzo and Florence. The base, a three-foot cube, bears the legend: *In Campaldino in the name of Dante, who was here a soldier for his commune, Florence and Arezzo, with the unhappy memories of civil wars, dedicate this pact of fraternity promised by national peace.*

CHAPTER II

THE AUTHOR AND THE BOOK

O glorious stars, O light impregnated
With mighty virtue, from which I acknowledge
All of my genius, whatso'er it be.

— *Paradiso* XXII.112–115

hat blood runs in the veins of this Dante whose coming stirred the heavens? What are the known facts of his life, two thirds of which (1265–1302) was lived in his native Florence, the other third "imprisoned in the wide world" after his exile; what kind of man was he whose personality was sufficiently powerful to capture all the divergent strands of an era as complex as the thirteenth century and fuse them into that perfect unity which is the *Divine Comedy?* All of these questions Dante himself answers more or less completely in the *Comedy* itself and in his other works, even those works which seem least subjective. A careful search of all these writings as well as of the historical records of the time, discloses evidence from which the story of his life can be reconstructed.

That Dante's ancestors belonged to the old nobility of Florence is proved unequivocally by the fact that their houses stood in what was then the center of the city (*Par.* XVI:40–42), opposite the Torre della Castagna, which stands on a narrow street now called Via Dante Alighieri. No traces of the ancient city houses are left: all the city property of the family was burned and confiscated when Dante went into exile in 1302. There is, however, a section of a country house still standing in Camerata between Florence and Fiesole.[1] That the Florentine stock stems from the old Romans is probably true; there is ample proof also that in Dante's blood stream ran Germanic blood.

The only specific statements about his ancestry made by Dante in any of his works he puts upon the lips of Cacciaguida (c. 1091–1150) his great-great-grandfather, when he meets him in the Heaven of Mars (*Par.* XV:88–148). From Cacciaguida, the first name we have in Dante's family tree, his paternity stems. Of his mother, Donna Gabriella, we know little except that she belonged to that Abati family to which Bocca (*Inf.* XXXII:76–112) who betrayed the Guelph cause at the battle of Montaperti also belonged.

Cacciaguida gives Dante many facts about his life. He tells him first that the Alighieri surname came from his son, Dante's great-grandfather, that he himself was born in Florence as were his brothers, that he was baptized in the ancient baptistery there, that his wife came from the Po valley and that from her Dante's surname really was derived, that he became a crusader under the Emperor Conrad (Conrad III), that he died while on the Crusade, a martyr for the Christian cause and came, therefore, directly to eternal peace (*Par.* XV:133–148). He asserts that he acquitted himself so creditably under Conrad, who had knighted him, that he advanced greatly in his favor which fact accounts, it would seem, for his being given a wife from the Alighieri family of Ferrara; for the Alighieri were court jurists in the suite of the Emperor. Cacciaguida, therefore, knew imperial favor, as did the Alighieri family into which he married.

Another strain in Dante's blood allies him with the famous Conti Guidi. When the Emperor Otho I, after he had been crowned with the Iron Crown in Rome in 961, paused for some time in Florence on his way back to Germany, he conferred territories in Italy upon some of his barons and left them behind as feudal lords. Among them were Uberto, founder of the great Uberti family; Lamberto, the ancestor of the Lamberti; and Guido, the founder of the long line of Guidi counts who pushed out in all directions and by 1100 were exceedingly important throughout Tuscany, particularly in the Casentino valley and the city of Florence. Of these Guido V, a brave warrior and supporter of the emperors, went on the second crusade in 1147 under Conrad III, the same crusade in which Cacciaguida participated. It was his son, Guidoguerra IV (*Inf.* XVI: 37), who married "La Bella Gualdrada" daughter of Bellincione Berti, the sturdy citizen clothed in simple leather, of whom Cacciaguida speaks (*Par.* XV:112–114). Guidoguerra IV and the good Gualdrada had eight children, five sons and three daughters. All three of the daughters married well, all three into families which in Dante's generation touched his life closely. One married into the illustrious Donati family, another into the Adinari family. The third married Alighiero, the great-grandfather of Dante.

To follow the fortunes of the Donati, Adinari, and Alighieri families through the three generations which lie between the daughters of Guidoguerra and Gualdrada and Dante is to understand Dante better, but that is a study in itself. The families lived close together in old Florence. The Donati and Adinari lived on the Via del Corso, where stood also the houses of the Portinari, the distinguished family to which belonged Beatrice (Chapter III), the girl who stirred Dante's heart so deeply that she became the most profound influence in his life.

The Donati family was important to Dante for many reasons. According to tradition, his mother died when he was not more than six years old; his father, probably before he was twelve. His father had married again shortly after the death of Dante's mother, and Dante remained with his stepmother; however, after his father's death, Manetto Donati became his guardian. Dante at the age of nine (some say twelve, because the dowry papers are dated 1277) had been betrothed to Gemma, Manetto's daughter, which may explain the guardianship. Tradition has it that when Dante was exiled in 1302, Gemma stayed on in Florence and raised his children, Jacopo, Pietro, Antonia, and possibly another son and daughter. Though Dante had considerable property both in and outside of Florence, he seems before the time of his exile to have contracted many debts which were only liquidated from his estate after his death in 1321. For these Manetto went surety. It is said also that five years after the edict of exile those who had claims against the estates of any of the exiles had the privilege of demanding their rights from those who had come into possession of forfeited property and that Gemma recovered her dowry rights. The fidelity of Gemma and her father to Dante and his children speaks well for that branch of the Donati family.

Another branch of the family included three persons who also had extraordinary importance in the life of Dante, the exquisite Piccarda and her brothers Corso and Forese. Piccarda became a Poor Clare nun and was torn from her cloister by Corso. We meet her in the Heaven of the Moon where she solves several of Dante's problems. Upon her lips Dante puts what has become the most famous line in the whole *Divine Comedy* (though Dante borrows it from Saint Augustine), compressing as it does into a few words the central thought of the poem: *His will is our peace* (*Par.* III:85). Dante's last year in Florence was spent in conflict with the proud, restless Corso, the tragic end of whose turbulent life he foretells in *Purgatorio* XXIV:82–87 and whom, by the lips of his brother Forese, he assigns to Hell (XXIV:85).

The Adinari family into which the second daughter of the good Gualdrada married produced Cavicciuli Adinari, one of the most violent opposers of Dante's return to Florence, and one of those who demanded the confiscation of his property. But we have run ahead of our story.

From the time in 1295 that Dante joined the Guild of Physicians and Apothecaries his name appears in the city records. In May, 1300, he was chosen to go as an ambassador to the neighboring city of San Gimignano to invite the citizens to join the Guelph league, a proposal which they accepted. Shortly after, he was elected as one of the six Priors, chosen annually for the government of Florence, the highest civil office in the commune. Each of the six exercised his office in turn for two months, Dante's term of service being from June 15 to August 15, 1300. The months of his term, as things developed, were fateful for Florence and for Dante. Florence was Guelph. In 1300, as the result of a quarrel between two branches of the Cancellieri family the Guelph party split into two factions. The quarrel was imported from Pistoia, a neighbor of Florence, politically allied with her, where descendants from the two wives of the original Cancellieri were in open hostility because of a murder.

One group became known as the Bianchi, the Whites, after the name of the first wife Bianca; the other, in opposition, was the Neri, the Blacks. Suffice it to say that when Florence intervened, the quarrel spread to Florence and was espoused there by two powerful families, the Cerchi and the Donati.

Vieri de Cerchi and Corso Donati had together pushed back the Ghibelline forces at Campaldino, but had later become bitterly antagonistic on social grounds. The Cerchi, a new-rich family, had gradually become owners of almost the whole Sesto di San Piero. Their arrogant display of wealth roused envy and hatred in other families, for example, the Donati, who, though not so rich, were of older nobility.[2] For a student of Dante the important thing about the conflict is that after the famous — or infamous — incidents of May Day and of the eve of the feast of Saint John the Baptist, June 24, of the year 1300 — both days of special festivity in Florence — the Priors made a decree to banish the leaders of both sides. Dante, who was a White, though his wife's family was Black — as indeed were most of his family friends because they were scions of the old Florentine nobility — set his hand to the exile of his friend and fellow poet, Guido Cavalcanti, and of his wife's kinsman, Corso Donati.

During his term as Prior, Dante was also to come into conflict with the Papacy. Believing as he did, that pope and emperor should operate each in his own sphere, it is not surprising that he should cross swords with Boniface VIII, the scholarly and imperial-minded occupant of Peter's chair at the time. Dante had seen him face to face when he had gone to Rome in 1300 for the year of Jubilee and must have recognized him for what his contemporaries knew him to be, a man with splendid qualities of leadership. He was a distinguished canonist, a man of culture, an astute statesman, born, however, into troublous times when nationalism was rising all over Europe. For years he had been talked of in Florence as a meddler. Undoubtedly he based his idea of the right to interfere in Florentine politics upon the general claim of papal supremacy over all Christian peoples and kingdoms; it may be that the growing power of Florence was a source of uneasiness to the Pope who believed one of his duties was to think of the whole balance of power in Europe.

In 1300 some of the Florentine Guelphs, fearing that the increasing conflicts between Blacks and Whites might encourage a return of the Ghibellines to Florence, had appealed to the Pope to interfere as mediator. Accordingly, Boniface had sent Cardinal Matteo d' Acquasparta to act as peacemaker. He had demanded that the offices of government be equally divided between Blacks and Whites; but the Priors, Dante among them, had refused his demand; wherefore he put the city under an interdict. This occurred just before the Priors, taking matters into their own hands, had banished the leaders of both factions.

Boniface, on March 15, 1301,[3] launched against the citizens of Florence the bull *Perlato pridem* in which, following the tradition of Gregory VII, Innocent II, and Gregory IX, he asserts the absolute sovereignty of the pope over cities, kings, princes, and every living creature. He invited Charles of Valois to enter Florence, nominally as a peacemaker; he was won over by the Blacks and, as Dante believed, showed himself to be a partisan by receiving Corso Donati. In October, 1301, Dante and two others were dispatched to Rome to try to make peace with Boniface. The other two returned to Florence; Dante was detained in Rome. During his absence, November 1, 1301, Charles presented himself at the gates of Florence and was received without opposition because of his promise to arbitrate impartially. But he turned the city over to the Blacks, who set up a Black government. Corso Donati returned in triumph with the rest of the exiled Blacks, pillaged the homes of the Whites, brought suit against Dante and other prominent Whites, charging them with malfeasance in office; of conspiracy against the Pope; the Guelph party; Charles of Valois, the Pope's agent; and in general against the peace of Florence. Dante never saw Florence again.

Three decrees of banishment were launched against Dante. The first decree, that of January 27, 1302, reached him, tradition says, in Siena on his way back from Rome. The decree did not particularize; all those who were exiled were lumped in one malediction as they had been upon the return of Corso Donati. Dante and sundry others were condemned to pay a fine of 5,000 florins, to restore all monies *illegally* exacted, payment to be made within three days of promulgation of the sentence, in default of which all their goods were to be forfeited and destroyed. In addition to payment of the fine the *delinquents* were sentenced to banishment from Tuscany for two years and to perpetual deprivation from office in Florence, their names to that end being recorded in the book of Statutes of the People as peculators and malversators in office. This sentence having been disregarded, probably because those concerned knew it to be unjust, on March 10, 1302, the same year, a second and more severe sentence was pronounced against Dante and fourteen others, condemning them to be burned alive should they at any time fall into the hands of the Republic. On November 6, 1315, Dante and those named with him were branded as Ghibellines and rebels and condemned, if captured, to be beheaded in the place of public execution. This time Dante's sons were included with him.[4]

So did the age-long struggle between Papacy and Empire divide Boniface and Dante, two of the ablest, keenest, most imperious men of their era, men whose interests and capacities intersected at many points and who under other circumstances might have been friends. The exiled Dante, dying in Ravenna in 1321, could never have dreamed that after six hundred years the Pope in the person of Benedict XV would send from Rome a delegate to participate in the celebration held in that city to honor him and that the only encyclical ever issued by any pope in honor of any poet would be published throughout the Christian world to urge all mankind to read the poem which was the fruit of his exiled years.[5]

> *Thou shalt abandon everything beloved*
> *Most tenderly, and this the arrow is*
> *Which first the bow of banishment shoots forth.*
> — *Paradiso* XVII:55-57

Dante had lived in Florence for thirty-seven years. His roots were there. He never took root again. Though there is considerable evidence that much had happened to make his early years unhappy, he was passionately devoted to his native commune and would never of his own volition have severed himself from her. His works seem to indicate that he was often lonely, for he was left an orphan at an early age; the sonnets of Forese suggest that his father was not such a man as the son could take pride in either for quality of mind or importance of position; his love for Beatrice and her apparent disregard of him caused him intense suffering: but his life in Florence had been full and active and he never recovered from the wound of the edict of exile.

It is clear from Dante's writings that he was not the dour, humorless, unsocial person he is sometimes pictured as being. The *New Life* shows that he was a part of all the social life of his times. In all his works he wrote knowingly of troubadours, carols, falconry, archery, love-making, pageantry, and the manifold activities of his era. He tells us (*Inf.* XXII:5–10) that he had experienced the shock of tournaments and jousts with trumpets and bells and drums and castle signals. He must have thrilled to the excitement of the *Palio*, run every year in Florence on the feast of Saint John the Baptist, her patron saint, as the riderless horses dashed through the old market and into the second ward of the city at the beginning of which was the Via degli Speziali where stood the houses of the Eliseo in one of which Cacciaguida was born (*Par.* XVI:40–43). Dante was himself a horseman: we find him a cavalryman at Campaldino; it is almost certain from *Inferno* XXI:94–96 that in August of the same year he took part in the war against Pisa when the Tuscan Guelphs captured the Castle of Caprona. We see him as the ambassador spurring on to San Gimignano heralded by silver trumpets and the banners of Florence, and on to Rome.

He participated in the public life of his commune in a variety of ways. We find him riding magnificently about Florence as one of the Captains of the People. We find him in charge of the widening of the streets in his native city. Florentines still point out the stone on which he sat long hours watching the beginning of the building of the cathedral. He was skilled in the arts. Tradition says that he sang well, that Casella wrote the music for many of his verses (*Purg.* II:91; 106–114) and that Belacqua (*Purg.* IV:106–126) made the musical instruments on which he played.

In the *New Life* (XII) love directs him to set his verses to pleasant music, and (XXXV) he is interrupted while drawing an angel. He exchanges bantering verses with fellow poets. He is not a lovelorn loiterer mooning over poetic effusions. For all things human he had a zest.

It was in Florence that Dante began his serious studies and acquired much of that encyclopedic learning which is the amazement of all who read him closely. He was torn from those persons and places associated with his studies. There is some justification, though no certitude, for the claim that part of his elementary education was received under the Friars Minor at Santa Croce. Wherever he had his early training, he must, like other boys of his era, have learned the Latin Psalter by heart, mastered the moral lessons in the Fables of Aesop and the Distichs of Cato and the summaries of the teachings of Saint Augustine and Boethius. Possibly under the tutelage of Brunetto Latini, in addition to the study of rhetoric — which included the study of Latin classics (Virgil, Ovid, Cicero, *et al.*), public speaking, and letter-writing in Latin — he may have been introduced to those scientific studies which were a major interest of his master. Brunetto probably inspired the young Dante with the desire to achieve fame through the use of words; there is a sonnet extant which Dante sent to Brunetto with a copy of the *New Life*. Brunetto may have taught him French, for he wrote his *Tesoro* in Provençal.

It was in Florence, too, that Dante studied philosophy and theology and came to know so well Aristotle and Saint Thomas at Santa Maria Novella under Fra Remigio, and the Franciscan philosophy under Pier Giovanni Olivi, who taught at Santa Croce. At the Augustinian studium at Santo Spirito he may have studied Saint Augustine, Saint Bernard, and the Victorines. Much of his omnivorous reading must have been done while he was pursuing these studies. According to his own statement (*Banq.* III, ix, 6), after the death of Beatrice he had so overtaxed his eyes with reading that all the stars seemed to have their light obscured by some white mist.

Whenever it was that he did his vast amount of reading, and whatever the circumstances were under which he did it, the quantity is staggering when one ponders the difficulties under which such vast learning was acquired. If it was done in learned leisure under the best of contemporary circumstances it would be amazing. But when one pauses to consider, as Moore points out, that it was done before the advent of printing, when books were available only in manuscripts which were difficult of access, that Dante's life was so occupied with political struggles in the early years in Florence as to seem to leave little time for serious study, that at last it was a wandering unsettled life — then his achievement is astounding.[6] He must have found it extremely difficult to be cut off abruptly from the opportunities for securing manuscripts that the fine studia in Florence accorded him.

It was in Florence that the gifted young poet wrote those first sonnets and *canzone* to Beatrice; and as a result was able to make the acquaintance of poets of his own and neighboring communes who exchanged sonnets and other lyrics and were critical of each other's work. Dante calls Guido Cavalcanti (*New Life* XXXI; *Inf.* X:61–63), proud aristocrat, ten years his senior, the "first" or "chief" of his friends: he knew him in 1283; Guido's devotion to the vernacular as against Latin seems to have made a deep impression on the eighteen-year-old Dante. Cino da Pistoia, a lecturer in jurisprudence; Lapo Gianni, a Florentine notary whose name is associated with Dante's during the period of his priorate; and Dino Frescobaldi are perhaps the most important of those men who have left lyric poetry which bears witness to their friendship with Dante. Dante names Cino and Lapo and Dino as the only poets besides himself who really understood the beauty of the vernacular. The last of these friends, Dino Frescobaldi, was to do Dante and the world a singular service.

Dante had begun the *Divine Comedy* before his exile and had, according to tradition, written seven cantos. They and his other writings were among the many "loved things" he had left behind in Florence. At the time of the edict of exile Gemma had hurriedly concealed them in certain strongboxes, where five years later in her search among his papers for legal documents necessary to recover her dowry, which had been confiscated with Dante's property, she found them. It was Dino Frescobaldi who is said to have brought it about that these first cantos were restored to Dante and he was persuaded to proceed with the writing.[7]

Dante went into exile bearing with him nothing but the great treasures of his learning; the vivid memories of the fair city on the Arno — her people, her buildings, her brilliant and versatile life of which he had been so vital a part; his experience as a soldier, an ambassador, and as an executive in various government positions. These were his only possessions, these and his unusual capacity to observe, to assimilate, to suffer, and to capture and hold all things in words. Exile widened his horizons, deepened his knowledge, and made of the Florentine a citizen of Christendom.

Thou shalt have proof how savoreth of salt
The bread of others, and how hard a road
The going down and up another's stairs.
— Paradiso XVII: 58–60

Like to a pilgrim who would fain return.
— Paradiso I: 51

There is much dispute among Dante scholars concerning his whereabouts during different years of his exile, but this does not concern us particularly. Some dates are fixed by documentary evidence; others are largely a matter of conjecture. We find him in the early years of exile engaged in various attempts to retrieve his fortune. We know that he was present with some others at San Godenzo on June 8, 1302, when the Bianchi allied themselves with the Ghibelline Ubaldini to make war upon Florence. We know, for he tells us (*Par.* XVII:67–69), that he broke altogether with his fellow exiles who contrived in various ways to re-establish themselves in Florence.

There are many conjectures as to the reasons for the break; perhaps it came because of Dante's unwillingness to fall in with the opinions and schemes of the party, eager at any cost to return to their native commune. We surmise that the break may have come in 1303 after the defeat of the Whites at Lastra. In any case Dante made a party of himself early in his exile. He may have been in Bologna in 1304 and 1305, for until they made a pact with the Neri in March, 1306, the Bolognese were hospitable to the White exiles. Many think the *Banquet* and the *Concerning Eloquence* were begun in Bologna between 1304 and 1306. Neither book was finished. There is a legal document which says he was in Padua on August 27, 1306, and when there was the guest of Giotto. One likes to think of Giotto and Dante planning together those still vivid frescoes in the Arena chapel.

In the *Banquet* I, iii, 1, Dante calls himself a pilgrim, almost a beggar, displaying against his will the wounds of fortune, wandering through almost every part of Italy, "a pilgrim (*Banq.* IV, xii, 6) . . . who is going by a road he has never traveled, who believes each house that he sees from afar to be his inn, and disappointed in this one puts faith in the next and so on from house to house. . . ." His status, though that of a wanderer, is not that of a beggar. He writes of the courtesy of the great Lombard (*Par.* XVII:71), whose giving foreran the asking, he praises the magnanimity of the Malaspina family (*Purg.* VIII:118–133). Actually his life was that of a courtier. He was, it is true, a wanderer whose lot it was to go from castle to castle, from town to town, to the houses of great lords who were famous for their liberality toward pilgrims of all sorts — troubadours and entertainers, as well as men of learning. His proud spirit must have rebelled at being one of the hangers-on among those who flattered their hosts.

We know from Dante's own writings the names of four of his hosts. In the *Paradiso* XVII:70 he tells us that his first refuge was in Verona with the great Lombard whose coat of arms represented an eagle on a ladder: Bartolommeo della Scala, if he was there before 1304; his brother Albuino, if he was there between 1304 and 1311. Here he met the young prince Can Grande della Scala (*Par.* XVII: 76–92) on whom he fixed his hopes as emperor after the death of Henry VII of Luxembourg at Buonconvento near Siena on August 24, 1313, whose guest he was more than a decade later, probably in 1316 and 1317, and to whom at its completion in 1320 or 1321, shortly before his death, he dedicated the *Divine Comedy*.

There are numerous references to the splendor of the court of the Scaligers, especially to the court of Can Grande, of the elaborate hospitality shown to banished men, each being assigned a special apartment, decorated especially for him, given his own servants and his private table, and provided with musicians, jugglers, and jesters for his amusement.[8] Just when Dante left Verona the first time is not known; nor is it certain when he left after Can Grande succeeded Bartolommeo and his brother. At any rate he was not there in the fall of 1306 and he seems to have left the court of Can Grande in 1316. In spite of the royal hospitality and special favors bestowed upon him by his host, such as dining at Can Grande's own table, Dante went away. It is possible that a man working on the *Divine Comedy* found the court life too distracting. The fact that he dedicated the *Paradiso* to Can Grande and that he sent him cantos of the poem as he finished them indicates that there was no severance of good will between guest and host.

The second great family which entertained Dante was the Malaspina family to which he pays glowing tribute in the *Purgatorio* (VIII:118–133). Eight members of this noble house are named in the *Divine Comedy*. That Dante was with them in October, 1306, is certain because he witnessed a signature at Lunigiana, the castle of Moroello Malaspina. It was to Lunigiana that Dino Frescobaldi sent or brought from Florence the cantos of the *Inferno* which Gemma had found in Dante's strongbox in Florence. With them he got into the hands of Moroello a letter strongly urging him to persuade Dante to continue so great a work. Dino's letter and Moroello's plea prevailed and Dante resumed the writing with the significant words, "I say continuing," the first words of the eighth canto. Raag in *Dante and His Italy* suggests that many ideas for the topography of the *Inferno* came from the region of Lunigiana; since the work on the *Inferno* was resumed there the suggestion has probability.[9]

The third great family to harbor Dante was the Conti Guidi in the Casentino valley near Florence, all of them lineal descendants of the good Gualdrada and Guidiguerra IV and therefore Dante's third cousins or second cousins once removed. When or how often he came to the Casentino no one knows; the only assured dates are in the spring of 1311. On March 31 he addressed a letter (Letter VI) to the "arrant scoundrels within the city" (of Florence) who bar from their doors the Emperor who has come to check the delirium of Italy; and on April 17, a letter (Letter VII) to "the most glorious Lord Henry by divine providence King of the Romans and ever Augustus."[10] Both letters are signed by Dante Alighieri, a Florentine in undeserved exile; both are further identified as *Written in Tuscany below the source of the Arno*. Here, too, were written several *canzone*, important in another connection.

The Casentino and its castles were not unfamiliar to Dante. He had fought in the valley in the battle of Campaldino, and from his familiarity with the whole countryside as evidenced in the *Divine Comedy* and the *canzone* he must have walked and ridden over it many times. Where he stayed in the Casentino is not certain; perhaps in only one or probably in all three of the castles which are there today, Romena, Porciano, and Poppi. As one drives from Florence over the Consuma Pass, the scarred towers of Romena (*Inf.* XXX:73) rear themselves above the domelike hill which rises from the lush green of the valley. One pauses on the highest point of the pass to see how it dominates the countryside and to think of Master Adam of Brescia who was "consumed" at the stake here in 1281 for false coinage of Florentine florins for the Conti Guidi of Romena (*Inf.* XXX:73–77), a flaming lesson to all who might be tempted. Henceforth the road out of Florence is called the Consuma Road. What an impression the event must have made upon the mind of the sixteen-year-old Dante! And later when the exiled Dante was a guest at Romena with this same edict of fire against him, how he must have reflected upon Adam as he looked at the pass from the momentary security of Romena!

Romena is the most forlorn and aloof of the castles today. Poppi still has its quaint supporting village, its Badia reminiscent of Frederick Barbarossa, its great battlemented wall. The ancient castle high on its hill houses the officials of the little town of Dante's day and of the modern town at its foot; Porciana has the charming village of Stia on the steep street climbing its way to the old castle; it is befriended, too, by the Romanesque church built by the great Matilda of Tuscany. But the village that supported Romena has disappeared;

she has but a fragment of one of her three sets of enclosing walls; and of the fourteen splendid towers of Dante's time only three broken towers remain. One approaches the castle over a rutted byroad past contemporary farm buildings to a charming villa at the base of the highest part of the knoll, near which is one of the towers still guarding a hidden stairway and subterranean passage to the countryside and to the river for escape in time of trouble. Perhaps the Conti Guidi escaped there when poor Adam was arrested. The present owner of Romena, the Countess de Goretti, tells charming legends of the castle and the Casentino and of Dante which have gone "from Tuscan lip to Tuscan ear for twenty lineal generations." One can walk across the ancient drawbridge over which is a marble tablet with the inscription, "Here the Guidi Counts entertained Dante Alighieri in the early part of his exile."

One legend tells us that while Dante was visiting at Romena in 1304 Margherita Malateste, daughter of Paolo, lover of Francesca da Rimini, was also a guest. The tragic death of Paolo and Francesca had occurred only nineteen years before (*Inf.* V:73–142). Margherita was nine years old at the time. Could she have given Dante some of the details? Dante must have remembered Paolo, who was one of the Captains of the People in Florence in his boyhood. Some say that Romena gave Dante the suggestion of the noble castle in Limbo, seven times encircled with lofty walls and defended by a river (*Inf.* IV:106–112). Perhaps it did. The green courtyard inside the circuit of the walls is still there. But there is a road which spirals up the mountain – or which did spiral up in Dante's time, now only parts of it remain – and a gate at the foot of the first level; and it seems quite possible that Dante's transforming imagination made of Romena his mountain of Purgatory. The air is singularly pure; even today the trees are abundant and very beautiful. It is easy to see the ocean in the lush green fields from which Romena rises abruptly, and looking to the east to visualize on the glistening Arno a boat crowded with penitent souls. It seems probable that Dante was at Porciano also, for the description of the course of the Arno (*Purg.* XIV:24–54) may well have been written there where the river rises.

Several Dante scholars hold that the fiery letters[11] which riveted the chains of the exile were written at Poppi, though Porciano is more directly *below the source of the Arno*. They believe that Dante came to Poppi in the spring of 1311, fresh from the coronation of Henry VII at Milan, and that he returned there from Pisa in the spring of 1312, where with other Florentine nobles he had greeted the Emperor. Among these others was the father of Petrarch, exiled with Dante, who had with him his little boy Francesco to whom he pointed out Dante as the most famous poet of the imperial cause.[12]

Several cantos of the *Divine Comedy* must have been written in the Casentino, possibly at Poppi, and probably at this period. Four or five years had elapsed since Dino Frescobaldi restored to Dante the beginning cantos of the *Inferno* and he must have continued to write. It would seem that the story of Adamo was written there, and perhaps the story of Francesca was inserted or revised. It seems probable, too, if the legends are true, that the famous Canto XXXIII of the *Inferno* was written at Poppi, for Dante's hostess was the Countess della Gherardesca, the daughter of the tragic Ugolino, who had been starved to death with his two sons and two grandsons twenty-two years before. Beyond any shadow of a doubt, some, if not all, of the story of Buonconte da Montefeltro (*Purg.* V:85–129) was conceived in the Casentino, a fourth vivid episode which would seem to have originated in the valley.

Pappini suggests (following, as he says, Zingarelli) that in the fierce battle of Campaldino, where Dante fought in the front ranks on the Florentine side and Buonconte as a leader on the Arentine side, it is quite possible that Dante killed Montefeltro and that here in the Casentino years later he may have recalled the incident, "not with remorse since Montefeltro had been killed in just warfare, but with compassionate regret, increased by the mysterious disappearance of the body." In the castle of Poppi, which commands at the northeast a view of the battlefield and at the south the lower valley where beyond the hills of Bibbiana the Archiano joins the Arno, he might well imagine the flight of the man pierced in the throat bloodying the plain, the loss of vision, the headlong plunge, the name of Mary, and the arms crossed in an act of faith. One visualizes the episode vividly at Poppi where the Arno runs its silver course between patches of careful gardens and vineyards. One can imagine, too, the storm at sunset along the low mountains of the Apennines (*Purg.* V: 109–123).

Possibly here in the Casentino Dante wrote the eulogy to Saint Francis (*Par.* XI); for La Verna is south and east of Poppi and he must have visited its grottos and monastery, endeared to all the world by the Poverello. He must have gone to Camaldoli, a monastery of reformed Benedictines also nearby; for his vision of the contemplatives is substantially that of Saint Romuald whom he presents with other Camaldolese and Benedictine saints in the heaven of Saturn (*Par.* XXII). Or did he hold these images in mind and write the cantos in Ravenna?

It may be that here in the Casentino Dante was the guest of Guido Battifolle when he wrote Epistles VIII and IX — the first, Epistle VIII, to the cardinals assembled near Avignon in 1314, in which he beseeches them to return the Papacy to Rome; the second, Epistle IX, to a friend in Florence in which he writes the touching passage about his refusal to return to Florence under the humiliating conditions offered to him. On June 2, 1316, the Florentine government issued a recall of exiles under a threefold condition: the payment of a fine, a merely formal imprisonment in one of the public prisons, and the "oblation" in the Baptistery, a ceremony in which the offender asked to be offered, as a redeemed prisoner, to God and to Saint John. These conditions Dante indignantly rejected in a letter (Letter IX) written to a friend in Florence, evidently a priest — possibly Fra Remigio, who was "an affectionate father of Dante during his years of exile"[13] — and preserved by Boccaccio.

Is this the glorious recall whereby Dante Alighieri is summoned back to his fatherland after suffering well-nigh fifteen years of exile? Is this the reward of innocence manifest to all the world, of unbroken sweat and toil in study? Far be it from the familiar of philosophy, this abject self-abasement of a soul of clay! To allow himself to be presented at the altar, as a prisoner, after the fashion of some Ciolo or other infamous wretch. Far be it from the preacher of justice, when he hath suffered a wrong, to pay his coin to them that inflicted it as though they had deserved well of him.

Not this the way of return to my country, O my father! but if another may hereafter be found by you, or any other, which hurts not Dante's fair fame and honor, that will I accept with no lagging feet. If no such path leads back to Florence, then will I never enter Florence more. What then? May I not gaze upon the mirror of the sun and stars wherever I may be? Can I not ponder on the sweetest truths wherever I may be beneath the heaven, but I must first make me inglorious, nay infamous, before the people and the state of Florence? Nor shall I lack for bread.[14]

> *And I, who . . . see*
> *How exiles great as these*
> *Are grieved and comforted*
> *Henceforth my banishment an honor deem;*
>
> . . . .
>
> *To fall among the great is worthy praise.*
>   — *Minor Poems*
>   "Tre donne intorno al cor mi son venute"
>
> *Ravenna stands as many years she stood.*
>   — *Inferno* XXVII:40

Dante's last host was Guido da Polenta, the lord of Ravenna, a nephew of Francesca da Rimini, who fancying himself a poet begged as a special favor that the exile come to be his guest. Whether Dante came to Ravenna from the Casentino or from Verona we shall probably never know. Some believe that shortly after the death of the Emperor in 1313, he appealed to the generosity of Can Grande Della Scala and spent some time again with the Scaligers. What we do know is that in Ravenna he found relative peace and security in the last years of his life. Most scholars place the year of his arrival as 1317. He died there in 1321. It seems significant to some that in the melancholy city in which according to Dante the Roman Empire began (*Par.* VI:61–63) — for it was from Ravenna Caesar moved to cross the Rubicon — the city which was the refuge also of the last of the emperors, a city which had in his time lost even its seaboard, Dante the political exile who so greatly desired the restoration of the empire should have found his last refuge.

Dante, who was by his very nature somewhat of a professor — all of his major works are from time to time full of miniature lectures — may have had a professorship in Ravenna or have been a teacher of rhetoric.[15] It is to this period that the *Eclogues* belong, those strange Latin poems written in response to a letter in Latin hexameters in which Giovanni del Virgilio of Bologna requested Dante to write something in Latin on some political subject. Then Del Virgilio would be proud to place the laurel crown on Dante's head before the applauding students of Bologna, if Dante would deem him worthy. Dante, tongue in cheek, became an Arcadian. He proved to Virgilio and to the world that he was a master of Latin prosody; in a sense, however, the *Eclogues* seem to have been written to uphold the superior possibilities of the vernacular, for Dante promises (*Ec.* I, 1. 57 ff.) to send Virgilio ten cantos of the *Paradiso* to prove his contention. He hopes (ll. 43–47) to return with his verses to Florence (*Par.* XXV:1–9), where alone he is willing to have his "triumphant locks hide beneath the green (of laurel) their hoariness."[16]

It is from Ravenna that Dante is called in 1320 to deliver at Verona on February 13 a lecture on physical geography entitled *Quaestio de Aqua et Terra* (freely translated, *On the Nature of the Two Elements Water and Earth*), a topic which was the subject of lively discussion in the schools and among writers. Dante's lecture concerned itself from both a scientific and philosophic point of view with the problem as to whether water in its sphere is in any place higher than the land which emerges from the water in what was commonly called the habitable fourth of our world. Europe and Asia with the northern part of Africa comprise the emerging continent described in Dante's treatise. With the men of his time Dante shared an interest in exploration in the narrow sense of that word as well as in the intellectual and creative realm. Probably for that reason, among others, he casts the *Divine Comedy* into the form of a journey; and, though ostensibly he is exploring the purlieus of the dead, he gives the journey extraordinary verisimilitude by embedding in it all the geographical and astronomical knowledge of his era. The crusades had brought about a new vigorous contact between East and West; missionaries, ambassadors, merchants, and explorers penetrated little known lands. Just before Dante's time when Mongolian hordes had swept across the whole of Asia and eastern Europe and were threatening the West, Pope Innocent IV and King Louis IX of France had sent two remarkable Franciscans, John of Carpini and William of Rubruk, separately and at different times, to the court of the great Khan. Both men left careful and brilliant records of their travels.[17]

Records of these and other travels fired the imaginations of contemporary writers. From the ports of northern Italy went explorers and travelers. From Genoa between 1280 and 1290 expeditions set out to explore the southern hemisphere in the direction that Dante makes Ulysses take (*Inf.* XXVI:55–142; *Purg.* XIX:19–23; *Par.* XXVII:82–83) and like Ulysses were never heard of again. The greatest of these travelers, Marco Polo, came from Venice; no book was more copied by scribes than his *Milione,* the record of his adventures and the marvels he encountered on his long journeys to regions of which the West of his day had only vague notions, and others of the existence of which it had no knowledge whatsoever. It is highly probable that a copy of the *Milione* had come to Dante's hand in Florence before his exile or at some castle where he was a guest. Marco Polo (1254–1325) and Dante (1265–1321) were precise contemporaries; he had traversed much of the area with which Dante deals in his treatise on "Water and Earth"; he is known to have lived in Venice in the first quarter of the fourteenth century when Dante lived in Ravenna. It is not too absurd, therefore, to picture the great Florentine and the great Venetian in conversation concerning an interest which they had in common, especially since Dante, during his sojourn in Ravenna, had considerable prestige in northern Italy.

In Ravenna, Dante was able to have his children with him, Pietro and Jacopo and his daughter Antonia, who became Sister Beatrice in the Dominican convent of San Stefano dell' Uliva there and who in 1350 was visited by Boccaccio who was sent by the Captains of the "Compagnia dei Landesi," a religious confraternity of Or San Michele in Florence, to place in her hands ten gold florins as a token of the appreciation of these guildsmen for the care she had given her father in his last days. It may well be that from

Sister Beatrice, Boccaccio heard many of the details which he later incorporated into his *Life of Dante*. According to Michele Barbi, it is probable that Gemma, his wife, joined him here too; tradition says that in Ravenna were his grandchildren, the children of Pietro. Here he seems to have been honored by all around him. But he was still an exile, his spirit yearning for Florence.

Here in Ravenna Dante finished and brought to perfection the *Divine Comedy*. Here he wandered in the Pineta (*Purg.* XXVIII: 19–21), the ancient pine wood on the Adriatic and listened to the mournful wind soughing through the trees and thought out the verses of the Earthly Paradise. The old trees still stand, though today to get to them, one must buy his way through many gates. Here his subtle intellect explored the courses of the stars where today space ships rove; his brave spirit soared beyond all eastern fronts to the home of eternal Light and touched the Infinite; here he wrote the matchless cantos of the *Paradiso*. Here, too, he ended the epic story of his life, significantly on the feast of the Exaltation of the Holy Cross, September 14, 1321. His life like that of his Master seemed to all his world a failure. Even his last mission as an ambassador from Guido da Polenta to the Doge of Venice lacked success.

But he had known prophetically that he had not failed altogether. He knew that his *Divine Comedy* would find its place among the greatest poems of the world. He had dared to say so in the opening cantos (*Inf.* IV:94–102) when he saw assembled in Limbo the "masters of highest song who like eagles soar above the rest," for they honored him and made him sixth among their number. Knowing this, he had labored all his exiled years to bring the poem to completion and had done so in the face of grave difficulties. During the delirium of the malarial fever which brought his death was he conscious of failure or success? He could not have foreseen that the Western world would rank him second or possibly first among her supreme poets, his only contestant for first place being Homer, whom he himself calls the sovereign poet.

Guido da Polenta buried his friend with every solemnity in the Lady Chapel of the church of the Franciscan friars across from his palace and after the obsequies he himself pronounced at Dante's home a funeral oration. The tomb was one already prepared for another; Guido planned for Dante later a splendid monument, but the next year he had to retire to Bologna to escape his cousin's machinations and the tomb was never built, though in subsequent centuries the citizens of Ravenna and of Venice, into whose jurisdiction Ravenna passed, did much to renovate and improve the chapel of Braccioforte in which the tomb stood as well as the tomb itself.

Florence made many attempts to recover the bones of her most illustrious son; but, quite rightly, Ravenna would not surrender them. The splendid tomb erected in Santa Croce to receive them stands empty. In 1519 Pope Leo X commanded that they be returned to Florence; the Franciscans of Ravenna, jealous of their treasure, removed them from the sarcophagus and hid them. In June, 1677, Fra Antonio visited the bones in their hiding place and verified them, but eventually the secret of the hiding place was lost. However, so the story runs, the tradition persisted among the friars that they were in the possession of a great treasure. As late as the nineteenth century, one Angelo Grillo, the sacristan of the Franciscan confraternity known as La Confraternita della Mercede, who was accustomed to sleep in the ancient chapel of Braccioforte, declared that he had seen in a dream a shade clad in the red gown of a scholar issue from the spot where the skeleton was later found and that its passed through the chapel into the cemetery. It approached him and, when he asked who it was, replied, "I am Dante." The sacristan died in May, 1865, a few days before the bones were found.

It seems that in October, 1677, just a few months after the bones had been verified by Fra Antonio, the box containing them had been built into a new wall where the old entrance to the Braccioforte chapel had been. On May 27, 1865 — May 27 is Dante's birthday — when all the world was preparing to celebrate the sixth centenary of Dante's birth, the pickax of a workman engaged in breaking through the wall to make some necessary repairs struck the wood of a small brown box on which were the hastily scrawled words Ossa Dantis. The bones were returned to the sarcophagus from which they had been taken; later in 1921, after being subjected to careful scientific examination by Professor Fabio Frassetto of Bologna — who in his book *Ossa Dantis* has set forth his findings — they were placed in the new tomb in which they are today.

And what of the poem? There is a legend about that, too, told by Boccaccio. As we know, Dante's Letter X dedicates his *Paradiso* to Can Grande at Verona: it was his custom, says Boccaccio, to send the cantos to him by installments. Dante died, however, without sending the last thirteen. For eight months following the death of their father, Jacopo and Piero[18] and the friends and disciples of Dante searched carefully among all his papers for these thirteen missing cantos. Moved by their friends, Dante's two sons, both "poets in rhyme," decided to complete the work as best they could, when to Jacopo there appeared a wondrous vision, "which not only checked his foolish presumption" but showed him where the thirteen cantos were.

Boccaccio has the story, he says, from Piero Giardino, "long time a disciple of Dante's" who told him that eight months after the death of his master, Jacopo came to him one night near to the hour of Matins (midnight) and told him that that same night a little earlier in his sleep he had seen his father draw near to him.

He was clad in whitest raiment, and his face shone with unwonted light. The son in his dream asked him if he were living, and heard him reply, "Yes, not in our life, but in the true." Again he seemed to question him, asking if he had finished his poem before passing to that true life, and, if he had completed it, where was the missing part which they had never been able to find. And again he seemed to hear in answer, "Yes, I finished it." And then it seemed to him that his father took him by the hand and led him to the room where he was wont to sleep when alive, and touching a spot there, said, "Here is that for which thou hast so long sought." And with these words his sleep and his father left him.

Jacopo said that he could not postpone coming to Messer Piero to tell him what he had seen, in order that together they might go and search the place. . . . While there still remained a good part of the night they set out together, and, coming to the designated spot, they found a matting fastened to the wall. Gently lifting this, they discovered a little opening which neither of them had ever seen or known of before. Therein they found some writings, all mildewed by the dampness of the wall, and on the point of rotting had they remained there a little longer. Carefully cleaning them of the mold, they read them, and found that they were the long sought thirteen cantos. With great joy, therefore, they copied them, and sent them first, according to the custom of the author, to Messer Cane, and then attached them, as was fitting, to the incomplete work. In such wise the poem that had been many years in composition was completed.[19]

Whatever one may say about the vision — and there seems little reason to doubt it — the fact remains that in the spring of 1322 Jacopo presented a complete copy of the poem to Guido da Polenta, who was then Captain of the People at Bologna.

And so, according to Boccaccio, we have the *Divine Comedy* complete — rounded out in its hundred cantos — because of a vision. Dante wrote it, he said, because of a vision (*New Life* XLIII; *Par.* XVII:128); it is a "sacred poem to which heaven and earth have set hand" (*Par.* XXV:1–9). But the paradox about Dante is this: though his poem had its inception in a vision, it is in no way visionary in the popular sense of that word; though Longfellow rightly calls it a medieval miracle of song, it is not medieval in spite of the fact that it gives the best summary we have of the life and thought of the Middle Ages; though it is more completely of its age than any other poem is of any age, it is of no age and of all ages. It is timeless as man is timeless, as Hell and Heaven, which Dante portrays with such vividness, are timeless, as God and eternity are timeless, as love is timeless. No other poem has such scope; no other poet makes so clear within the confines of one work what he believes about the meaning of the whole universe, about the meaning of life and of death and of immortality.

It was not until 1373, fifty-one years after Dante's death, that the *Divine Comedy* was first expounded to a Florentine audience, when — "at the request of the people" — Boccaccio was given permission to hold a course of lectures officially described as "a moral and rhetorical exposition for the benefit of the unlearned of the book vulgarly known as *el Dante.*" The first lecture was given on October 23 of that year. Boccaccio is first in the long line of distinguished lecturers on the *Commedia* whose names on marble plaques line the walls of the Guild Hall above Or San Michele.

NOTES

1. That Dante had country property is attested by Leonardo Bruni in his life of Dante and by other records. Bruni asserts that Dante had "possessions in Camerata, in the Piacentina, and in the plain of Ripoli." See James Robinson Smith, *The Earliest Lives of Dante*, trans. from the Italian of Giovanni Boccaccio and Lionardo Bruni Aretino, Yale Studies in English, No. X (New York, 1901), p. 90.

   A tower section of the old house in Camerata still stands, forming part of the lovely villa known as *Il Garofalo* (The Carnation), situated on the Via Forbici, halfway between Florence and Fiesole. *Forbici* is the Italian for *scissors;* the villa is located between the blades of Via Forbici and the old Fiesole highway. The entrance is in the old Alighieri section, which from the garden presents a stolid towerlike aspect. The Contessa Rimbotti, the present owner, says that her papers certify that the villa was owned by the Alighieri family, by Dante, in fact, and that after his death in Ravenna when his sons returned to Florence was sold by them to the Portinari family. It had not been confiscated at the time of Dante's exile, as had the city houses, because it was not within the jurisdiction of Florence.

   In the entrance hall on the left wall as one enters are the coats of arms of the Alighieri and Portinari families and medallions of Dante and Beatrice. In the court is a well, now filled in; the masonry with the bucket arrangement is said to have been constructed by the Portinari.

2. For further information about the Cerchi and Donati families and the feud, read Amerigo Parrini, *With Dante in Florence* (Florence: Giannini, 1930), pp. 165–167.

3. In Florence in the thirteenth century as in many other Italian cities and in some other parts of the world, the year began *ab incarnatione,* that is on the feast of the Annunciation and Incarnation, celebrated on March 25. In fact, in spite of the decree of Gregory XIII in 1582 and that of Innocent XII in 1691 abolishing the ancient calendars throughout the Christian world, Florence did not begin her year on January 1 until 1750. On the wall of the Loggia in the Palazzo Signoria is a marble tablet recording this important event.

   In discussing events in the life of Dante, it is necessary, therefore, to observe whether an author is using a contemporary calendar or that of the Middle Ages. Many Dante scholars write dates indicating both, for example, Toynbee writes 1300[1]. Dates are used here according to contemporary reckoning.

4. This material on the decrees of banishment is condensed from the discussion in Paget Toynbee, *A Dictionary of Proper Names and Notable Matters in the Works of Dante*, 4 ed. (Oxford, 1910). See entry under "Dante."

5. The encyclical of Benedict XV is known as *In Praeclara*. It is addressed to *Our beloved sons, the professors and students of all Catholic institutions for instruction in literature and higher culture on the sixth centenary of the death of Dante Alighieri*. It can be found, among other places, in *The Catholic World*, Vol. CXIII (September, 1921), pp. 867–872; and in Patrick Cummins, O.S.B., *Dante Theologian* (Saint Louis, 1948).

6. Edward Moore, *Studies in Dante, First Series*, "Scripture and Classical Authors in Dante" (Oxford, 1896), pp. 1–3.

7. Boccaccio in relating a variant of this incident names the poet Dino di Messer

Lambertuccio. See Smith, *op. cit.*

8. Material on the court of the Scaligers is quoted from various sources and discussed in some detail in Toynbee, *op. cit.*, p. 116 seq.

9. Lonsdale Ragg, *Dante and His Italy* (London, 1907), p. 322. The material on Dante's hosts was drawn from many sources: discussions with scholars and people who live in the places where Dante is known to have been and personal observations — all of which are compared with the scholarly writing of Barbi, Wicksteed, and Gardner; from Ragg and Toynbee; and from two books on the Casentino, namely, Beni, *Guide Illustrate del Casentino* (Florence, 1889) and Ella Noyes, *The Casentino and Its Story* (New York, 1905).

10. For excellent commentaries on the letters of Dante see *A Translation of the Latin Works of Dante Alighieri*, The Temple Classics (London, 1934).

11. Note the close of Letters VI and VII.

12. Ragg, *op. cit.*, p. 313, speaks of the incident as being recorded in Petrarch's *Letters*.

13. See Chapter I, above, Note 8. For other suggestions regarding the identity of Dante's correspondent, see P. H. Wicksteed and E. G. Gardner, *Dante and Giovanni del Virgilio* (Westminster, 1902), p. 72.

14. Since the letter of recall excluded certain groups of exiles, three of which groups would include Dante, the editor of the translation cited above suggests, pp. 341–342, that the priest who wrote Dante and whose letter Dante answered in Letter IX may have received private assurances that grace would be extended to Dante if he would "express application" and would submit himself to the conditions.

15. Note 2, Chapter I, above, discusses Dante's qualifications for a chair in Ravenna. Catherine Mary Phillimore, *Dante at Ravenna* (London, 1898), p. 46, quotes from a codex in the Laurentian library cited by Bandini which states: *It is commonly reported that Dante, being studying in Ravenna, and giving lectures as a Doctor to his pupils upon various works, the schools became the resort of many learned men.* She further asserts that the matter of the lectures was his *Concerning Vernacular Eloquence.* For the development of this point see Chapters III and IV, pp. 43–120.

16. For a discussion of the *Eclogues* read the section "Dante and Del Virgilio" in The Temple Classics translation of the *Latin Works*, 371–385. See also Wicksteed and Gardner, *op. cit.*

17. *The Mongol Mission, Narratives and Letters of the Franciscan Missionaries in Mongolia and China in the Thirteenth and Fourteenth Centuries*, trans. by a nun of Stanbrook Abbey, ed. Christopher Dawson (New York, 1955).

18. There is a discrepancy in the spelling of the name of Dante's second son. Modern biographers spell it *Pietro*; Boccaccio spells it *Piero*.

19. James Robinson Smith, *op. cit.*, pp. 65, 66.

CHAPTER III

THE DIVINE IN HUMAN LOVE

Antiphon. *It is not good for man to be alone.*

God knew the loneliness of Adam's gladness,
And, setting seal like harvest after dearth,
Touching our dawn like music out of sadness,
Came Eve to be the mother of the earth.
Then first man felt the beauty of a maiden
Bound the dim ocean of desire with shore:
The Polestar leads our breathless vessels laden
With hardy cargo home, but she leads more.*

— James J. Donohue
Exile in the Stars, A Book of Hours

ven people who have little or no knowledge of either Dante or Beatrice know that they were lovers. The names are everywhere linked: there are Dante and Beatrice book ends and Dante and Beatrice plaques; and there is the popular picture in living rooms and libraries of the meeting near the bridge Santa Trinità in Florence where Beatrice and two other maidens are coming toward the Florentine scholar, who stands with his hand upon his heart. Many of these folk have never heard of the *New Life* or the *Banquet* or even of the *Divine Comedy,* three books which form a trilogy in which Dante sets before us the whole story of the meaning of Beatrice in his life. And since love is universal, even in those aspects which seem most particular and individual, he shows, too, especially in the *Commedia,* what love is in the life of any man and any woman.

Volumes have been written about Dante and Beatrice. Some nineteenth-century critics would prove that the woman Beatrice did not exist, that since Dante is a medieval man and worked with

* (New York: The Macmillan Company, 1945.)

57

symbols, Beatrice is merely a symbol. They allow that in the first instance an actual person, possibly her name was Beatrice, flashed an ideal into Dante's mind; but they maintain that all the details of the *New Life* are purely fictitious. In the *Divine Comedy,* according to some of them, Dante's devotion to Beatrice means his devotion to Wisdom, just as his devotion to the "gentle lady" in the *Banquet* means devotion to Philosophy. There is a group, too, which holds that Beatrice is a personification of the ideal of womanhood, the *ewige weibliche* of Goethe. She is to these the embodiment of female perfection, not realized and impossible to be realized on earth.[1]

The best critics of the twentieth century hold with the early commentators in affirming that Beatrice was an historical personage. They find no reason for believing that Dante did not mean what he said. For four hundred years after the death of Dante no one questioned the actual existence of Beatrice. Boccaccio had identified her as Beatrice Portinari, the daughter of Folco, a prominent citizen of Florence; Dante's son Pietro confirmed Boccaccio's statement, and there is extant a sonnet by Cino da Pistoia sympathizing with Dante upon her death. Folco Portinari is said to have had twelve children — Beatrice had five brothers and six sisters — several of whom must have been living in Florence at the time of Boccaccio's lectures. One of her brothers is reputed to have been that "second friend" for whom Dante wrote the two lyrics of Sections XXXIII and XXXIV of the *New Life.* If Boccaccio's statement were untrue, someone would surely have risen up to say so.

Contemporary scholars, accepting the evidence of Dante's friends that the lady of the *New Life* was Beatrice Portinari, also accept as essentially true the episodes. There is in these moderns a fusion of the attitudes of the nineteenth-century critics plus a new psychological element: they hold, as the early realists did, the historical validity of the recorded events and of Dante's assertions relative to their effect on him; they see that the image of Beatrice enlarges and that she becomes a symbol while she remains in every sense a real woman, the "Beatrician image" — to borrow the phrase of Charles Williams in his *The Figure of Beatrice*[2] — enlarging and extending itself into Dante's political and religious life; they see that in the *Divine*

Comedy Beatrice is in a sense the eternal feminine as Dante is the universal man. But in this age so profoundly interested in psychology, many of these contemporary critics are inclined in addition to these points of view to analyze the book for its metaphysical and psychological implications; because it is so detailed a record of the inner life of a master poet, they endeavor to study the growth and clarification of the meaning of Dante's love of Beatrice in his life and writings.

These contemporary scholars are puzzled particularly by the *New Life*. They ask whether such simple episodes as it records could be fraught with such extraordinary results. They ask whether the work was conceived and planned for itself, reporting things just as they happened so far as the memory of them is accurate, or whether at a later date it was revised and altered and adjusted to the other two works of the so-called trilogy. One nineteenth-century critic goes so far as to say that the whole thing was fabricated to serve as a basis for the place of Beatrice in the *Divine Comedy*.[3] Michele Barbi, however, Italy's pre-eminent Dante scholar, to whom was confided the editing of the definitive edition of the works of Dante published in Florence in 1921 on the occasion of the sixth centenary of Dante's death, makes this statement:

> The most trustworthy opinion among so many guesses is that the *Vita Nuova* is to be read literally without hidden meanings, and that it has never had any other form than the one we know; and that since the facts related in it do not take us beyond 1292, the plan and the completion of it must not have occurred much later than that year.[4]

Dante wrote the *New Life* for his "chief friend" Guido Cavalcanti (XXXI), writing it in the vulgar tongue as Guido desired. It is a collection of poems, thirty in all, linked by prose passages which tell the occasion of each poem, analyze each, and explain its meaning. The poems, which in their personification of love and other conventional stylistic devices reflect the troubadour lyrics of the day, were written over a period of eight or nine years: the first dates from 1283, the last probably from 1292. As Dante set the writing down it was continuous and remained so until the nineteenth century. The breakdown into forty-three sections seems to have been made by some nineteenth-century editor who did not catch Dante's sense of structure; since throughout the book Dante carefully uses three, nine, and ten as he did later in the *Divine Comedy,* he would surely have made divisions on that basis — if, indeed, he wished to make any.

The *New Life* seems to consist of a Prelude, three major parts, and an Epilogue. Dante closes each major part with a statement that he is moving on to another matter more noble or more significant. He explains his reason for the use of three in Section XXX — the reason, of course, having its foundation in the Blessed Trinity.[5] The whole is a soul-searching love story filled with mysticism which places in juxtaposition natural and supernatural episodes. Gardner calls it "a spotless lily of a book, the most spiritual and ethereal romance of love that exists." But its purity comes, he continues, "not from innocent simplicity of soul, but from self-repression."[6] Both here and in the *Divine Comedy* Dante says that his love was ever under the control of reason.

The very title of the book is delicate and significant. Dante had had a wound of love from which he never recovered; it came early in his life before which in "the book of memory" little was written. He recognized when he wrote these things down eighteen years after the first incident occurred, that for him on that day in his childhood there had begun a *new life;* that is, after he received this wound of love, he could never again be the same. The facts are few and very simple: his reactions to them are singularly vivid and poignant.

The book begins with a simple quite ordinary external happening and a deep inner reaction which Dante recalls and sets down with vibrant vividness. He was at the end of his ninth year and Beatrice at the beginning of hers when he saw her for the first time. She was wearing a crimson dress girdled and adorned; and when he saw her, the "spirit of life which has its dwelling in the *secretest chamber of the heart"* began to tremble so violently that his whole body shook and he heard these words, "Here is a deity stronger than I: who, coming, shall rule over me." At this moment the experience was also *intellectual,* stirring "the lofty chamber whither the senses carry their perceptions" (that is, the brain) filling it with wonder and saying, "Your beatitude hath now been manifest to you." At that moment, too, *the natural spirit* (that is, the liver) the seat of *organic life* was quickened and said, "Woe is me for that I shall be disturbed from this time forth." Then Dante quotes from the *Iliad,* "She seemed to be not the daughter of a mortal man but of God." To put it all quite simply, Dante's whole person was stirred: he was quickened spiritually, intellectually, and physically. A whole new life was stirred. He experienced love at first sight. He carried the image of Beatrice with him until the day of his death.

> *I am one who when Love breathes in me note it and write as he dictates.*
> — *Purgatorio* XXIV:52–54

Though Dante must have seen Beatrice frequently during the next nine years — they lived but a short distance apart in old Florence — and in his "boyhood often went in search of her" (*New Life* II), she did not speak to him until a day when he met her on the street walking between two other ladies, the meeting portrayed in the popular picture. This episode marks the beginning of the first section. On that day she was clothed in white, the color of faith. He was moved even more profoundly than he had been when he saw her first; he was eighteen now and she was seventeen, the age when the blood runs warm and sensibilities are easily stirred. The night after this meeting and salutation, he dreamed that Love appeared to him in visible form, a joyous lord clothed in a color of flame, and spoke to him. But of all that Love said, Dante understood only, "I am thy master." Love was carrying Beatrice in his arms; in his hand he held something all aflame and he said to Dante, "Behold thy heart." Then Love wakened Beatrice and made her eat of the heart and she did so, fearing. Then Love wept and gathered the Lady in his arms and ascended with her toward heaven. Dante was now possessed wholly by love; he grew thin and irksome to his friends who questioned him.

Following this episode there are the episodes of the two screen

ladies, a device (like that of personifying love) taken from troubadour poetry, nothing new, nothing old. One who deals with adoles-
cents sees the device used again and again. The first screen lady
was between him and Beatrice in church, and catching Dante's
intense gaze, thought he was looking at her. He resolved to use
her to throw his friends off the track. However, before long she
left Florence and he was again at a loss. At the time of her departure he wrote a sorrowful poem, the fashion for a would-be
troubadour. But one day Love appeared to him again, this time
in guise of a traveler, for Dante was on the highway in a goodly
company. Love proposed another screen lady, but the second screen
lady did not work out so satisfactorily, and Dante found himself in
the midst of complications.

However, all the days between, the tender love which Dante
felt for Beatrice so extended his heart and gave him such elation
of spirit that he would have pardoned anyone for any injury. And
this is as it should be; for, as Dante shows us, true love brings with
it nobility and gentleness. True nobility, he says, does not lie in
"ancient wealth" but in the perfection of nature. Dante discusses
the matter at considerable length in the fourth book of the *Banquet,*
Chapters XV, XVI, and XVII. Nobility exists where virtue dwells:
the moral virtues, that is, which are within the power of man to
achieve. Love is expansive; it splits the ego and reaches out beyond
the self. Else it is not really love. However, this growth in virtue
does not necessarily bar difficulties.

The second screen lady whom Love suggested was annoyed at
Dante's attentions and said so to her neighbors and friends; tongues
began to wag and gossip spread evil rumors which came to the
ears of Beatrice. She, being the "destroyer of all evil" and the "queen
of all good," refused to speak to Dante; he, being disconsolate, wept
bitterly. Love appeared a third time and after weeping, too, and
hinting darkly at the death of Beatrice told Dante why Beatrice
had refused to greet him, suggesting that despite the screen ladies
his secret must have become known to her from familiar observation (how utterly human and feminine this is) and urged Dante
to write certain poems in which he was to make clear what a
strong mastery love had had over him even from childhood because

of her; these verses, Love said, would discredit the gossips. But he must write the verses as though they were the work of a third person and set them to appropriate music so that they could be sung where Beatrice would surely hear them.

During this time Dante was very troublesome to himself and to his friends. His poor heart had no peace. While he was battling with his thoughts, as every man must, not knowing whether to be done with love or to "bow with mind and sense," he was taken by a friend to a social gathering. The friend intended well. There might be safety and diversion in numbers. There would be many beautiful women at the gathering and Dante, never impervious to beauty, might be brought out of his doldrums. But he was only submerged in them. The gathering was in honor of a gentlewoman who had that day been given in marriage; some commentators identify her as Beatrice herself and the occasion that of her marriage to Simone dei Bardi. When Dante saw Beatrice on that day, he was so overcome that he found it necessary to lean against the wall for support; several ladies, among them Beatrice, seeing his confusion, whispered among themselves and mocked him. Their derision so overwhelmed him emotionally that he excused himself to his friend and went home to weep.

There is one more episode in this first section, the decisive one, the climax in the drama; possibly it marks the climax in Dante's emotional life. Dante's distress after the incident of the wedding, his continued grief because of his lady's refusal to salute him had worn him out emotionally. He had sung of what her beauty and her salutation had done to him. Then one day in a social gathering (the number of the social affairs of which he is a part indicates that he did not spend his time feeling sorry for himself; whatever his interior life may have been he participated in the life about him) where Beatrice was not present but where many ladies were laughing with one another, one soft-spoken lady addressed Dante by name and all fastened their eyes on him, waiting his reply, when she asked him why he loved his lady so deeply and to what end. These may be the same gossipy ladies who had discussed Dante and the second screen lady; if they are not identical, they are of the same kind. When he had answered that all he desired of his lady was her salutation, that in that alone was his beatitude, they, like many knowing ladies today, put their heads together, and then the lady with the soft voice asked, "Pray, wherein abideth this beatitude?" When he had answered, "In those words which praise my Lady," she said that his words must have been written with another intent.

Dante was put to shame at the suggestion in her words and left the gathering. As he walked, he resolved that henceforth he would choose for his theme only the praise of Beatrice; in other words, his love songs would no longer be self-centered. His love for Beatrice would be purely spiritual; he would no longer sing of her beauty except to extol her beauty of soul. Beatrice became at that point not only herself but the personification of all beauty and nobility, the perfect woman who leads man to God.

How familiar most of this is in its external episodes, how easily transferred from thirteenth-century Florence to any twentieth-century city or town or village! It is familiar except for the fact that Dante never sees Beatrice alone. There is always that circle of feminine faces surrounding her against a medieval background. But the women themselves easily find their counterpart in upper-class twentieth-century society or middle-class society or on a college campus. Boy meets girl. He is profoundly stirred spiritually and physically. He is unhappy when he sees her, unhappy when he does not see her, quite lifted out of himself when she smiles at him or speaks to him. He may not, he often does not, want her to know how deeply moved he is. He may even in his own way, in his own environment, find screen girls. Gossips and meddlers may spoil the relationship. And from that point the decisions he will make will depend largely upon his temperament; perhaps his environment will determine them as far as externals are concerned. The wound of love may last a lifetime; any of us can name cases where it did, though at the time we called the love "puppy love" and did not understand.

None of the adolescent episodes confound the critics. What does confound them is the first one, the one when Dante was nine. They do not understand why so casual a meeting should enkindle so unquenchable a flame. The answer lies probably in the kind of boy Dante was. He was a prodigy, a genius in the arts capable of being profoundly stirred emotionally. We have in the field of music records of such prodigies: Beethoven, Mozart, Mendelssohn. In her *Valiant Pilgrim*, writing of John Bunyan, Vera Brittain remarks that one danger inherent in modern psychology is a tendency to regard inspired departures from the average as forms of psychiatric aberration, that individuals who pride themselves upon their own normality are likely to be baffled by exceptions. Great literature outside of the *New Life* deals with the thesis of love at first sight very early in life. Juliet was only fourteen. The glance of the child Beatrice fell without her knowing it on the highly inflammable material which was the heart of Dante. The intensity of the reaction at the age of nine may be extraordinary. So was Dante. Apparently he knew on that day with a surety that he never doubted all his life long that Beatrice had awakened in him a powerful creative force. The most significant thing about it is that it was always under the control of reason.

> My Lady, God shall ask, "What daredst thou?"
> (When my soul stands with all her acts reviewed)
> "Thou passedst Heaven, into My sight, as now,
> To make Me of vain love similitude.
> To Me doth praise belong,
> And to the Queen of all the realm of grace
> Who slayeth fraud and wrong."
> Then may I plead: "As though from Thee he came,
> Love wore an angel's face:
> Lord, if I loved her, count it not my shame."
>
> — Guido Guinizelli
> from "Of the Gentle Heart"
> (Rossetti's translation)

Young readers always ask, "If Dante loved Beatrice so devotedly, why did he not marry her?" Or the question may take this form:

"After Dante was married to Gemma Donati how could he still continue to love Beatrice? Wasn't he unfaithful?" The thirteenth century understood the answers to these questions in a way difficult for the twentieth century to grasp. The simplest answer to the first question, of course, is that Dante was never free to marry Beatrice. Dante knew from the time he was a child of nine, or possibly, twelve, that he was betrothed to Gemma Donati. Beatrice, too, was probably spoken for. Marriages were arranged in those days. It is not easy to make these young people see that, notwithstanding, most of them turned out quite as happily as the romantic twentieth-century alliances. Dante accepted the fact that he could not contemplate marriage with Beatrice; nowhere is there any suggestion that he considered himself unfortunate. He seems never to have had the remotest desire to marry Beatrice. The average twentieth-century reader knows little about the position of woman in the symbolism of the Middle Ages and is often unable to adjust his thinking to the sublimation which could lift her from the level of the senses to the realm of the spirit, which is precisely what Dante does in the second section of the *New Life* and in the *Divine Comedy*.

Dante's love had from the beginning been unique in its self-effacement. Saint Thomas distinguishes the love of friendship from the love of desire; in the love of friendship that which is loved is loved simply for its own sake. Such love can exist between people of the same sex or those of the opposite sex. It can exist on a natural and supernatural level. The supernaturalized love of friendship as defined by Saint Thomas finds concrete expression in the allegorical figure of Love in Dante's *New Life*. When God is the reason for the love, it becomes charity. According to Saint Thomas the image of God belongs to both sexes, since it is in the mind, wherein there is no sexual distinction. It is for this reason that there is no infidelity in Dante's love of Beatrice after her marriage to Simone dei Bardi and after his own marriage to Gemma Donati.[7]

The lyrics of the second part of the *New Life* greatly surpass in every way those of the first. In the first great poem "Ladies Who Have Intelligence in Love," Dante exalts Beatrice as the example of all womanhood at its best. She is desired in heaven, but she is permitted to remain on earth; whoever gazes on her will be ennobled; when such a one deserves to be raised on high, her power comes to proof; whoever speaks with her can never come to an evil end; she is the pinnacle of all God's creation, "a fair woman . . . is as high as Nature's skill can soar."

All that was personal in Dante's devotion is now past; his love has become a transcendental rapture; self is annihilated. There are episodes here, too, that are important: the death of the father of Beatrice and "her face bowed with the grief that Love makes full of grace," Dante's own illness and the premonition of the death of Beatrice herself, the dream in which he

> Saw the angels, like a rain of manna
> In a long flight flying back Heavenward
> Having a little cloud in front of them.

The imagery becomes daring in this section as it is in the *Divine Comedy*, particularly so in the episode involving Joan, the loved lady of Guido Cavalcanti, and Beatrice. Joan is called here Primavera, Spring, because of her comeliness. She comes first because her name, Joan, was taken from John who went before the True Light. Love speaking again said, "I am the voice of one crying in the wilderness, 'Prepare ye the way of the Lord.'" The implication is clear; though Dante does not quite say so, Beatrice is in a sense to be Dante's savior. Beatrice represents Love. Human love is the way to Divine Love. She is the vehicle who will draw him to God because of her gentleness and humility. Again and again Dante stresses these virtues in Beatrice, virtues by which all men are drawn to God.

To draw men to God because of her virtue and her love is the function of woman in whatever capacity she live out her life. Fashioned neither from the head of man to rule over him nor from his foot to be trampled by him but from his side near his heart to be loved by him, woman is man's spiritual as well as material helpmate. This concept of woman, a Christian heritage from Scripture and theology (cf. *Summa* I, q. 92, a. 3), lies behind Dante's idea of Beatrice. Beatrice could have been an Eve, not a cause of a fall but at least an occasion. But she was not. She leads Dante to Mary, who gains for him the vision of God. On the cornice of the lustful, those who are purging their souls sing of chastity in young virgins who have not yet decided on their way of life, in consecrated virgins, and in chaste wives and husbands. The Middle Ages understood that all these can know love well: they understood the chaste love of Francis for Clare and of Clare for Francis; the love of Gertrude for Mechtilde; the conjugal love of Elizabeth of Hungary and the princely Louis. All of these were "real flesh" (*Purg.* XXVI:12) whose lives were dedicated to love.

> *Love appears in all literature, not as a passing episode, but as the marrow of it. But with what a bewildering variety of incident and type!*
> — M. C. D'Arcy, S.J.
> *The Mind and Heart of Love*

It is important here to make a little detour. It is important to point out that the dedication to love as Dante understood it, as is clear from all his writing, and as the aforenamed men and women understood it, differed altogether in essence from the erotic courtly love which was introduced into literature by the troubadours of the south of France in the first half of the twelfth century and which permeates the lyrics and romances of the next three hundred years. In fact, in the Arthurian romances as retold by Tennyson there is a residue of this eroticism. In the thirteenth century it was the departure from this erotic concept of love that distinguished Dante and the other poets of the *sweet new style.* Like the troubadours, Guido Guinizelli and his school believed that human love is an ennobling force, but they freed themselves from those aspects of courtly love which created a dichotomy between it and Christian thought. Though the cult of courtly love maintained that its desire was union of heart and mind rather than physical possession, it nevertheless condoned — the word is an understatement — fornication and adultery; its whole outlook was in that area which Saint Thomas classifies as the love of concupiscence.

There are several theories as to the origin of the cult of courtly love as it is found in the songs of the troubadours, the metrical romances of the Arthurian Cycle, and the *Romance of the Rose*. Whether it came through Avicenna and the Arabs and was Oriental in its origin, or whether it came through the *Ars Amatoria* of Ovid and was Greco-Roman is, in this connection, of little importance. What is important is that the doctrine of courtly love had two fundamental un-Christian points of view. The first of these is that same "double truth" that the schoolmen fought in the Averroism of the Faculty of Arts at the University of Paris, the principle that what is true in philosophy may be false in theology or Divine Revelation; the second is the building of a sort of love-religion with a ritual borrowed from that of the Church. The involvement of "double truth" in the question of love lies in the philosophy of the nature of man as a pure creature of nature or as a supernatural creature of grace as well. The second point of view took two forms: sometimes the ritual became a mere jest or parody of the Church; sometimes it was a serious travesty on religion in which Love is a deity who enslaves only the noblest hearts and demands of those whom he deigns to admit to his court utter self-surrender. Both the "double truth" and the love-religion are irreconcilable with the tenets of the Christian faith.

The textbook of courtly love was the *De Arte Honeste Amandi* of Andreas Capellanus (Andrè the chaplain), who at the end of the twelfth century officiated at the court of Marie of Champagne, herself an "authority" on all amatory questions. She was the patron of Chrétien de Troyes, who, at her bidding, put into action in his metrical stories the developed theory of love as Andreas put it into Latin prose. Both Andreas and Chrétien, however, saw the dichotomy between Christian ethics and the precepts of the Court of Love as they set them down in their works, and ultimately in later writings showed that they did.[8]

The book of Andreas as it has come down to us falls into three parts, the last of which contradicts the other two. The first part, the *De Amore,* in a series of ideal dialogues gives methodical instruction in the art of love-making; it discusses for a certain Walter the conventions and rules which he must follow and points out the errors he must avoid. The second part deals with the problem of retaining love. On this Andreas has little to say. The third part, known as the *De Reprobatione Amoris,* tears down all that the first has built up. In the *De Amore,* on purely rational grounds, Andreas presents the thesis that from a purely natural point of view, all men are irresistibly drawn to love. All that is good in this present world depends solely upon love. Since it is wrong to oppose nature, it is wrong to oppose love: whatever is done under the compulsion of nature cannot be called wrong. However, rationality lifts man above the animals; his love is, therefore, set apart and ennobles him. In the *De Reprobatione* Andreas presents the Christian concept of man as a *super*natural creature, a child of God by grace, with an end wholly different from the purely natural happiness proposed in the *De Amore.* Behind, above, and beyond any secular or temporal good, there is eternal good before which the temporal must give way. From the supernatural point of view, Andreas, too, recognizes the truth that the teachings of the Court of Love may prove as disastrous as they did to Francesca and Tristran and the "more than thousand shades" (*Inf.* V:68) which Virgil pointed out to Dante in Hell.

Dante's calling attention to the Lancelot story (*Inf.* V:127–129) reminds one that just as Dante revolts from the attitudes toward love in the medieval romances and points out their danger, so, too, did some of the romancers themselves, among them Chrétien whose *Lancelot* in all probability Paola and Francesca were reading. Chrétien's *Lancelot,* written at the command of the Countess of Champagne, was left unfinished, perhaps in protest to the cult of romantic adultery. Like Andreas, Chrétien testified to his recognition of the irremediable rift between the precepts of the Court of Love and the teaching of the Church. He closed his writing career with the *Percival,* in which — as in the *Parzifal* of his contemporary, Wolfram von Eschenbach — the quest of man becomes what it is in the *Divine Comedy,* the quest for God and the things of God.[9] Perhaps Chrétien and Wolfram did not wish their books or themselves to prove a "Gallehaut" (*Inf.* V:137) — a panderer — to other Francescas. In Wolfram's work particularly, there is full-blooded living in forms of decency and loyalty; there is conjugal fidelity in body and spirit.

It is no wonder that the schoolmen made war on Averroism with its doctrine of "double truth" which was cutting its way into every area of man's thought and activity.[10] Nor is it a wonder that Dante with his passion for social reform should make war on the romancing of the poets of the Court of Love. The *New Life* and the *Divine Comedy* represent in poetry that noble fusion of the rational and religious, of faith and reason, of the human and divine which we find in Saint Thomas Aquinas. In their own field they stand in as stout opposition to Averroism and eroticism as the writings of the greatest of the schoolmen.[11]

> *O, excellent soul! how blessed is he that now looketh upon thee.*
>
> — *New Life* XXIII

The poems of the third part of the *New Life*, as Dante promised, deal with the manner by which he was subject to the influence of Beatrice. The major episode is that of her death, of which he had had so sure a premonition. She was carried by the angels to the Heaven of Humility where Mary is, from which she will come to win help for Dante and to which she will lead him in due time. The city of Florence is desolate. So is Dante's heart. On the first anniversary of her death, he wrote, at the request of his "second friend," two poems. Following the discussion of the sonnets, he told of the lady who pitied him in his grief for Beatrice and for whom he wrote several lyrics, thinking that perchance Love had set her in his path. However, one day, about the ninth hour, he had a vision of Beatrice, dressed in crimson as she had been when he first saw her. Retracing in memory all those episodes of which she was a part, he repented of his lapse of fidelity, contrary to the constancy of reason, and from that hour thought constantly of Beatrice with a *humbled and shamed heart*. He wept so that his eyes were circled about with red. Never, he said, did he permit them to look upon the beauty of any face that might bring him to evil desires and vain temptations.

The third part closes with the pilgrim folk on their way to Rome to see the *Veronica*, that is, the towel which Veronica offered to Jesus on his way to Calvary and on which he left the imprint of his holy face — that Face upon which his dear Lady now looks continually. These pilgrim folk pass without sorrow through the desolated city of Florence because they do not know that she is bereft of Beatrice. There is a touch of irony in this passage, written in 1292, because of Dante's first definition of a pilgrim as *anyone who leaveth the place of his birth*. A decade later, Dante will be a pilgrim and remain a pilgrim for the rest of his life. In the *Banquet* he will enlarge upon the definition of pilgrim which he gives here.

The epilogue has but one poem, one of the most significant of all Dante's lyrics. Some gentle ladies asked Dante to bestow upon them certain of his rhymes, and he, resolving to write some new thing to send with those others, wrote the memorable sonnet of the epilogue which presaged the *Divine Comedy*:

> Beyond the sphere which spreads to widest space
> Now soars the sigh that my heart sends above;
> A new perception born of grieving Love
> Guideth it upward the untrodden ways.
> When it hath reached unto the end, and stays,
> It sees a lady round whom splendors move
> In homage; till, by the great light thereof
> Abashed, the pilgrim spirit stands at gaze.
> It sees her such, that when it tells me this
> Which it hath seen, I understand it not,
> It hath a speech so subtle and so fine.
> And yet I know its voice within my thought
> Often remembereth me of Beatrice:
> So that I understand it, ladies mine.

"After writing this sonnet," Dante says, "I beheld a very wonderful vision which determined me that I would write no further of this most blessed one, until such time as I could discourse more worthily concerning her. And to this end I labor all I can; as she well knoweth." According to the statement by Barbi, already quoted, this sonnet was written not later than 1292. Dante's study of philosophy either at Bologna or at Santa Maria Novella (see Chapter I, Notes 2 and 8) is part of the meaning of the labor. Then follows the promise of the *Commedia*. "Wherefore if it be his pleasure through whom is the life of all things, that my life continue with me a few years, it is my hope that I shall write concerning her what hath not before been written of any woman. After the which, may it seem good unto Him who is the Master of Grace, that my spirit should go hence to behold the glory of its lady: to wit of that blessed Beatrice who now gazeth continually on his countenance *qui est per omnia saecula benedictus. Laus Deo.*"[12] The *Divine Comedy* is the fulfillment of that promise.

The beauty and unity and significance of the *New Life* rise from the intensity of the emotion with which Dante looks back upon the early poems and experiences and which fuses them into an aesthetic and spiritual oneness. The writing is filled, to be sure, with conventions of the love poetry of the time, the screen ladies, the visions. But the prose sections which explain the significance of the verses and many of the verses themselves rise above all conventional love literature; the work as a whole has a ring of sincerity and finality which make it a thing apart, the most ethereal romance of love in all the literature of the world.

> *Lady, why do you put him to such shame.*
> — *Purgatorio* XXX:96

If woman is the inspiration of man, what happens if she dies and he is left desolate? How then shall she lead him to God? Dante answers this question the first time in the third part of the *New Life*; in one sense the whole of the *Commedia* is a dramatized answer. In the *New Life* when he rallies with the "piteous lady," Beatrice, though dead, calls him back. He is repentant: she shows him a wonderful vision of the meaning of love, a vision, the light of which never ceased to burn in the depths of his soul. In the *Divine Comedy* he shows how it was the love of Beatrice which brought to him in Virgil the personification of the constancy of reason of which he wrote in the third part of the *New Life;* Virgil who points out the full meaning of disordered love. Beatrice, who had begun in Dante a new life, who had quickened his creative powers, will not permit him to squander his gifts. He must teach the whole world what she has taught him, namely, that love is the center of spiritual gravity in the universe. Death should have made no essential difference in their relationship; in fact, Beatrice tells him (*Purg.* XXX:128) that her added beauty after death should have given him increased incentive for virtue. When the relationship is utterly spiritual, death can make no real difference.

Fallen human nature, however, is weak. After the close of the *New Life* and before he finishes the *Divine Comedy,* perhaps before he begins it, Dante is again unfaithful — and this time possibly in the commonly accepted sense of the word. The so-called *Pietra Canzone,* probably written in the Casentino, express passion very different from the sublime sentiment of the *New Life.* Possibly, as Alice Curtayne maintains,[13] they convey nothing more definite than Dante's understanding of the passion to which his friends at the various courts succumbed and with which he was frequently surrounded in the great houses in which he was a guest. She suggests that he may have thought a description of that fire worth incorporating into poetry but that he revised this opinion in later days. Miss Curtayne's point of view is that of Umberto Cosmo, who points out that a poet's experiences are often a matter of his imagination.[14] Perhaps Papini is right: he maintains that the sensuousness which Dante had silenced but had not mastered swept him off his feet more than once.[15] Boccaccio had made a like statement. Whatever the facts may be, none of the lyrics deviate from a high level of decency; Dante was not corrupt, and nothing morally impure went from his heart into any of his writing. There is nowhere in Dante even a trickle of that unclean stream which runs through parts of the *Romance of the Rose* and some of the other medieval romances.

There are other conjectures about the nature of Dante's fall from grace: his infidelity to Beatrice. We have been dealing with Beatrice chiefly in the literal historic sense. But Beatrice may be considered in the fourfold sense in which Dante says all things in poetry should be considered. Since there is Beatrice in the symbolic sense as Divine Wisdom or Divine Revelation, in the moral sense as Love always under the command of reason, in the anagogic or mystical sense as Love which kindles in the soul the love of God, it follows that Dante's infidelity to Beatrice need not have been infidelity to the historic woman whom he knew and loved in Florence. There may have been moral lapses which were not precisely lapses against chastity. The *Tenzone* offer hints of an unworthy friendship which would obscure the memory of Beatrice. There is in the *Banquet* the definite statement of his being ashamed of the early lyrics and of his replacing the Lady Beatrice with the Lady Philosophy. Some would interpret this replacement to mean that Dante for a period had temptations or lapses against religious faith, the Divine Revelation and heavenly Wisdom of which Beatrice is the symbol. He may have wandered from grace and divine love through sins of the intellect rather than through sins of the flesh. Certainly he reproaches himself for his lack of fidelity to his creative genius.

Dante may have lapsed in all these ways. If he began the *Divine Comedy* in 1300 — as he suggests — at the time that he was lost in the dark wood, he was not a wanderer, an exile, a man dispossessed and poor. He was a successful and honored citizen of Florence, lost perhaps in politics, confused concerning which was the right party; seeing a conflict between his religious faith and his scientific and philosophical studies. The lady of Dante's second love, Philosophy, had by his own admission so enamored him as to draw his heart away from Beatrice. There is a long thread to follow through the fabric of the *Banquet* and the *Monarchy* before it leads to that union which we find in the *Paradiso* between the knowledge and philosophical devotion of the *Banquet,* the theological surety of the *Summa Theologica* which he made his own, and the self-effacing love of the *New Life*. In the years of suffering and wandering and loss while Dante was working on the cantos of the *Divine Comedy,* he assimilated and reviewed and added to all the concepts he had when he was thrust out of Florence; his speculations on things human and divine brought him back to the idealism of the epilogue of the *New Life* and forward to the perfect knowledge and love of the Supreme and Uncreated Good of the *Paradiso*.

Whatever Dante's lapses were, we know from the *Commedia* that he regretted them bitterly. That there was a great discrepancy between what he had loved and what he had been is apparent. Dante understood very well the standards and ideals of the artist and the saint, but he had not always lived by them. He had never accepted the standards of the men of the world, but he had sometimes followed them. His severest condemnation is based upon his own confession of unworthiness when he meets his Lady in the Earthly Paradise. He puts upon her lips the biting denunciation he must have pronounced upon himself: that he of so great talent had not made the most of his abilities, that he had followed false visions of good, that he had paid no heed to the inspirations and warnings she had sent him in dreams and in other ways.

The reader must not forget that in this memorable scene of the meeting with Beatrice in the Earthly Paradise it is Dante who brings himself before the bar of judgment. Though he represents the angels as asking Beatrice in pity why she shames him so, he recognizes the justice of her stern rebuke. He understands that because she loves him she has taken the measure of his gifts, many of which he has not brought to fruition; she had inspired him to great things because of these gifts and he had failed her. Now while there is still time for repentance, she demands as she did in the *New Life* when he turned from her, that he face the issues, see them clearly, recognize them for what they are, confess his guilt, and repent. She will be with him in the Heaven of Mars when he is given his mission. She will prepare him for it now. There, knowing she has made him ready for it and that he will not fail her again, she will smile her approval and promise to be ever at his side (*Par.* XVIII:1–9).

The function of woman is to help man, even in spite of himself, to fulfill his complete function in the universe by using his talents to work out his salvation in his unique way with his unique gifts. Beatrice has by the intensity of the love with which she inspired

Dante set free his creative power. Because she is to lead him to the ultimate ends of being, to the Beatific Vision, she must lift him out of himself. That is why when he dallied with those things which are not God and do not lead to him, she appealed to Virgil to take him through Hell to learn what dallying means. That is why she instructed Virgil to lead him all the way up the mountain, to purify all the internal and external senses, to learn all the disciplines of mind and body, to study the way of all the arts. She would have him crowned and mitered, master of himself and all his powers. She knew he could not achieve the mastery without pain. Love is not afraid of pain. Divine Love in human form redeemed man on Calvary. Crucifixion is the forerunner of resurrection in every life. Beatrice is always on the farther side of the purifying flame.

True love never seeks self; it never stops in self. Beatrice leads Dante from virtue to virtue, from truth to truth, from light to light. She shows him things which afterwards he is to write for the world. She brings to him all those who can assist in his illumination. When he looks too deeply or too long into her eyes she cries, "Too fixed a gaze!" or "These eyes are not thy only Paradise" (Par. XVIII:20–22); or "Why does my face so enamor thee? Turn . . ." (Par. XXIII:70). In the Heaven of the Sun when his heart is so filled with the love of the Trinity that he forgets her utterly, she smiles well pleased (Par. X:58–63). Her eyes reflect deep and ever widening vistas of truth which lead him to Ultimate Truth; her smile reflects the joy of Infinite Love.

Blessed sister, holy mother, spirit of the fountain, spirit of the garden,
Suffer us not to mock ourselves with falsehood.*
— T. S. Eliot in Ash Wednesday

* (New York: Harcourt, Brace & Co., 1930.)

*Shall I at least set my lands in order?**
— T. S. Eliot in *The Waste Land*

When the real function of woman is not understood by a civilization, that civilization becomes a wasteland. From a human as well as from a creative and poetic standpoint Dante's handling of the creative theme is worthy of study. He says there are three steps. First, there is inspiration: that which stirs profoundly comes not from within but from without. Second, one takes note. Third, one studies the significance. Love must be investigated rationally. It matters little that in the *New Life* Dante arrives at the essential qualities of what love is by a series of visions in which he dramatizes love. The significant thing is that he is able to say of the beginning and of the end as he writes it all down after the death of Beatrice, "And albeit her image that was with me always, was an exultation of love to subdue me, it was yet of so perfect a quality that it never allowed me to be overruled by Love without the faithful counsel of reason." His love in the first section may have been egocentric — he writes how he was stirred by the beauty of Beatrice — but it was never uncontrolled. In the *Inferno* he will show us men and women who did not follow the counsel of reason: Francesca, Paris, Tristan, Lancelot. Having taken note of what true love is, one knows what it is not.

But when love is directed by reason it is one of the most ennobling of all human experiences. It carries one quite beyond one's self and teaches true courtesy and humility and gentleness. It reaches out to encompass the whole of humankind and folds all men in its charity. It operates this way, says Dante, in both men and women. "Women feel the same for worthy men" (*New Life* XX). Such love is "smokeless flame."

In the first part of the *New Life,* Love weeping had said to

---

* (New York: Harcourt, Brace & Co., 1930.)

Dante (XII), "I am the center of a circle to which all parts of the circumference bear an equal relation, but with thee it is not so." When Dante pressed Love for the meaning, Love told him, "Demand no more than may be useful to thee." It is only in the last canto of the *Paradiso* that Dante understands what Love had said. With the vision of the Incarnation Dante understands in a flash how love is the center of all that exists, human and divine. This wondrous vision of the meaning of love has its prelude in the *New Life* (XXIV), where Dante sees in Beatrice his savior. All through the *Divine Comedy* she is the God-bearing image: it is in her eyes that he sees reflected divine Truth; it is through her smile that he feels the warmth of divine Love.

Because of this function of Beatrice in the life of Dante, the colors associated with her throughout both the *New Life* and the *Divine Comedy* are those identified with the theological virtues. When Dante saw Beatrice first she was dressed in a subdued and goodly crimson; in the first dream she was covered in the arms of Love with a blood-red cloth; when he returned to his room the first time she spoke to him, the room was filled with a mist the color of fire. When he saw her in the fantasy come as a reproach for his dallying with the lady at the window, she was again clothed in crimson. In the Earthly Paradise when she came again and stirred him so that there was no dram of blood that did not quiver in him, when he felt all the power of ancient love grow strong within him and he recalled the piercing experience of childhood, she was again dressed in crimson: the "living flame" of the Holy Spirit; this time she wore a white veil and a green mantle.

In the adolescent episode in the *New Life,* when Dante saw Beatrice on the bridge and she smiled upon him, she was dressed in white, the color of faith. Her soul went to heaven in his dream as a little white cloud before white angels; when he went to behold her in death, certain ladies were covering her head with a white veil. In the triumph car in the Earthly Paradise, she is wearing this white veil. The veil and the lilies falling from the hands of the hundred angels obscure Dante's vision of her eyes. There is exact parallelism in many of the details of these two scenes: the veil, the angels, the lilies which would surely surround Beatrice as they did the other friend whom he describes in death. The white of faith covers the head of her who is clothed in the flame-red of the Spirit of Love; Divine Revelation demands faith. In the white rose where faith becomes vision, the white-robed, unveiled Beatrice smiles upon Dante.

Nowhere in the *New Life* is there specific mention of green, yet everywhere there is a springtime air which would suggest green. The very title speaks of hope. Almost all of the episodes look forward. Especially is there a ring of hope in the episode in which Joan, who walks before Beatrice, is compared with Saint John the Baptist, not only because of her name but because she is the forerunner of the Light of Dante's life. When Beatrice appears in the triumph car, it is right that she who long ago brought Dante new life, who quickened in him creative activity, who is to lead him to the Beatific Vision, should be enveloped in a mantle of green and crowned with Minerva's olive leaves, the symbol of the creativity of the ancient goddess of wisdom. Beatrice represents to the struggling, sinful Dante the hope of forgiveness, of salvation, of beatitude. In the Earthly Paradise, though she rebukes him so that he looks down in shame and confusion before her veiled face, at the end of the journey he looks up into her unveiled eyes, grateful because she had kept his hope alive along the difficult stretches of the Purgatory and through the vast planetary spaces of the Paradise, and makes to her his prayer addressing her as the "Lady in whom his hope is strong."

For all true lovers the colors are significant. Red is the color of charity, that charity which is patient and kind, which is not puffed up, which does not envy, nor seek its own advantage, nor deal perversely. It is the color of that love which never falls away. Red is the color of blood — the courage of the martyrs, the color of sacrifice. Love always means sacrifice. Where it is unwilling to sacrifice it cannot be love. For a man to fulfill his function in this life and the next demands courage and sacrifice.

White is the color of purity as well as faith. When love is not pure it cannot have integrity. Love demands faith in the beloved. There are hidden things in all love which the eye cannot penetrate until the veils are rent away. Love which is pure, which has integrity, which is characterized by faith in the beloved accepts much that it cannot in this life understand.

Love is always forward-looking: it is always the beginning of a new life. Each day for lovers marks a new effort to conquer new realms of the spirit. Love hopefully leads the beloved out of darkness, along the difficult way of self-mastery, from virtue to virtue, from star to star, to the vision of God.

Beatrician love has all these qualities. Because it is strong and courageous, chaste and ever faithful, forward-looking and upward-moving, it fulfills perfectly the function of woman: it helps man to fulfill his function in this life and the next. It leads him to perfect Truth and perfect Love, the ultimate ends of being.

NOTES

1. For a discussion of nineteenth-century points of view summarized here, see the study on Beatrice in Edward Moore, *Studies in Dante*, Second Series (Oxford, 1889), pp. 78–151.
2. Charles Williams, *The Figure of Beatrice*, 5 ed. (London, 1950).
3. John Earle, "Vita Nuova," *Quarterly Review*, No. 367 (July, 1896).
4. Michele Barbi, *Life of Dante*, trans. and ed. Paul G. Ruggiers (Berkeley, 1954), p. 36.
5. "And touching the reason why this number was so closely allied unto her, it may peradventure be this. According to Ptolemy (and also to the Christian verity), the revolving heavens are nine; and according to the common opinion among astrologers, these nine heavens together have influence over the earth. Wherefore it would appear that this number was thus allied unto her for the purpose of signifying that, at her birth, all these nine heavens were at perfect unity with each other as to their influence. This is one reason that may be brought: but more narrowly considering, and according to the infallible truth, this number was her own self: that is to say, by similitude. As thus. The number three is the root of the number nine; seeing that without the interposition of any other number, being multiplied merely by itself, it produceth nine, as we manifestly perceive that three times three are nine. Thus three being by itself the efficient of nine, and the Great Efficient of Miracles being of Himself Three Persons (to wit: the Father, the Son and the Holy Spirit), which, being Three, are also One: this lady was accompanied by the number nine to the end that men might clearly perceive her to be a nine, that is, a miracle, whose only root is the Holy Trinity. It may be that a more subtile person would find for this thing a reason of greater subtility: but such is the reason that I find and that liketh me best." *New Life*, XXX, trans. Dante Gabriel Rossetti.
6. Edmund G. Gardner, *Dante*, rev. ed. (New York, 1923), p. 56.
7. Saint Thomas Aquinas, *Summa Theologica* I–II, q. 26, a. 4. This matter of the difference of love of friendship and love of concupiscence as presented in Saint Thomas is discussed at some length in I. J. Semper, "Dante's Creed of Spiritual Life," *Catholic World*, Vol. 169 (April, 1949), pp. 27–33.

8. Andreae Capellani regii Francorum, *De Amore, libri tres,* recensuit E. Trojel (Havniae, 1892), trans. John Jay Parry, *The Art of Courtly Love* (New York: Columbia University Press, 1941).

9. For a discussion of courtly love see Alexander J. Denomy, *The Heresy of Courtly Love* (New York: The Declan X. McMullen Company, 1947), pp. 33–40, and Hermann J. Weigand, *Three Chapters on Courtly Love in Arthurian France and Germany* (Chapel Hill, 1956), pp. 18–25.

10. The *De Amore* of Andreas was condemned at the University of Paris in 1277 at the same time that the writings of Siger of Brabant were condemned and on the same basis, namely, that it claimed that things may be true according to philosophy but not according to faith, just as if there were two contradictory truths.

11. Mr. C. S. Lewis points out that Dante's *New Life* is at the extreme of those romances which deal with love according to the complete Christian teaching and that there are authors dotted about in every sort of intermediate position. C. S. Lewis, *The Allegory of Love, A Study in Medieval Tradition,* 6 ed. (Oxford, 1951), p. 21.

12. . . . *who is blessed throughout all ages. Praise be to God.*

13. Alice Curtayne, *A Recall to Dante* (New York, 1932).

14. Umberto Cosmo, *A Handbook to Dante Studies,* trans. David Moore (New York, 1947), pp. 53–55.

15. Giovanni Papini, *Dante Vivo,* trans. Eleanor H. Broadus and Anna Benedetti (New York, 1935), Chap. 32.

CHAPTER IV

CHARTING THE JOURNEY

> They who would present something by way of
> introduction to a portion of any work, find it
> necessary to give some idea of the whole work to
> which that portion belongs. . . .
>
> — Letter to Can Grande

etween the time in 1292 when Dante had the vision
which determined him to write the *Divine Comedy* and
the year 1321 after its completion when he wrote the
dedicatory letter to Can Grande, much had happened to
him and to his world. Precisely what the vision was no man can
say; neither can any man doubt that it deepened and intensified
and clarified as the years advanced and the mind and soul of Dante
were enriched. We know from the *New Life* that the vision had
to do with the other world, for Dante was to say to the doomed in
Hell that he had "looked on that for which God's chosen pray"
(XIX); we know from the command of Cacciaguida (*Par.* XVII:
127–129)

> . . . all falsehood laid aside
> Make manifest the vision utterly
> And let them scratch wherever is the itch

that the object of the vision was reform; the statement in the
letter to Can Grande indicates that the object of the reform was to
bring peace. Dante's major objective in writing the *Divine Comedy*
was not, then, to produce a literary masterpiece but to create a

83

practical work which would change the world and bring mankind from misery to happiness. He had had a revelation. He must construct his poem so that he can announce for the saving of misguided humanity those things which God had helped him to see and hear.

Dante has said many things about poetry in general and the *Commedia* in particular which throw light upon his objectives and his method. In the dedicatory letter to Can Grande he gives his reasons for calling his work a comedy; twentieth-century students often find the title somewhat incongruous for a poem dealing with a vision of Hell and Heaven. Dante begins by differentiating comedy and tragedy in mood and style, indicating that whereas the beginning of tragedy is "quiet and admirable" and its end "horrible," the reverse is true of comedy, for it ends prosperously. His *Commedia,* he explains, is in the beginning "horrible and fetid, being Hell": in the end it is "prosperous, desirable, and pleasant, being Paradise." In language, *comedy* with the ancients was a *rustic song;* the manner of the speech "humble"; Dante writes his poem in the humble vernacular, "which even women use." In general, it may be said that in Dante's time any serious piece of writing in which things ended happily for the protagonist might be called a *comedy;* the word had none of the connotations of humor and levity which it conveys to the modern mind.

Frequently today the *Divine Comedy* is classified as an epic: some speak of it as the *Danteid.* From the literal point of view, Dante is, of course, the chief personage. But there are difficulties in placing his poem in the same category as the *Iliad* and the *Aeneid.* Homer and Virgil each had a story to tell: each wrote a long narrative poem centering about the exploits of a hero. Dante has a world to explain and to reform. He believes that order is the principle on which the universe is founded: he must show what has brought about the disorder in the world he sees and how order can be restored. He could have written an expository treatise as he did in the *Monarchy,* but he wanted all men to read what he wrote, and men are bored with explanations. He conceived a poem in which he could be not only narrator but actor and spectator. Such a poem is really not an epic.

He cast his poem into the form of a journey; in a journey he can keep his teaching in the background; he can observe and comment. People of his day, as indeed of ours, were interested not only in *bona fide* travels like Marco Polo's but in accounts of visions which included journeys to the other world. There is an immense literature all the way from Saint Augustine to C. S. Lewis concerning real and visionary journeys to such destinations as the Garden of Eden;[1] serious geographers in the Middle Ages placed the Earthly Paradise on their maps and serious explorers set out to find it. In fact, when Christopher Columbus discovered the New World, he thought he was close to the Earthly Paradise.

Visions of journeys to the Garden of Eden and to Hell, Purgatory, and Heaven filled not only the religious literature of the twelfth and thirteenth centuries; the romances, *chansons de geste*, and allegories portray frequent excursions into them. Dante's journey will include many familiar landmarks from other journeys: the dark wood, the mountain which one cannot climb, the rivers, the castle, the island. But they will all be very different in his journey. For his journey will be our journey, too; it will be every man's journey in the way of salvation.

His journey will be more than any single man's journey, much more. It will be the historical journey of the human race from the fall of Adam and Eve, brought into the focus of a single vision in the end of that journey — which is also the beginning — "where every *where* is *here* and every *when* is *now*" (XXIX:12). His journey he says in the dedicatory letter, like that of the Israelites out of Egypt, is an *allegory*. He will show that there is a possibility of a journey to God even in this life. According to Dante, then, his poem is a *vision*, a *journey*, an *allegory*, a poem in honor of Beatrice. He had promised to sing of her. The poem may also in one sense be a romance: it will surely be lyrical; part of it will be lyrical poetry of the highest order.

Modern critics, among them Mr. Allen Tate, Mr. Francis Fergusson, Mr. Erich Auerbach, find much of the *Divine Comedy* to be essentially drama.[2] Surely in the *Inferno*, as they point out, there are hundreds of "played-out tragedies" combined in one great play in which Dante unfolds the history of Florence, of Italy, and of the world. Each character stands before us differing from every other in the category of sinners to which God's judgment has consigned him, each manifesting by his speech and actions the essential qualities of his own personality, each revealing for all eternity the decisive actions and traits of character which brought him where he is. Francesca retains her courtesy and her charm as well as the evasiveness which made her fail to face the reality of her guilt; Farinata is the strong leader still interested in politics and holding in high scorn even Hell; Ulysses still spins a travel tale. The whole drama of each is represented in microcosm: the tragic flaw in character, the tragic decision, the denouement.

The *Purgatorio*, too, is filled with action; in fact, here the action is in progress. What the end of each drama will be we know in essence, for the climax has been passed. The characters here also retain their peculiar qualities: Belacqua, his laziness; Manfred, his ready leadership; Guido Guinizelli, his poetic discernment. Often, especially in the Ante-Purgatory, they display the old flaws; but the admirable intellectual or social qualities which in Hell merely serve to intensify the tragedy here become part of the reason for the mercy shown them.

In still another sense the *Divine Comedy* is dramatic, for in displaying his own progress as the chief protagonist, Dante shows himself to be a dramatist of rare skill. The whole episode of the meeting with Beatrice in the Earthly Paradise is filled with the tensions of great drama as is the episode in the Heaven of Mars in which he receives his commission. Scattered all through the last two canticles there is a variety of dramatic forms: masques, pageants, tableaux — all of them handled with sensitivity and adroitness, all of them tributary to the central dramatic progress of the chief character.

Other critics find other incipient literary forms in the *Commedia*: qualities of the novel, of didactic poetry, of the short story. Jacques Maritain finds all of these and makes the observation that the poem is so difficult to classify, that it has qualities of so great a variety of modern literary types, solely for the reason that in Dante's day literature had not yet been broken down into the genres which we now have and that, therefore, Dante could embrace in the substantial unity of his single masterpiece forms of creative expression which in our time demand separate treatment.[3]

To Dante, of course, the last-mentioned literary types could have no meaning because they were not known in his day. Why, one is sometimes asked, when Dante set out to present a vision, a journey, an allegory, did he choose to write in poetry? The answer is probably twofold: he was writing of and for Beatrice and he was above all a poet. A love song must be poetry. Whatever else Dante was at any period of his life he was always a poet. When he was a soldier, a statesman, an ambassador, a city counselor, a philosopher in Florence he was engaged in writing poetry and in studying the craft of poetry. From the time when, at the age of eighteen, he sent out the first sonnet to Guido Cavalcanti — and certainly he was writing verse before that — he was an attentive student of the art of poetry. His *New Life* is a select grouping of his earliest lyrics; his *Banquet* was designed as a commentary on later lyrics; his *Concerning Vernacular Eloquence* is a discussion of language and of the art of poetry. From this treatise alone one learns how great a student of poetic craftsmanship he was. The *Purgatorio*, in which he suggests the disciplines in all the arts, is filled with observations about poetry as an art.

Dante always believed that artistic expression demands discipline; inspiration is not enough. He closes the *New Life* with the statement that he studies all he can. He is convinced that a poet must be a scholar and a scientist so that he may set in verse things hard to conceive (*Purg.* XXIX:42); he must labor to perfect his craft (*New Life* XVIII; *Eloquence* II, IV) and he must gain help from God. All of Dante's work is filled with prayer. When his spirit was inflamed with important things to be said, he would, of course, present them in the medium best adapted to the saying and with expert craftsmanship. The vehicle for impassioned utterance has always been poetry.

Sapientis est ordinare.
*The wise man's gift is for putting things
in order.*

Dante has many things to say. In the method characteristic of
the Middle Ages he says them on four levels. These four levels —
the literal, the allegorical, the moral, and the anagogical or mystical — are frequently discussed by medieval writers; Saint Thomas
expounds them at some length in the *Summa* (I, q. 1, a. 10) and
Durandus in his *Proem*. Dante presents them in the *Banquet* (II, i)
and in the dedicatory letter to Can Grande. Saint Thomas and
Durandus are speaking specifically about the reading of Sacred Scripture; Dante is applying the principle to the reading of the *Divine
Comedy*. It is logical to infer that if the *Divine Comedy* is to be
read on four levels, it was written so to be read. In fact, Dante
points out in part what meaning each level conveys. At a first
reading we may find it necessary to look intently and separately at
each meaning as a beginner in music looks carefully at each note
in a chord. But so masterful is Dante in his work, that after repeated readings we get all meanings as it were in a single glance
as we hear only the chord, unconscious of the separate notes which
compose it.

The many ideas which Dante wishes to present he fits into
this fourfold scheme. The *literal* meaning is, he says, a presentation
of the state of souls after death, the simple record of his journey
through the three realms of the afterlife. He shows us in Hell
the souls of the damned in ever deepening circles of depravity; we
meet in Purgatory those who, having repented of their sins, are
endeavoring to cast out the roots of evil and to acquire the virtues
opposed to the root sins; we behold in Heaven the souls of the
just, the angelic hosts, and the vision of the Triune God.

Dante explains that according to the *allegorical* meaning the
subject of the *Commedia* is man subjected, insofar as by the freedom
of the will he deserves it, to just reward or punishment. Dante has
now risen to a philosophical level of thought. Man is made up of
body and soul and must work out his salvation in the temporal
and spiritual order. Historically, the establishment of the means for

this end was ordained by God to come through Aeneas and David: from the one would come in God's good time the founders of the Roman Empire; from the other, Christ who would found his Church. Christ's birth and death would take place under Roman law, to which he would be subject, thereby setting his seal on the Roman Empire and on Roman law. Dante will show the ravages brought about by the lack of right guidance on the part of both Empire and Church, the two guides appointed by God for the well-being of mankind.

Men have spoiled God's plan; the world has gone wrong because of bad leadership in both State and Church. There has been no leader in the Empire for fifty years; the Papacy has usurped the mission of the Emperor and neglected its own mission. Aeneas, the founder of Rome, had made a journey into the next world to learn about the Roman Empire; Paul, a Roman citizen, chosen by Christ to spread the Christian faith among the Gentiles, had been lifted to the heavens to see the glory to which the Church leads mankind. Dante, too, will make a journey guided by Reason and Divine Wisdom and Revelation, to discover what is wrong with the world and to learn how it must be set right. He will see in Hell the reason why the world is plunged into confusion: the *Inferno* is a portrayal of this corrupt society. He will then show in the *Purgatorio* the way in which society must set itself in order, that right order in which civil jurisdiction will be restored to the Empire and in which the Church will return to her mission of guiding men to Heaven, reopened to them by Christ. He will portray in the *Paradiso* a society in which love and justice prevail and where the proper hierarchial order is maintained. Man is a social being and must work out his salvation in both the political and ecclesiastical orders; however, he does so with difficulty when the sword is grafted upon the crook (*Purg.* XVI:109–112).

In the third or moral order Dante will present to the individual man the way in which he should walk. He will show him the real nature of sin by which he turns away from the Uncreated Good; he will follow sin to greater and greater depths — from concupiscence of the flesh to the perversion of the intellect and of the powers of love in sins of fraud and treachery. He will show man his capacity for evil. Then, when man has seen sin in its essence, he will show him how to turn about and go through the dark way of remorse until he comes out to begin a new day and walk a new way and learn to put love in order. He will show him the beauty of discipline and teach him through the arts the great art of right living. He will lead him by right reason back to that Garden of Eden from which Adam and Eve were driven when they set themselves against the law of the Most High. He will then show him the beauty of spirit which it is possible for man to achieve if he will place himself under the guidance of Divine Revelation. He will lead him to the vision of God.

"*Anagogue,*" says Durandus, "is so called from *ana,* which is upwards, and *goge,* a leading: as it were *an upward leading.* Whence the anagogic sense is that which leadeth the mind upwards to the invisible. . . . *Anagogue,* therefore, is that sense which leadeth the mind upwards to heavenly things: that is, to the Trinity and the orders of angels, and speaketh concerning future rewards, and the future life which is in heaven."[4] In the *Divine Comedy* Dante teaches man on the anagogical or mystical level the way by which, even while engaged actively in the affairs of earth, he can rise to the heights of contemplation.

The way leads through an understanding of the heinousness of sin as it is contemplated in the light of the infinite purity of God. It follows on through the purgation of the soul — first through the dark night of the senses to purify it from all attachment to earthly things, and then through the dark night of the soul to cleanse the intellect and the will from all inordinate attachment to the things of self so that one may submit one's intellect by faith to the incomprehensible things of God and one's will to the Divine Will. Along the purgative way man will find illumination from time to time to aid him in the disciplines to which he submits himself that he may reach the pristine beauty of Adam before the fall.

The way leads then along the effortless way of illumination from supernatural height to supernatural height, to deeper and deeper comprehension of philosophical and theological truths, to ever increasing brightness in the revelation of divine mysteries, to the complete restoration of the Divine Likeness through the passive purification of faith, hope, and charity. It comes at last to the unitive way where the soul attains to heights of contemplative prayer, that simple gaze into the Divine Essence which is the peak of religious experience. In effect this movement along the illuminative way to the union of the soul with God in contemplation is the meaning of religion; the very word means to bind back, to bind the creature back to his Creator. It is possible for man even in the flesh to reach the heights of contemplation. Man is led to such heights by Divine Revelation and by Love. Beatrice will show Dante the way.

> Let every one . . . when he purposes to sing of these three subjects (love, politics, and righteousness) . . . drink of Helicon and then, after adjusting the strings, boldly take up his plectrum and begin to ply it. But it is in the exercise of the needful caution and discernment that the real difficulty lies; for this can never be attained to without strenuous efforts of genius, constant practice in the art, and the habit of the sciences.
>
> — Concerning Vernacular Eloquence
> Book II, Chapter V

Dante, who says in the *Eloquence* that there are three fit subjects for poetry, is enabled in the *Divine Comedy*, because of the intensity and clarity with which he conceived it, to fuse these three into a perfect unity. Perhaps this is true because of the circumstances of his life. He suggests that no other poet had been so deeply wounded by love; few poets have been so wounded by politics and have had such strong convictions concerning national and international problems; few have had so great a sense of justice and of moral rectitude. Love was the inception of the *Divine Comedy*; love gives it its emotional intensity. Always there is the love for Beatrice. But love of Beatrice broadens into love for Florence; for Rome; for the Empire and Henry of Luxembourg, the unfortunate

prince on whom Dante had set his hope; and above all and absorb-
ing all, the Church. This love encompasses suffering humanity,
reaches beyond the confines of time and encompasses God and the
angels and the whole Communion of Saints. It gives everywhere to
each part an inner feeling which transcends the meaning of the
lines — even when they quicken another emotion, love is there;
often it is there in its antithesis, for love of the good is hatred of
evil. Love is all about the poem, in each episode, in its every fiber.

Love makes of Dante a true philosopher and leads him back to
God, the First Cause, according to his analysis in the Banquet;
for "philosophy is a loving use of Wisdom, which exists above all
in God (III, xii, 4) because in him is supreme Wisdom, and
supreme Love and supreme Power which cannot exist elsewhere
except as it proceeds from him. Therefore the Divine Philosophy
is of the Divine Essence, because in him can be nothing added to
his essence and she is most noble because the Divine Essence is
most noble and she exists in him perfectly and truly as it were
by eternal wedlock." Moreover, philosophy "aids our faith, which
more than other things is useful to humanity as that by which we
escape eternal death and gain eternal life" (Banq. III, vii, 8). For
this reason, in keeping with the practice of Saint Thomas, Beatrice,
the symbol of Divine Wisdom and Divine Revelation, discusses with
Dante along the illuminative way philosophical questions in close
connection with theology.

In the Eloquence Dante had said (Book II, ii) that he had not
found any Italian who had written poetry on the subject of arms
(politics). In the Divine Comedy he will set forth his whole
political doctrine. As we have already noted, by the time that he is
well into the writing of the Divine Comedy, Dante is neither Guelph
nor Ghibelline (Par. VI:31–33; 103–109); his program is to restore
universal world order and bring the world to peace. Again and again
in the Divine Comedy, but particularly in Canto VI of the Paradiso
through the mouth of Justinian, Dante praises Roman law; he raises
the imperial standard as the point about which kings and princes
can rally to restore law and order in a world rent by avarice and
greed.

In his letter to the Italian cardinals (Letter VIII) assembled at

Carpentras near Avignon in 1314 to elect a successor to Pope Clement V, we get the concentrated statement of Dante's political thought as he finally formulated it. We see how, in his thinking, Rome, Italy, the Church, and the world are welded together in such indissoluble unity that the life of one is the life of all; the evil in one, the misfortune of all. He is disconsolate because the Papal chair has been removed from Rome, because the Papacy is "committing fornication with kings" (*Inf.* XIX:108). Here and in the *Commedia* he shows his great reverence for the Papal dignity and his chagrin with those unworthy churchmen who have dallied with the she-wolf of avarice and in their lust for power and riches have proved to be unworthy shepherds, who have indeed made themselves wolves and have worked havoc in the work of Redemption (*Inf.* I:100; XIX:112; *Purg.* XX:10–12; XXXII:148–160; *Par.* IX:127–132; XXVII:121–123). Both popes and emperors have dallied with the Siren and have been lured from their rightful course. This figure of the Siren is as important in the *Purgatorio* as the Geryon figure of fraud is in the *Inferno*. Luxury and deceit involve both State and Church.

Both Guelphs and Ghibellines are wrong. Dante does not choose between Church and Empire. He distributes through the blackest circles of Hell the enemies of both — enemies, by their evil leadership of the institutions designed by God to remedy the havoc wrought in human nature by the sin of Adam (*Purg.* XVI:94–108). Just as the Redemption did not restore man to original justice but through the foundation of the Church gave him the means to work out his salvation and attain eternal happiness, so the Empire by restoring law and order would give man the means for temporal happiness. Dante does not wish the Emperor to be controlled by the Pope nor does he wish the Pope to usurp the prerogatives of the Emperor. When the sword is joined to the crook, both the spiritual and the temporal order go ill because being joined neither can check the other (*Purg.* XVI:109–112). One guide should serve as a curb to the other. This thought is central to Dante's political creed and is therefore placed in the central cantos of his poem. Beatrice insists (*Purg.* XXXII:103–105; XXXIII:52–54) that it is Dante's duty to understand and promulgate this creed for "the good of the world that liveth ill." The empire envisioned by Dante is, therefore, not the pagan Roman Empire of Caesar Augustus but the Christian empire of Justinian which he lauds in *Paradiso* VI.

Several times in the *Divine Comedy* Dante turns prophet. His language in these sections is as obscure as that of the Greek oracles or that of some of the prophets in Sacred Scripture. That better times will come he promises at the beginning of the poem (*Inf.* I:101–111) and in the *Paradiso* (XXVII:145–148) as he enters the Primum Mobile. The prophecies of the Greyhound and the Veltro (*Inf.* I:105) and particularly that of the DXV, The Five-Hundred-Ten-and-Five (*Purg.* XXXIII:43–49), have concerned scholars across the centuries and brought about much controversy which need not be discussed here.[5]

In the development of the third subject for poetry, that of righteousness, Dante calls upon his knowledge of theology and Divine Revelation. So great is his mastery in the field of theology and Sacred Scripture that Giovanni del Virgilio of Bologna in writing Dante's epitaph called him "Dante the theologian, skilled in every branch of knowledge." Raphael in his *Disputa* places him as the only layman among the most eminent theologians of the Church. All of the matters in the *Divine Comedy* which have to do with love and politics, in certain of their aspects, also involve righteousness.[6]

In Dante's thought the two most momentous events in human history are the fall of Adam, which brought sin into the world and closed Heaven to mankind, and the Redemption, by which the gates were reopened. The free will of man, God's supreme gift (*Par.* V:19–24), makes it possible for him to sin and to practice virtue: God's perfect justice demands punishment for sin (Hell); but God's mercy and love which brought a Redeemer and which give man grace make it possible for him to regain innocence if by reason and free will he co-operates by prayer and penance (Purgatory). He can then reach eternal happiness (Heaven). To assist him in the attainment of this goal man has the Church, the custodian of Truth in Sacred Scripture and in philosophy and theology. Dante has faith in the authority of the Church; his faith explains his sure judgment in matters of morality and doctrine, his consistency, his clarity. Dante never dissembles, never supposes, never just thinks. He always writes with assurance: he knows.

> Think, Reader, if the story begun here
> did not continue, what desire you would
> have to know more.
>
> — *Paradiso* V:109–111

Perhaps because of the vision and perhaps because of the nature of the ideas he had to express, the general form of the poem must have been present to Dante's mind from the outset. He would have three poems in one poem, three canticles, each dealing with one of the three realms after death. Because it was to be written in honor of Beatrice who was a three (*New Life* XXX; compare Chapter III, Note 5) and whose life was dominated by nine which has its root in three, the architecture of the poem must everywhere be three and multiples of three, moving always from three to one, the symbol of unity, and then to ten and one hundred, the symbols of perfection.

Within the pattern of the *Divine Comedy* this use of three and multiples of three; of one, ten, and one hundred is manifest again and again. One student listed almost four hundred instances of the use of three; there are probably more. All that can be done here is to give the general scheme and call attention to a few particulars. There is first the over-all plan: in the one work called *La Divina Commedia* there are three poems — the *Inferno*, the *Purgatorio*, the *Paradiso*. There are in all one hundred cantos — thirty-three in each part — giving a total of ninety-nine, and one introductory canto, bringing the total to one hundred. Each major part of the poem is again divided into three parts: the *Inferno* into upper, middle, and lower Hell; the *Purgatorio* into Ante-Purgatory, Purgatory proper, and the Earthly Paradise; the *Paradiso* into the heavens of the shadowed planets, the heavens of the unshadowed planets called the heavens of honor, and the upper heavens comprising the Stellar Heaven, the Primum Mobile, and the Empyrean. Each major part is a nine plus one, which brings it to the perfect number: the *Inferno* is made up of nine circles and Ante-Hell; the *Purgatorio* of the Ante-Purgatory, the cornices of the seven capital sins, and the Earthly Paradise — but the underground passage leading from Hell to the base of the mountain brings the number to ten; the *Paradiso* of the three shadowed planets, the four unshadowed planets, the Stellar Heaven, the Primum Mobile, which make nine, and the Empyrean, the real heaven, which brings the number to ten.

The stanza form which Dante forges for his poem is called *terza rima;* it is in the *Divine Comedy* a three-line stanza made up of three perfect unbroken eleven-syllable lines. In Book II, Chapter V, of the *Eloquence* Dante discusses at some length the perfection of this *endecasillabo;* he had used it frequently in his earlier poems but he uses it exclusively in the *Commedia* because of its unity. The first and third lines of each stanza rhyme, the middle rhyme being carried over to be the first and third rhymes of the following stanza, "triple hooks of silver" they have been called. Each stanza, made up of three perfect unbroken eleven-syllable lines has in all thirty-three syllables. The following terza rima from *Purgatorio* XXX (31–39), which describes Beatrice as Dante sees her in the Earthly Paradise after his "ten years' thirst," will give an idea of the structure of the verse.

> Sopra candido vel, cinta d' oliva,
> donna m' apparve, sotto verde manto,
> vestita di color di fiamma viva.
>
> E lo spirito mio, che già cotanto
> tempo era stato che alla sua presenza
> non era di stupor, tremando, affranto,
>
> senza degli occhi aver più conoscenza,
> per occulta virtù che da lei mosse,
> d' antico amor sentì la gran potenza.

In his *Dante Theologian* Patrick Cummins, O.S.B., points out, in connection with Dante's verse structure, how superb an architect he is. He calls attention to the fact that one line and only one line is broken, verse 125 of Canto XVII of the *Purgatorio.* "Why," he asks, "is that line broken?" and proceeds to answer his question:

Because that line is the keystone line. Its number in the whole poem is 7,117. Hence, in a poem of 14,233 lines, that line is mathematically central. The divine poem is a rainbow arch. The keystone of the arch must look both ways, toward both half-arches, backward to the ascending, forward to the descending. To mark the keystone line, Dante linked it both ways. Its first part looks back, its second part looks forward.[7]

> Questo triforme amor quaggiù di sotto
> si piange; or vo' che tu dell' altro intende,*
> che corre al ben con ordine corrotto.

> This triform love three-circled here below us
> beweeps itself.
> But now turn thy attention*
> to where in good we outdo or beslow us.

In his commentary on this line, Father Cummins makes the observation that Virgil who in the first part of the line has been pointing below, turns at the break to point ahead and above. "*Terza rima,* you will find in other poets," he says in the introduction to his book, "the unbroken line and keystone architecture are Dante's idiosyncratic distinction." A detailed study of the structure of the *Divine Comedy* is most rewarding in revealing the precision with which it is built. One finds evidence everywhere of the power of a mind which organizes and orders and has the capacity for taking infinite pains.

Apart from the architecture of the poem but closely integrated with it are other important uses of three. Three beasts — the leopard, the lion, and the she-wolf — imperil Dante when he would ascend the mountain; three intangibles — light, sound, motion, and their antitheses — produce the atmosphere; three women — the Virgin Mary, Saint Lucy, and Beatrice — are instrumental in bringing him help in the crisis; and three guides — Virgil, Beatrice, and Saint Bernard — help him on his road to God. To discuss all of these groups of three would be profitable if space allowed; however, in order to understand some of the aspects of the journey it is necessary to know something about Dante's reasons for choosing the three guides.

Both Virgil and Saint Bernard come to guide Dante at the request of Beatrice (*Inf.* II:52–118; *Par.* XXXI:65–66). Why Dante makes Beatrice his guide and why he places the choice of the other guides in her hands we already know; why she chooses Virgil and Saint Bernard is not so self-evident. She herself stands in the middle way: Virgil leads Dante to her in the Earthly Paradise; she leaves him in the care of Saint Bernard when he is ready for the unitive way after she has led him into the Empyrean.

For the choice of Virgil as a guide there are many reasons, some growing out of the peculiar place he filled in the thought of the Middle Ages; some out of Dante's own personal attitudes toward him. In Dante's time Virgil was held in high esteem as a writer, a sort of magician, and a quasi-prophet. His *Aeneid* was one of the classics studied assiduously. The power which in the sixth book Virgil represented Aeneas as exercising over Hades and its denizens gave him the reputation of having supernatural powers; his fourth *Eclogue* (ll. 5–63) was frequently considered as a prophecy of the coming of Christ and was compared with the Messianic prophecies of Isaias. He was looked upon as the poet-philosopher beyond all others, an example of the natural nobility of man, a type of reason unillumined by Divine Revelation, who could point out what sin makes of a man and what steps man must take to live a life of natural virtue. Since, according to Saint Thomas, reason directs each individual man to faith (Revelation) and since there can be no quarrel between faith and reason, faith beginning where reason ends, Virgil will lead Dante to Beatrice (Revelation, Theology), for all Christian antiquity saw in him a prophet of Christ.

Dante had many personal reasons for making Virgil his guide. He says clearly (*Inf.* I:79–87) that careful study of the *Aeneid* taught him how to write, gave him his style. A gifted poet is a good guide for a gifted poet. Virgil had been in Hell: in the sixth book of the *Aeneid* he shows us its topography and the torments of the damned. There are in the same book hints of the need of penance and purgation. All through the epic there is an exaltation of discipline: Aeneas fulfills his mission because he is obedient to the gods. That mission, too, is of grave interest to Dante; Virgil taught him to believe in the divine origin of the Roman Empire, taught him, too, that its greatness and dominion gave peace to the world. Both as a symbol and as a poet Virgil fulfills Dante's need for a guide through Hell and Purgatory.

Anyone who has studied the life of Saint Bernard knows that he was a master of both the active and the contemplative life. "He found ways," says Gilson, "to remain a man of letters and to become a saint in the bargain."[8] He came from his cloister to preach a crusade, to admonish and advise popes, emperors, and kings. He had a passion for reform. All these facets of his dynamic personality would appeal to Dante. But what appealed even more was his mysticism and the profundity of his theological teaching. He was an ardent lover of the Virgin, who according to various legends, taught him herself and led him along the upper reaches of contemplative prayer. For these last reasons he is a perfect guide for the last stage of Dante's journey; Bernard will ask the Virgin to lead Dante to the vision of the Trinity.

Each of these guides performs a distinct but vitally important function. Virgil and Beatrice discharge the function Dante attributes to Empire and Church: Virgil leads Dante to the Earthly Paradise, the symbol of earthly happiness; Beatrice leads him to eternal happiness. Saint Bernard gains for him the Beatific Vision, man's ultimate goal.

> *It is another journey you must take if you*
> *wish to escape from this wild place.*
> — *Inferno* I:91–93

Like many of the other medieval journeys into the next world, Dante's journey begins when he is lost in the dark wood, "gone from the path" which in drowsiness and confusion of mind he has somehow left. Before him is a mountain, the usual mountain of the allegories, which he tries to climb but is kept from climbing by the three beasts. Virgil comes to him when he is endeavoring to climb the mountain; since the beasts will not permit them to ascend, Dante and Virgil must take the long way around, and so we have the journey — and the poem.

Dante would impress upon us the idea that his journey is a real journey made at a definite time and in a definite place. Therefore, his time references are frequent and precise. Critics differ on some aspects of the chronology. All agree, for Dante is very specific on this point, that the journey begins in Holy Week of his thirty-fifth year. According to most interpreters that would be in the year 1300, though a few hold out for 1301. It is possible, since Dante's birthday fell in May, to assume either year.

All agree that the action begins on Holy Thursday night. But other data which Dante gives — though all associated in our minds with Easter — do not combine to correspond to any actual day in the calendar for either 1300 or 1301. Good Friday fell on April 8 in 1300; on March 31 in 1301. But those who take the year 1301 argue that Dante for reasons important to his poem assumes an ideal date for the date of his vision, chooses March 25, and represents it as Good Friday.[9] In the Church calendar, March 25 is the feast of the Annunciation; as we have seen, it was in Florence the day for the beginning of the new year. Should March 25 fall on Friday in Holy Week, it gives way to Good Friday and is celebrated later on some appointed day; nevertheless, it would combine in the reader's mind three important concepts: the feast of the Annunciation, which is also the feast of the Incarnation; the feast of the Redemption; and the beginning of a new year: all significant for Dante's poetic purpose.[10]

Whatever the date, it is clear that Dante was lost in the dark forest on the night preceding the anniversary of the death of Christ; he attempted to climb the mountain on Good Friday morning, started with Virgil on the journey on Good Friday evening, and entered the gate of Hell at midnight. At six o'clock on Holy Saturday night they reached the depths of Hell where Lucifer is waist-deep in the ice of Cocytus. By careful astronomical calculations Dante tells us that they spent an hour and a half clambering down the sides of Satan to the center of the universe, the center of physical gravity. Here they must of necessity make a complete turn-about — the symbolism is evident — and move up toward the antipodes of Jerusalem or retrace their steps through Hell. They turn and begin their ascent through the dark passage worn in the rock by the River Lethe, which Dante represents as flowing from the mountain of Purgatory to join the Cocytus in the frozen depths of Dis where Satan is fast in the ice. They set their feet on the upward road at seven-thirty in the evening.

What is seven-thirty in the evening in the hemisphere they have left is seven-thirty in the morning in the hemisphere under which they now are. The period of ascent through the dark passage takes all Friday night and all day Saturday, Jerusalem time. Dante and Virgil come out into the light at the foot of the mountain of Purgatory "when it began to dawn" (Mt. 28:1) on Easter Sunday morning. Dante has spent four nights and three days in Hell; like Christ he rises on Easter Sunday at dawn. It is clear that he spends three days and three nights on the mountain of Purgatory (Sunday, Monday, and Tuesday); six hours of the next day in the Earthly Paradise, and enters Paradise on Wednesday at noon.[11]

There is little reference to time in the *Paradiso;* in fact, there are only two very obscure references. Dr. Franz Hettinger, one of the most quoted German Dantists, says that Dante's whole pilgrimage lasted ten days: three days and four nights in Hell, four days and three nights in Purgatory, three days and three nights in Heaven.[12] Most commentators, among them Andrea Gustarelli whose three-volume summary outline[13] seems to be used as a study guide in all Italian schools and universities, calculate that the journey took seven days; some suggest that the ascent through the Spheres into the Empyrean took twenty-four hours. According to their calculations Dante would come to the Beatific Vision on the eighth day.

From all the discussions in patristic and scholastic literature concerning the meaning of the octave, much of which would have been familiar to Dante, it is quite in keeping with his plan to have the journey close on the eighth day. Saint Augustine in the *City of God* calls the eighth "the eternal day"; Saint Thomas says, "the number seven is succeeded by the octave, that is, by the resurrection of the body and soul." Dante arrives in the heavens on the seventh day, the day of rest; he has the vision of the Church Triumphant and of the Blessed Trinity on the eighth day, where the world of time and the world of eternity meet in the life of contemplative prayer.[14]

> *If thine own fingers unto such a knot*
> *Be insufficient, it is no great wonder*
> *So hard hath it become from want of trying.*
> — *Paradiso* XXVIII:58–60

Dante's journey in space took him through the whole universe. It is impossible to follow him intelligently without some understanding of his conception of the structure of the universe; in his poem he does not separate the here from the hereafter, for in his mind, the physical and moral universe have definite interrelationships. Since the whole universe is, as the word implies, *one*, he builds his philosophical and theological structure into his physical structure. Throughout all its parts there is perfect order unless that order is destroyed by the free agent, man.

To Dante as to every other medieval man the earth was literally God's footstool. In the *Banquet* (III, v, 5–6) he quotes Aristotle as his authority for holding that the earth is immovable and does not revolve, that with the sea it is the center of the heavens, and that the heavens revolve continually around this center. In Book II, iii, he has discussed the errors into which Aristotle had fallen in his concept of the number and relative positions of these heavens and asserts that he has accepted the correction made by Ptolemy that there are nine heavens and that the order of the planets is the Moon, Mercury, Venus, the Sun, Mars, Jupiter, and Saturn; that beyond these there is the eighth, the heaven of the Fixed Stars, and the ninth, the Primum Mobile or Crystalline heaven which moves with immense velocity. Beyond these, Dante says, Christians have placed a tenth, the Empyrean heaven, which they hold to be immovable (*Banq*. II, iv, 1) "because it has within itself in every part that which its matter demands. This is the heaven of perfect contemplation and rest . . . the abode of that Supreme Deity who alone doth perfectly behold himself. This is the abode of the beatified spirits . . . this is the supreme edifice of the universe in which all the world is included and beyond which there is nothing."

Astronomy occupies a prominent place in the works of Dante; to him, as to other men of his age, the subject had exceptional interest for many reasons which would not concern us today. The conviction that stellar influence on human affairs and character was very considerable gave astronomy and astrology (the words were used interchangeably) a very important and practical philosophical interest. The belief that there was a mystical interrelationship between the physical world and the sphere of moral and mental activity gave rise to detailed discussions of the relationship between the subjects of the Trivium and the Quadrivium and the other subjects of the medieval university with the heavenly bodies (*Banq*. II, xiv). In theology the functions of the angelic choirs in relation to the heavens were given much consideration. All these matters are a part of the fabric of the *Divine Comedy*.[15]

For a complete understanding of Dante's thought one should follow, too, his discussions of the magnitude of planets, problems of planetary motions, measurement of time, precession of equinoxes, cycles and epicycles, signs of the zodiac, and many other matters which throw light on the philosophical and metaphysical and theological problems of the *Divine Comedy*. Much learned work has been done in the field.[16]

The medieval man had definite notions of the geographical position of Heaven, Hell, and Purgatory; these were predicated upon his notions of the physical universe. As we have seen, he placed our world at the center of the universe. He believed it to be divided into a hemisphere of land and a hemisphere of water; he confined the habitable portion to the northern hemisphere, which he divided symmetrically into two parts, Asia in the East and Europe and Africa in the West. Asia, in which Europe was included, was held to be equal in size to Europe and Africa together.

Jerusalem was the center of that portion of the periphery of the earth which is the hemisphere of land. It was the Greenwich of the Middle Ages, the center in latitude as well as in longitude. On either side of Jerusalem — at a distance of ninety degrees were the Ganges on the east and the Pillars of Hercules (the Strait of Gibraltar) on the west. Halfway between Jerusalem and Spain, and therefore in the center of the Mediterranean, was Rome: forty-five degrees west of Jerusalem, central between it and the Pillars of Hercules. For Dante, Jerusalem was the center of the inhabited world; Rome, the center of the Western or Christian world.

There was a popular notion in Dante's time that when Saint Michael expelled Lucifer and the rebellious angels from Heaven they came hurtling down through the nine heavens and through the circles of air and fire which surround our world. Having lost their center of spiritual gravity which held them in the Empyrean, they fell to the center of physical gravity at the center of the earth. The earth being a faithful creature of God, recoiled from these rebellious creatures and a yawning funnel-like abyss was formed to receive them. This funnel is Hell. Weighted with his load of sin, Lucifer struck the earth with such force that he pierced it to its center: the upper part of his vast frame (several Italian commentators calculate his height as roughly one and one third miles) stuck fast in one hemisphere; the lower half is in the other.

It is a law of the physical universe that matter is indestructible; hence the matter which was displaced rose in the hemisphere of water to form the Mountain of Purgatory (*Inf.* XXXIV:121–126). On the top of the mountain, Dante places the Earthly Paradise, an idea completely original with him. (Most of the medieval writers, including Saint Thomas, place it in Asia Minor in the fertile crescent, though some locate it in India or other parts of the Far East.) Antipodal to the Mountain of Purgatory is Jerusalem; therefore, Calvary, where sin was expiated confronts the mountain of purgation. Heaven is presented in the seven planets which whirl about the earth, the Stellar Heaven, the Primum Mobile, and the Empyrean — the seat of the Deity — which is really the only true Heaven.

We to the place have come, where I have told thee
Thou shalt behold the people dolorous
Who have foregone the good of intellect.
                                              — *Inferno* III:16–18

According to Dante's own statement (*Inf.* XI:80–82) he bases his threefold division of Hell upon the three dispositions opposed to morality treated by Aristotle in his *Ethics* (VII, I): incontinence, bestiality, and malice. With the bestiality of Aristotle he equates the violence of Cicero (*De Officiis* I, 13); with his malice he equates fraud (XI:22–23), thus designating sins in the three major divisions of Hell as sins of incontinence, violence, and fraud. Sins of incontinence, proceeding from the irrational or animal nature of man are punished in five circles of the upper Hell, Limbo forming the sixth and Ante-Hell the seventh section of this first division; sins of bestiality and violence are in the middle Hell; and sins of fraud and treachery in the lower Hell.

The inscription over the gate of Hell (*Inf.* III:1–9) tells the reader that he is entering a doleful city of eternal pain, where dwell a people without hope, lost forever. Hell was made, the legend reads, by the Blessed Trinity — Divine Power, Supreme Wisdom, and Primal Love. One may expect, therefore, to find it as well ordered, in its own way, as either Purgatory or Heaven. The landscape of this subterranean funnel with its rivers, deserts, mountains, cliffs, abysses, forests, morasses — though extraordinary creations of Dante's imagination and intentionally exaggerated so as to serve as the eternal abode of demons — is not without its savage counterpart in the great natural caves explored by men in the Bermudas or Dante's own Italy near Naples or Mammoth Cave and Cudjo's Cave in the southern United States. The fire and ice, the hurricanes, the darkness which are part of the punishment spell disaster also for living men.

In the seven divisions of the upper Hell are found the pusillanimous, the unbaptized, the unchaste, the gluttonous, the avaricious, the angry, and the Epicurean heretics. In Ante-Hell, which is just inside the gate, Dante shows us that great mass of people who never did their own thinking, trimmers who followed whatever banner was raised, pusillanimous souls who merely followed the crowd. Because he scorns such souls utterly, he places them inside the gate on the near side of Acheron, suggesting that since they had lived without "praise or blame" neither rebellious against God nor actively faithful to him, they are claimed by neither God nor the devil (*Inf.* III:34–42). From this point the circles are ever descending narrowing circles which go to the bottom of the funnel where, at the center of the earth, stuck fast between the two hemispheres is the gigantic figure of Lucifer.

Limbo, the first circle proper, seems in a sense not to be a part of Hell. The souls here experience a natural happiness, their only suffering being to desire what they can never have. There is here the natural light of earthly existence and the pleasure of intellectual discussion, for Dante places in Limbo not only unbaptized infants but virtuous pagans.[17] Though here in the *Inferno*, he says nothing about the infants, he names them in *Purgatorio* V:31–33 as being here. It is from Limbo that Virgil has come to be Dante's guide; it is in Limbo that we meet Aristotle, Averroës, Plato, and other non-Christian thinkers in all the areas of human knowledge.

In the next five circles Dante places those who permitted their animal nature to gain the ascendancy over their rational nature and were not guided by reason in their desire for and use of things which in themselves are good or even necessary. In the second circle, the first of these five, are the unchaste, swept off their feet forever by violent winds symbolic of violent passion: the sex appetite, essential for the life of the race, may if unbridled, lead to fornication or adultery. The food appetite uncontrolled may become gluttony: in the third circle the gluttons wallow in a virtual pigsty. The property appetite may be perverted to avarice or prodigality; the rolling up or the rolling away of wealth are symbolized by the laborious rolling of huge masses of rock in opposite directions. The gift of anger bestowed upon man to help him protect his person, his sustenance, his property may be used unjustly to harm his fellow men: the angry are submerged forever in a Stygian morass where they rend each other asunder or, stuck in the mud at the bottom, are unable to rise, their punishment depending on which type of anger they displayed on earth.

The sixth circle, the last of the upper Hell, is entered through a gate set in the ramparts which completely surround the whole Nether Hell to which it is closely related; for though heresy is a sin of the intellect, it may be prompted by one of the sins of human weakness. The gate is guarded by a thousand insolent demons, who at first refuse to permit Dante and Virgil to enter. The Epicurean heretics placed in this circle in fiery tombs because of their denial of the immortality of the soul may have been led into error, Dante seems to suggest by the position he gives them, by their desire to enjoy the pleasures of this world without the restraints of considerations of a life beyond the grave. Among the souls here in the fire-filled tombs on the great plain are leaders prominent in Church and Empire — Pope Anastasius, Frederick II, Farinata degli Uberti among them. Here, too, is Cavalcante Cavalcanti, the father of Guido, the "first" of Dante's friends.

In the upper Hell the scenery, though representing elements hostile to man, is not perverted; in the middle Hell where Dante places those guilty of sins of violence and bestiality we have nature not only hostile and savage but also seemingly alive and conscious. Here in this seventh circle in three rounds are those who were violent against their neighbor in his person or in his property — murderers, pillagers, and the like; against themselves — suicides, squanderers of their talents or fortunes; and against God, nature, and art — blasphemers, sodomites, and usurers. These men used their powers to defeat the end of love, love of neighbor, of self, of God. To symbolize this perversion of love Dante perverts the whole landscape in which they act. These, like those in the upper Hell, have for all eternity precisely what they wanted, that which made them turn from God and his law.

In a natural landscape man likes water and trees and a meadow; a waterfall, perhaps; fish in the stream if it be a river; and little animals and birds to enliven the scene. But here the river is a river of boiling blood in which murderers are immersed to varying depths signifying their degree of guilt: some only to the ankles, some to the eyebrows, these last with their brains covered being for the most part those who plotted extensive purges. The wood is the gnarled trees of the suicides, who not having wanted their bodies are now forever deprived of them. The meadow is a sandy plain where sodomites pace forever, where usurers sit with their pouches around their necks, where blasphemers lie prone looking up to God whom they defied. Upon them all instead of dew from heaven fall flakes of the fire of God's wrath. Here the animals who are part men — or men who are part beast: the minotaur, the centaurs, the harpies — serve as guardians and as representatives of the bestiality of some of the sins.

Lower Hell is separated from middle Hell by a vast chasm from which Geryon, the symbol of fraud, rises — a sort of demoniac air plane — to carry Virgil and Dante through the black air to the depths of Hell to the eighth and ninth circles where simple fraud and treachery are found. In the eighth circle, in ten evil pits in ever descending gradations, are those who practiced fraud against any neighbor; in the ninth are those who deceived and wrought evil against those who had a right to place special trust in them. In this lower Hell sin reaches its depth: man is lower than any beast; here is the worst perversion of all, for man who was given his gift of intellect to discover truth has used it to deceive.

In the first of the evil pits of the eighth circle are panderers and seducers; moving down in order, we find flatterers; churchmen guilty of simony or nepotism; false prophets — soothsayers, diviners, and magicians; barrators and political grafters; hypocrites of all sorts (Dante like Molière hits religious hypocrites hardest); thieves and robbers; and in the eighth, evil counselors. The ninth and tenth fosses are amazing travesties on surgery and medicine, showing the dreadful deformities and sicknesses of an evil society. Disease is to the physical order what sin is to the spiritual. In the ninth circle are sowers of scandal and schism and heresy, which rend society and violate its major institutions, Church and State, and the smaller institutions of which these are composed — the community and the family. In the tenth pit are the falsifiers of things and persons: alchemists who falsify metals, men who pretend to be persons they are not, counterfeiters who falsify coins, and liars who falsify words.

In the very bottom of Hell, the ninth circle, the intelligence is bedeviled; fraud becomes treachery. Dante presents here a field of ice guarded by giants; in four rings, frozen fast in the ice, are those who hardened their hearts and froze out the natural warmth of love which all men feel for family and country and friends and benefactors. In the very pit is Lucifer himself, once Heaven's brightest angel, now Emperor of this dark domain of evil, forced to spend eternity as the lowest creature in the chain of living beings champing in the jaws of his three faces Cassius and Brutus, who would destroy the Empire by bringing about the death of Caesar, and Judas who betrayed the founder of the Church; immobile except for the activity of the jaws and the futile movement of his vast wings, futile movement because it serves only to freeze the ice which holds him fast. Lucifer is a symbol of anti-Trinity, a negation of all the Trinity means. All about him under the ice, bent in court bows forever, are those who were traitors to their benefactors: the field of ice in the pit of darkness is the antithesis of the great white rose of the *Paradiso*, Dante's image of the Communion of Saints, where the angels and the souls of the blessed move forever in harmony with that Will which is forever active, where all is light and the glow of love.

The *Inferno* is not an account of how sin is punished; it is fundamentally a revelation of what sin is. And so Dante used his powerful imagination to depict concretely the essence of sin. He shows souls identified for all eternity with the activities which cut them off from God or with the symbols of these activities: gluttons in a pigsty, murderers in boiling blood, fornicators and adulterers swept off their feet by a whining whirlwind. He shows avaricious churchmen rolling up great material masses symbolizing wealth and moving forever in futile activity, or for their simony and nepotism stuffed head-first into evil pockets in the rock, because when they should have been looking up to the things of God they were looking down to earthly gain. He shows traitors to both Church and Empire in obeisance before Satan whom they have chosen for their leader, a frozen court forever encased in ice.

Why do you not climb the mountain of delight
Which is the beginning and the occasion of all joy?
— *Inferno* I:77–78

While the dawn stars are still in the sky, Dante and Virgil emerge from the underground passage worn by the River Lethe as it descends from the Earthly Paradise to empty into the depths of Cocytus, and in the beauty of the Italian springtime stand on the beach of the island of Purgatory, which rears its gray height above them. Dante is now where he would have been at the beginning if he could have come by the direct route. The mood has changed from despair to hope. He had descended into Hell on Good Friday night; he has risen with Christ on Easter morning.

The landscape and seascape of Purgatory are the familiar scenery of our world; some of it like the valley of the princes and the Earthly Paradise restful and charming; much of it, especially along the ledges or cornices, austere and difficult to conquer, but none of it savage or malignant. There is the light of the stars and of the moon to make the nights beautiful; the days have all the familiar lights and shadows from dawn to gloaming. There is hard going in the upward climb and there is pain. But there is the will to advance and there is joy; for these repentant souls desire the discipline which will make them ready for the Beatific Vision. The way leads to God; his grace is with them each difficult step of the journey; the pain is curative pain which comes from the identification of the soul with the virtue opposed to the sin being uprooted.

In the Ante-Purgatory Dante places two major groups, the excommunicated and the late-repentant. Of the late-repentant there are three divisions: the indolent, those who have put off going about their Father's business because of inertia or sheer laziness; the energetic, all of whom were overtaken by sudden death; and the negligent princes, those who were, for various reasons, lacking in right qualities of leadership chiefly because they were egocentric, preoccupied with their own affairs.

The second major division is separated from the first by the gate of Saint Peter and the three steps of penitence; on the threshold of the closed gate sits the bright angel confessor who with the tip of his sword inscribes seven *P's* (*Peccata*) on Dante's forehead, symbolizing the seven capital sins, and who commands him that he wash the scars away. The resistance to entrance at this gate is not the violent opposition offered by the demons at the entrance gate to the City of Dis in the *Inferno,* but a calm resistance which the penitent must overcome by obedience and submission to lawful authority, the first act always of one who has transgressed and wishes reinstatement. When the angel is sure that Dante's dispositions are right, he turns the key and the gate swings wide. There is a burst of melody because of the joy of the angels that a soul is to begin his penance.

On the seven cornices or terraces which constitute Purgatory proper, souls purge themselves of the seven capital sins, which can lead to the actual sins depicted in the *Inferno.* Pride can lead to any of the sins of the upper, middle, or lower Hell, as can envy or anger or any one of the remaining four. In the *Inferno* sin was shown in its effects on the sinner as well as in its essence; here in the Purgatory it is considered in its cause, disordered love. The sequence of capital sins which Dante follows is that of Saint Bonaventure, the order being pride, envy, anger, sloth, avarice, gluttony, and lust.[18]

Along the cornices Dante meets representatives of Church and Empire as well as humble citizens of his native Florence. Through various arts he presents characters from Scripture, profane history, and literature as examples of those who have practiced valiantly the virtues these souls are trying to practice; for instance, the first historical example of humility is David, the next Trajan. The Virgin Mary is always presented as the first and most perfect example. These personages are the call to the virtue. Dante also chooses from Scripture and history examples for meditation from among those who fell because of the vice, meditation on whom should be effective in curbing it — for instance, Lucifer, Saul, Cyrus, and the people of Troy who fell because of pride. This pattern of call and curb is found on all the cornices. The souls making their way up the mountain practice disciplines to help them acquire the virtues opposed to the seven capital sins: humility to overcome pride; brotherly love or generosity to supplant envy; meekness to counteract anger; zeal to cast out sloth; poverty of spirit and liberality to replace avarice and prodigality; temperance to rectify gluttony; chastity to burn out lust.

When Dante has passed through the purging fire on the last cornice and is free from the slavery of every evil tendency, Virgil pronounces him upright and whole, and crowns and miters him sovereign of himself, signifying that he now needs neither civil nor ecclesiastical law to direct him. Purified from sin, he has regained the state of innocence which Adam knew and is ready to enter the Garden of Eden which Adam lost because of his transgressions. The Earthly Paradise which he is about to enter, a sort of tableland on the blunted top of the mountain, represents not only Paradise Regained and the state of innocence; but also the temporal blessedness which Adam and Eve knew before they set their wills against the will of God. By discipline, prayer, and the grace of God, Dante's will has been made perfectly conformable to the Divine Will and has won perfect liberty. Matilda, the third subsidiary guide of the *Purgatorio*, whom he meets when he enter the Garden of Eden and who symbolizes the active Christian life (some commenators say ecclesiastical guidance), will assist Beatrice in his final purification.

The action in the Earthly Paradise, the very heart of the *Divine Comedy*, and therefore outlined here in some detail, consists mainl of two allegorical presentations: the pageant of the Church an the regeneration of Dante. The pageant of the Church is divided into two masques between which Dante has placed the dramati episode of his reunion with Beatrice. The first masque represent the coming of the Church: the Old Testament books which promis the Messias, the Gospels which give the record of his coming an of his teaching, and the remainder of the New Testament represent ing the work of his Apostles and disciples. The second masqu presents the history of the Church from apostolic time to Dante own day, chiefly in the relationship between the Church and th Empire. It is significant that the episode of the regeneration c Dante follows that section of the pageant which represents th coming of the Redeemer and the founding of his Church for th salvation of fallen man. For it must be remembered that Dante not only himself but universal man. The second masque shows that the evils which persist in the world and which prevent the Church from accomplishing her divine mission rise chiefly, in Dante's opinion, from wrong relationships between the Church and the Empire.

Dante has set the stage very carefully. The scenery is taken from the Pineta of Classe (XXVIII:19), the ancient pine forest on the Adriatic near Ravenna, once the great port for the Roman fleet. Through the forest — as Dante transfers it to the Earthly Para dise — run two rivers: Lethe, the classical river of forgetfulness, which is used here to destroy all memory of sin and the sin itself; and Eunoë, a river of Dante's own invention, which restores re membrance of the sin as a fact, only that it may serve to quicken gratitude for the mercy of God and subsequent blessedness. At the end of the last canto of the *Purgatorio*, Dante seems to see the two rivers as the Tigris and Euphrates, which run through the fertile crescent, the traditional site of the Earthly Paradise, and to equate them with Lethe and Eunoë (*Purg*. XXXIII:112–129). Hence Dante has brought together here in his setting scenery associated with the Roman Empire and with the fall of Adam, which necessitated the foundation of the Church which came into being under Roman rule.

With ineffable melody the pageant moves upon the scene. Its formation is that of a Roman cross, for in a sense it is a pageant of the Redemption. The procession is headed by seven golden candlesticks (Apoc. 1:12), which even today head every formal Papal procession, the rainbow pennants of light which stream from them signifying the seven gifts of the Holy Ghost as they are enumerated in *Isaias* (11:2): wisdom and understanding, counsel and fortitude, knowledge and piety, and fear of the Lord. Immedi ately following these are the twenty-four elders (Apoc. 4:4), who represent the books of the Old Testament in the grouping used by most Jewish scholars and/or by Saint Jerome;[19] these Old Testament books form the base of the Roman cross. After them, in the center at the crossbeams, forming a body guard, as it were, or the triumph car, which represents the Church, are the four living creatures, traditional symbols in both Testaments of the four evangelists (Ezech. 1:4–14; Apoc. 4:6–8). Every medieval city had its *carroccio* or triumph car: this is the carroccio of the city of God.[20] It rolls on two wheels, symbolizing Saint Dominic and Saint Francis – cherubic knowledge and seraphic love (*Par.* XII:44–111). It is drawn by a griffin, a classical and heraldic creature whose forepart is an eagle and whose hindpart is a lion, used in medieval art as a symbol of Christ in his twofold nature, human and divine – the hypostatic union of the Incarnation. His golden wings signifying divinity, stretch up far out of sight.

Forming the right arm of the cross and dancing at the right wheel of the chariot are three maidens representing the theological virtues; forming the left arm and dancing at the left wheel are four nymphs representing the cardinal virtues, who in the *Paradiso* are stars in the heavens of honor (*Purg.* XXXI:106). Following the chariot and the four evangelists who flank it and forming the last segment of the cross are seven elders, symbolic of the remaining books of the New Testament, *Acts,* the epistles, and the *Apocalypse.*

Within the triumph car, surrounded by a hundred angels who are singing and scattering flowers, is Beatrice, who is both her historic self and a symbol of that which is most precious within the Church – some say Theology, some Divine Revelation. Dorothy Sayers interprets Beatrice as the Eucharist, Christ veiled in the Sacramental Species, this last a symbol difficult to sustain throughout the *Commedia.*[21] The sight of Beatrice wakens in Dante all the power of the old love, and, deeply moved, he turns to address Virgil. But Virgil, the symbol of natural reason, has gone: where faith begins reason ends. Whether Beatrice represents Divine Revelation, Divine Wisdom, Theology, the Eucharist, or all of these she must be met with faith.

The part played by Beatrice in the regeneration of Dante has already been discussed in the third chapter; further aspects will be presented in the ninth. After "the thorn of repentance" has pierced Dante (XXXI:85) so that he has fallen vanquished by remorse, after Matilda has drawn him through the waters of Lethe and his sin and the remembrance of sin have been erased, she takes him to the breast of the Griffin, and reflected in the eyes of Beatrice, the mirror of Revelation or Divine Wisdom or Theology he sees the double nature of Incarnate Love, the unity of which he is to comprehend in the Empyrean in the vision of the God-Man in the Trinity.

Following the revelation of the meaning of the Incarnation, Dante witnesses the historical-political masque, much of the imagery of which as well as of the first masque is taken from the *Apocalypse*. In the first masque Dante has seen the divine origin of the Church; now he will witness what has happened to it because of the machinations of men. While his eyes were fixed upon Beatrice and the Griffin, the procession had wheeled to the right. Dante now joins it, following it through the divine forest until it reaches a desolate and despoiled tree, the tree of the knowledge of good and evil, desolated by the sin of Adam and here representing Adam in his fallen nature. When the Griffin comes to the tree and touches it and binds to it the chariot pole (the Cross), which had been formed from it (XXXII:49–52) — there was a tradition that the wood of the Cross came from the tree of the knowledge of good and evil — the desolated tree bursts into leaf and flower (58–60), symbolizing the redemption of man's ruined nature.

Dante falls asleep, he knows not how, and wakes as did the Apostles on Mount Tabor at the Transfiguration to find the procession and the Griffin gone and Beatrice seated on the roots of the tree. She is guarding the chariot, which was tied to the tree by the Griffin, the seven nymphs with the lighted candles forming a ring around her. The tree now becomes the symbol of the Empire; it, too, had burst into bloom when the chariot of the Church touched it and should have sheltered the Church and Christianity, symbolized by Beatrice. The root of the imperial tree on which Beatrice is seated symbolizes Rome.

In a series of tableaux Dante sees now the whole history of the Church in its relation to the Empire: the early persecutions and heresies; the donation of Constantine; the schism caused by Mohammed; the monstrous transformation of the chariot caused by the riches as it assumes secular power; its usurpation by the harlot who represents corrupt ecclesiastical authority based on Decretals; and finally its abduction by a giant, representing the royal house of France, who alternately caresses and scourges the harlot, unbinds the chariot from the tree, and finally drags it away from the forest.

This last scene symbolizes, of course, the transfer of the Apostolic See from Rome to Avignon. In terms of the *Comedy*, Dante turns prophet here, for the abduction took place in 1305 and the date he assigns for the vision is 1300.

Dante's prophecies in the next terza rima run beyond his lifetime. He puts upon the lips of Beatrice a promise of punishment of offenders against both Church and Empire and of the regeneration of both. Beatrice commands Dante to promulgate to the whole world what has been revealed to him, urges Matilda to draw him through the waters of Eunoë which will sharpen the remembrance of good. When Matilda has done so, he is pure and ready to mount with Beatrice to the stars.

> Lift up then, Reader, to the lofty wheels
> With me thy vision straight unto that part
> Where the one motion on the other strikes,
>
> And there begin to contemplate with joy
> That Master's art, who in himself so loves it
> That never doth his eye depart therefrom.
>
> — Paradiso X:7–12

The atmosphere of the *Paradiso* is for the most part suprasensible: there is no need for angels and saints to see in the forms of earth or to question and reply. All things are evident to them; they see and know everything, not directly, but in God (*Par.* IX:73). Again and again the whole panorama appears and vanishes, having shaped itself only to clarify for Dante things purely suprasensitive because purely spiritual.

With the rapidity of light, Dante and Beatrice make their way through the nine heavens into the Empyrean. As they do so, groups of spirits come out of the Empyrean to meet them, just as delegations come to meet an important personage who is coming home. Dante is careful to inform his reader that the souls he meets in the various heavens are really in the Empyrean, where there is an eternal here and now but are shown to him in the lower heavens which mark stages of his journey toward God so that he may ask them questions. Their answers to his questions help him to understand degrees of holiness and the roads that lead to the Beatific Vision.

In the infrasolar or shadowed planets — the moon, Mercury, and Venus — Dante meets souls whom some imperfection has made fall short of their spiritual potentialities; though they are perfectly happy, their joy is of a lesser intensity than it would be if they had been perfectly true to their better selves. Usually these heavens are known as the heavens of imperfect fortitude, imperfect justice, and imperfect temperance. Souls in the *Paradiso* are represented as jewels dancing in the light; these are pearls which refract the light less brilliantly than diamonds or topazes or sapphires. Nor are there here the magnificent emblems one finds in the heavens of honor.

In the second division, the heavens of honor, Dante meets those who have practiced the cardinal virtues in an extraordinary manner: the first three groups in the active life of the pen, the sword, and the scepter; the last in the life of contemplation. In the Heaven of the Sun he finds the great teachers — those who have taught well by word, spoken or written, and by example. The virtue here is prudence, which according to Aristotle and Saint Thomas is the great virtue of the intellect. In the Earthly Paradise, where the cardinal virtues were presented as nymphs at the left wheel of the chariot, Prudence has three eyes: teachers must have one eye on the past, one on the present, and one on the future. The emblem here is the circle, for the teachers in this university of the eternities compass all knowledge.

In the Heaven of Mars, which is next, are martyrs and crusaders of all kinds who have fought valiantly for Christ; they are shown on a great cross, two milky ways at right angles. The virtue here is, of course, fortitude. From this cross comes Cacciaguida to give Dante his mission, an episode developed in detail in subsequent chapters. In Jupiter, the emblem is the Roman eagle; here are gathered those who lived well the active life of the scepter; the virtue is heroic justice. In Saturn, Dante presents the contemplatives; their outstanding virtue is temperance, their emblem a ladder reaching into the Empyrean which they ascend and descend.

When Dante has studied the cardinal virtues by meeting souls who were distinguished in their practice, and is ready for his examination in the theological virtues, up from all the heavens where he has met them moves the procession of the blessed back through the Heaven of the Fixed Stars and the Primum Mobile to the Empyrean where they really *are* and where in the vision of the white rose he sees them. In the Stellar Heaven as in a wonderful garden he has a glimpse of Christ and sees the Virgin and all the other saints; here Peter, James, and John examine him in faith, hope, and charity. In the Primum Mobile, he has a close-up of the nine choirs of angels; in the Empyrean, he sees the angels and saints together in the mystic rose and is vouchsafed the vision of the Trinity.

Even at this height, Dante is mindful of the three themes which he blends in his *Commedia*. Remembering that he undertook the journey to discover what is wrong with the world and how it can be set right, he turns his thought to Pope and Emperor, who should be leading men to this high joy; he sings here one of his finest lyrics in honor of Beatrice. Just before he enters the Empyrean, he puts upon the lips of Saint Peter a fearful denunciation of his unworthy successors (*Par.* XXVII:46–66); in the mystic rose, he sees the empty seat reserved for the unfortunate Prince Henry to whom he had for a time looked as the Emperor who would bring peace to his country and the world at large. When Beatrice has guided him along the illuminative way and brought him to the Empyrean, she leaves him in the care of Saint Bernard, without any warning of her going. He looks for her as he had looked for Virgil when he had vanished, his work — like hers now — being done. Saint Bernard points her out to Dante in the place in the Communion of Saints to which her merits have assigned her. She looking down on Dante from that great height gives him her last beautiful smile. Knowing that he will never look upon her face again until he himself will have passed the judgment, he sings to her his last lyric in her honor. The lyric is a prayer of gratitude and petition to a saint in heaven, Dante's own particular saint, the woman he has loved from childhood. It must have been written only a few months before Dante's death. The translation is Cary's.

O Lady! thou in whom my hopes have rest;
Who, for my safety, hast not scorned, in hell
To leave the traces of thy footsteps marked;
For all mine eyes have seen, I to thy power
And goodness, virtue owe and grace. Of slave
Thou hast to freedom brought me: and no means,
For my deliverance apt, hast left untried.
Thy liberal bounty still toward me keep:
That, when by spirit, which thou madest whole,
Is loosened from this body, it may find
Favor with thee.

Then follows Saint Bernard's exposition of the mystic rose, his prayer to the Virgin, and Dante's prayer to the Trinity as he is vouchsafed the glorious vision of the Three Persons in One God and the mystery of the Incarnate Word.

NOTES

1. For a survey of literature dealing with preternatural and supernatural journeys in the Middle Ages consult Howard Rollin Patch, *The Other World According to Descriptions in Medieval Literature* (Cambridge, 1950). Chapter V discusses journeys to the Earthly Paradise.
2. See "The Dante Number" of *The Kenyon Review*, Vol. XIV, Spring, 1952, for articles by these and other critics.
3. Jacques Maritain, "Dante's Innocence and Luck," *ibid.*, Part III, pp. 319–323.
4. William Durandus, *Rationale Divinorum Officiorum*, trans. John Mason Neale and Benjamin Webb, under the title *The Symbolism of Churches* and *Church Ornaments* (London: Gibbings & Company, 1906).
5. Edward Moore, *Studies in Dante*, Third Series (Oxford, 1903), "The DXV Prophecy," pp. 253–283. See also Edmund Gardner, *Dante and the Mystics* (New York, 1913), "Dante, Joachim, and Siger," especially the paragraph on page 329 beginning, *Nowhere in any of his sources.* . . . Consult also Giovanni Papini, *Dante Vivo*, tr. E. Broodus and A. Benedetti (New York, 1935), pp. 280–302.
6. Dante's ability in the various branches of theology is presented in succeeding chapters.
7. Patrick Cummins, O.S.B., *Dante Theologian* (St. Louis, 1948), pp. 2, 3.
8. Etienne Gilson, *The Mystical Theology of Saint Bernard* (New York, 1955), p. 7.
9. Moore, *op. cit.*, "The Date Assumed by Dante for the Vision of the *Divina Commedia*," pp. 144–177.
10. Edmund G. Gardner, *Dante* (New York, 1923), p. 114. Gardner points out that the crucifixion was believed to have taken place on March 25 on the thirty-fourth anniversary of the Annunciation (*Inf.* XXI:112; *Purg.* II:98, i.e., three months from Christmas Day).
11. Carefully worked-out timetables for the *Inferno* appear in William Warren Vernon, *Readings on the Inferno of Dante* (New York, 1894), Vol. I, pp.

lviii–lxxix, and *Readings on the Purgatorio* (New York, 1897), Vol. I, pp. xxix–xlvi. In Vernon, April 8, 1300, is the assumed date for Good Friday.
12. Franz Hettinger, *Dante's Divine Commedia,* trans. Henry Sebastian Bowden, 2 ed., rev. (London, 1894), p. 69.
13. Andrea Gustarelli, *Il Poema Sacro. Riassunti E. Schemi Per Lo Studio della Divina Commedia* (Milan: Carlo Signorelli, n.d.), three volumes.
14. Saint Augustine, *The City of God,* trans. Marcus Dods (Edinburgh, 1934), eighth impression, two-volume edition, Vol. II, Book XXII, Chap. 30, pp. 543–545:

> "There shall be the great Sabbath which has no evening, which God celebrated among his first works. . . . The first age, as the first day, extends from Adam to the deluge; the second from the deluge to Abraham. . . . From Abraham to the advent of Christ there are, as the evangelist Matthew calculates, three periods, in each of which are fourteen generations – one period from Abraham to David, a second from David to the captivity, a third from the captivity to the birth of Christ in the flesh. There are thus five ages in all. The sixth is now passing and cannot be measured by any number of generations. . . . After this period God shall rest as on the the seventh day, when he shall give us (who shall be the seventh day) rest in himself. . . . The seventh shall be our Sabbath which shall be brought to a close, not by an evening, but by the Lord's day, as an eighth and eternal day, consecrated by the resurrection of Christ, and prefiguring the eternal purpose not only of the spirit, but also of the body. . . . This is what shall be in the end without end."

Saint Thomas, *Commentary on the Psalms* (*Opera Omnia,* Parma ed.), Vol. XIV, p. 164.

> "Whence there is another reason why the Resurrection is signified by the octave, since in the present age there are two types of life. One is that in which a man is occupied by corporal things; the other that in which a man is occupied with spiritual things. The first life is signified by the number 4 . . . the second which is spiritual is signified by the number 3. . . . The number 7 which is constituted from the 4 and 3 is succeeded by the octave, that is the resurrection of the body and the soul."

15. Chapter V, "Dante and the Angels," discusses, among other things, the functions of the angelic choirs, pp. 162–170.
16. See Moore, *op. cit.,* "The Astronomy of Dante," pp. 1–108; and "The Geography of Dante," pp. 109–143.
17. It would seem that there is no matter of Christian theology more disputed than that relative to the eternal disposition of children who die in the state of original sin and of adult infidels. In dealing with the problem of adult infidels, Dante, who has been recognized by the Church as a master theologian (see Chapter II, Note 5, and Chapter VII, Note 2, relative to the encyclical *In Praeclara* of Benedict XV) presents a point of view contrary to that usually held by theologians. It is probably from Saint Thomas that he received the concept of Limbo as a place in which the punishment inflicted consists simply and solely in the exclusion of unregenerated souls from the Beatific Vision of God and not in any physical suffering, a concept which he concretizes in the fourth canto of the *Inferno.* He differs from Saint Thomas, however, in detaining in Limbo unbaptized pagans after the Harrowing of Hell.

As has already been indicated, the discussion of Limbo centers about the disposition of both unbaptized children and adult infidels. Many early theologians, among them Saint Augustine, and a few of the schoolmen held that though the punishment of unbaptized children is "the mildest punishment of all," yet it is a punishment of *ignis aeternus* (eternal fire). It is pointed out in *God, The Author of Nature and the Supernatural, A Dogmatic Treatise* by Joseph Pohle, adapted and edited by Arthur Preuss, 4th ed. (Saint Louis, 1923), pp. 301–302, that toward the end of his life Saint Augustine seems to have held that for unbaptized children "as between reward and punishment there may be a neutral sentence of the judge," which suggests that ultimately Saint Augustine was in virtual agreement with what, centuries later, was taught by Saint Thomas and held by Dante. However, in Dante's day and, in fact, even to our day, the two dissenting groups are known as the Augustinians and the Thomists. For a detailed survey of the controversy see George J. Dyer, "Limbo: A Theological Evaluation," *Theological Studies*, Vol. 19 (March 1958), pp. 32–49.

In their treatment of the salvation of uncircumcised children of the Old Law and of Gentile children, who were outside the Mosaic Law, most theologians — probably Dante among them — held that there was a remedy for original sin in what was known as a *sacrament of nature*, some externalized ritual ceremony based on a belief in a future Redeemer and performed by those holding such belief for those who had not reached the age of reason. In the Mystic Rose of Paradise, which represents the Communion of Saints (*Par.* XXXIII:58–84) Dante places infants of both Testaments — those of the New Law having been baptized — each group in the proper half of the Rose.

The salvation of adult infidels poses quite a different problem. In his retention of certain "virtuous" pagans in Limbo after the Harrowing of Hell, Dante, as has already been said, differs from the teaching of Saint Thomas, though in regard to the salvation of *some* pagans, for example, Cato, Trajan, and Rhipeus, he follows the great scholastic. For Saint Thomas and theologians in general, it is impossible for adult infidels to be in *original* sin alone. It is their problem to explain how grace and the means of salvation come to these infidels. They hold that a man may prepare himself by natural reason for receiving faith and that "if anyone born in barbarous nations do what lieth in him, God will reveal to him what is necessary for salvation either by inspiration or by sending a teacher." Dante holds with this teaching in regard to the pagans named above. (See Chapter VII, p. 224 and footnote 7 at the end of the chapter for a discussion of the view as presented by Saint Thomas.) Dante, however, envisions the problem otherwise for many infidels. He assumes the possibility of their dying in original sin alone and therefore consigns them to Limbo.

The two-volume historical survey of this problem of the salvation of infidels — Louis Capéran, *Le Problème du Salut des Infidèles*, Nouvelle Edition, Revue et Mise a Jour (Toulouse, Grand Séminaire, 9 Rue des Teinfuriers, 9, 1934) — gives seven pages (pp. 206–212) to Dante's discussion of this problem, commenting on his presentation of all of its aspects in the *Divine Comedy* and concluding with the following statement:

> In summing up the evidence from Dante, the following points are important. His testimony is especially valuable, first of all, because the poet in submitting his inventive genius to the matters treated in theology bears witness to the fact that these matters have significance for everyone without exception; he has presented to us in concrete form and with vivid colors those truths which the Commentators on the *Sentences* repeated dryly. Furthermore, do we not hear in the poem of Dante an echo not only of scholastic teaching but of popular ideas, sentiments, and beliefs? In particular, the description of the lot of pagans in Limbo is not exclusively the fruit of the poet's dreams; rather the description translates and reveals for what they are the aspirations which were latent in the souls of those about

him. Thus can we explain why certain theologians studying the state of souls after death have allocated to them five different places of sojourn: Heaven, Hell, Purgatory, Limbo, and the Elysian Fields.

There are theologians later than Dante who admit adult pagans into the Limbo of children. They are discussed in Capéran and are listed in the *Dictionaire de Théologie Catholique* (Paris, Librairie Letouzey et Anè, 1923), Vol. VII, seconde partie, cols. 1894–1898.

18. See Edward Moore, *Studies in Dante*, Second Series (Oxford, 1899), "The Classification of Sins in the *Inferno* and *Purgatorio*." The table on p. 208a will prove especially helpful in giving the order followed by major theologians prior to Dante's time.

19. Dante uses the number twenty-four for the books of the Old Testament, the number given by Saint John in the *Apocalypse*. Saint John probably has the number from the Jews of his day. The matter is discussed in John E. Steinmueller and Kathryn Sullivan, *A Companion to the Old Testament* (New York, 1946), p. 2:

"The Jews of old never adopted the words *Bible* and *Testament*. They preferred to designate the Old Testament according to three divisions of its books: *Torah*, or the Law . . . *Nebiim*, or the Prophets; and *Kethubim*, or the sacred writings. Occasionally they used the term 'The Twenty-Four Books,' for by combining several books as one (e.g., the twelve Prophets as one book) they reduced the number of books from thirty-eight to twenty-four, or even twenty-two, to correspond with the number of letters in their alphabet."

Saint John probably has in mind this grouping made by the Palestinian Jews; Dante, however, may be thinking not only of this but of the grouping used by Saint Jerome, which also gave a total of twenty-four books. He, too, called the twelve minor prophets one book as he did *Paralipomenon* (*Chronicles*), *Kings*, and others.

20. For the use of the war chariot or *carroccio* in the life of a medieval city, see numerous references in William Heywood, *Palio and Ponte* (London, 1904).

21. Dorothy Sayers in her *Translation of the Purgatory*, Penguin Books (Edinburg, 1955), p. 305, interprets Beatrice as the Eucharist.

PART TWO

Ideas Central to Dante's Thought

CHAPTER V

DANTE AND THE ANGELS

> Not where the wheeling systems darken
> And our benumbed conceiving soars!
> The drift of pinions, would we hearken,
> Beats at our own clay-shuttered doors.
>
> The angels keep their ancient places;
> Turn but a stone and start a wing!
> 'Tis ye, 'tis your estranged faces,
> That miss the many-splendored thing.
>
> — Francis Thompson
> "The Kingdom of God"
> (*In No Strange Land*)

ll three divisions of the *Divine Comedy* are peopled with angels, each of whom is a distinct person with a particular office. In the *Inferno*, with the single exception of the sublime angel who commands that the gates of the city of Dis be opened, the angels are those evil spirits who, led by Lucifer, fell from heaven before the sword of Saint Michael in the very hour of their creation and were hurled into the abyss of Hell which yawned before them and who in the capacity of guardians and tormentors are still Satan's votaries. In the Ante-Purgatory, along all the cornices, and in the Earthly Paradise we meet angels who minister to the souls of good will who are on their way to God. In the *Paradiso* Dante puts into matchless verse the traditional philosophical and theological elaborations about the legions of angels of which the Scriptures speak, in the nine choirs whose names the Scriptures give. Any reader of Dante is aware that angels are as real to him as

125

men; in all of his major works, he speaks of them with the same casual assurance with which he speaks of men or things.

Though the medieval man based his belief in angels primarily on Scripture, he did much speculating about them and presented various philosophical arguments for their existence, their nature, and their function in the universe. Following Aristotle he said that there must be a First Cause, himself uncaused, an *intelligent* First Cause who ordered the universe. All things in it are subject to change: they are in the process of becoming; they pass from potential being to actual being. An acorn has the potentiality of becoming an oak, a block of marble of becoming a statue, a bolt of black voile of becoming an evening gown or the veil of a cloistered nun. But anything at all that passes from potency to act — that is, from potential being to actual being, supposes in the last analysis — though there may be a long chain of intermediate causes — an uncaused cause, something that is simply act with no mixture of potentiality, of imperfection. That which is pure act is the uncaused cause — the first mover, the first intelligible, the first good, whom the medieval Christian called God. God, he said, is the only unconditioned reality. All other reality derives from him in one of three ways: either immediately because he *created* it as it is; or *engendered,* as the acorn is engendered by the oak; or *manufactured* by one of his creatures, as the statue or the evening gown. God, he said, is at the peak of the hierarchy of being.

All through the *Divine Comedy,* but chiefly in Cantos II, XIII, XXVIII, XXIX of the *Paradiso,* Dante presents the framework into which the man of faith and philosophy saw the angels fit in the hierarchy of being. The medieval man pondered why God, ultimate reality, absolutely complete in himself, absolutely happy, should create a universe of beings. Dante (*Par.* XXIX:13–36) has Beatrice, looking into the depths of this Ultimate Reality, sum up the reasons. It was not that he might acquire any benefit for himself, which cannot be, because God is all in all to whom nothing can be added, but that other beings derived from him, each a separate entity, might participate in his glory and realize their own destiny by reflecting back to him the splendor of the creative rays — the joy, the beauty, and the majesty — all of the divine attributes of the One who brought them into existence.

The chief argument for the existence of angels grew out of the medieval concept of hierarchy, the so-called chain of being which rises from the lowest order of inanimate things in the material universe to the highest created things, namely, men and angels. This hierarchical order, implicit everywhere in the *Divine Comedy*, is explicit in several sections, notably in the first canto of the *Paradiso* (103–120). The medieval philosopher argued that in every class of beings, the imperfect presupposes the perfect; this principle must hold true of rational as well as of irrational beings. It is true that man, the highest crown of the material universe, mirrors God in his highest attributes, his intellect and free will. It is true that he has power to order things and in a sense has power to create in that he can make one thing from another according to the intelligible image in his mind. It is also true that he has power to reflect and to arrive at truth, that he has power to love. But in all these activities man is dependent upon his body, upon matter. Human intelligence is for this reason an imperfect grade of intelligence, so far removed from God's perfect intellectual knowledge that it is fitting — the medieval philosopher argued — that there be a missing link between man and God, created beings completely spiritual but finite, who mirror the infinite more perfectly. To these creatures next to God in the hierarchy of beings he gave the name of angels.[1]

Individual things throughout the whole chain of being, says Dante (*Par.* I:103–108), from stones to angels — that is, the whole range of inanimate and living creatures are ordained to make up the order and beauty of the universe, "the form that makes the universe resemble God." All creatures, irrational as well as rational, serve the end for which God made them by reflecting each in its own way, within its own capacity, some facet of the infinite and varied splendor comprised within the unity of the One. But the difference in capacities is astounding, for even when a thing is perfect according to its capacity, capacities differ. There is the splendor of an ant or lily; there is the splendor of an angel. Since angels are highest among created beings, they reflect most perfectly the Divine attributes, the highest among them reflecting the light to those next in rank (*Par.* II:112–148).

Since the perfection of God is infinite and these spiritual creatures were made to contemplate this infinite perfection and to manifest it to the rest of creation (*Par.* II:136–139; XXIX:13–18), each individual angel manifesting it in his own way, Dante and the schoolmen argued that there must be legions of angels, each angel showing forth some aspect of infinite perfection. So perfect is the angelic nature in its separateness that angels are as different from each other as a snowflake is from a mountain.[2] In this manifold diversity each angel can and does mirror some aspect of the infinite perfection of God. But among these legions of individual angels there must be order as there is order throughout the universe, hierarchical order. In both the *Banquet* and the *Divine Comedy*, Dante discusses what this order is and what its gradations are (*Banq.* II, vi, 3; *Par.* II:112–148; XXVIII:16–36; XXXI:17).

From the seventh century down to the time of Dante and beyond it, the work of a certain Dionysius, which he entitled *On the Celestial Hierarchy*, was considered authoritative by such men as Saint Bernard, Saint Thomas, and others upon whom Dante leaned for his theological concepts.[3] This authority was based upon the uncritical assumption of an identity between Dionysius the author and Dionysius the Areopagite — that convert, friend, and companion of Saint Paul who "adhered" to him at Athens (Acts 17:34). It was alleged that Saint Paul, who had been lifted up to the third heaven (2 Cor. 12:1–4), and had therefore seen the angels, had instructed Dionysius directly concerning the hierarchies (*Par.* X:115–117; XXVIII:130–139).

In his book Dionysius divides the nine choirs of angels into three hierarchies of three choirs each: the first — beginning with the highest and moving to the lowest — consists of the Seraphim, Cherubim, and Thrones (*Par.* XXVIII:98–106); the second, of Dominations, Virtues, and Powers (121–123); and the third, of Principalities, Archangels, and Angels (124–126).[4] In the *Banquet* in the section cited above Dante discusses at length the relation of these three orders of angels to the three Divine Persons, showing why there must be nine choirs, and three orders of angels in each hierarchy.

Following Dionysius, Dante teaches (*Banq.* II, vi, 5; *Par.* II:127–138) that the nine heavens are moved by the nine choirs of angels, the angels being the *Intelligences* signified by Aristotle in his *Of the Heavens and the Earth*. Since an angel is immaterial, this power to move the spheres is independent of physical contact; it is the operation of intellect alone and arises from contemplating the Divine Mind. What Aristotle taught was that all motion originates in the Divine Mind and that as creatures participate in that mind, they have power to move or act. This idea of the importance of contemplation and its relation to the active life (*Banq.* II, v, 3) was a very significant medieval teaching, finding an excellent exposition in the *De Consideratione* of Saint Bernard.

In *Paradiso* XIII, Dante discusses how the divine, the living Light, comes into our world. The Light streams from the Father upon the Son, Divine Wisdom, whom the Father sees from all eternity and to whom he gives expression in the Word; it streams thence upon the Holy Spirit, who is the mutual love of the Father and the Son; and in such a way that the Light is never divided from the Father nor from the Holy Spirit, the rays of the Divine Wisdom are mirrored in the nine orders of angels, remaining, however, eternally One (*Par.* XIII:52–60). All the orders of angels *gaze upward to the Light and prevail downward* (*Par.* XXVIII:127–129), the Seraphim as the highest created intelligence pouring out upon the ninth heaven, the Primum Mobile, the full volume of Power, Wisdom, and Love which they receive from the Blessed Trinity. They pass it on to the Cherubim who govern the Fixed Stars, from whom it passes down to the lower heavens and to the world of men (*Par.* XIII:60–66; *Banq.* II, vi, 3; *Summa* I, qq. 106–108).

Since it is by the Divine Wisdom, the second Person of the Blessed Trinity, that all hierarchies are enlightened, the great chain is completed for men by the Incarnation. Saint Paul, the New Testament writer who is concerned most with the angelic choirs, writes in *Ephesians*, 1:16–23, that the Father of glory has set Christ on his right hand in the heavenly places above all principality and power and virtue and dominion and every name that is named, not only in this world but also in that which is to come. Since the Divine Wisdom, the Eternal Idea begotten of the Father from all eternity, gives the hierarchies of angels knowledge of the whole Trinity, it is by the Word made flesh, who is Head of his mystical body the Church, that human hierarchies within that Church are rendered able to receive enlightenment which passes down to men from the angels.

> *Bless the Lord, all ye his angels; you that are mighty in strength and execute his word, hearkening to the voice of his orders.*
> *Bless the Lord, all ye his hosts: you ministers of his that do his will.*
> *Bless the Lord, all his works in every place of his dominion; O my soul, bless thou the Lord.*
>
> — Psalm 102:20–22

The men who did all this philosophical and theological speculating about angels were essentially men of faith, men like Dante whose vigorous intellects delighted in a tightly knit argument but who believed that the greatest truths are given to man by revelation. Therefore it is significant that in the very section of the *Banquet* in which Dante gives his philosophical arguments for the existence of angels (II, vi) he writes:

> For want of instruction the ancients knew not the truth concerning spiritual beings, although the people of Israel were taught it in part by the prophets. . . . But we have been instructed by him who came from God; by him who created them (the angels); by him who preserves them; that is, by the Emperor of the universe, which is Christ . . . who was the Light that shined for us in darkness, and who taught us the truth concerning those things which without him we could not have known, nor have seen truly. . . . Our Savior said with his own lips that the Father could give him many legions of angels.

In Scripture these medieval men found confirmation of their speculations concerning the existence of angels and of their numbers and functions. They found the names of the nine choirs of intelligences: Isaias (6:2, 3) describes the Seraphim with their six wings, who sing "Holy, Holy, Holy"; Ezechiel (X, XI) goes into detail about the Cherubim; Saint Paul writing to the Ephesians (1:20, 21) names Principalities, Powers, Virtues, and Dominations; in his letter to the Colossians (1:16), among others he names Thrones; and in the first epistle to the Thessalonians, speaks of an archangel (4:15) as does Saint Jude in his epistle (1:9).

The angelic world as depicted in Holy Scripture exceeds human enumerations and dimensions. In Scriptural texts angels are numbered in multitudes; revelation, therefore, substantiates the philosophical concept that a vast army of angels was necessary. In the vision of Daniel (7:9,10) "thousands of thousands" of angels ministered to God and "ten thousand times a hundred thousand" stood before him; in that of Isaias (6:1) his "train" filled the temple; Saint John heard the voice of many angels round about the throne and "the number of them was a thousand thousands" (Apoc. 5:11); and in 19:13, 14 he saw the *armies* of heaven follow the Word on white horses; Saint Matthew (26:53) writes of more than twelve legions.

As a philosopher, a theologian, and a poet, Dante had meditated deeply on these concepts. He has carried them over into the *Divine Comedy* in the "flying multitudes" of the great white rose (*Par.* XXXI:19); the "number greater than that reached by doubling in succession the squares of the chessboard who echoed *Hosanna* from choir to choir" as they circled round the Point of Light in the Primum Mobile (*Par.* XXVIII:91–96); the "more than thousand rejoicing angels" with widespread wings against the pacific oriflamme, which is Mary's banner in the highest heaven where she reigns as queen (*Par.* XXXI:127–133). The angelic natures mount to so high a number, he says, that never did mortal speech or concept go so far (*Par.* XXIX:130–132).

The Scripture is clear, too, about the function of the angels in their relationship to God and man. Their chief function, their proper work, is to adore, praise, and glorify God. "*Adore* him all you his angels" (Ps. 96:7); "*praise* ye him, all his angels" (Ps. 148:2); "O ye angels of the Lord, *bless* the Lord; *praise* and *exalt* him above all forever" (Dan. 3:58). Scripture suggests that the angels make up God's court. Since his glory and all his infinite attributes are to be known and loved by rational creatures, the angels who radiate that glory from higher to lower choirs and down to men are always with him. In the Gospel Jesus speaks of the angels, who forever look upon the face of his Father (Mt. 18:10); in the *Divine Comedy* Dante says that since the angels first gathered joy from the face of God, they have never removed their gaze from it (*Par.* XIX:76–78). In the sublime passage with which Dante begins his description of the white rose of Paradise (*Par.* XXXI:1–12) he gives in matchless imagery these concepts of angels adoring God and singing his glory:

> In fashion then as of a snow-white rose
> Displayed itself to me the saintly host,
> Whom Christ in his own blood had made his bride,
>
> But the other host, that flying sees and sings
> The glory of him who doth enamor it,
> And the goodness that created it so noble,
>
> Even as a swarm of bees, that sinks in flowers
> One moment, and the next returns again
> To where its labor is to sweetness turned,
>
> Sank into the great flower, that is adorned
> With leaves so many, and thence reascended
> To where its love abideth evermore.

*Are they not all ministering spirits, sent
to minister for them, who shall receive
the inheritance of salvation?*
— Heb. 1:14

*For indeed we owe them praise and honor
for many reasons. They are our guar-
dians, our ministers, our brothers and
fellow citizens, they bear our souls to
Heaven, they present our prayers to
God, and they console the afflicted.*
— The Golden Legend
From September 29
Saint Michael the Archangel

Angels and ministers of grace, defend us.
— Hamlet I, iv, 39

The services of angels to man are diverse and numerous; in performing them angels sweep across the Old and New Testaments
from *Genesis* to the *Apocalypse*. All of the manifold services depicted
in Scripture angels also perform in the *Divine Comedy,* most of
them in the *Purgatorio,* where Dante represents mankind on its
way to God and where angelic ministrations would be most fitting.
The word *angel* comes from a Greek word meaning messenger;
in the Bible there are many instances in which God uses these
pure spirits to communicate his will to man. An angel stays the
hand of Abraham when he is ready to sacrifice Isaac (Gen. 22:11);
an angel finds Agar in the desert and sends her back to Sarai
(Gen. 16:9). Angels as messengers play an important part in the
life of Christ: the Archangel Gabriel announces his coming; angelic
choirs herald his birth to the shepherds; an angel tells Joseph to
take the Child and his mother and flee into Egypt. In the *Divine
Comedy* it is no surprise to meet angels who point the way from
cornice to cornice and who speak words of encouragement.

In Sacred Scripture angels serve as ministers of God's mercy or
his wrath. They deliver the youths from the fiery furnace (Dan.
3:49); a seraph cleanses the lips of the prophet Isaias with a
burning coal to free him from his iniquities so that he can go to

convert his people. They comfort Jesus after the temptation in the desert and strengthen him in his agony (Mt. 4:11; Lk. 22:43). They minister to his apostles and disciples also: twice an angel frees Peter from the prison in Jerusalem, once when he and John were in prison together and were led out (Acts 5:19); and later when the angel broke his chains and delivered him (Acts 12:7, 8), to the amazement of the Christian family to whose house he came in the middle of the night. An angel arranges for Philip to meet the eunuch of Queen Candace of the Ethiopians (Acts 8:26–40) and baptize him; an angel assures Paul that all on the wrecked ship with him will escape with their lives (Acts 27:23–24). As ministers of the wrath of God they slay the idolatrous citizens of the city of Jerusalem (Ezech. 9:1–10); and they kill the wicked Herod (Acts 12:23).

Throughout the *Purgatorio* from the time in the second canto (28–30) when Virgil tells Dante to bend his knees before the angel of faith who is conducting the souls across the sea to the strand of the island, Dante and Virgil meet ministering angels. There is in the *Divine Comedy* but one instance of an angel who is a minister of the wrath of God, the majestic angel before whom a thousand demons flee as he flings wide the gates of the city of Dis, which these demons have clanged shut before the two pilgrims.

Since angels in Scripture act as guardians of nations and of specific places, it is not surprising that each circle of Hell, each precinct of Purgatory, and each of the stellar heavens has its own angel or group of angels. That Michael was the guardian spirit of Israel we are told in *Daniel* (10:13); in the same chapter we learn that there was a guardian angel of the nation of the Persians. The "man of Macedonia" who appeared to Saint Paul at Troas urging him to pass into his country to help the people (Acts 16:9) is usually interpreted as the guardian angel of Greece or of that section of Greece. Saint John in the Apocalypse (1:20) writes of the "angels of the seven churches" and *Genesis* (3:23) tells us that when Adam and Eve were cast out of Eden, God placed before the gate Cherubim and a flaming sword turning every way to guard the tree of life.

We know, too, from Scripture that angels have charge of individual souls. The familiar quotation from Saint Matthew (18:10) about the little children whose angels always see the face of God in heaven is one of the principal bases for the belief that each individual man has his own guardian angel. When Judith returns to the people of Israel after beheading Holofernes (Jud. 13:20), she tells them that God's angel, usually interpreted as her special guardian, had protected her in her coming and going and when she was within the camp of the enemy. Quite literally, Dante must have applied to himself the Scripture texts from Psalm 90, which were familiar household words to the men of his time, for he assumes that "God has given his angels charge over him to keep him in all his ways."

Angels serve in other important capacities which Dante does not overlook. Saint John saw them acting as divine agents governing the elements: fire, wind, earth, water (Apoc. 7:2, 3; 14:18; 16:5); they protect the faithful as sentinels watching over the enemy on the walls of Jerusalem (Isa. 62:6); they have power over evil spirits (Tob. 8:3; 12:14). They present the prayers of the faithful to God as they did those of Sara (Tob. 12:12–15), and they console and comfort the children of God as they comforted Daniel and innumerable others. At the last, they bear the souls of the just to heaven as they did the soul of the beggar Lazarus (Lk. 16:22); and Christ tells us that they will be witnesses before his Father for those who confessed him before men (Lk. 12:8, 9).

Following these Scriptural leads, Dante describes how the dark angel brought the storm after the battle of Campaldino; he has angels stand as sentinels on the hills which rise above the valley of the princes; win over the evil garrison who closed the gate of the city of Dis; present manifold helps on the mountain of purgation; and act as witnesses to his confession and repentance in the Earthly Paradise. One of the loveliest scenes in the New Life is the one in Dante's dream of the death of Beatrice where he beholds a multitude of angels like a rain of manna flying back to heaven bearing the soul of his lady.

Perhaps before proceeding further it may be useful to review the concepts of angels which are found in Scripture and which were held by Dante and his contemporaries as well as by their predecessors down the Christian centuries. Modern art has distorted Scriptural angels into the cherubic children with wings and long dresses with which the modern reader of Dante is familiar on Christmas greeting cards and in cheap sculpture and fresco. He needs to quicken his imagination to leap from these notions of angels to those with which Dante was familiar.

The angels depicted in the Old and New Testaments carried about them the majesty and authority of the Most High, for they came as representatives of the Almighty One. In the Old Testament when they came as messengers, they were received with fear and reverence as befitted ambassadors of the King of Kings. Lot (Gen. 19:1), seeing them, rose up and went to meet them and worshiped prostrate on the ground in true Oriental fashion; David (1 Par. 21:16), seeing the angel of the Lord standing between heaven and earth with a drawn sword in his hand, fell flat upon the ground.

And well he might! Terrifying indeed are the angels of God's wrath who make visible to men something of the power bestowed on them by the Almighty whose majesty and omnipotence they reflect. Among these are the angel horseman (2 Mach. 3:25) who rode fiercely against Heliodorus and whose charger struck him with his forefeet; the swift angel who slew the first-born of the Egyptians in one night (Exod. 12:23); and the magnificent angel, probably Michael, an angel with a strong military background, who came and slew in the camp of the Assyrians in one night a hundred and eighty-five thousand (4 Kings 19:35)!

In the New Testament even when they bear messages of great joy, they inspire fear. "Fear not," said the angel Gabriel to Zachary when he came to foretell the birth of John the Baptist. "Fear not, Mary," he said at Nazareth before he announced her part in the Incarnation. "Fear not," said the bright angel to the shepherds who feared with a great fear as the brightness of God shone round about them on the field at Bethlehem. "Fear not you," said the angel at the tomb, whose face was like lightning, to the holy women on Easter morning, when after the earthquake which announced his descent from heaven he had rolled back the stone from the empty tomb and sat upon it, having struck the guards with terror so that they became as dead men (Mt. 28:2–5).

These angels of the Old and New Testaments represent in action the seraphim of the glorious vision of Isaias, the giant cherubim of Solomon's temple, ten cubits high with wings five cubits in length and overlaid with gold (3 Kings 6:23–28). It is angels with this stature, this majesty, that we find in the giant mosaic figures of the Baptistery of Florence, of Cefalu and Monreale, in the sculptures of Chartres, and in the poetry of Dante.

> How art thou fallen from heaven, O
> Lucifer, who didst rise in the morning?
> how art thou fallen to the earth, that
> didst wound the nations?
> And thou saidst in thy heart: I will ascend
> into heaven, I will exalt my throne
> above the stars of God, I will sit in the
> mountain of the covenant in the sides
> of the north.
> I will ascend above the height of the
> clouds, I will be like the most High.
> But yet thou shalt be brought down to
> hell, into the depth of the pit.
> — Isa. 14:12–15

From Scripture, too, men took their proofs for the existence of the devil, a belief which no writer portrays more dramatically than Dante. In the Old Testament there is first of all in *Genesis* 3 that episode of the serpent in the garden of Eden. The Archangel Raphael not only led young Tobias to the home of Sara, chosen by God to be his wife, he bound Asmodeus, the devil that possessed her and had killed the seven suitors who had wished to marry her (Tob. 3; 6; 8:3). It was Satan that brought about the sufferings of Job (1; 2). The New Testament has a parade of devils as well as of angels. The evil spirit tempted Christ in the desert (Lk. 4:1–12; Mt. 4:1–11) before the good angels ministered to him; and there are numerous instances of his casting out devils and of their crying as they went, "Thou art the Son of God" (Lk. 4:41; 8:28), displaying in this manner their knowledge superior to that of men, who did not yet know the identity of Jesus.

Of the number of fallen angels who can be in one place there is Scriptural evidence. From the young man whom chains could not bind, Jesus drove a legion of devils, who entreated him not to command them to go back to the abyss (Lk. 8:27–35); from Mary Magdalen he drove seven; and he speaks of the evil spirit who, when he has gone out of a man, will bring seven devils more evil than himself and repossess him (Mt. 12:45).

Medieval literature is filled with examples of the struggle between the evil spirit and the angel of God for the possession of a man's soul at the moment of death. The *Divine Comedy* has two memorable examples of such a struggle in the death of a father and a son, Guido and Buonconte da Montefeltro. In the pit of the evil counselors in the circle of the fraudulent (*Inf.* XXVII), Guido tells the story of how the black demon snatched him away from the hand of Saint Francis because, though in outward semblance in joining the Franciscan order he had lived a life of penance misled by Boniface VIII, he had again dissembled, died unrepentant, and was, therefore, lost. His son Buonconte, who died pierced in the throat on the field of Campaldino, had seemingly no time for repentance. But he tells Dante in the Ante-Purgatory (*Purg.* V:103–107) where Dante meets him, how for one poor tear of real sorrow, God's angel snatched his soul while the disappointed devil exclaimed in dismay that he was cheated and gave vent to his fury by rousing the elements. Saint Paul (Eph. 2:2) speaks of the demon as "the prince of the power of the air," and though Dante may be describing here a storm which did actually follow the battle of Campaldino in which he had fought, it is quite possible that he is more interested in showing how the intellect of the fallen angel and his knowledge of the elements, joined to an evil will, made him a terrible agent of destruction (V:112–129).

The questions of when the angels were created, and when and why some of the angels fell were frequently debated in Dante's time. In the story of creation in *Genesis* nothing is said about angels.

Saint Augustine had taught that though there is no direct mention in Scripture of the creation of the angels, it must be regarded as signified in the creation of light on the first day because angels were partakers of the eternal light.[5] Saint Jerome, according to Dante (*Par.* XXIX:37–39), held that they existed ages before the rest of the world; Dante and Saint Thomas hold (*Par.* XXIX:20–33; *Summa* I, q. 46, a. 3, 1) that *in the beginning,* that is to say, before all things, when the Spirit of God moved over the waters and *God created heaven and earth,* four things were created together: *the empyrean heaven, corporeal matter* (by which is meant the earth), *time,* and *the angelic nature.* For, Dante argues (43–45), the angels, being governors of the corporeal heavens, must have been created with them. Therefore, the angels were flashed into being not *before* time but when time *first was,* in that split second when time began. He and Saint Thomas agree, too, in the brevity of the time between the creation and the fall of the angels. Dante makes the concept concrete (*Par.* XXIX:50): "Before one could count to twenty," he says, "part of the angels fell." In the *Banquet* II, vi, 4, he specifies that the *part* that fell was probably a tenth of the total number.[6]

> The greatest gift that God made
> through his liberality in creating
> and most conformable to his goodness
>
> was free will, with which
> intelligent creatures, all and severally,
> were and are alone endowed.
>
> — Paradiso V:19–24

One cannot discuss the fall of the angels without touching upon the question of free will, a question central to the whole concept of sin and hell, as indeed it is to the whole *Comedy.* Since Dante taught that God brought all creatures into being so that each might mirror the glory of the Creator to the ultimate extent of its capacity, no creature at any moment of its existence was, in the right order of things, to consider itself as being the end for which it was made. True, each creature was to serve God by *being totally itself*, by acting completely according to the nature that God had given it. To angels and men God had given intelligence; in varying degrees they can contemplate God and comprehend his beauty and majesty. He gave to each of these highest of his creatures the power to *assent* to serving him by recognizing that its very selfhood and existence came from him, and the power to love him as its creator and last end. Having given to angels and men the power of assent, of free choice, God could not at any time force the will of any angel or any man. The freedom of the will is God's greatest gift to rational creatures. Without free will neither hell nor heaven makes sense: there would be no justice in the punishment of the one or the joys of the other (*Purg.* XVI:70–72).

For this reason, in the very heart of the *Divine Comedy*, the middle cantos of the *Purgatorio*, Dante discusses the nature of free will and of love; for like other scholastics he holds that love lies in the will. In Cantos XVII and XVIII he shows how sin is the turning away of the creature from the laws written in its nature or from the expressed will of its creator. It is a refusal of assent. Inanimate creatures like stones and stars are true to the laws of their nature: bound, as we say, by the laws of the physical universe, they cannot dissent. Irrational animate creatures like roses and rabbits inevitably follow the laws of their natures and so grow and increase and multiply according to the laws of botany and biology; they cannot dissent. All the lower forms of creation praise the Lord of the universe by harmonious accord with the laws of their being. Only for men and angels is it possible to refuse to revolve in the light and harmony of law; only they can disturb the order of the universe, seek independence from the will which preserves this order and harmony, and by dissenting whirl off into that exterior darkness which is life apart from their maker. Even then, they are bearing witness to that justice and order against which they have rebelled.

But as the whole *Divine Comedy* teaches, freedom to choose — for angels as for men — does not include freedom to choose the consequences of their choice. The consequences are determined by the laws of the universe, as Dante is at great pains to make clear. The meaning of Hell is that the angels and men who turned from God have eternally the consequences of their choice. All sin is essentially an effort either to *gain* something against or apart from the will of God or to *be* something apart from his will: sin is the assertion of creature against Creator. Since God called angels and men, like everything else in the universe, out of nothingness, he sustains them in being or they would fall back into that nothingness. God's being is infinite; to choose God is to choose the infinite; to choose anything apart from God is to choose nothingness. Between God and that nothingness is an abyss. To choose self is the greatest of folly; hence pride is in its naked essence the greatest of sins. Pride closed the gates of Heaven to Lucifer and his followers, and to Adam and his progeny.

According to Dante and Saint Thomas, angels, as well as Adam and Eve, were given grace and the theological virtue of infused love (*Par.* XXIX:64–66; *Summa* I, q. 62, a. 4) from which they could turn away by an act of the will. Like men, the angels had to be tried. God looked upon his creation of the angels and it was good: they were perfect in intellect — their knowledge was complete; their desires, following perfect knowledge, were perfect. They had perfect *natural* happiness because they were in perfect possession of *natural* good. But God could give them a perfection *above* nature: he could raise them to supernatural happiness. But that goal above nature had to be won. In that moment of trial some of the angels fell. Dante with Saint Thomas distinguishes three instants in that little time: the instant of creation, the instant of probation and choice, and the instant of beatitude or reprobation.

There was, however, an essential difference between the fall of Lucifer and that of Adam and Eve. Though both men and angels were created in the image and likeness of God, inasmuch as both were endowed with intelligence and free will, the nature of an angel is not the nature of man, and it is the nature of the angels which determined the nature of their fall. An angel is pure spirit; man has a body; he is a combination of matter and spirit. Man uses his intellect to move from sense impressions to abstractions, from principles to conclusions; it is possible for him to make mistakes and to form wrong judgments. But an angel needs no such intellectual process. The essence of a thing is immediately present to the intellect of an angel by intuition. An angel sees in one penetrating glance. Infused ideas, which Plato and the transcendentalists falsely ascribed to man are characteristic of angels. There can be no possibility of a hesitant judgment, for there is no deliberation involved in intuitive knowledge. An angel's knowledge is infallibly certain knowledge, for it mirrors directly the knowledge of God.

Nor is the *will* of an angel like the will of man. In man there are two appetites present: the sensitive appetite, which may be called instinctive appetite; and the intellectual appetite, which we call will. Because man is an animal — a rational animal, it is true, but an animal — he is aware of his biological or sensible appetites and of the difficulty of keeping them under the control of his reason. All the desires of the animal nature of man must be directed by the light of reason so that the will, which is a blind faculty, will not desire or choose anything opposed to reason. That is man's major problem — to keep his house from being divided against itself.

Now, as the object of sight is color, the object of the will is the good. It is possible for the mind of man to propose a false good as a real good (*Purg.* XVIII:19–39); such a judgment is impossible to an angel. Part of man's powers go forth intermittently as act; part remain inactive as potentiality, waiting to be called into play. Angels, on the other hand, when they look upon things ". . . at once behold all things whatsoever that can be known in them" (*Summa* I, q. 58, a. 3). An act of the will in an angel follows immediately upon vision. "An angel," says Saint Thomas (*Summa* I, q. 63, a. 8), "has nothing in him to retard his action, and with his whole might he is moved to whatever he is moved, be it good or bad." The nature of angelic will is to adhere immovably to its first election; choice in an angel is irrevocable. The will of man is flexible even after sin, and repentance and conversion are possible to him. The first election is to angels what death is to man — the end of all probation (*Summa* I, q. 64, a. 2).

The trial of the angels was the acceptance or nonacceptance of life with God: in that instant of seeing and of choice, the good angels by an act of love — and, Dante suggests, of humility in acknowledging that they owed their very existence to the Goodness which now made them ready for so great understanding — merited (*Par.* XXIX:59–63) higher vision of God and the absolute confirmation of their wills in goodness; the others, who did not lay their affections open to this grace, having lost their center of spiritual gravity, whirled off into exterior darkness, causing confusion to our elements (that is, to earth, water, air, and fire) as under the leadership of Lucifer they fell to the center of physical gravity and Hell came into being (*Par.* XXIX:50–51). In *Luke* (10:18) Christ says, "I saw Satan like lightning falling from heaven." The angels who failed the test refused to be *in-Godded*, to use Dante's daring phrase (*Par.* IV:28), and chose as supreme that which they could obtain by their own natural powers. Therefore, their sin was the sin of pride. It was the sin of naturalism. Having cast themselves apart from the will of God they became forever opposed to that will; and since the activity of the will in harmony with the Divine Will is love, the wills of the evil spirits turned actively to hate, hate being nothing but perverted love.

Having themselves refused to assent to the Divine Reality, having nothing but hatred for God and hatred for each other, and hatred for man who will supplant them in Heaven, Lucifer and his fallen legions endeavor to make man fall also. That is the meaning of Saint Paul's dictum that our wrestling is not against flesh and blood but against principalities and powers. In *Purgatorio* XIV:145–150 Virgil says to Dante,

> ... you mortals take the bait, so that the hook
> of the ancient adversary pulls you to him,
> and checks and lures avail little.

> The heavens call you and circle around,
> showing you their eternal beauties,
> And still your eyes gaze at the ground.

Yet, says Saint Paul, "All things work together unto good for them that love God." This wrestling with animal appetites and with the temptations sent by demons is in the nature of a scrimmage between the first and second teams in college football: through wrestling, man gains power to win. Merit comes from the winning (*Purg.* XVIII: 66–68).

To afford man the opportunity to prove his love of God by warring against temptation is the chief function the fallen angels serve in the divine scheme of things. Though the angels be fallen angels, they stand in their own nature between God and man. Saint Thomas summarizes the matter succinctly in the *Summa* (I, q. 64, a. 4).

> Now the order of Divine Providence so disposes that it procures the welfare of the inferior orders through the superior. But man's welfare is disposed by Divine Providence in two ways: first of all, directly, when a man is brought unto good and withheld from evil and this is fittingly done through the good angels; in another way, indirectly, as when anyone assailed is exercised by fighting against opposition. It was fitting for this procuring of man's welfare to be brought about through the wicked spirits, lest they should cease to be of service in the natural order.

By performing this service, the angels though damned in Hell are still ministers of the Most High and despite themselves perform a function for which they were created. Even in their rebellion they contribute to God's glory.[7]

> And when Josue was in the field of the
> city of Jericho he lifted up his eyes, and
> saw a man standing over against him
> with a drawn sword, and he went to
> him and said: Art thou one of ours, or
> of our adversaries?
> And he answered: No: but I am prince
> of the host of the Lord, and now I am
> come.
> Josue fell on his face to the ground. And
> worshipping, said: What saith my lord
> to his servant?
>   — Jos. 5:13–15

How can men see angels or devils who are spirits and therefore immaterial? The answer is that ordinarily we do not see them. Sometimes we are aware of them by what they do. By their "fruits," their effects, we know them. An angel is where he acts. He acts where he wills, neither moving through space nor taking up room. The laughter of the eighteenth-century rationalists at the idea of the schoolmen playing with the concept of the number of angels who could dance on the point of a pin seems a little hollow to the modern man, made aware of the terrifying intangibles of even one split atom. No one saw the legion of angels that possessed the young man described by Saint Luke. Yet the young man could not be bound by chains; he could not be incarcerated because of the power of the demons who possessed him.

Sometimes, however, the angels or devils appear in some corporeal form. Satan appeared to Eve as a serpent. The Scripture says that Raphael accompanied Tobias as a personable young man. Mary saw Gabriel when he told her she was chosen to be the mother of the Redeemer; Peter saw the angel who loosed him from his chains. When an angel has a mission to fulfill that requires a body, he assumes a body, usually the body of a youth. Because in the description of the Cherubim in Solomon's temple, in the revelations of Isaias, and in other places in Scripture, the angels have wings, in the best periods of Christian art angels were portrayed as young men with wings. In the *Paradiso* IV:40–48, Dante comments on the fact that since men grasp through sense impressions that which afterward they understand abstractly, Scripture condescends to man's capacity and attributes hands and feet to God and human faces to Gabriel, Michael, and Raphael. In all medieval art forms from the pages of *The Golden Legend* to the façades and walls of the great cathedrals, angels and devils are set before our eyes with such vividness that we know that to men of these centuries the spirit world was as real as the material world.

Outcasts of heaven, despicable creatures!
— Inferno IX:91

Even in Hell angels, though fallen, perform the ministries to men for which they were created. There are guardians of each circle and guardians of the precincts within the circles. In the eighth and ninth circles ministers of mercy are perverted to ministers of torture; all of the demons, in a sense, are ministers of God's wrath; all are witnesses of his justice. The demon guardians of the circles are false gods and personages of heathen mythology; for Dante — like Milton, who follows his lead — conceives of these mythological characters as fallen angels, a point of view held by churchmen of the Middle Ages.

They make a vivid group. The guardians of the upper Hell are Charon, the infernal ferryman of the woolly cheeks and eyes like wheels of flame, who rows the damned to the sad bank of Acheron; Minos the judge, whose index tail is long enough to swing around him a sufficient number of times to indicate the circle to which a soul is condemned (*Inf.* XXVII:124–127); Cerberus, the three-throated dog who rends the gluttons; Plutus, who as the pagan god of wealth presides over the avaricious and the prodigal; and Phlegyas, the irascible boatman who conducts souls from the circle of the wrathful to the city of Dis. On the red-hot iron walls of the city stand the guardians of the sixth circle, Medusa, the fearsome Gorgon who changes men into stone if they but glance at her, and the dread Erinnyes — Alecto, Megaera, and Tisiphone — ancient ministers of justice, with their hydra-wreathed heads and their garments of flame. Silhouetted against the dark sky by the flames licking over the walls are the thousand black demons who form the garrison guarding the massive gate. Guardian demon of the seventh circle is the Minotaur "the infamy of Crete," who has as subsidiary guardians for the three rounds the centaurs, harpies and huge female mastiffs. Up from the abyss comes Geryon, the guardian of the eighth circle, that of fraud. The monster has the head of a man; the rest is serpent. The giants, the first of whom is a Biblical not a mythological character, guard the circle of traitors: Nimrod, who attempted to build the tower of Babel, Ephialtes, Antaeus, and Briareus. These demon guardians of the nine circles are as imposing a group of figures as are to be found in the whole *Commedia*.

The lesser demons who are ministers of torture infest all divisions of the lower Hell. For these much of Dante's imagery is taken from popular notions of his day. Some of the activities in which they indulge in punishing sinners seem to have been suggested by the punishment of criminals or enemies in Dante's Italy, punishments which Dante must have considered diabolic. Of these the keen-taloned fiends with the fleshhooks, guardians of the boiling pitch where the barrators are immersed, are perhaps the most vivid. Some of them have tusks with which they rip the sinners or flay them; some have tails to lash them. These fiends are named by Dante; several of them are carefully characterized. They rush upon him but do not catch him, for Virgil snatches him up and races along the cliff and saves him. Dante had been accused of political graft at the time of his exile; perhaps for that reason he makes these demons pursue him but because of his innocence fail to overtake him.

In an extraordinary number of instances, serpents are used in connection with the demons: Cacus the Centaur has serpents for hair; hydras and asps are the locks of the Erinnyes; the pit of the thieves is filled with demons who are serpents. All of the demons are intelligent and quick; they still possess their "swift intellects"; all of them are diligent ministers in their supervision of sinners. Many of them are blasphemers and liars. Many of them are insolent and cruel. Repeatedly Virgil overcomes their insolence by telling them that it is impossible for them to thwart his purpose, for it is willed "where will and power are one." Everywhere throughout the *Inferno* Dante makes his reader aware that God rules in Hell as he rules in Heaven.

No place is there greater evidence of God's dominion over Hell than at the gates of the city of Dis. The demon guards after a brief parley with Virgil rush into the city and clang the iron gates behind them, leaving Dante terrorized by their insolence. Virgil, too, is momentarily shaken. Suddenly, down the steep way, speeding over the turbid waters of the Stygian lake with unwet feet, heralded by a crash so full of terror that both shores tremble as when a whirl-wind rends a forest, beats down the trees, and makes beasts and shepherds flee; waving the gross air from his countenance blazing with indignation, comes a sublime angel — a minister of the wrath of God (*Inf.* IX:64–102). Before him a thousand devils flee like frogs before a serpent; at a touch of his wand the gates of Dis fly open. Then, having rebuked the insolent demons, quite unmindful of Virgil and Dante, as though occupied with more important matters, he turns and soars away. He is the only minister of God's wrath in the *Divine Comedy.* To have him assert power over the demons at the very entrance to their stronghold is a stroke of genius. Carroll is probably right in claiming that this strong angel is Gabriel, the Angel of the Annunciation, who would no more be named in Hell than Christ or Mary, and that the rod in his right hand represents specifically the power of the Virgin Mary over the demons.[8]

> *Behold I will send my angel, who shall go*
> *before thee and keep thee in thy journey*
> *and bring thee into the place that I have*
> *prepared.*
> *Take notice of him, and hear his voice, and*
> *do not think him one to be contemned. . . .*
> — Exod. 23:20, 21
>
> *Bend, bend your knees;*
> *here is the angel of God; fold your hands!*
> *From now on you will see such ministers.*
> — Purgatorio II:28–30

In the *Purgatorio* — as we have already noted — angels serve in all the capacities in which they serve in Scripture. Here are angel guardians of the gate, guardians of the cornices, and guardians of other precincts of the mountain. Here are angel sentinels who protect the faithful; angel choirs and artists who make the way lightsome by song and sculpture and story; angels of mercy and benediction who exemplify the virtues in which the penitent souls must perfect themselves as they mount from terrace to terrace; and angel witnesses whose sympathetic presence gives support.

The first angel of the Ante-Purgatory is the vigorous angel of faith, who pilots a hundred singing souls from the mouth of the Tiber to the shore of Purgatory. He heralds the sunrise, for the beginning of life with God in the morning of the supernatural day is faith. At first he and his boat are but a ruddy glow on the eastern horizon;

in the brief moment in which Dante turns to question Virgil the boat has come so near that he sees the strong white wings raised toward the sky and observes that their movement makes the light vessel skim over the surface of the water. Virgil identifies the angel and tells Dante to bend his knees before him. The angel, without a word, makes the sign of the Holy Cross upon his hundred passengers, waits for them to gather on the shore, then leaves as rapidly as he had come. The powerful, silent angel in white signifies the vigor and purity of faith which should characterize those who, without questioning the cost, enter wholeheartedly upon the way which leads to salvation.

As faith is followed by *hope* that God will answer humble prayer and earnest endeavor, and in his merciful *love* watch over those who are determined to climb to him, the next angels suggest these two virtues. They are the sentinel angels who sweep down from Heaven in answer to the prayers of the souls in the Valley of the Princes: their flowing garments, as green as new leaves in spring, blown in the quiet evening air by the swift movement of green-feathered wings, are obviously symbolic of the newly quickened hope of salvation in these waiting souls; their flaming swords suggest the red of charity. Their "blond heads bright with heaven's light" suggest searchlights flooding the valley from the opposing hills on which they take their stand; and when, after night has fallen, the serpent glides into the valley illumined by the light of vigilant faith, the flaming swords of love fly into action to expel him. Then the angels return to their posts to keep watch over the quiet valley, serene in the light of the newly risen moon.

The first of the angel guardians in Purgatory proper is the majestic angel, who, with a naked sword reflecting rays of intense brightness, sits upon the solid rock in which the closed gate of Purgatory is set. The gate is Saint Peter's gate, to which in the beginning of the poem (*Inf.* I:134), Dante had begged Virgil to lead him; the angel and his accouterments dramatize several aspects of the words of Christ in *Matthew* (16:18, 19):

. . . thou art Peter: and upon this rock I will build my church, and the gates of hell shall not prevail against it.

And I will give to thee the keys of the kingdom of heaven. And whatsoever thou shalt bind upon earth, it shall be bound also in heaven and whatsoever thou shalt loose on earth, it shall be loosed also in heaven.

Dante works out a parallelism. On the occasion upon which these words were pronounced Peter had just made his profession of faith, saying, "Thou art Christ, the Son of the living God"; Jesus, after giving him the keys, had admonished him to put Satan behind him and had told the disciples that if anyone would come after him he must take up his cross and follow him. Upon his entrance into Purgatory, Dante had encountered first the angel of faith to whom he had bent his knees; subsequently, in the Valley of the Princes, he had been protected by the sentinel angels who had routed Satan. Now he is ready to submit himself to the bright angel of the Church, the Church being represented by the solid rock upon which the angel is seated.

This angel at Purgatory gate wears an ash-gray robe symbolizing penance in a twofold sense: the sacrament of Penance; and, as on Ash Wednesday, the spirit of prayer and mortification, the taking up of the Cross. From under this robe he draws the keys of authority (or power) and wisdom (or discernment), both of which he needs in binding or loosing. He represents the ideal confessor, a bishop, who has the plenitude of the priesthood. He passes judgment on the penitent Dante, who after acknowledging his sins, asks humbly that the gate be unlocked. Before the angel opens it, with the point of his sword he inscribes upon Dante's forehead seven P's, each representing one of the capital sins (P signifying *peccatum*, the Latin for "sin") and admonishes him to wash the wounds away. Then he swings the gate open. As the pivots begin to turn on their strong metal hinges Dante hears a voice singing the *Te Deum Laudamus*, accompanied, as it were, by an organ. The voice is that of an angel (Lk. 15:7) rejoicing because a sinner has set his feet upon the penitential way.[9]

The signing on the forehead is certainly suggested by the liturgy of the Church. Much of the symbolism in the first two cantos is taken from the liturgy of the Sacrament of Baptism; the whole of Canto IX details the five steps in the worthy reception of the Sacrament of Penance. Here at the Purgatory gate Dante may very well have in mind the Sacrament of Confirmation, always administered by a bishop, which presupposes and complements Baptism and advances the Christian to adult standing in the Church. In the ritual which tradition has ascribed to Pope Gelasius I (492–496) and which has been used down the Christian centuries appears this prayer, said by the bishop over those who are to be confirmed:

> Almighty, everlasting God, who hast deigned to bring these thy servants to a new life by water and the Holy Ghost and hast granted them remission of all their sins, send forth upon them Thy sevenfold Spirit of Holiness, the Paraclete from heaven.

Then follow the seven specific prayers for the seven gifts of the Holy Ghost, in the order in which they are given in *Isaias* (11:2). Since the gifts of the Holy Spirit cannot dwell in a soul given over to the seven capital sins, and since at the top of the mountain of Purgatory, when Dante has fulfilled the command to wash the scars of the sword point away, he sees the streaming pennants of light, which symbolize the gifts of the Holy Spirit, it would seem that here as everywhere in the *Commedia* there is a sequence in symbolism to indicate the sequence of ideas.

The guardian angels of the seven cornices represent in a strikingly graphic way the essence of the virtues which the souls are striving to practice as they purge out the seven capital sins. The vigorous beauty of each angel shouts of fulfillment as he pronounces the benediction upon the soul ready to leave the cornice of which he is guardian, the benediction being given in the words of one of the Beatitudes (Mt. 5:3–10). As he gives it, his wings brush from the forehead the scar of one of the seven P's; often he speaks words of hope and encouragement as he points the way to the cornice ahead. The angels do not appear until a man has perfected himself in the virtue which the angel represents: he does not see the angel of humility until he has eradicated pride; the angel of brotherly love until he has cast out envy; the angel of meekness, until he is rid of anger; of zeal, until he has overcome sloth; of temperance, until he has conquered gluttony; of chastity, until he has vanquished lust. On the fifth cornice, that of avarice, he hears the voice of the angel of poverty of spirit though he does not see him.

The angel of humility appears to Dante shortly after noon. In the *Banquet* (IV, xxiii, 8), Dante says that the sixth hour (that of noon) is the most noble of the whole day and has the most virtue. Since nothing in the *Divine Comedy* is without symbolic significance, it is not by accident that the hour of noon is chosen for three important milestones on Dante's way to God: the deliverance from the bondage of pride, which is the root of all evil; the final cleansing in Eunoë on the mountaintop; and the entrance into Heaven.

The image for the angel of humility is taken from the appearance of the moon or a star when the sun has risen and its lesser light is no longer needed. The man who has learned the virtue of humility has learned to sublimate his ego, to be in evidence when his leadership is needed, to be unobtrusive when he can no longer serve. "Clothed in white and tremulous as a star at dawn" (*Purg.* XII:88–111), the angel comes toward Dante, opens his arms and then his wings, points the way to the next steps with the encouraging words that the climbing will be easy now, touches Dante's forehead with his wings so lightly that Dante is unaware until later that the first *P* has been brushed away, promises safe passage, and disappears. As the light of a star is lost in the light of the sun, the humble spirit hides its light in the light of God. As Dante moves onto the next cornice where the sin of envy is expiated, he hears the voice of the angel blend with the voices of the other angels singing "Blessed are the poor in spirit" in melody so sweet that words cannot describe it.

The time spent on the cornice of the envious is about three hours, for at three o'clock that same afternoon the poets encounter the angel of brotherly love, "generous and merciful" love, Romano Guardini calls it.[10] As the two men circle the mountain (*Purg.* XV:6–39), they are at this point traveling due west, and the rays of the sun strike them "in the middle of their noses." Suddenly Dante is dazed by such extraordinary splendor that he raises his hand to shield his eyes, thinking that the light comes from above. He is surprised to discover that the radiance leaps at him from the ground as a light reflected from water or a mirror rises in the opposite direction from which it descends, making an equal angle with the perpendicular. This powerful light blinds him utterly;

disconcerted he asks Virgil what it is from which he cannot screen his eyes and which seems to be moving toward them. "Rejoice, thou that conquerest," exclaims a radiant angel. "Enter upon a stairway that is less steep!" And then, as they climb to the next terrace, Dante and Virgil hear sung behind them, "Blessed are the merciful." This angel of generosity is the brightest of the angels of the virtues because of the way his light joins with the light of the sun to strike the eyes with a double brilliance. When envy has been routed utterly and the love of God and love of neighbor are joined in a soul, there is exceeding brightness. Other souls, like mirrors catch the light and it is reflected everywhere.

The angel of meekness on the third cornice is so hidden in his own radiance that Dante's powers of vision cannot rightly discern him. Seeing that help is needed, he "does as man should" do — proffers assistance before Dante and Virgil are aware that they need it. Unjust anger often hides its intent to injure and refuses aid where it should be given; the angel of meekness gives aid before its need is recognized.

Dante's use of light in the description of these angels of the cornices clarifies the meaning of the virtues: the fading light of the angel of humility, reflected light casting back its radiance where brotherly love has been perfected, the hiddenness of the angel who comes to those who have conquered anger. When the P is erased, Dante feels the angel's wings fan his face. The faces of the angry are often flushed; we sometimes tell an angry person to "cool off." The benediction here adds a note of distinction between just and unjust anger: "Blessed are the peacemakers *who are without sinful anger,*" sings the angel of meekness. Dante hints that this same bright angel can blaze with just indignation should God make him a messenger of his wrath.

On this cornice, too, the time of day is significant. The benediction is pronounced just before sunset: Dante has not let the sun go down on his wrath. Filled with the peace of the angel's benediction, Dante and Virgil sit at the top of the stairs leading to the cornice of the slothful talking through the quiet evening hours and on until nearly midnight. As Dante meditates on the meaning of Virgil's words, the moon rises, looking like a bucket all aglow with fire, making the stars seem few. His thoughts are interrupted suddenly by zealous souls rushing past him in the moonlight seeking the mountain pass. When the crowd has moved on, he closes his eyes and falls asleep.

That Dante oversleeps on the cornice of the slothful is significant. He has stayed up too long the night before and is not ready for the next day's work! The sun is already risen when Virgil wakens him, urging that they seek the pass to the fifth terrace. As though he had come in answer to Virgil's proposal, the angel of zeal or alacrity speaks to them, and suddenly with open swanlike wings appears before them ready for action. In a tone so kind and gracious that Dante had never heard the like he says, "Come; here is the pass!" Three qualities which characterize perfect zeal characterize this angel: he is kindly; he is instant in alacrity; he points upward, oblivious of self. As the broad white pinions stir for flight, their movement fans away the P of sloth from Dante's forehead; the angel declares that those who mourn are blessed, and soars away.

Dante does not describe the angel of the fifth cornice (*Purg.* XXII:1-6), who had directed the poets to the sixth ledge and who having erased the P of avarice or prodigality had pronounced the beatitude: "Blessed are those who thirst for justice." Dante comments on the fact that the angel uses only the word *thirst*, the word *hunger* being reserved for the cornice of the gluttonous onto which he points the way. Since there is always a reason for Dante's omissions as well as for his descriptions, it may be that because detachment from worldly goods is purely interior and has nothing to do with the number of one's possessions, he does not externalize the virtue by depicting it in the angel. Liberality, too, should be hidden: the right hand should not know what the left hand does.

"Of what are you thinking, you three going by yourselves" (*Purg.* XXIV:133), cries a voice just ahead of Dante, Virgil, and Statius (a Latin poet who had joined them on the last terrace and who acts as a subsidiary guide) as they move to the last section of the sixth cornice. So natural seems the query that Dante is startled to find that the words were uttered by a supernatural creature, one glowing so red that never glass or metal in a furnace glowed as he did. As usual, Dante is blinded by the brilliance of the angel's countenance; in following his admonition to ascend to the next terrace he must find his way by hearing and not by sight as he moves on behind his guides. "This way he goes who seeks peace," says the angel, and moving his pinions like a May breeze which brings fragrance of grass and flowers or of ambrosia, he wafts away the sixth scar.

The benediction pronounced by the angel of temperance, whom Dante has just encountered, is a paraphrase of the remainder of the beatitude used on the last cornice (*Purg.* XXIV:151–154):

> ... Blessed are those whom grace
> so enlightens that the love of taste does
> not kindle excessive desire in their breasts
>
> And who hunger always in right measure.

The "right measure" in the angel's benediction indicates that temperance may be violated not only by excessive eating and drinking but by excessive fasting. In the *Banquet* (IV, xvii, 4), Dante defines temperance as a law and curb for overgreediness or for excessive abstinence in the things which preserve our life. William Vernon suggests[11] that this angel has a strong kinship with the angel that watched over the youths cast into the fiery furnace in Babylon, as they walked unharmed through the fire singing their hymn of praise; for the image invoking metal in a glowing furnace and the fragrant breeze are reminiscent of the episode in *Daniel* where the flame became "like the blowing of a wind bringing dew" (3:50). But the walking in fire and the singing are even more suggestive of the seventh cornice where the souls sing as sexual intemperance is burned away by fire hotter than molten glass; and since the angel of temperance not only erases the P of gluttony but points the way to the next terrace, Dante may well have had this Old Testament angel in mind. The red color of the fiery furnace is also the red of charity: the fire of the love of God must be set against the burning thirst of the gluttons and the fire of carnal passion.

When God cast out Adam and Eve from the Earthly Paradise, which Dante is now approaching, he placed "before the paradise of pleasure Cherubim, and a flaming sword, turning every way, to keep the way of the tree of life" (Gen. 3:24). The fire turning every way around the mountain, making a wall of fire on the seventh cornice, is doubtless made by the flaming sword "turning every way," and the glad angel (*Purg.* XXVII:6–12) who stands on the bank out of the flames singing "Blessed are the clean of heart" is one of the Cherubim placed by God to guard the Garden of Eden. The angel singing beyond the fire (XXVII:55–63), whose voice guides the poets to where the ascent begins, is another of the Cherubim.

These angels, whose voices ring clear beyond all earthly music, are the most persuasive of the angels of Purgatory. Dante, who on the other cornices has responded with alacrity to the invitations to ascend, remains as irresponsive as a dead man when the angel on the bank urges him to enter the fire. He leans over his clasped hands, re-calling vividly (XXVII:15–18) the burned human bodies he has seen, like that of Adam of Brescia on the Consuma Pass; mindful, too, no doubt, of the edict of death by fire which his native Florence had pronounced against him. It is not the angels, however, who break his resistance but Virgil, who reminds him with urgency and paternal kindness that Beatrice is on the other side of the wall of fire. "Come, ye blessed of my father," sings the angel of chastity, shrouded in a radiance of blinding light, "the sun is near to sinking and it will soon be dark. Do not linger; press on." Before night enfolds the mountain, the poets are safe on the topmost steps. Though there is no mention of the removal of the final P from Dante's brow, we know it is gone, burned away by the fire "hotter than molten glass."

All along the cornices — as well as in the Ante-Purgatory and the Earthly Paradise — we are aware of angels that we do not see. Repeatedly we hear them sing; Purgatory is filled with the music of men and angels. But on each cornice angels minister to the penitents through some other art as well as music. According to Saint Thomas, angels act upon the intellect and will of man through the imagination or the senses. On the pavement of the cornice of the proud, they have sculptured characters from sacred and profane history, from legend and mythology, who have fallen because of pride; into the side of the mountain they have cut majestic figures three times the height of a man which exemplify humility. Two of these sculptured figures are angels: the fallen Lucifer, and the Archangel Gabriel bringing the message to Mary. On the cornice of the envious, angel voices tell stories of envy and brotherly love; on that of the avaricious and the prodigal, they give through song and story examples of these vices and of the opposing virtues of poverty of spirit and liberality. They present visions and dreams on the third and fourth terraces and quote poetry from the tree of the knowledge of good and evil on the sixth.

Dante's Florence knew many stories of angel artists, the favorite being that told of Bartolomeo, a Florentine artist, who in the year 1252 was commissioned to paint an Annunciation for the Servite church in Florence, now known as the Basilica of the Annunciation. Skillfully and to his satisfaction, Bartolomeo executed the figure of the angel Gabriel and that of the Virgin, but he had made the face of Gabriel so beautiful that he doubted that he could make the face of Mary more lovely, as he knew he should. Discouraged, he fell into a troubled sleep from which he waked to find that the Virgin's face was completed, having been painted by an angel. It is indeed a strikingly beautiful face. At the rear of the basilica, a chapel of gold has been built, above the marble altar of which the painting is enshrined. The heavy gates of the chapel are locked and the picture kept veiled except on special feast days, when the church becomes a place of pilgrimage.

> *You watch in the eternal day*
> *so that neither night nor sleep hides from you*
> *a step taken on the ways of the world;*
>
> *therefore, my answer takes greater care*
> *that he, weeping over there, should understand,*
> *and that his sin and sorrow should be equal.*
>
> — *Purgatorio* XXX:103–108

The hundred angels in the Earthly Paradise, who participate in the pageant of the Church and in the drama of the reunion of Dante and Beatrice, the focal episode of the whole *Divine Comedy*,

fulfill all the functions of the chorus in a Greek play: they help
establish the mood; they furnish the music; they serve as witnesses
and as an ideal audience; they further the action by asking pertinent
questions or making pertinent comments or providing a necessary
link between past and present. First of all, they furnish the music.
Though the melody which runs through the luminous air before
the procession comes into view may be the harmonious chant of the
twenty-four elders who immediately follow the candlesticks, it seems
almost certain that the *Hosanna* is sung by the angels. Much of
the meaning of the meeting of Dante and Beatrice in the *Commedia*
hinges upon passages in the *New Life* for complete understanding,
since the *Commedia* is the fulfillment of the promise made at the
close of the early book. These angels who know all things in an
eternal present are, says Beatrice (XXX:103–106), in possession
of all the facts in this drama of love and infidelity to love; therefore
they are used to bind the past with the present.

In his dream of the death of Beatrice (*New Life* XXIII), Dante
saw "a multitude of angels," who sang *Hosanna in excelsis* "gloriously," as they returned to Heaven bearing before them the little
white cloud, which intuition tells him is the soul of Beatrice. Though
the meaning of the coming of Beatrice is enlarged here to include
not only the return of the historic Beatrice but also the coming of
the symbolic Beatrice, Dante keeps the personal Beatrice always
in the foreground. When one of the elders thrice intones, "Come,
from Libanus, my spouse" (XXX:11; Cant. 4:8), referring here as
was the tradition in the Church to Mary, Bride of the Holy
Spirit and Mother of the Messias, the hundred-voiced choir rising
on the chariot of the Church answers, *Benedictus qui venis*, meaning
that he who comes will be the Griffin, Christ. But the meaning is
also that Beatrice will come; Beatrice the woman; Beatrice, Divine
Wisdom and Divine Revelation; Beatrice, Theology; but, most of
all, at this moment Beatrice dressed as a bride; Beatrice of the *New
Life*, who brought inspiration and love to Dante; Beatrice, who will
bring him to God. In the liturgy of the Mass, Christ, who long
ago ascended into Heaven, descends upon the altar between the
singing of the *Hosanna in excelsis* and the *Benedictus*.

As the angels sing the *Benedictus*, they scatter flowers above them and around them; they continue to toss the blossoms as they sing the lovely line from Virgil's *Aeneid*, "Oh, give lilies with full hands!" This line has a twofold significance here. Dante may have seen lilies on the body of the dead Beatrice. At any rate, lilies are associated with the death of the young. In the *Aeneid* the quoted line referred to the death of Marcellus, the nephew and adopted son of the Emperor Augustus, who had commissioned Virgil to write his epic; here we associate it with the going of Virgil, commissioned by Beatrice to bring Dante to her. There is sadness at his going. Beatrice had sought Virgil in Limbo; now that his task is accomplished, he must return to Limbo. Dante loves Virgil. He is, perhaps, next to Beatrice in his affections. Bound up in this one *terza rima* is much of the joy and "the tears of things."

From this point in the drama, the angels act as witnesses of the confession and regeneration of Dante. In the churches of Dante's Italy angels were often painted or wrought in mosaic as attendant witnesses of the great activities of the sanctuary whereby men received grace that was a presage of salvation. Here they listen sympathetically to the dialogue between Dante and Beatrice, chief actors in the drama. Their sympathy as they sing the second verse of Psalm 30, "In thee, O Lord, have I hoped," melts the ice about Dante's heart as does their pity when they ask Beatrice why she shames him so. To them Beatrice addresses the whole story of Dante's infidelity to the high gifts with which he was endowed and to the ideals with which she had inspired him, of her repeated attempts to recall him to the life he should be leading, of her request to Virgil, telling them that though they who live in God's eternal present know these things, she tells them in Dante's presence so that he may be moved to perfect sorrow. When, sobbing, he makes his full confession, they hear the commendation by Beatrice for his complete admission of his infidelity and they witness his remorse when he lifts his head to look at her. They chant the *Asperges me*[18] when Matilda draws him through the waters of Lethe; and when the procession moves through the divine forest to the tree of the knowledge of good and evil, it is to the tones of angelic music that the steps are timed. Then when the procession moves back to heaven, the angels, too, disappear.

Though Dante does not say so, it is probable that these angels of the Earthly Paradise are Cherubim, for Cherubim had been sent by God to guard the Garden of Eden. The Cherubim, according to Saint Bernard, draw from the very fountain of Wisdom; Saint Thomas says that they have fullness of knowledge. They appear in the chariot of the Church surrounding Beatrice, who is the symbol of Divine Wisdom or Revelation or Theology, all associated with the Second Person of the Blessed Trinity. They disappear with the Griffin, the symbol of Christ, who appears in the Stellar Heaven (that moved by the Cherubim) at the head of the triumphal procession of the Church.

> *You must know that all have delight*
> *insofar as their sight penetrates*
> *into the truth which quiets doubt.*
>
> *Hence one can see how happiness*
> *is founded on the act of beholding,*
> *not on that of loving, which follows later.*
> — *Paradiso* XXVIII:106–111

One who approaches the *Paradiso* for the first time is surprised to find that until he reaches the Stellar Heaven (Canto XXVIII) he sees no angels. In the second Canto (112–148) Beatrice tells Dante how the nine choirs of "blessed movers" cause the revolution of the spheres; but along the illuminative way as he ascends from star to star those who come to enlighten him are saints, not angels. At the close of his letter to Can Grande, Dante says that in this section of the *Commedia*, which he dedicates to him, he will *speak of the blessed souls discovered in each sphere*; and *to show the glory of the beatitude of these souls, many things will be asked of them as the beholders of all truth, things which in themselves are profitable and delightful.* The questions which Dante asks in each sphere relate to those aspects of human life controlled by the choir of angels which move that sphere and whose function it is to exercise jurisdiction over human affairs in that area. For the functions of the various choirs he leans heavily on the *De Consideratione* of Saint Bernard,[13] which he names in the same section of the dedicatory letter.

In the *Paradiso* the saints are as eager to assist Dante as were the angels in the *Purgatorio*. They respond to his questions joyously, often before he puts them into words; for they wish him to increase in knowledge so that he may increase in love. In the Heaven of Venus (*Par.* VIII:32–39) Charles Martel says,

> We are ready, all of us, for your pleasure,
> so that you may delight in us
>
> . . . .
>
> And we are so full of love that to please you,
> A little pause (in the dance among the Seraphim)
> will not be less sweet to us.

In the Heaven of Mercury (*Par.* V:118–120) Justinian had said, "By the light which spreads through all of Heaven we are illuminated; therefore if you want to be enlightened by us, satisfy yourself at your pleasure."

Those who do not understand the concept of beatitude held by Dante are sometimes annoyed with him for introducing into the *Paradiso* discussions about scientific, political, philosophical, and theological matters. To Dante, Heaven is the home of Infinite Truth, the place where all the answers to perplexing questions are to be had. To him the Beatific Vision means direct intellectual knowledge, direct contemplation of God who is Absolute Truth; therefore he puts to those who come direct from this contemplation the problems which vex him. He believes that for men, as for angels, the answers to these questions come through vision: they are found by looking into Infinite Truth in the vision of God. The intensity of the activity of love is proportionate to the intensity of the keenness of this vision: happiness has its root in *seeing* not in *loving*, which is the aftergrowth of seeing (*Par.* XXVIII:109–111).

When one understands Dante's consistent teaching that love is dependent upon knowledge; that perfect happiness consists in the perfect satisfaction of man's intellectual powers; that the more one knows of divine truth the greater — here in the Paradise — will be one's love of the Supreme Goodness, who is Absolute Truth, then one understands the place of these discussions involving the whole range of human and divine science as Dante moves along the illuminative way in his progress toward God. These basic concepts of knowledge and love Beatrice explains to Dante as they advance toward the Empyrean, chiefly in the Crystalline or ninth heaven where he sees the nine choirs of angels revolving around the Point of Light, Dante's first glimpse of the Divine Essence. It is right, however, that she should hint at them in the first heaven, that of the moon.

> See how the Angels feel through far-off space,
> How keenly and unceasingly they feel.
> Beside their red flame our white-heat is cool —
> See how the Angels glow through distant space.
>
> — through their vast radiant spheres they go.
>
> — Rainer Maria Rilke
> "Angels"
> (translated by Jessie Lemont)*

The Heaven of the Moon is moved by the lowest order of angels in the lowest triad; they are known simply as the ANGELS. As we have seen, Scripture teaches that an angel is assigned to each man as his guardian and accompanies him in all his ways throughout his whole lifetime. For this reason, the matters discussed in the heaven moved by these angels are problems of peculiar significance to individuals: the making and breaking of vows and the related problems of free will.

Above the angels in the first triad are the ARCHANGELS who, like the angels, act as messengers and guardians. They are entrusted, however, with matters of graver import, and are known as "exalted" messengers and "exalted" guardians. Saint Bernard says that they are aware of the divine mysteries and are charged with messages of special importance and sacredness. Gabriel announced the coming of the Redeemer, "than which there could be no more

---

* (New York: Columbia University Press, 1943.)

important message." Michael was thought of as the special monitor of the Holy Roman emperors and as the guardian of the Empire, than which there could be no more important national guardianship.[14] Under the old dispensation he had been the guardian of the Jewish nation. For these reasons, in the Heaven of Mercury, Beatrice explains to Dante the mystery and necessity of the Incarnation and Redemption, and the Emperor Justinian gives a magnificent review of the glories of Rome.

Above angels and archangels are the PRINCIPALITIES. Evidently in the medieval mind a connection had been established between the words *principalities* and *princes;* for it is the function of the Principalities *to establish, rule, limit, transfer, and curtail nations and by their management and wisdom to exercise jurisdiction over earthly principalities.* They represent the lordship of God; their major function is to attract earthly rulers to imitate the Divine Ruler so that love may join rulers to their subjects, and ruler to ruler. Since these rulers in the Middle Ages were often churchmen as well as civil rulers, in this third heaven, that of Venus, bishops appear as well as kings and emperors.

The discussion in the Heaven of Venus centers on matters related to good government and the way in which God provides for the diversity of gifts and aptitudes which are needed in a well-ordered society. The heavenly bodies and the choirs of angels who rule them are the instruments of the Prime Intelligence in distributing talents without reference to family or social rank; so one is born a Solon (a lawgiver); one, a Xerxes (a military genius); another, a Melchisedech (a priest); another, a Daedalus (an inventor). Much confusion and evil arise in the world because men are forced into places in society for which they are not equipped by nature. Here, as elsewhere in the *Commedia,* it is evident that Dante gives some credence to the influence of the stars on human life; in Canto XXII: 112–115, he expresses his gratitude for being born under "lucky stars."

It must be remembered that all the souls in the lower heavens, those of the shadowed planets — though ultimately they attained beatitude — during much of their lives were diverted from the right path by the allurements of the world and the flesh. Those who are untrue to their high calling in Church or State commit spiritual adultery and are shown in this Heaven of Venus with lovers who were guilty of carnal infidelity. In this heaven as well as in other places in the *Divine Comedy* Dante takes up the cudgels against avarice, his point of departure here being that avarice in the hearts of rulers leads to such major national catastrophes as the Sicilian Vespers (*Par.* VIII:73–75).[15]

The first three of the four heavens of honor, to which Dante and Beatrice are now ascending, are moved by the angels of the second triad — the Powers, Virtues, and Dominations. These choirs are concerned with the active life in its three major areas, that of the pen, the sword, and the scepter; therefore in the fourth heaven, that of the sun, teachers come forth to meet them; in Mars, crusaders in the broad and narrow sense; in Jupiter, kings and princes, who during their time on earth were engaged primarily with works of justice and administration.

The Heaven of the Sun is moved by the POWERS, to whom are assigned the special functions of combating the powers of darkness and of healing diseases. Since good teaching, correct philosophical and theological training, must precede and direct all aspects of the active life, it is fitting that in this first heaven of that life, Dante should meet the eminent teachers of all the rival schools. Teaching by word, spoken or written, and teaching by example is combating the powers of darkness in dispelling spiritual maladies of sin and ignorance; because the sun is the giver of light and the preserver of health in the literal sense and the symbol of knowledge and virtue in the figurative sense, it is clear why Dante and other medieval scholars put the Powers in control of the sun.

The scholars who come to meet Dante appear in two circles. Since in Dante's day the Dominicans and Franciscans had co-operated with the angelic Powers and flooded the Church with the light of learning and virtue, Dante makes the most distinguished theologian of each order the leader of his circle. He puts upon the lips of Saint Thomas a eulogy of Saint Francis, the founder of the Franciscans, and upon the lips of Saint Bonaventure the praises of Saint Dominic. Each founder in his own way had done much to combat the powers of darkness: Francis by his remedy of poverty had helped to heal the plague of avarice; Dominic by his preaching of sound doctrine had removed the cancer of heresy. The discussion in this heaven concerns two major theological questions, the hypostatic union and the resurrection of the body.

The Heaven of Mars is moved by the VIRTUES. For the purpose of stirring men up, the angels in this choir work signs and prodigies in the elements; they are conspicuous for their valor, their function being to make men endure gloriously in the combat against the world, the flesh, and the devil. As he enters this fifth heaven, Dante is moved to make a holocaust of himself as a man must who enters a conflict. The emblem formed by the saints in Mars is an enormous crusader's cross stretching across the heavens; on the cross Christ flashes forth, and from top to bottom and left to right move the lights, those who have fought under the standard of the cross and who have in a sense been crusaders yielding the sword figuratively or literally against the enemies of Christ and his Church. From among those on the right arm a light moves like a falling star to the foot of the cross and addresses Dante, identifying himself as Cacciaguida, Dante's great-great-grandfather. Cacciaguida co-operates with the Virtues by announcing to Dante his mission to fight and condemn vice, especially in high places; to rebuke and admonish his contemporaries, and to teach eternal truths to future ages. He foretells Dante's unjust exile and warns him of the fortitude he will need to support him in the bitter years ahead.

The DOMINATIONS, who rule Jupiter, the heaven of the just rulers, are, according to Saint Bernard, masters of all those ministering spirits who move the heavens of the active life. *To them, as to masters, are referred the guiding activity of the Principalities, the protecting activity of the Powers, the works of the Virtues, the revelations of the Archangels, and the care and foresight of the Angels.* In the *Banquet* II, xiv, where he is comparing Jupiter to geometry, Dante quotes Ptolemy as saying that Jupiter is a temperate star midway between the coldness of Saturn and the heat of Mars. Among all the stars it shows white, almost as if silvered (*Par.* XVIII:67, 96). The temperate aspect of the star may symbolize to Dante that quality of a just ruler which Saint Thomas calls *clemency,* a moderation in inflicting penalties; its whiteness the impeccable justice, which like geometry is "without spot of error and most exact in itself and in its handmaid, perspective."

The souls of the rulers come to Dante as lights, singing and flying like birds as they form themselves into the first verse of the book of *Wisdom: Diligite justitiam qui judicatis terram* (Love justice you that are the judges of the earth). There is significance in the fact that *Wisdom* was written by Solomon, the prototype of the just ruler. The lights, which at first form the many letters of the verse, settle into a huge M, obviously indicating *Monarchy*, the kind of government Dante deems best; then with but slight change they resolve themselves into a Roman eagle, the emblem of the Empire. The Dominations, the ministers of the one just dominion of God, have the function of drawing all rulers to unity of subjection and obedience to this one lordship. The earthly symbolism is clear. Dante had written in the *Monarchy* (I:ix), "It is obvious that the world's well-being demands a Monarch or single government know as the Empire." Here he has all just kings and emperors form an imperial eagle, the most significant of these rulers forming the eye of the bird, ever vigilant against aggression or disunion. The discussions in the Heaven of Jupiter all bear upon justice: the justice of God in requiring Baptism for salvation, of the manner of saving souls born outside the Hebrew or Christian dispensation, the inability of the finite mind to comprehend the justice of God, the need for man to conform his will to the will of God, which is and must be always just.

The "cold" Heaven of Saturn, that of the contemplatives, is presided over by the THRONES, the lowest choir in the final hierarchy. They are called Thrones, says Saint Bernard, because they sit, and they are sitting because God sits among them. The sitting means *the highest tranquility, the most gentle serenity, the peace which surpasses all understanding. Such is the Lord of armies, who sits among the Thrones judging all things with tranquility, most gentle, most serene, most peaceful. Such a Lord has created the Thrones for himself, very like himself. By means of the Thrones* God will execute his judgments.

The emblem in the heaven of the contemplatives is a ladder of golden light reaching into the highest heaven. Down this ladder come two saints, Benedict and Peter Damian, to speak with Dante, who, not having found a satisfactory answer to his question concerning the justice of damning souls who seemingly have had no opportunity to know the true way of salvation, now raises the problem of predestination. Saint Peter Damian checks him, telling him that what he asks goes so deep into the abyss of God's eternal law that even the highest Seraph with his vision most wrapt in God could not answer him. Dante does, however, get his answer in the Empyrean. From this serene and tranquil "seventh heaven" Beatrice invites Dante to look down upon our world, "the threshing floor" upon which the foot of the ladder rests, the rungs of which he has climbed through Purgatory and the lower heavens.

> Forth from the last corporeal are we come
> Into the heaven that is unbodied light;
> Light intellectual, replete with love;
> Love of true happiness, replete with joy;
> Joy that transcends all sweetness of delight.
>
> — *Paradiso* XXX:39–43
> (Translation by Cary)

From the heavens of honor, Dante and Beatrice pass into the Stellar Heaven, the Primum Mobile, and then into the Empyrean. The Stellar Heaven, sometimes called the Heaven of the Fixed Stars or the Firmament, is the celestial counterpart of the Earthly Paradise, which it parallels in numerous details and completes in others. As the CHERUBIM guarded the Earthly Paradise, so do they rule this eighth heaven. In the Earthly Paradise Dante saw the masque of the Church in which they participated; here he witnesses the magnificent procession on the perpendicular, the completion of the procession which disappeared into the heavens from the Earthly Paradise. This is the procession of the Church Triumphant, the entry into the City of God, of Christ, the Conqueror of sin and death, who is leading home to his Father the fruits of his Passion: his Virgin Mother, the Apostles, and the vast army of saints, "the harvest gathered from the circling spheres" (*Par.* XXIII: 19–21).

In the Stellar Heaven, as in the Earthly Paradise, Dante is put to the test, this time the final comprehensive test. As in the Earthly Paradise he was "examined" by Beatrice and made his confession after the procession of the Church had moved back to Heaven, the angels remaining as witnesses; so now after the triumphal army of saints has ascended into the Empyrean and Peter, James, and John examine him in faith, hope, and charity, we may assume that in the sphere which they rule the Cherubim rejoice with his examiners when he passes the tests. In the Earthly Paradise he saw the despoiled tree and meditated upon the sin of Adam and the need of the Incarnation; here after he has seen the triumph of the Redemption, he meets Adam, whom he questions about the time and nature of the fall. Here in the figure of her assumption into Heaven, Mary, the new Eve, is crowned by the Archangel Gabriel who descends circling from the Empyrean and revolves around her welcoming her as *Regina Coeli*, the Queen of Heaven, who in fulfillment of the proto-Messianic prophecy made in the Garden of Eden has, through her Son, crushed the head of the serpent.

The Crystalline Heaven, the Primum Mobile, the ninth and swiftest heaven, is governed by the Seraphim, spirits wholly set aflame with divine fire. Because of the fervent desire of all of its parts to be united with the Empyrean Heaven, the quiet heaven of peace, the Crystalline Heaven burns with the greatest intensity and moves the most rapidly. It is in this heaven that Dante sees the Point of Light around which revolve the nine choirs of angels and in which Beatrice gives him instruction about the hierarchies. These hierarchies sing *Hosanna* to the Point on which the Heavens and all Nature depend; it represents the unity of God and of all creation. It is the center of spiritual gravity which will hold the angels where they have always been (*Par.* XXVIII:94–96); the bond which holds them being their immediate vision and possession of God, which constitutes Beatitude.

In the Primum Mobile there are no saints; these having moved into the Empyrean in the triumphal procession will be seen again in the places in the great white rose to which their merit assigns them. Dante sees in the Primum Mobile no spirits but the angels themselves; the discussions deal with the angelic nature and all the contingent problems discussed at the beginning of this chapter.

As at daybreak before the growing glow of sunrise the stars fade, so the nine circles which played around the Point disappear little by little and Dante finds himself with Beatrice in the Empyrean, the Heaven of Pure Light, "Here," she says, "you will see both hosts of Paradise," meaning the hosts of angels successful in the trial and the victorious "soldiery" of mankind. Suddenly a brilliant light shines around him and he sees light in the likeness of a river, an image of time, flowing between banks covered with flowers. This river is the river of illuminating grace; the flowers are the souls of the saints. "The Cherubim," says Saint Bernard, "drinking from the very font of wisdom from the mouth of the Most High pour out streams of knowledge upon all his citizenry, and this is perhaps what the Psalmist (Ps. 45:5) meant by the force of the river making the City of God joyful." From this river, as sparks of the glowing light, fly the angels like bees to settle among the flowers, carrying to the saints the knowledge and the grace of God. Then as if intoxicated with the fragrance of the flowers, they fly back to the river, filled with the odors of holiness. Dante drinks of this river of light with his eyelid's rim (*In thy light we shall see light* [Ps. 35:10]) and finds the river transformed into a sea of light, the *lumen gloriae* of Saint Thomas, by which the intellect is strengthened to see God (*Summa* I, q. 12, a. 4; a. 5). The flowers change into the bodies of the saints as they will be after the Day of Judgment and he sees both courts of heaven in the height and vastness of the white rose.

In the image of the rose the angels are again likened to bees (an image which Dante uses frequently probably since it was an image loved by Virgil) who descend into the flower and fly upward to the light under which it blossoms. They all have faces of living flame and wings of gold; the rest is whiter than the purest snow. The flame probably signifies their intense love; the gold, their everlasting integrity; the white, their purity beyond that of the saints; for the angels were never touched by sin, original or actual.

When they sank into the flower
from rank to rank, they bestowed
the peace and ardor acquired as they flew,

nor did such a flying multitude
between the flower and what was above
obscure the vision of the splendor,

for divine light penetrates through the universe
in proportion to its merit,
so that there nothing can obscure it.

The essential happiness of both angels and saints is, of course, the Beatific Vision. But each "soldiery" may receive an accidental happiness from the other: the angels from the knowledge that they have aided many souls to attain salvation and have therefore participated in bringing to the Vision of God another order of creatures, who throughout eternity will take the places of the angels who fell; the saints, by witnessing the active joy of the angels as they dip into the petals of the rose and then fly back to contemplate the Divine Essence; and by observing the manifold perfection of the innumerable species in the nine choirs. In the Empyrean Heaven, as Carroll points out, the antagonism which seems to exist on earth between the active and the contemplative life is resolved; here in the angels *who flying see and sing* is the perfect union of the two forms of life, "the vision of God that is never lost in the swiftest flight of service, and the song of praise issuing from both, praise for what God is and for what he has created them to be."[16]

The last presentation of the angels comes in the vision of Mary: Mary the Aurora, Mary the Peacemaker, Mary the Queen of angels and men. Against a radiant background as of a far-flung banner of flame on a ground of gold like the unconquerable oriflamme of the ancient French kings, exalted above all the elect, in the midst of thousands of angels, is she who is the Dawn because she brought forth the "Sun of justice"; she who is our peacemaker with the angels (who were offended with us who had offended God), she who "made the ranks of the angels whole again," because through her Son the souls of men have been redeemed to take the places in Heaven left vacant by Lucifer and his followers. This oriflamme, like the flaming morning sky, is a pacific oriflamme because Mary is the Queen of peace who brought into the world the Prince of peace. Against this regal banner "which shone brighter in the middle, and on either side gradually and equally decreased its light" Dante sees more than a thousand rejoicing angels with widespread wings, each distinct in effulgence and function, smiling at their games and joyous in their songs, a delight to the eyes of all the saints. Their festival brings a rain of joy upon Mary, Queen of both courts. When Gabriel spreads his wings in front of her and sings *Ave Maria gratia plena,* the salutation which marked the dawn of joy for all mankind and increased the joy of all the angels, the blessed court of angels and of saints sing the response, their faces growing brighter as they commemorate that blessed central moment in time which united angels and men in the peace of God.

NOTES

1. *Summa,* I, q. 50, a. 1. "There must be some incorporeal creatures. For what is principally intended by God in creatures is good, and this consists in assimilation to God himself. And the perfect assimilation of an effect to a cause is accomplished when the effect imitates the cause according to that whereby the cause produces the effect; as heat makes heat. Now, God produces the creature by his intellect and will (q. 14, a. 8; q. 19, a. 4). Hence the perfection of the universe requires that there should be intellectual creatures. Now intelligence cannot be the action of a body, nor of any corporeal faculty; for every body is limited to *here* and *now*. Hence the perfection of the universe requires the existence of an incorporeal creature."
2. Saint Thomas discusses these matters relative to the angelic nature in *Summa,* I, q. 50, a. 3, 4.
3. See Dionysius the Areopagite, *The Mystical Theology and the Celestial Hierarchies,* trans. and ed. by Editors of The Shrine of Wisdom (Fintry, Brook, Nr. Gadalming, Surrey, 1949), for matter referred to here and on succeeding pages. For comments on the identity of Dionysius and his importance in shaping the thought of theologians see the "Proemial" of this book and Baring-Gould, *Lives of the Saints* (Edinburgh: John Grant, 1914), new and rev. ed., Vol. XI, p. 190 seq.
   It would appear that at least three different persons have been confounded under the name Dionysius: the convert of Saint Paul; Dionysius, the martyr and patron saint of France, commonly known as Saint Denis; and Dionysius, the author of the so-called works of Dionysius. "Modern scholarship," say the Editors of The Shrine of Wisdom, (p. 7) "has settled the fact that . . . *The Mystical Theology* and other Dionysian writings did not come into existence until centuries after St. Paul's Athenian convert." They continue:
   "In fact, it is almost certain that the writer was either a pupil of Proclus or, as is more probable, of Damascius, the second in succession of the Athenian school. It was natural that when he became a Christian writer

he should assume a name which had sacred memories of Athenian faith, and which was also a link with Greek culture.

"But whatever his origin, the writings of this master mind early became the form and type of mystical religion within the Church. . . . This anonymous, mysterious, monastic genuis taught the foremost Christians for ten centuries both in the East and West, for nearly every great medieval scholar made use of his writings, and his authority came to be almost final. A modern writer says that even the *Summa Theologiae* of St. Thomas Aquinas — the Angelic Doctor — is but a 'hive in whose varied cells he duly stored the honey which he gathered' from the writings of Dionysius, and he became the bee-bread on which all the great mystics fed."

Baring-Gould, in commenting on the influence exercised by *The Mystical Theology, The Celestial Hierarchies* and the other works of Dionysius says:

"It is scarcely possible to speak too highly of the value and importance of the works long attributed to Dionysius, and thought by leading scholars of the early and late Middle Ages to have been written by him. These works which laid the foundation in the West of both mystical and scholastic theology are now attributed by modern critics to an unknown genius of the fourth and fifth centuries and are called the work of the pseudo-Dionysius."

In Chapter IX of this book, "Purgation for Perfection," the influence of Dionysius upon mystical and ascetical theology is discussed in some detail. Much of the terminology used by mystical and ascetical writers down the Christian centuries is taken from the writings of Dionysius.

4. In the *Divine Comedy* Dante follows precisely the order of Dionysius, as does Saint Thomas in the *Summa*, q. 108. In the *Banquet* Dante follows the system of Saint Gregory, an "error" for which (*Par.* XXVIII:135–137) Gregory must smile at himself in heaven where he now sees things as they are. Saint Bernard, on whose *De Consideratione* Dante leans for some considerations of the functions of the choirs, follows also the order given by Gregory.

5. Saint Augustine, *op. cit.*, Vol. I, Book XI, 19, p. 458.

6. Saint Thomas deals with the problem of the number of angels who fell and from what choirs, *Summa*, I, q. 63, a. 9.

7. In *The Golden Legend* of Jacobus de Varagine in the discussion of the angels there is a succinct statement of a concept prevalent in the Middle Ages. *To every man, indeed, two angels are given, one a bad angel to try him, the other a good angel to guard him.* — *The Golden Legend* of Jacobus de Varagine, trans. and adapted from the Latin by Granger Ryan and Helmut Ripperger (New York, 1941), Part II, p. 585.

8. See John S. Carroll, *Exiles of Eternity* (London, 1911 or 1924), Preface to the third edition. The Preface to the third edition is reprinted in the 1924 edition.

9. The *Te Deum Laudamus*, which is said in the Divine Office at the end of Matins, is used in many extraliturgical functions as a hymn of thanksgiving. Some commentators say that it is sung here not by the angels but by penitents inside the gate of Purgatory.

10. Romano Guardini, *Der Engel in Dante's göttlicher Komodie*, 2nd ed. (Munich, 1951), p. 59.

11. William Warren Vernon, *Readings on the Purgatorio of Dante* (London, 1897), Vol. II, p. 337.

12. The *Asperges me* is sung before High Mass except during the Paschal season when it is supplanted by the *Vidi Aquam*. Intoning the ninth verse of Psalm 50, the penitential psalm known as the *Miserere*, the celebrant passes down the main aisle of the church saying the psalm in a quiet voice while the

choir finishes the verse he has intoned. In the Vulgate translation the verse reads: "Thou shalt sprinkle me with hyssop, O Lord, and I shall be cleansed; Thou shalt wash me and I shall be made whiter than snow." The significance of the use of the *Asperges* here is self-evident.

13. Throughout the *Paradiso*, though Dante does not follow the arrangement of the choirs used by Saint Bernard in the *De Consideratione*, he does follow closely Saint Bernard's assignment of functions to the various choirs, the evidence being the discussions he introduces in the various spheres. For the complete text see Bernard of Clairvaux, *"De Consideratione Libri Quinque ad Eugenium Tertium,"* Migne, P.L., 182, col. 792, B,C. See also Dionysius, *op. cit.*, Chapters VI–IX, pp. 45–57.

14. Usually Michael and Gabriel are called archangels. Dante so classifies them, as do Saint Thomas, Saint Bernard, and Saint Dionysius who are Dante's mentors. Because in *Luke* (1:19) Gabriel identifies himself as "Gabriel who stands before God" (Raphael so identifies himself also when he speaks to Tobias) some later theologians place Gabriel, Raphael, and Michael among the seven privileged spirits who stand before the throne (Apoc. 1:4; 8:2). The seven, these theologians argue, would belong to the highest of the angelic choirs. For a discussion of this matter see Joseph Husslein, S.J., *The Spirit World About Us* (Milwaukee, 1934), p. 116. Dante, too, in *Par.* XXXII:109–111 seems to give Gabriel the highest possible rank.

15. Dante refers here to the imperial schemes of Charles of Anjou and to the opposition they aroused, particularly in Sicily. On Easter Monday, 1282, there was an uprising in Palermo and throughout the island fomented by Aragonese and Hohenstaufen interests against the hated French whom they looked upon as usurpers, and between three and four thousand French were slaughtered.

16. John S. Carroll, *In Patria* (London, 1911), p. 483.

CHAPTER VI

DANTE AND THE VIRGIN MARY

> As the honor of the male sex is in the flesh of
> Christ, the honor of the female sex is in the
> Mother of Christ.
>
> — Saint Augustine

> Fair Virgin,
>   Vestured with the sun!
> Bright shining one,
>   Star-crowned:
> Who such sweet ultimate favor found
>   From all eternity
> With the great primal Sun
>   That from the height
> He stooped in thee to hide the light
>   Of his Divinity:
>   Now shall my love upraise
>   New measures in thy praise,
> Though to begin without thy aid were vain
>   And without his,
> Who, joined with thee in love, shall ever reign.
>   Thee I invoke who never turned deaf ear
> When ardent faith called to thee without fear.*
>
> — Petrarch
> "Ode to the Virgin"
> (From the Italian by
> Helen Lee Peabody)

ante's understanding of the Virgin Mary as a woman,
a mother, and a religious force is that of any true
Christian of the Middle Ages. In the twelfth, thirteenth, and fourteenth centuries, she held a unique
place in the personal and social lives of the people, whose work
and play, study and prayer were permeated by devotion to her.

* From *I Sing of a Maiden*, Sr. M. Thérèse (New York: The Macmillan Co.,
1947).

Guildsmen and soldiers were as ardent in their service as monks and bishops; kings and popes were as humble in her vassalage as the lowliest serfs. Princes and artisans from Paris and Chartres to Palermo and Constantinople vied with each other in erecting cathedrals and abbey churches in her honor. Schoolmen like Saint Albert the Great argued whether she possessed perfectly the seven liberal arts and decided that since she is the Mother of Divine Wisdom, she is that House of Wisdom of Scripture (Prov. 9:1) with the seven sculptured columns (the seven liberal arts) and is, therefore, master of the sciences. She was invoked by Saint Dominic against the heresy of the Albigenses, by Crusaders against the Moslems. Her banners floated from merchant ships and the towers of castles and were raised aloft in battles on land and on sea. In Siena, *Il Palio*, one of the most famous of these banners, used even to the present day, was borne in the triumph car in the procession preceding the famous horse race run on two of her feast days; instead of a cup or other trophy it is still given to the winning contrada or ward of the city. She was the refuge of women in childbirth, of the dispossessed living in exile, of the unshriven dying by violence. The mighty and the lowly turned to her in all the vicissitudes of life.

In Florence, or wherever else he went, Dante was aware of places dedicated to the Virgin and of persons devoted to her. She was present in every home, in every church, on every street corner. Her flowers brightened the fields. In the *New Life* (V) he saw Beatrice in a church "where words could be heard of the Queen of Glory." He was familiar with the hymns, sequences, and antiphons sung in her honor. He knew her prayers. All these he built into the fabric of his writings. He invoked her name both night and morning (*Par.* XXIII:88), probably at the ringing of the Angelus bell. She was to him what she was to every other medieval Christian, *Notre Dame*, "Our Lady." He had for her the intimate affection of every medieval — and modern — Italian: she is *Madonna*, "My Lady." Because in him love was always ruled by reason (*New Life* II), he had for her the intellectual love of the schoolmen and like them studied her prerogatives and the consequent position she held in relation to the Trinity and sinful, though redeemed, mankind. He meditated with them on her virtues. He contemplated her high dignity. It is altogether understandable, therefore, that she played her part in the development of his poetic powers as she played a part in all the other art of the Middle Ages.

> Mother of virtue, light eternal, thou
>   Of whom was born the meek benignant fruit,
>   That suffered on the cross a bitter death,
>   To save us sinners from the dark abyss:
> Thou, queen of heaven, and of this world, supreme,
>   Vouchsafe to entreat thy ever-worthy Son
>   To bring me to his heavenly kingdom's joys,
>   By virtue of his never-failing grace.
> Thou knowest my hope was ever placed in thee;
>   Thou knowest in thee was ever my delight;
>   O goodness infinite, support me now;
> Help me, for at the bourn I am arrived
>   Which I must soon inevitably pass;
>   O now, chief comforter, forsake me not:
> For every fault committed here on earth
>   My soul deplores, and contrite is my heart.
>
>   — Dante
>   "Sonnet XLIX"
>   (Translation of Charles Lyell)

From apostolic times, historians and theologians had concerned themselves with the place of Mary in the Christian dispensation. Upon the Gospel story recorded in *Luke* (1; 2) her virginity and divine maternity were predicated. Built on these chapters in *Luke* and other passages in the Old and New Testaments, there developed in the Church a vast theological structure known as *Mariology*, an integration of countless biblical, patristic, papal, and liturgical documents which set forth Mary's position in the scheme of salvation. Theologians of the twelfth and thirteenth centuries were exceedingly active in this integration: the air of Dante's time was charged with Mariological discussion.[1] It is only against this rich background, so vigorous a part of the time in which Dante lived, that his life and works can be understood.

It is impossible here to review in any detail the growth of the teaching of the solemn and ordinary *magisterium* of the Church in regard to Mary, but it is essential that the reader of Dante be familiar with the fundamental beliefs which permeate his thought. First of all, it is necessary to be clear about the way in which he thought she should be honored; then it is necessary to know the eight prerogatives which entitled her to this honor.

The medieval man was not confused in his theology as he is sometimes accused of being. The *Divine Comedy* illustrates well just where he stood. Though he honored Mary, even her greatest devotee did not adore her; adoration was reserved for the Trinity. Between Mary and the Trinity, the gap was infinite. He never forgot that Mary is completely human; he knew that adoration belongs only to Divinity. Since, however, God had bestowed upon Mary privileges beyond those given to any other creature, angel or man, she is, he reasoned, entitled to special honor from angels and men: whereas man gives to other saints the honor known as *dulia*, to Mary he gives *hyperdulia* (*Summa* II, II, q. 103).

Though for centuries some of the privileges of Mary had been matters of faith for all Christians, having been formulated at early councils such as Nicaea (325) and Ephesus (431), some, however, like the belief in the Assumption were not declared dogmas and made matters of faith. The Assumption was not declared a dogma until the twentieth century; on some others, Rome has not yet spoken. The eight privileges discussed in detail by Saint Bernard and other theologians and set forth in the *Speculum Beatae Mariae Virginis* (*The Mirror of the Blessed Virgin Mary*)[2] of Saint Bonaventure are her Divine Maternity, her Perpetual Virginity, and her Eminent Sanctity — all of which had been promulgated in the early councils; her Spiritual Maternity, her role as Coredemptrix, her power as Mediatrix, and her Assumption and Queenship, about which Rome had not spoken *ex cathedra*. In all eight, Dante had unquestioned faith, as his writings, especially the *Divine Comedy*, testify. In his Mariology he leans heavily on the writings of both Saint Bernard and Saint Bonaventure.

Theologians teach that the ultimate cause of Mary's privileges is her DIVINE MATERNITY. "Because she is the Mother of God," says Saint Thomas (*Summa* I, q. 25, a. 6, a. obj. 4), "the Blessed Virgin has a kind of infinite dignity from the infinite good which is God." From this single revealed truth from Scripture all the other seven beliefs were drawn. Scripture, in prophecy in the Old Testament and in historical record in the New, had said that the birth of Christ was a virgin birth; the Church after centuries of controversy — though Tradition had always affirmed it — at the first Lateran Council held in 649, pronounced upon Mary's PER-PETUAL VIRGINITY. The angel of the Annunciation had addressed Mary as *full of grace:* upon that premise her EMINENT SANCTITY was predicated, some theologians, Duns Scotus for instance, arguing for her Immaculate Conception — all declaring that even before her birth and until the time of her death she was free from all stain of sin, original and actual.

Though Rome had not proclaimed her eminent sanctity or the remaining five of the prerogatives of Mary as *de fide*, that is, matters of faith, Dante and most other medieval Christians believed in them as they believed in the first two. Many of the most eminent theologians, among them Saint Albert and Saint Bonaventure, argued ardently for Mary's SPIRITUAL MATERNITY, asserting that when Christ on the Cross gave Mary to Saint John as his spiritual mother (Jn. 19:26–27), he gave her through John to the universal Church and that at once she assumed the role of mother. For that reason she was with the Apostles in the Cenacle (Acts 1:12–14; 2:1–4) on the first Pentecost; for that reason she is the tender, long-suffering, always approachable mother of all mankind.[3]

Because Mary as the Mother of the Incarnate Word knew from the moment of her *Fiat* that she was the Mother of the Redeemer and co-operated with Christ all his life in his preparation for the sacrifice on Calvary and was present at the foot of the Cross where the sacrifice was consummated, she is the COREDEMPTRIX. Be cause the Redeemer came to man by the free assent of Mary to become the Mother of God and because she was associated in the

Redemption, she has almost unlimited power in the distribution of the graces that flow from the Redemption; the graces of the Redemption are distributed through her hands, for since Christ came to men through Mary, it is fitting that his graces should come to men through Mary. She is, therefore, the MEDIATRIX OF ALL GRACES — the Mediatrix with her Son, who is the Mediator with the Father. This was the consistent teaching of Saint Albert, Saint Bonaventure, and Saint Anthony — to say nothing of Saint Bernard, who is known as the *Doctor of Mediation* and who in season and out of season preached of Mary as Mediatrix. In one of his sermons for the feast of Mary's Nativity there is a characteristic statement: "Let us honor Mary because it is his will that we should have all through Mary."[4] "It is by the hands of this Lady," writes Saint Bonaventure, "that we have whatever good we possess."[5]

The doctrines of the ASSUMPTION of Mary into heaven and her QUEENSHIP were matters of ardent belief in the Middle Ages and are woven by Dante into the superb poetry of the *Paradiso*. The medieval man made a careful distinction between the *ascension* of Christ, who, as God, rose to Heaven *by his own power*, and the *assumption* of Mary whose virginal body *was taken* into Heaven by the power of God, there to be crowned Queen of angels and men by her divine Son. "We truly confess her to be the Queen of Heaven," wrote Saint Augustine, "because she brought forth the King of angels."[6]

So rooted in Scripture and Tradition was this concept of the Queenship of Mary that no medieval Christian had any doubt that Mary was the Queen of all creatures. The builders of the cathedrals of Chartres and Paris wrote it in stone a century before Dante wrote it in verse in the *Divine Comedy*.[7] But it is much older in Christian art than the French builders or Dante. In a picture in the catacombs of Priscilla, painted probably in the first quarter of the second century, the Blessed Mother, represented as showing her Son to the Magi, wears a headdress similar to that of the Empresses of that period. Pope John VII (705–707) commanded that in the Marian Chapel of the old Vatican Basilica, a representation be made of Mary wearing a royal crown, with himself, Pope John, at her right. In the inscription he calls himself: *Johannes . . . Beatae Dei*

Genetricis servus — "John . . . the servant (or slave) of the Blessed Mother of God."[3]

The above-named eight prerogatives of Mary form the theological framework upon which the position of Mary in the *Divine Comedy* is built. The poem was written for Beatrice — and her role in it is exceedingly important; but the central role in the regeneration of Dante is played by the Virgin Mary. She seems always to be associated with Beatrice in the mind of Dante, for she is the mother of fair love; she is, moreover, the only perfect woman, "our tainted nature's solitary boast," as Wordsworth put it centuries after Dante. When Beatrice dies, God has taken her to himself so "that she might be glorious under the banner of that blessed Queen Mary, whose name has always a deep reverence in the words of holy Beatrice" (*New Life* XXIX); when Dante writes the poem on the anniversary of her death, he thinks of her in the new abode (XXXV) "in the heaven of humility, where Mary is."

In the last sonnet of the *New Life* which is the forerunner of the vision which "determined" him to write the *Divine Comedy* he gives a picture quite like that in the last cantos of the *Paradiso* where he shows Mary enthroned:

> Beyond the sphere which spreads to widest space
>   Now soars the sigh that my heart sends above;
>   A new perception born of grieving Love
> Guideth it upward the untrodden ways.
> When it hath reached unto the end, and stays,
>   It sees a lady round whom splendors move
>   In homage; till, by the great light thereof
> Abashed, the pilgrim spirit stands at gaze.
> It sees her such, that when it tells me this
>   Which it hath seen, I understand it not,
>   It hath a speech so subtile and so fine.
> And yet I know its voice within my thought
>   Often remembereth me of Beatrice:
>   So that I understand it, ladies mine.

Whether the Vision was, as some commentators claim, a vision of Hell, Purgatory, and Heaven, or a vision of Mary enthroned and of Beatrice among the blessed spirits, where like bees the angels "fly and sing," we shall never know. The evidence seems to be in favor of the latter; for, when ten years later Dante fulfills the promise made after the vision to write of Beatrice what never had been written of any woman, he makes Mary the fulcrum for the action of the poem and directly or indirectly the major influence in each of the canticles. He seems to have held in mind the image presented in that final sonnet of the *New Life* so that he might make it the climax of the promised poem. He makes Mary bring Beatrice to his aid, first through Virgil and then in person; he has Beatrice lead him to the vision of Mary so that the poem comes full circle.

> *There is a Lady above who wins grace for us.*
>
> — *Purgatorio* XXVI:59

Because of Dante's belief in the spiritual maternity of Mary, his conviction that as the Mother of the Redeemer, given from the Cross, she is forever associated in the work of saving souls, he pictures her as coming to his rescue in the dark wood even before he asks her help. A mother is ever mindful of her child, especially when she sees him in need. In other parts of the poem he shows her coming immediately to the succor of those who do call upon her. Notable among these is Buonconte da Montefeltro (*Purg.* V:85– 130), whom he meets in the Ante-Purgatory among those who died by violence with little time to repent, "sinners to the last hour." Pierced in the throat, bloodying the plain, he fled the battle of Campaldino. His vision failing, he fell, crossed his arms upon his breast, and said the name of Mary. Instantly, as we saw in the last chapter, Mary sends an angel to bear his soul to safety, almost snatching it from the hands of the demon. Because Dante believes in the eminent sanctity of Mary "full of grace" he turns repeatedly to the *Speculum* for its extended meditation on the "Angelical Saluta- tion." Following this text, he sets Mary before the souls trying to eradicate the seven capital sins, as the perfect example of the virtues they are trying to acquire.

Often in the *New Life* and in all his subsequent writings Dante professes his belief in the Queenship of Mary. In the *Divine Comedy* he shows her Assumption and later her enthronement in the court of the Most High, where angels and saints honor her as befits her dignity. Because Bernard more than any other Doctor of the Church extolled the exalted office of Mary as Mediatrix between God and man, Dante makes him — before the whole heavenly court — petition her to gain for him the Beatific Vision. And because he is convinced that all these beliefs are grounded in Scripture, he has all the books of the Old and New Testament sing her praises in the glorious pageant of the Church in the Earthly Paradise.

The Madonna of the *Divine Comedy* in whatever aspect she is portrayed is majestic — approachable always, but majestic as befits her great dignity. In Dante as in the best sculpture and painting and mosaic of the earlier centuries, she is rather an empress than a queen. And this is fitting since she has four domains under her control. She is Queen of Heaven, crowned in the Empyrean by the King of kings and holding court among angels and saints. She is Queen of Purgatory and is so represented in activity or symbolism in each of the major divisions. Strange as it may seem to some, she is Queen of Hell and its demons:[9] of this belief Dante makes important use. She is Queen of Earth, the compassionate, often imperious Queen of the medieval legends, put into verse by Gaultier de Coincy and told by Jacobus de Varagine in *The Golden Legend* before Dante's time and in the fifteenth century by Johannes Herolt in *Miracles of the Blessed Virgin Mary:* the Queen who stooped, as did Elizabeth of Hungary and other saintly medieval queens, to release prisoners; to wipe the face of the tumbler who had done his best tricks to entertain her; to take the place in a tourney and win the jousts for a knight who had paused to do her homage; or, on occasion, to insist on better treatment for a weak or ne'er-do-well client to whom a lesser ruler had meted out justice — not knowing, as she did, all the secrets of his heart.[10] "She typified," says Adams, "an authority which the people wanted, and the fiefs feared; the Pax Romana, the omnipotence of God in government. In all Europe, at that time, there was no power except Christ and his Mother and the Imperial Crown."[11]

Lady of Heaven and earth, and therewithal
Crowned Empress of the nether clefts of Hell.

— François Villon
"His Mother's Service to Our Lady"
(Translation of Dante Gabriel Rossetti)

The power of Mary in both Heaven and Hell comes to us in one
flash at the very beginning of the *Divine Comedy* when she sets
the poem moving. In the second canto Dante represents her as
breaking "the sharp judgment on high" when, moved to pity because
of his predicament in the dark wood, she appeals to Lucia to do
something for her "faithful one." Lucia goes to Beatrice who appeals
to Virgil. The significant point is that as Queen of Hell as well as
of Heaven she not only permits Beatrice to go to Limbo to make
the appeal to Virgil but permits Virgil to absent himself from this
first circle of the damned to act as Dante's guide through the infernal
regions and through the first two sections of Purgatory. Her authority
in Hell is shown again at the gate of the city of Dis when she sends
Gabriel to scatter the garrison of the demons who would keep Dante
and Virgil from entering and who opens the gate with his rod. In
the *Speculum*, Mary is identified as the "rod of power" of Psalm
109, the "rod of Aaron" (Num. 17) flowering by her virginity, a rod
of power against infernal enemies, whom she dominates by her great
power.[12] Gabriel would not be named in Hell any more than Christ
or the Virgin because of his intimate association with them.

In the Ante-Purgatory, another episode — that of the serpent and
the angel sentinels — shows the power of Mary over Satan. The
negligent princes in the lovely valley carved out of the mountainside have gone to rest after having finished Compline and sung the
Salve Regina (*Purg.* VII:84) to ask the protection of Mary during
the night. When the green-clad sentinel angels with the flaming
swords take their places on opposite banks to guard the valley,
Sordello tells Dante and Virgil that they "came from Mary's bosom
because of the serpent who straightway will come" (VIII:37). When
the serpent does come, as we know, the angels put him to flight
and resume their guard until dawn when they will return to the
snow-white rose of Paradise where Mary reigns.

> Now therefore, ye children hear me:
> Blessed are they that keep my ways.
> Hear instruction and be wise, and refuse it not.
>
> Blessed is the man that heareth me, and that
> watcheth daily at my gates, and waiteth
> at the posts of my doors.
>
> He that shall find me shall find life
> and shall have salvation from the Lord.
>
> — Prov. 8:32–35

In the purification of souls in the *Purgatorio* on the cornices of the seven capital sins Mary plays a fundamental part. The *Divine Comedy* represents not only Dante's struggle to attain perfection; it represents every man's struggle. In order to acquire perfect love, the prerequisite for the Beatific Vision, a man must cast out the seven capital sins, supplanting them by the virtues opposed to the sins. It would seem that Dante's idea for using the life of the Virgin to present on each cornice of the Purgatory the perfect example of the virtue which serves as the antidote for the capital sin the soul is striving to overcome was also suggested by the *Speculum,* since Dante follows the order of Saint Bonaventure and not that found in other theologians, notably Saint Thomas, whom he usually follows in such matters.[13] In earlier chapters of his book Saint Bonaventure has been expounding the first phrases of the *Ave Maria;* now in Chapters XIV and XV he is discussing the phrase *Blessed art thou among women.* Chapter XV presents the thesis that Mary is blessed by the seven virtues against the seven capital vices; it sets forth the virtues and vices in the introductory paragraph and develops the idea throughout the remainder of the chapter:

> The world incurred malediction by the seven capital vices; but Mary obtained blessing by contrary virtues. Blessed, therefore, art thou among women, O Mary. Blessed by *humility against pride,* by *charity against envy,* by *meekness against anger,* by *diligence against sloth,* by *temperance against gluttony,* by *chastity against lust.*[14]

In this introductory paragraph Saint Bonaventure names only six of the capital sins, omitting avarice; however, on succeeding pages when he develops the ideas here presented he discusses (p. 155) the liberality of Mary, beginning his paragraph, "fifthly, hear how blessed is Mary by her liberality against avarice." Though on each cornice, Dante cites several examples of those who have practiced with heroism the virtue opposed to the capital sin, Mary is always cited first; for she alone practiced the virtue perfectly. It must be remembered that in the *Purgatorio* Dante is emphasizing the importance of time; he is teaching men how to live here and now. A man *ought* so to live that he need not spend time after death in Purgatory. He *should* when he dies be ready for Heaven; in fact, any man who co-operates perfectly with all the graces he receives, as Mary did, will not go to Purgatory. To urge a man to fidelity to grace, to teach him how to acquire the virtues, Dante selects events from Mary's life and shows how in all of them she is a model to be followed.

In the Gospels Mary speaks four times. The incidents associated with these four times, and with the Nativity where her silence is eloquent, are the incidents Dante uses for meditation on the seven cornices; two of them twice, with a different emphasis each time. Mary speaks to Gabriel at the time of the Annunciation, to Elizabeth when she goes to visit her, to the Child when she finds him in the temple, and to her grown Son at the marriage feast of Cana just before he enters upon his public life. It is as though Dante would urge the soul striving for perfection to learn Mary's words perfectly and make them the center of his living.

> I am the mother of fair love
> And of fear, and of knowledge
> And of holy hope.
>
> In me is all grace of the way
> and of truth.
>
> In me is all hope of life and
> of virtue.
>
> — Ecclus. 24:24-25

All Christendom is familiar with the details of the five events in the life of Mary chosen by Dante to suggest the virtues she mastered perfectly; so all that he does on each cornice is recall the incident by word or some sort of representation. On the first terrace, that of the proud, where he uses sculptured figures about eighteen feet high carved into the mountainside to give examples of humility, he presents first the Annunciation group. So realistic are the figures that Dante seems to hear Gabriel say "Hail" and Mary respond, "Behold the handmaid of the Lord." The Incarnation is the greatest rebuke to man's pride: pondering the profound humility of Christ and the humility of the young Virgin, who so simply and completely submitted her intellect and will to the mystery she could not understand, will teach humility, the basic lesson of the Christian life.

On the cornice of the envious where we meet souls who have been blind to the good of their neighbor, Dante presents the Madonna of the First Miracle to exemplify fraternal charity. The perfection of the virtue lies in awareness of the needs of one's neighbor, the forethought which will save him shame and confusion. With one line Dante brings before us the whole scene: "They have no wine." Mary at Cana was alert to the need of the young bride and groom before they were, and she did something about it.

To show Mary's meekness and gentleness, the antidote to anger, Dante chooses the incident at the temple when, after the three-day search, she finds the Child seated among the doctors. Our gall is likely to rise against those who put us to great trouble and anxiety, who make no explanation when it seems logical that they should make one. Mary's patient search, her simple question when it is ended so that her Son may have an opportunity to explain, her humble acceptance of his answer in which there is no shadow of an apology for the anguished hours he has occasioned: all these show how practiced Mary was in the humble submission of her judgment and will. The choleric man like Dante may well study the Madonna of the Finding of the Child in the Temple.

To the phlegmatic, the slothful, the person with a "don't care" philosophy, the Madonna of the Visitation presents an excellent study. Mary sets the clear pattern for virtuous action: she "rose up in haste and went into the hill country." In the whole of the *Purgatorio* Dante is concerned with the blending of action and meditation or contemplation in the Christian life. In the incident of the Visi-

tation, Mary's canticle, the *Magnificat* (Lk. 1:46–56), shows the
fruits of her contemplation of the wonder wrought within her as
well as her zeal in rising up without hesitation to visit Elizabeth
and congratulate her at a time when she might surely have held
herself excused. Mary's going to greet Elizabeth brought an extraordinary grace to the unborn John, a good she could not have contemplated. Dante would have the slothful meditate on all the
contingent goods which are never attained because of sloth.

Mary's poverty at Bethlehem is a perfect example of the virtue
of detachment and poverty of spirit. In obedience she had left
Nazareth and all that she had in readiness for the birth of her
Child. The kings who came to Bethlehem were wealthy among men
of the East. But they, too, had poverty of spirit: they were not
inordinately attached to their possessions. They gave liberally of
themselves and their wealth. Even the very poor can be avaricious
in spirit. Against the spirit of avarice in men of every station, the
spirit which more than any other Dante thinks destroys in individuals
and in society the peace which Christ was born to bring into the
world, Dante places the Madonna of the Nativity.

Here on this fifth cornice there is implicit, hidden, another
Madonna. An earthquake "such as is wont to grip one who is going
to his death" (*Purg.* XX:128–130) sends a chill through Dante.
There is a wealth of symbolism in this earthquake. Over the Crib
there was the shadow of the Cross. Even as Mary pressed her infant
to her breast she knew for what a bitter end she nourished him.
The poverty of Bethlehem's Crib and Calvary's Cross are the same.
The participation of Mary in both is what gives her, by a divine
paradox, her riches. The Madonna of the Nativity suggested on this
cornice by the singing of the *Gloria in excelsis Deo* marks her
physical maternity of the Redeemer; an earthquake like that of Good
Friday suggests her spiritual maternity of all men begun on Calvary.
The Madonna of Calvary is known as the Mater Dolorosa, the
Mother of Sorrows.

On the sixth cornice, where gluttony is being expiated, Dante
again uses Mary at the wedding feast at Cana, a favorite theme in
the Middle Ages. Here she is the Madonna of Temperance, one
who delighted in good company and who did not want the party

to be spoiled; therefore she asked for what was needed to make the feast "honorable and complete." Mary's request is for more wine. The response of her divine Son is to provide more wine — one hundred fifty-three gallons more![15] Temperance does not lie in abstinence but in the rational control of appetite.

On the last cornice, that of the lustful, Dante goes back to the Annunciation. This time, however, instead of stressing humility he stresses cleanness of heart. Mary, the Immaculate Virgin and Mother, is the supreme example of chastity. When she made the statement *I know not man* quoted here by Dante (*Purg.* XXV:128), she expressed, according to theologians, not only a fact but an intention solemnized by a vow with which her husband Joseph was in complete accord. Dante praises this case as a unique supernatural incident; but he takes care to honor also the natural inclination to chastity typified by Diana, and "wives and husbands who were chaste as the virtue and marriage vow require" (*Purg.* XXV:133–135).

The significance of the events in Mary's life upon which Dante invites those seeking perfection to meditate lies in the fact that, despite the supernatural elements involved in each of them, they can easily be transferred into the everyday life of the average man and woman. No one, Dante frequently points out, can attain to the eminent sanctity of Mary, but all are called to sanctity. Men who aspire to be with Mary in glory must follow her in the humdrum of daily living and joyously, if laboriously, climb the mountain with her virtues ever before them. Christ is the Way which Mary followed. But, as Dante and the *Speculum* point out, Mary, who is altogether human, shows weak and erring humankind the way through discipline and prayer and pain that leads to glory. In the ancient Byzantine liturgy Mary is hailed as the Heavenly Ladder whereby God came down to earth; Saint Bernard and other writers of the Western Church call her the *sinners' ladder* whose top touched the heavens and passed through them until it reached the well of living waters, a ladder which, rung by rung, men may mount to God.

There is no rose of swich vertu
As is the rose that bare Jesu.
Alleluial

— Medieval Carol

Since man's hope of salvation lies in the Incarnation, and since Mary's assent to Gabriel's message made the Incarnation possible, Dante persists in keeping before us Mary's Divine Maternity, the source of all her prerogatives and of our Redemption. It is not strange, therefore, that in the third major division of the *Purgatorio,* the Earthly Paradise, in which the regeneration of Dante takes place, we are again reminded of the Incarnation and of Mary's part in it. The purgative way began with a meditation on the Virgin of the Annunciation; it proceeded through meditations on Mary's words in some of the chief episodes in her life with her divine Son. The reinstatement of Dante in grace in the Earthly Paradise takes up that first scene of the Annunciation again and carries it forward to the scene of the Visitation and the purification of Saint John the Baptist. "Blessed art thou among the daughters of Adam," sing the writers of the Old and New Testaments who make up the pageant of the Church, words of Gabriel and Elizabeth (Lk. 1:28, 42) spoken at the time of the Incarnation, Gabriel's words being spoken just before and Elizabeth's soon after.

The flowers which crown these singers also praise Mary, the woman promised in the Garden of Eden, whose seed would crush the serpent's head. "I am the flower of the field (the Rose of Sharon) and the Lily of the Valleys," sang the inspired Solomon in the *Canticle* (2:1, 2), words which the Church has always applied to Mary. The writers are all dressed in white, emblematic of their faith in the Messias promised to Adam and Eve: the writers of the Old Testament looking *forward* to the Incarnation wear Mary's lilies symbolic of her purity and of their faith in the Redeemer to come; those of the New Testament wear roses and other red flowers symbolic of her love and their own love of the Saviour who gave his life for them. As at the beginning of the poem, Mary inaugurated the coming of Beatrice to Virgil to save Dante from the dark wood, here in the pageant, in song and symbol, she foreruns the coming of Beatrice to Dante himself to prepare him through his confession and purification to mount to the stars. Throughout the *Divine Comedy*, Mary initiates each new step toward beatitude.

The *Paradiso*, too, begins with a reminder of the Incarnation and of Mary's part in it. In the Heaven of the Moon, the first of the ten Heavens, Piccarda Donati, one of Dante's old Florentine friends who appears to him there, gives him further insight into the profound lesson of humble conformity to the divine will — which was the first meditation proposed on the first cornice of the *Purgatorio* — and as she vanishes into the higher heavens chants the *Ave Maria*. Dante has asked her whether the souls in the lowest heaven, that of the moon where he meets her as a symbol of those lowest in beatitude, yearn for a higher place and has received from her the memorable answer that the essence of blessedness is conformity to the divine will. This being true, the beginning of the Paradise — life with God — like the beginning of the way to Paradise, the first rung of the Purgatorial ladder, is in the *Fiat* of the soul, exemplified in Mary's "Behold the handmaid of the Lord." The *Ave Maria* of Piccarda is a sort of prelude to the Marian symphony of the other parts of the *Paradiso*, for in the last section Dante makes clear that Mary's splendor rises from her Divine Maternity.

Our Queen has gone before us;
she has gone before us and has been so gloriously
received that her servants may confidently cry out,
"Draw me after thee!"

— Saint Bernard

In the *Purgatorio*, Dante has walked in the way of the Virgin by faith; in the last division of the *Paradiso*, faith is rewarded by vision. He sees Mary three times in the three relationships in which she is honored. In the Stellar Heaven he sees her in relation to the Incarnate Word, the God-man, the Redeemer, the Conqueror over sin and death. "Behold the hosts of Christ's triumph," says Beatrice, "and all the fruit gathered from the circling spheres" (*Par.* XXIII: 19–21). Mary here is the most glorious fruit of Christ's Passion, one of the saints; for Mary, like the rest of the human race, was saved by the Saviour of the world. In the second vision he sees her in her relation to the angels and the other saints, the Regina Coeli, the Queen of Heaven. In the last vision, in the last canto of the poem, he sees her in relation to the Godhead, to each person of the Blessed Trinity. Through Mary the vision of the Trinity is given to Dante; through the vision of the face of Mary he is prepared for the vision of the mystery of the divine and human in Christ.

The Starry Heaven in which Dante has the first vision of Mary is a traditional symbol of the Church. In the *Divine Comedy* it is also, as we know, the counterpart and fulfillment of the Earthly Paradise, the Garden of Eden. The pageant which represents the Church there is supplanted here by a tableau of the Church Triumphant. Nowhere is Dante's dramatic imagination more evident than in this suprasensible portrayal of ineffable truths. The hour is represented at first as dawn; one wonders whether Dante has in mind Mary, the Aurora, described in such detail in the *Speculum*. In order to make the proper psychological approach to the mystery he wishes to present, he has Beatrice stand tensely expectant as a bird on a branch of a tree and Dante hold his breath in suspense as they wait for this extraordinary sunrise.

In little time, the heavens grow resplendent with the light of the Sun of justice; spread before Dante's eyes is a vast garden of flowers which are lights, and of lights which are flowers like jewels — all of these lights kindled by the Sun which pours its noonday radiance upon them. Unspeakable joy brightens the face of Beatrice who, if she were not now Dante's guide, would participate in this triumph. All the colors of the jeweled emblems in the circling spheres through which Beatrice has led Dante are gathered here in this resplendent tableau, a horizontal rose window spread out frameless like a multicolored Oriental rug. This is the Garden of the New Eden into which the Christian life blossoms to show the rich variety in the individual lives of the members which make up the Mystical Body of Christ,[16] each manifesting in its own way the one spirit of Jesus their Head.

We must remind ourselves here of the place the Stellar Heaven holds in Dante's system of the universe. All power and virtue in the universe flow from the Empyrean Heaven, the mind of God, down through the ninth heaven ruled by the Seraphim, into this Starry Heaven. It is the function of the Cherubim who move this heaven to distribute this virtue and power through the seven lower heavens and thence into our world, each man receiving the special endowment proper to the star under which he is born so that there will be the diversity of gifts and abilities needed in human society. Up from these seven lower spheres have come the souls Dante has seen in them to take their places here in this triumphal tableau. Ingathered are all the human hierarchies named in the Litany of Saints: patriarchs, levites and prophets; martyrs, penitents, and confessors; monks, hermits, bishops; holy matrons of the Old Law and virgins, wives and widows of the New Dispensation; in fact, all the holy ones of all times and all places triumphing here with Christ by whom they were saved, the rays of whose noonday light blinds the eyes of Dante.[17]

Soon, however, the Sun moves up into the farther heavens (the ascension of Christ, Acts 1:9) and Dante's eyes can see more clearly the greatest flame-flower among the remaining lights, "a living star," a beautiful "sapphire" which makes the whole heaven blue.[18] The shifting colors of the tableau — from dawn to the brilliance of high noon and now to this blue after the disappearance of the sun — give lighting effects upon the tableau which excel all devices of the modern theater. In this change of light we have Dante's dramatic exposition of the eternal day. The sun in disappearing has risen; the blue — though it suggests the lovely blue of gloaming — is a bright blue, a live daytime blue which sharpens the integrity of all the other colors, the blue of thirteenth-century stained glass in afternoon light. The sapphire star — though it is the evening star — shines with a light bright enough to illumine the whole garden of this New Eden.

The tableau breaks into action when Gabriel descends circling and crowns the star, singing of the Incarnation. While he sings, Mary the crowned light follows the Sun which has risen to the Empyrean, where, Dante says, she will make the highest heaven more beautiful by entering it. As she moves up, all the other lights sound her name, and, in a striking image of mother and child, reach up to her, stretching out their arms to her as infants who have nursed reach out to their mothers. Up beyond Dante's sight she passes into the Primum Mobile, the ninth heaven, which like a royal mantle folds in the eight circling spheres below it (*Par.* XXIII:112) — still reaching up to her the saints with unforgettable sweetness sing *Regina Coeli* (*Queen of Heaven*), which in the time of Dante was the Easter Vesper antiphon, *de sancta Maria*.

This episode of the Starry Heaven, in a microcosm in dramatic form, portrays most of Dante's fundamental beliefs about Mary. Her Divine Maternity is suggested by Gabriel's song; her spiritual maternity as the new Eve in this New Eden by the reaching out of the whole body of the blessed as infants to a mother; her Assumption and Coronation by her rising crowned into the Empyrean and by the words of the *Regina Coeli*. That she was saved by the Redeemer of the world is attested by her place as one of the saints in the triumph of her Son; that she is the *felix coeli porta* (happy portal — or gate — of heaven) of the medieval processional hymn *Ave Maris Stella* and of the *Alma Redemptoris Mater*, the Marian antiphon of Advent and the Christmas season, is suggested by the rising of the star — *Miriam*, the Hebrew form of Mary's name being thought in Dante's time to mean *star of the sea*. There are other implications, too, in this scene which strictly speaking are not Marian and can better be discussed elsewhere.

> *Let us rejoice in the Lord, keeping holiday in honor of the blessed Virgin Mary at whose festival . . . the angels rejoice and give praise to the Son of God.*
>
> — Introit of the Mass for several feasts of the Virgin, including that of the Assumption

Of Mary enthroned in the white rose of Paradise, we have had a glimpse in the preceding chapter where we watched the angels in revel about her. The rose is first made visible to Dante by a ray of God from the outer rim of the Primum Mobile (*Par.* XXX:107); as he moves into the Empyrean he sees reflected in the sea of light which forms its center (XXX:109–114)

> As in a mirror, on more than a thousand tiers
> All who have returned on high.

Beatrice, who has led him through all the spheres of the illuminative way, now leads him into the center of this sea of light, this *lumen gloriae* or light of glory (124–132); and as the rose takes form before his eyes, he looks upon the height and vastness of the City of God flowering under "the three-fold Light which in a single star" shines upon it. To their places in this rose have come all whom he saw in the Stellar Heaven, all the holy people of God enumerated in the hierarchies of the Litany of Saints. In this new tableau of the Empyrean, which like that in the Stellar Heaven breaks very soon into active drama, are the two courts, those of angels and of saints; enthroned above them is Mary, whom her Litany calls Queen of angels, Queen of prophets, Queen of apostles, Queen of confessors, of martyrs, of virgins, of all saints. Turning to ask Beatrice a question, Dante is surprised to find that she is replaced by one who had "grown beautiful through Mary as the morning star does through the sun" (XXXII:106–108) and who identifies himself to Dante as "the faithful Bernard of the Queen of Heaven" (XXXI:103–105). He will be Dante's guide on the unitive way.[19]

Dante's image of the White Rose as the Church Triumphant is one of the most significant and most pregnant with meaning in all literature. His choice of a rose as the symbol was not unique; what is unique is the position of the rose, its color, its magnitude, and the richness of its symbolic meaning. Throughout the Christian centuries Mary had been called the *mystical rose*; artists and architects and writers had used the symbol in fresco, mosaic, stained glass, and the spoken and written word. In the rose windows and the half domes of the cathedrals and other great churches she appears frequently as Queen of the Mystical Body of Christ. Sometimes Christ appears in the center as in the half dome of Monreale; sometimes she is in the center as in the rose of France window at Chartres.

All of these blaze with color like the triumph in the garden in the Stellar Heaven.

In a very real sense, because of her Divine Maternity ("the rose in which the Word Divine made itself flesh," *Par.* XXIII:73), the image of Mary as the *mystical rose* is related to her as Queen of the Church — militant, suffering, triumphant; that is, on Earth, in Purgatory, in Heaven — because in the minds of the theologians beginning with Saint Paul (Gal. 3:28; Eph. 2:14–17; 1 Cor. 1:13, 1 Cor. 12) the Church is the unity of redeemed humanity, a unity made possible by the Incarnation, mankind as a whole, the many as one, the Mystical Body of Christ, the Communion of Saints.[20] Because of her spiritual maternity Mary has brought forth the Mystical Body of Christ as well as the physical body; she has nursed it with the milk of her virtues. Dante, therefore, like other artists of his era presents her flower as the symbol of the Church in triumph. What Dante has done with the image in relation to the angels, to the saints, to Mary, to the Trinity shows his originality and his power in the use of symbols.

The color of the rose is important for many reasons. The most obvious reason for its whiteness would be that white suggests purity: Mary's virginal purity — not only at the time of the Incarnation but throughout her life — and the purity demanded of all the saints. White is the color used by medieval artists in all representations of Mary's Assumption. White, as we have seen repeatedly in the *Divine Comedy*, is the symbolic color of faith. The rose is divided on the basis of faith, faith of Old Testament and New Testament saints. Mary occupies the central point in the perimeter of the rose — Mary at the top and Saint John the Baptist at the bottom. Born under the Old Law, they are key persons in the New Dispensation, both tied up significantly with the Incarnation, which is the central point in time; both related to the work of Redemption — Mary as the Mother of the Redeemer and Coredemptrix, and John as the precursor whose penance and preaching prepared the way of the Lord. All those ranged in semicircles on the left of Mary and of John were saved by faith in the Redeemer to come; those in semicircles at the right, by following his Gospel. In various dramatic ways Dante, all through the *Divine Comedy*, has emphasized the difference between the Old and New Testaments. There remain at least two other reasons for Dante's use of white, both of which are clarified in the *Banquet* (IV, xxii, 8). White, Dante says, symbolizes contemplation; contemplation is the "work" of the Church Triumphant. White is more full of light than any other color. This perhaps is the most significant reason of all.

All through the *Divine Comedy* there is evidence of Dante's knowledge of the physics of light. Everywhere there is evidence, too, of his passion for unity. These combine in his major reason for using white for the color of the rose. In the Stellar Heaven where Mary is likened to a rose and the apostles to lilies, she is probably represented as a red rose, the red of the rose of Sharon of the Earthly Paradise. In the first portrayal of the Church Triumphant, color and variety are emphasized to portray the *individuality* among the members of the Church. In the Empyrean, Dante wishes to emphasize the *unity* of the Church and blends the infinite variety of colors he has shown us in the Stellar Heaven into the radiant white of the rose; for white is the sum of all colors as the Truth found in the Empyrean is the sum of all knowledge and the Love is the sum of all virtues and the Church is the unity of all saints. The unity among angels and men, their oneness in contemplating the Oneness of the Triune God shining upon them in one ray: all these thoughts and more must have been in Dante's mind in his use of white in the Rose of the Paradise.

> *O Messias, our God . . . Thou who hast glorified*
> *the memory of the Assumption of thy mother,*
> *the Immaculate Virgin, accept the perfume*
> *of our incense . . . Grant that this may be*
> *in honor of thy Mother, Queen of Angels*
> *and* Empress *of Saints.*
>
> — Incensation prayer for the Assumption
> in the ancient Antioch liturgy

Throughout the poem Dante has shown Mary's regal power. He has portrayed her as Queen of Hell, of Purgatory, of Earth, and of

Heaven: she is Queen of angels and men wherever they are; therefore she is Queen of the Universe. At the end of the *Divine Comedy,* he makes Bernard call her *Empress.* Bernard has pointed out and named for Dante many saints; now he names "the *patricians*" (definitely Roman) "of this most just and devout empire": Eve at Mary's feet, Adam at her left hand and Peter at her right, Saint John the Evangelist at Peter's right, Moses, Saint Anne, and Saint Lucy. It is not the importance of the seven names — though they are important — that concerns us here, but that they form a noble symbolic group singled out as important to the Empress.

Back in the Earthly Paradise when Beatrice was guarding the chariot of the Church after the procession had returned to the heavens, she said to Dante, prior to the presentation of the tableaux which portray the history of the Church and the empire (*Purg.* XXXII:100–106):

> You will be for a while a forest dweller [on earth]
> And then you will be with me forever a citizen
> of that Rome in which Christ is a Roman.
>
> Therefore for the good of the badly living world
> keep your eyes on the chariot, and be careful
> that you write down what you see after you return.

When in the *Paradiso* she has taken him into the heart of the white rose and shown him the height and vastness of the City of God, she identifies for him one seat only, a seat with a crown above it, the seat reserved for Henry VII in whom Dante had placed his hope for the restoration of the Empire. Her last words, before she takes her place on the throne in the rose to which her merit raises her, are words of reproach for Pope Clement V, who uses his papal office to work against Henry. Surely the city which Beatrice shows Dante is the City of God of Saint Augustine; surely it is the Heavenly Jerusalem of the Church Fathers and theologians. But it is also Rome, the seat of the Church and Empire, Rome eternal in which men are forever citizens, Rome where "Christ is a Roman" and Mary his Mother is Empress.

In the *Banquet,* Book IV, Chapters iv, v, and vi, Dante has developed the idea that the Roman Empire had its especial birth and its especial growth from God and that the words of Virgil in the *Aeneid* (Book VI, 11:795–797): "To them (that is, to the Romans) I have set no limit of things nor of time; to them have I given an empire without end" are inspired words. He develops the thought that the divine election of the Roman Empire is made "very evident by the birth of the holy city (Rome), which was contemporaneous with that of the root from which sprang the race of Mary" — Jesse, from which root Mary sprang, being the father of David who was born at the same time that Rome was born. In other words, Aeneas came from Troy into Italy at the same time that David was born in Judea. Christ was born under Roman law and was crucified under Roman law: in both he was obedient to political decrees of Roman government. For these reasons Dante sees in Rome the seat of Church and State.[21]

Everywhere in the *Divine Comedy*, as well as in his other writings, Dante insists that man must work out his salvation in the two organizations ordained by God for his temporal and eternal welfare. Since earthly Rome was chosen by God as the seat of government of Church and State on earth, he would place as Empress over both, in the Rome of the Paradise, the woman whom John had seen in his vision before he saw the dragon and all the symbols of evil in Church and State which Dante uses in the pageant in the Earthly Paradise; the *woman clothed with the sun and crowned with twelve stars,* who brought forth the Saviour, the King of kings, the woman who in all Christian literature is symbolic of the Church. He trusts that she who had saved him in the dark wood by setting in motion all those persons necessary for his salvation will by her wisdom and power bring his lost world to the knowledge and love of justice, and therefore to peace. Like the builders of Chartres, who had enthroned Mary at the portal of the cathedral, he places her here at the portal of the last canto before he enters it for the vision of God.

As the knight or the peasant or the king or the courtier at Chartres or Paris paused before he mounted the steps of the cathedral to enter the doorway and gazed up at the face of the Queen Mother to murmur a prayer, so does Bernard bid Dante pause here to look upon her face. This is Dante's third vision of Mary, this close-up of her face. All the old legends assume that the resemblance between the Son and the Mother must have been perfect because Christ took all of his humanity from Mary. It is but one step from the vision of the Virgin to the vision of her Son, though the distance between them is immeasurable. That one step is taken by prayer to her, "lest in moving our wings, thinking to advance, we fall backward" (Par. XXXII:145–147).

Beatrice has led Dante to Bernard so that Bernard may lead him to Mary. Now with his eyes fixed on the Virgin's face, Bernard, speaking for Dante, petitions her to bring to a perfect close the long journey she initiated in the dark wood. As Bernard begins his prayer, Beatrice and the whole blessed court clasp their hands to pray with him, and the attentive eyes of Mary shine down upon their unanimity of desire!

> Virgin mother, daughter of thy son,
> humbled and exalted more than any creature,
> goal established by Eternal Counsel,
>
> thou art the one by whom human nature
> was so ennobled that its Maker
> did not disdain to become its creature.
>
> Within thy womb was rekindled the love
> through whose warmth this flower
> has blossomed in eternal peace.
>
> Here thou art for us a noonday torch
> of charity, and down below, among mortals
> a living fount of hope.
>
> My Lady, thou art so great and so triumphant
> that whoever wants and does not turn to thee
> would have his desire fly without wings.
>
> Thy benignity succors not only those
> Who ask, but many times
> freely anticipates the request.
>
> In thee is mercy, in thee pity,
> in thee magnificence; in thee whatever goodness
> can be found in creatures is resumed.
>
> Now, this man who from the deep well
> of the universe up to here
> has seen the spiritual lives, one after another,

> begs thee of thy grace for strength,
> so that he may lift his eyes
> still higher toward the ultimate salvation.
>
> And I who never for my own sight long more
> than I do for his, offer thee all my prayers,
> and may they not be insufficient,
>
> in order that thou, through thine, mayest dispel
> every cloud of his mortality, so that
> the Supreme Pleasure may reveal itself to him.
>
> I pray thee further, O Queen! thou who canst do
> what thou wilt, that thou keepest
> his affection sound after so great a vision.
>
> May thy protection overcome his human impulses.
> Behold Beatrice with so many of the blessed
> clasping their hands to aid my prayer.

The prayer falls into two parts: the apotheosis of the Virgin and the prayer for Dante. The apotheosis is in words what the dramatic scenes of the Starry Heaven and the Empyrean have been in tableaux, a summary of the Mariology of the Christian centuries. To this there is added the burning love of Mary's Bernard — and of the heart of Dante. In the beauty of the Italian it pulsates with emotion, so perfect a wedding of thought and exalted mood with sound and rhythm that the lines rank with the greatest in the literature of the world. Exposition there is. It is expressed in the extraordinary paradoxes of the first tercet: Virgin Mother, daughter of thy Son, humbled and exalted; in the lucid statement in the second, of Mary's relationship to the Trinity: that she had so exalted human nature that the Creator did not disdain to make himself its creature, that the Holy Spirit made her his spouse; in the third, of her relationship to angels and men — in Heaven the torch enkindling charity; on earth the fount of hope, the mediatrix, the advocate who helps not only those who ask as Bernard asks now, but those who have not asked as Dante had not asked when he was lost in the dark wood, the mother of pity and mercy, the epitome of all the goodness and magnificence which can be found in any creature. The second part is the prayer for Dante, not only that he may be granted the Beatific Vision but that ever after he may overcome all merely human impulses and be faithful to the grace vouchsafed.

Saint Bernard has said repeatedly that without doubt the Son will hear his Mother and the Father will hear the Son. In another of those breathless moments like that in the Starry Heaven before the light breaks over the garden of the blessed, we see all Heaven stop, awaiting the answer to Bernard's prayer. Mary shows how gratefully devout prayers are heard. She turns to the Eternal Light; and in a moment, Dante, finding that his sight has grown pure because Mary has won the grace for him, can penetrate the Light also. He penetrates into the divine life of the Triune God, where, as a final revelation, he beholds the Son of God and Son of Mary, the mystery of the Incarnation.

All of the beautiful cathedral churches of Europe were, of course, erected in honor of the Blessed Trinity. The object was to provide a fitting place — as nearly fitting as man could make it — for the celebration of the Divine Mysteries, the great Eucharistic renewal of the Sacrifice of Calvary, the Mass. Most of them were named for Mary by men of faith, who believed in Mary as the first tabernacle of the living God, Coredemptrix on Calvary, Mediatrix with her Son the great Mediator, spiritual Mother of all mankind, and Queen of the universe. In the symbolism of stone and jeweled windows they professed these beliefs. Hers is the figure carved over the portal, for she is the Gate of Heaven; hers are the glorious rose windows and windows of the nave lighting the way to the altar; hers is the resplendent Lady chapel behind the high altar where she is enthroned. Dante has said in words what his near contemporaries have said in glass and stone and precious metal. His words in her honor will endure beyond their craftsmanship; for men can carry words into the presence chamber of the Trinity, since the mind of man which retains them is immortal.

NOTES

1. For a discussion of the progress of Mariology in the Western Church, see Walter J. Burghardt, S.J., "Mary in Western Patristic Thought," in *Mariology*, ed. Juniper P. Carol (Milwaukee, 1954), I, pp. 109–155, and George W.

Shea, "Outline History of Mariology in the Middle Ages and Modern Times," *ibid.*, pp. 281–315.

2. Saint Bonaventure, *The Mirror of the Blessed Virgin Mary* (*Speculum Beatae Mariae Virginis*), trans. Sr. Mary Emmanuel, O.S.B. (Saint Louis, 1932). The *Speculum* or *The Mirror of the Blessed Virgin Mary* is now believed by some scholars to have been written by Conrad of Saxony. Since Dante believed it to be the work of Saint Bonaventure, whom he esteemed as a theologian, citations in this chapter and elsewhere are attributed to Saint Bonaventure.

3. Origen in the third century in his Preface to his Commentary on Saint John suggested this explanation and it has been accepted, especially from the twelfth century on, as the common teaching of theologians. For a discussion of the precise event which constituted Mary as the Mother of mankind, see R. Garrigou-Lagrange, O.P., *The Mother of the Saviour*, trans. Bernard J. Kelly, C.S.Sp. (Saint Louis, 1948), p. 165.

4. Sanctus Bernardus, *Sermones*, "Sermo in Nativitate B. Mariae Virginis," Migne, *P.L.*, 183, col. 441-B.

    The following fuller quotation has much bearing on Dante's thought in the *Divine Comedy* since it deals with Christ as the Mediator as well as with Mary the Mediatrix and clarifies Bernard's teaching in this matter:

    "Therefore, with the inmost part of our hearts, with all our devotion, with all our vows and affections, let us honor Mary because it is his will that we have all through Mary. I say it is his will, but it is for our benefit. . . .

    "(If) you fear to go to the Father, are afraid to be heard alone, take refuge in the prophecies; he has given you Jesus as a Mediator. What will such a Son not obtain from such a Father? Certainly he will be heard because of love, for the Father loves the Son. But perhaps you fear to go to the Son, though he is your brother and your flesh, tried in all things except sin so that he will be merciful. Mary gave him to you as a brother. Perhaps, however, in him also you fear the Divine Majesty because although he was made man, nevertheless he remained God.

    "Do you wish to have an advocate before him? Run to Mary. For there is pure humanity in Mary, not only pure from every contamination, but also pure in the singularity of her nature. Certainly the Father will hear the Son, and the Son will hear the Mother. My Sons, this is the ladder of sinners; this is my greatest hope; this is the whole reason of my hope. Is the Son able either to refuse or to be refused, not to hear or not to be heard? Indeed neither is possible. 'You have found,' said the angel, 'grace before God.' She always finds this grace, and it is grace alone of which we are in need. The prudent Virgin sought not wisdom as Solomon, not riches, not honors, not power, but grace. For by grace alone we are saved. What else do we desire, brothers? Let us seek grace and seek it through Mary, because what she seeks she finds; she cannot fail."

5. Saint Bonaventure, *op. cit.*, p. 26.

6. Quoted in Saint Bonaventure, *op. cit.*, p. 125.

7. For an interesting discussion of Mary as Queen and Empress in the work of architects and craftsmen, who put into stone and glass and metal the ideals of the generality of the people of the Middle Ages, see Henry Adams, *Mont-Saint-Michel and Chartres* (Boston, 1933), pp. 71–78, and Chaps. VI and X. See also Allan Temko, *Notre Dame of Paris* (New York, 1955), Chap. XIII.

8. Adapted from William G. Most, "Universal Queen," *Queen of All Hearts*, November-December, 1954, Vol. V, No. 4, pp. 3–10.

9. Saint Bonaventure, *op. cit.*, pp. 26, 27.

10. Johannes Herolt, *Miracles of the Blessed Virgin Mary*, trans. C. C. Swinton Bland (London, 1928), a volume in the Broadway Medieval Library Series, ed. G. G. Coulton and Eileen Power. The following excerpt from the introduction by Eileen Power, p. XXXV, makes an excellent interpretative comment on the miracles:

> "The instinct of the people was a just one. If behind all the superficiality and irresponsibility of the miracles we look closely at the Virgin of the Middle Ages, we shall perceive that she does represent the deepest and most essential side of the Christian religion, the insistence on faith, the power of love to blot away sin, above all the infinite mercy. . . . One of the most touching of the miracles shows her moving the Christ Child about in her arms, to make him turn his averted face towards her so that she may the better plead with him. . . . It is for this quality and because she mirrors for us the real religion of the people in the Middle Ages that the Virgin of the miracles deserves to be studied.

For a discussion of the miracles, see also Adams, *op. cit.*, Chapter XIII, "Les Miracles de Notre Dame," pp. 249–282.

11. Adams, *op. cit.*, p. 73.
12. Saint Bonaventure, *op. cit.*, p. 26.
13. The fact that Dante follows the order of the seven capital sins as given in the *Speculum* is interesting. Lists of capital sins are found as early as the fifth century; there is no evidence that the Church ever formally adopted any specific order of the capital sins or, for that matter, that it has ever settled upon seven as the exact number. Some of the early lists have eight sins, dividing pride into vainglory and pride. Down the centuries, however, though there is disagreement in the order of the sins, pride is always presented as the leader and root of them all. Usually where there is a difference of opinion among theologians, Dante follows the lead of Saint Thomas; this being one of the rare instances in which he deviates. The difference lies in the relative positions of sloth and avarice. The order with Dante, as with other theologians, is not negligible because it involves a judgment as to the relative gravity of the sins. The order of the *Speculum* and of the *Divina Comody* is as follows: pride, envy, anger, sloth, avarice, gluttony, lust. It must be observed that the same order — in reverse — is followed by Dante in the *Inferno*, insofar as the capital sins are named there.
14. Saint Bonaventure, *op. cit.*, p. 149.
15. Dom Bernard Orchard, *et al.*, ed. *A Catholic Commentary on Holy Scripture* (New York, 1954), see note 786c, p. 984.
16. Saint Paul, 1 Cor. 12. This chapter is the chief basis for the term *the Mystical Body of Christ* in common use in theological literature. It and other passages in the epistles of Saint Paul form the Scriptural foundation for several images in the *Paradiso*, notable among them images in Cantos XIV, XXIII — discussed at this point — and that of the mystic rose, Cantos XXX–XXXIII. The doctrine of the Mystical Body is discussed more fully in subsequent chapters.
17. Dante further arranges these human hierarchies, grouping them, in Canto XXIV:10–21. For a discussion of this matter see John S. Carroll, *In Patria* (London, 1911), p. 380.
18. In the art and symbolism of the Middle Ages the color blue signified wisdom. The wings of the Cherubim were, therefore, painted blue. Here the use of blue would seem to suggest the knowledge of God sent forth from the Mother of Divine Wisdom. For *blue* in stained glass see Adams, *op. cit.*, Chapter VIII. In his "The Blessed Virgin Compared to the Air We Breathe" Gerard Manley Hopkins makes use of the symbolic blue.

19. The three divisions of the road to God: the purgative, illuminative, and unitive are discussed in detail in Chapter IX.

20. For a readable comprehensive discussion of the "Communion of Saints" see Karl Adam, *The Spirit of Catholicism,* trans. Dom Justin McCann, O.S.B., rev. ed. (New York, 1944), Chaps. VII, VIII. The book is now available in Image Books, a paperback edition. Other chapters will throw light on some of the matters which are part of Dante's background of faith.

21. *Mon.* II, xi. Throughout the *Monarchy* Dante discusses his reasons for believing that Rome was elected by God as the seat of both Church and State and that the Roman Empire should continue as the political organ of government.

CHAPTER VII

DANTE AND THE DEITY

Dante, the theologian, skilled in every branch of
knowledge.

— Giovanni del Virgilio (Epitaph)

Uni trinoque Domino,
Sit sempiterna gloria:
Qui vitam sine termino
Nobis donet in patria.

(Eternal glory be to the Triune God, who giveth
us life without end in our fatherland.)

— Saint Thomas Aquinas
from *Verbum supernum*

ante's was a God-centered world. The essential and enduring characteristic of medieval thinking, as Henry
Adams saw it, and as he presented it in *Mont-Saint-
Michel and Chartres*,[1] is that its whole foundation
was God and God's active presence in the whole universe and especially in his Church. The medieval man pondered this divine activity,
not only within the vast creation of spirit and matter in time and
space but also within the Trinity itself. He kept in the forefront of
his mind the two basic tenets of his faith, the Trinity and the Incarnation and Redemption. He was firmly convinced that man in
his pride had been disobedient and had been driven from the
Garden of Eden and that the Saviour, promised on the day of the
fall, came in God's good time, when the Second Person of the Trinity
became man and satisfied divine justice by his death on the
cross. In his daily life medieval man professed his belief in the

Trinity and the Redemption, by beginning and closing all his activities by making the Sign of the Cross on his person, saying at the same time, "In the name of the Father and of the Son and of the Holy Ghost"; in all that he made or did he used the cross and the principle of three in one.

Why the medieval cathedrals were cruciform, a great nave and two great transepts; why they had three spires and three portals and three aisles; why even in minor details the triform and the cross were structural principles is understandable. That the thought of the greatest poet of the Middle Ages should flow in these channels is also understandable. As one might expect, the writings of Dante are based on this concept of the Triune God and the Christ of the Incarnation and Redemption.

The whole plan of the *Divine Comedy* is Trinitarian; it is theocentric and Christo-conscious. Indeed, in all of Dante's major works — perhaps it is accurate to say in all his works, even his minor lyrics and certainly in his letters — Dante is conscious of what transcends time and space, even while he deals with things in terms of time and space. Because his belief in God and eternity underlies all his thinking, he sees all created things in relation to the Trinity in the order which he believes the Trinity gave them when Infinite Power, Wisdom, and Love willed them into being. It is important, therefore, for the reader of Dante to be reminded of his concept of the Deity and his belief in the underlying unity of the vast creation. It is even more important for him to have a clear idea of Dante's Christology, which is the subject of the following chapter.

In the *Divine Comedy*, Dante has undertaken the tremendous task of glorifying these mysteries. To grasp the theological concepts which run through the whole poem, glinting like crystal in many scattered lines and shining brilliantly in some of the longer discourses, is not easy. Dante himself admits the difficulty of catching the concepts in words (*Inf.* XXXIV:24; *Par.* I:5, 6; XXXIII:55, 56, 106–108, 121–123); in fact, at one point (*Par.* II:1–6), he suggests that those who are in a little boat return to shore and do not try to follow him into the deep sea of theological thought. Perhaps he has reference to those readers who are loath to wrestle with profound truths, those Christians of his and every age who say that they will take the word of Scripture and/or the Church, and who are only irritated by rational approaches to mysteries which, they say, lie beyond reason anyway. Or Dante may mean those others who do not have sufficient humility to admit the existence of anything which reason cannot grasp in its entirety. To those who are eager for truth, that "bread of angels on which we feed below without being sated," he addresses himself.

In the *New Life* (XLIII) Dante says that he had a wonderful vision; later in the *Divine Comedy,* which he wrote as a result of the vision, he says (*Par.* 1:4–6) that he has seen God, who dwells in light inaccessible. In all probability he uses the word *see* in the sense in which we use it when we have grasped an idea: he has seen God by some intellectual flash, some flash of grace vouchsafed in meditation or contemplation. Whatever his experience was, he, like Saint Thomas, who in the field of dogmatic theology is his master, concerned himself ever after in answering the question, What is God? Thomas as a five-year-old child had put the question to his teacher; Thomas the intellectual giant had attempted to answer it in the *Summa.* Another intellectual giant, who was a theologian as well as a poet, pays tribute to Thomas by weaving through the whole *Commedia* the answers Thomas gave to the question. So true is this that any statement that Dante makes about the nature of God can be matched by a statement made by Saint Thomas.[2]

Dante, like Saint Thomas, believed in a reasoned approach to all questions. He goes as far as he can with reason, though he recognizes that thirst for the knowledge of God may be the source of problems which reason cannot solve and which may, therefore, give rise to difficulties. When they arise, he tries to solve them; failing, he humbly submits his intellect to the answers of revelation. He studied doctrine as God revealed it to get more light on the sure ground of revealed truth. He realized, as Saint Thomas did, that finite man by his own power cannot compass infinity; but he realized, too, that the mind can never be satisfied until it is illumined by the truth outside of which there is no further truth (*Par.* IV: 124–138). He taught that one can approach God by reason and by reason prove his existence and discover some of his attributes. He taught that to learn of the intimate life of God one must have recourse to revelation, which means knowing God by faith. He knew, however, as did Saint Thomas, that man cannot see God in himself except by vision, that is, by God's own light. Because of his belief that the "veils of ignorance" can be removed in these three ways, Dante has three guides in the *Divine Comedy*: Virgil, *reason*, directs man to Beatrice, *faith*; Beatrice, *revelation, faith,* directs him to Bernard, *vision, contemplation, sight,* who leads him to God.

> O triune Deity,
> we beseech thee that thou visit us
> as we adore thee;
> lead us by thy ways
> whither we direct our steps
> to the light wherein thou dost dwell.
>
> — Saint Thomas Aquinas
> "Sacris Solemniis"

When Saint Peter is examining Dante on faith, he asks him at the close of the questioning for a summary of his belief and the bases for it. Dante's Credo falls into two parts: his belief in God, "one God" and the basis for that belief; his belief in "three eternal Persons" and his foundation for that belief. Like Saint Paul (Rom. 1:20) and Saint Thomas (*Summa* I, q. 2, a. 3) Dante asserts (*Par.* XXIV:130–134) that man can, through his own effort, by the natural light of reason, ascend through creatures to a knowledge of God:

> I believe in one God
> alone and eternal who, not moved,
> moves all the heavens with love and with desire;
> and for such belief I have . . . proofs
> physical and metaphysical.

He goes on to say that there are proofs also in Sacred Scripture, both Testaments; but the important point here is that by observation of the physical universe and by philosophical reasoning, man can prove the existence of one God who is eternal. The physical and metaphysical proofs to which he refers doubtless go back to the *Physics* and *Metaphysics* of Aristotle and to the five famous proofs given in the *Summa* (I, q. 2, a. 3).[3]

With Saint Thomas, Dante believes in solid learning, an endeavor to penetrate the universe with the study of science (physics) through the data received through the senses; he believes that man must be proficient in metaphysics, the science of the first principles of all existence, before he can come to a knowledge of the nature of things through the closely knit reasoning of philosophy. But reason, though it can prove the existence of God, is inadequate: there are great horizons of truth which lie beyond the horizon of intellect (*Purg.* III:33–45); nevertheless, the study of philosophy (*Banq.* III, xiv, 5) should and does lead a man to faith. It brings man to the realization that there is such a thing as mystery, before which he needs intellectual humility. There is no quarrel between faith and reason: a man should use reason as far as it can take him. Where reason stops, faith begins.

Dante recognizes a problem here for the man gifted with superior intelligence. The problem is that of submitting one's mind to being perfected by God through revelation, a problem that in all probability he himself faced. He may even have succumbed to the temptation of following his own way of thinking when "the right way was lost" and he found himself in "the dark wood." The sin for which Beatrice (Divine Wisdom, Revelation) upbraids him in the Earthly Paradise may be pride of intellect, as many commentators think. At any rate, in the *Divine Comedy* in the eighth circle of Hell, where sins of the intellect are punished (*Inf.* XXVI:19–22), Dante represents himself as putting a check upon his intellect. He has come upon Ulysses, the mastermind among Homeric heroes, wrapped within the tongue of flame which represents the false light of his own intellect, the abuse of intelligence in giving evil counsel, and he recognizes within himself the danger to which Ulysses has succumbed:

> Then sorrowed I, and sorrow now again,
>   When I direct my mind to what I saw,
>   And curb my genius more than I am wont.
> That it may run not unless virtue guide it.

The keenest intellect, even more than the dullest, needs intellectual humility. Pasteur, who was a man of deep religious faith, was once asked by a skeptic why he held to the doctrines he had believed in his childhood — those of a Breton peasant. He answered that the more he probed the truths of physical science, the deeper became his faith in the Lord of the universe. "If God gives me more years for research and study," he said, "I shall soon have the faith of a Breton peasant woman." Pressed for his meaning he replied, "When they go to church to pray for rain, they carry their umbrellas." Philosophy, says Dante, can lead not only to faith in Eternal Power and the Prime Intelligence, the First Cause, the First Mover, it can lead to love (Par. XXVI:25) of the "Supreme Goodness," the "First Lover," "Infinite Worth," the "Eternal Pleasure."

In the second part of his Credo, Dante professes his belief in the Trinity, a belief which can be founded only on Divine Revelation (Summa I, q. 32, a. 1). Though man can prove the existence of God by reason, he arrives at his knowledge of the intimate life of God by Divine Revelation, through Sacred Scripture. In all of his works, Dante reveals his deep knowledge of and reverence for Sacred Scripture, "that truth . . . which rains down here through Moses, the prophets, the Psalms, the Gospels and through you (the apostles) who wrote after the ardent spirit made you holy" — he is speaking to Saint Peter (Par. XXIV:134–138); "the abundant rain of the Holy Spirit which is diffused over the old and new parchments" (Par. XXIV:91–96). In the Monarchy (III, iv) he expresses succinctly his reason for this reverence:

> For although those who write down the divine word are many, they all do so at the dictation of the one God, who has condescended to display his good pleasure towards us by employing the pens of many people.[4]

To Sacred Scripture as the work of God himself, Dante has submitted his intellect and his will.

Faith in God is a mysterious reciprocal bond between God and the human soul, which requires the direct participation of the human will. This point is clarified throughout the whole of Hebrews 11 the first verse of which Dante quotes as his definition of fai

(*Par.* XXIV:64–67): *Faith is the substance of things hoped for, the evidence of things that appear not.* Understanding of doctrine need not include an *acceptance* of the doctrine. Dante studied doctrine as God revealed it to get more light; but, as he says explicitly in many places in the *Divine Comedy* and implicitly in hundreds of others by his quotations and his references to Scriptural passages, the fact that he is dealing with revealed truth is sufficient reason for his wholehearted acceptance. He says (*Par.* XXV:83–90) that the New and Old Testaments set down the goal of our souls and point it out to us; that man has Scripture and the shepherd of the Church to guide him (*Par.* V:76–78), that when Scripture proclaims a truth there is no questioning it (*Par.* XIX:83–85), that every Scripture leads to that ultimate Good which contents the heavenly court, that is, all the angels and saints (*Par.* XXVI:16). The cantos of the *Divine Comedy* rise in a crescendo of faith to that heavenly court, where in that gratuitous light which the Supreme Good gives him (*Par.* XIV:47–49; *Summa* I, q. 12, a. 5) Dante enjoys the vision of God.[5]

> *I believe in three eternal Persons,*
>   *and these I believe one Essence, so unified*
>   *and threefold that they agree with both* are *and* is.
>
> *On the profound, divine state of being*
>   *of which I speak now, the evangelical doctrine*
>   *many times puts the seal.*
>
> *This is the source, this is the spark*
>   *which afterward grows into a living flame*
>   *and shines within me like a star in heaven.*
>   — *Paradiso* XXIV:139–147

As the first tenet of Dante's Creed was concerned with his belief in God, one eternal God, the second is a profession of faith in the Trinity, three Persons in one God, a profession which Dante makes repeatedly throughout the *Divine Comedy*. Although he realizes that anyone who hopes that reason can penetrate the profound mystery of one substance in three Persons is mad (*Purg.* III: 34–36), he brings into the narrative from time to time some aspect of Trinitarian doctrine: the relations of the Persons to each other, known as the procession of Persons; the operations of the Trinity upon the created universe; the appropriation of certain works to each person.

In the fourth heaven, that of the Sun, where Dante meets the theologians (*Par.* X:1–3) he states with great care the doctrine of the procession or origin of Persons, avoiding the teaching of the Greek theologians which led to the great schism of the eleventh century. The quarrel centered on what was known as the *filioque* doctrine, the Greeks maintaining that the Son and the Holy Spirit both proceeded from the Father, the Latins or Western theologians insisting that the Holy Ghost proceeded from the Father *and* the Son by spiration.[6] The Church — with which Dante, of course, holds — presents the doctrine this way: the Eternal Father "the beginning without a beginning," knowing himself, begot the Son, the Word, Infinite Wisdom, as the mind begets or generates an idea. The Father looking upon the Son and the Son looking upon the Father with reciprocal infinite love *breathed* forth Infinite Love, which is the Holy Spirit (*Summa* I, q. 27). In the Heaven of the Sun, Dante begins the discussion of the doctrine with the line, "Gazing at his Son with the Love which both eternally breathe forth," thus professing his belief in the *filioque* doctrine (*Par.* X:1). The most profound expression, however, comes in the final canto (*Par.* XXXIII:115–120) where in a single light there appeared to Dante three circles of three colors and one dimension:

> Within the deep and luminous subsistence
> Of the High Light appeared to me three circles,
> Of threefold color and of one dimension,
>
> And by the second seemed the first reflected
> As Iris is by Iris, and the third
> Seemed fire that equally from both is breathed.

To present graphically the theological concept that the three Persons in the Trinity are distinct but not separate, Dante speaks of "a three-fold light in a single ray" (*Par.* XXXI:28) so "One" and so "Trine" that *is* or *are* may be used in speaking of the Essence of God (*Par.* XXIV:140–141).

Another aspect of the relations of persons of the Trinity to each other implicit in Dante's profession of faith is that known as the Mission of the Divine Persons (*Par.* XXIV:145–147; *Summa* I, q. 43). The Father as principle or source sends but is never sent; he sends the Son; the Father and the Son send the Holy Spirit on temporal missions of salvation to mankind. By grace won for man by the Son, the Holy Spirit dwells in man *shining like a star* (*Par.* XXIV:147). Man's place is God (*Par.* I:116) and to rise to him is man's calling. Therefore (*Par.* X:79–85) the theologians in the Heaven of the Sun are represented in a dance of joy for the knowledge they have of the mystery of the Trinity and for the vision of God given them. They pause in the dance — a pause which may suggest meditation on or contemplation of the mystery — and then resume it.

During the pause, Saint Thomas speaks of the radiance of eternal Light which shines in him and which enables him to see Dante's desire for further knowledge. It is only by grace given by the Blessed Trinity that Dante has been able to ascend to this heaven and that the theologians participate in this joyous carol. Everywhere in the *Purgatorio* and *Paradiso* motion signifies longing for the Highest Good; therefore, their resumption of the dance is an indication of the desire of the theologians for even deeper knowledge and more intense love.

The teaching of Scripture and the Church relative to the operations of the Divine Persons on the created universe and the appropriation of certain works to each person is also explicit in the *Divine Comedy*. The teaching that there is no external operation of the Divine Nature which is the work of one Person as distinct from the others Dante presents in many passages, notable among them, the inscription over the gate of Hell (*Inf.* III:4–6) where he declares that the Creator of Hell was Divine Power, Supreme Wisdom, and Primal Love. However, he keeps before us also the teaching of Sacred Scripture and the Nicene Creed concerning the distinction in persons by calling the Father the Creator, the first ineffable

Power who made everything (*Par.* X:4–6) and who never removes his eyes from his creation, thereby holding all things in being (X:10–12); by attributing to the Son, who subsists by way of knowledge, all works of knowledge and wisdom (*Par.* XIII:49–60) and, of course, of Redemption which *is* the work of the Son *alone,* for he alone assumed human nature and *in that nature* died for us; and by calling the Holy Spirit the giver of faith (*Par.* XXIV: 92), the Holy Spirit of Love (*Par.* III:52–54), and dramatizing his sevenfold light (*Purg.* XXIX:43, 62). In this way Dante keeps before us the distinction in Persons, though often in the same passage, for example, that from *Paradiso* XIII, he makes us aware that the operation attributed to one Person is really the action of all Three.

For my thoughts are not your thoughts
Nor your ways my ways, saith the Lord.

For as the heavens are exalted above the earth
so my ways are exalted above your ways
and my thoughts above your thoughts.

— Isa. 55:8, 9

In answering the question, What is God? Saint Thomas, probing the nature of God, ascribed to him seven attributes: simplicity, perfection (goodness), infinity, immensity and ubiquity, immutability (changelessness), eternity, and unity, among which are several which Plato and Aristotle had already ascribed to the Ultimate Reality or First Cause. That Dante, who everywhere in his dogmatic theology follows Saint Thomas, had meditated deeply upon all of them is clear from numerous passages and images in the *Divine Comedy.*

Following Saint Thomas and the Greeks, Dante uses philosophical arguments for the *simplicity* of God. Saint Thomas had said (*Summa* I, q. 3) that the proof of the simplicity of God, in other words of his being pure spirit, lies in the fact that he is the First Mover himself unmoved, pure act, in no way in potentiality. From Aquinas and Aristotle Dante borrows many of his names for God: "First Mover" (*Purg.* XXV:70), "First Cause" (*Par.* XX:132), "Supreme Essence" (*Par.* XXI:87) — to cite only a few. But Dante, because he is a poet as well as a philosopher and theologian, and must therefore express these concepts graphically seizes upon the traditional image of light, long used for the portrayal of spirit. For Scriptural as well as scientific reasons it is a good one: in the New Testament particularly, God — especially the Second Person of the Trinity — is spoken of as Light; from the scientific point of view, light is as bodiless as anything imaginable. Dante uses this traditional image for God in highly original ways, the most memorable of which are the Point of Light upon which the whole universe depends for its being, which represents God as the All-Mover, the glory of whose Light penetrates the universe; the superabundant Light which makes the rose of the Empyrean radiant; the triple circles of three colors and one dimension, his principal image of the Trinity.

In a sense, the whole *Divine Comedy* is a profound commentary on the *perfection* or *goodness* of God, the second attribute in Saint Thomas' list of seven. Since the whole universe was created to mirror this goodness (*Par.* I:108), any individual creature is good in the degree to which it attains this end. Hell represents the failure of some creatures — angels and men — to fulfill this obligation; Purgatory is the dramatization of the struggle of fallen human nature to climb to this perfection; the joy of Heaven lies in the contemplation of this infinite Goodness forever.

This infinite perfection of God mirrored throughout his whole creation was to Dante a source of never ending wonder. Since God created all things, whatever perfection exists in them pre-exists in him; for whatever perfection exists in an effect must pre-exist in the efficient cause (*Banq.* II, v, 4; *Summa* I, q. 4, a. 2); however vast the creation may be, and whatever perfection created beings may attain, the Creator must remain in infinite excess of what he has created (*Par.* XIX:40–45). His perfection is infinitely more than that in any finite image of himself in his visible creation: whatever good is found outside his supreme excellence is nothing but a ray of its own light (*Par.* XXVI:31–33). This idea we found in the discussion of the angels, no two of whom are alike, each of whom mirrors down through the nine spheres some aspect of the mani-fold perfection of the Creator. But inanimate nature mirrors him too — the fury of a hurricane his power, the glimmering evening star his tranquillity.

This Supreme First Good whose joy is only in himself (*Purg.* XXVIII:91; *Summa* I, q. 26, a. 4) draws every creature to himself, the inanimate universe by physical necessity, the brute creation by instinct and man by knowledge and love (*Par.* I:109–117). The Supreme Goodness breathes forth the soul of man directly without secondary causes and so completely enamors it of itself that the soul ever after desires this Goodness (*Par.* VII:142–144). God speaking of himself to Moses (Exod. 33:19) said that whoever saw him saw all Worth (*Par.* XXVI:42); therefore he who attains the Beatific Vision has reached Infinite Worth (*Par.* XXXIII:81), though the grace of the Supreme Good does not descend equally on all (*Par.* III:89).

Consideration of the *infinity*, the *eternity*, the *immensity*, and the *ubiquity* of God stirred Dante no less profoundly than considera-tion of his goodness and perfection as is evident from the sublime images in which he attempts to portray these attributes: the limitless reaches of the river of grace, the uncharted sea of light, and the time-less, spaceless rose of the Empyrean. That this infinite, omnipotent God rules in Hell as he rules on Earth and in Heaven Dante shows dramatically throughout the *Inferno* by having Virgil warn the evil spirits again and again that Dante's passage through the lower regions is willed "where will and power are one" and that for them to resist that will is folly. God is that "Eternal Power" (*Par.* I:107) in which all creatures, even the fallen angels, move and have their being; he is the self-subsisting "Serene One" (*Par.* XIX:64) who is the "Eternal Pleasure" (*Par.* XX:77) of angels and saints.

Because God is infinite power which ordains and foresees (*Par.* IX:105), he is at the central point of the being of everything whatsoever. The word *infinite* in its derivation means *without limits or boundaries;* God, because of his actual contact with all things as he holds them in being, transcends time and space (*Par.* XIV:28–30):

That One and Two and Three which always lives and always reigns in Three and Two and One *uncircumscribed* and *circumscribing* all.

Because he is uncircumscribed, without boundaries, he is everywhere; because he circumscribes all, he has the attribute which Saint Thomas calls *ubiquity*. Because he is omnipresent, he acts everywhere; the whole universe is filled with the activity of the first Will, which never moved from itself.

As God is a spaceless being without limits or boundaries, so is he *changeless*: he *"always* lives and *always* reigns in Three and Two and One" (*Par.* XIV:28, 29; *Summa* I, q. 9). In the chapter on the angels (p. 139) we saw that, according to Dante, time and the universe began together in that split second of creation when God flashed into being the angels, the Empyrean Heaven, corporeal matter, and time (*Par.* XXIX:20–33; *Summa* I, q. 46, a. 3, 1). This occurred when the Divine Mind expressed the idea of the universe and the Divine Will of the Prime Mover set in motion the Primum Mobile (*Par.* XXVIII:70) — primary in nature if not in time — from which motion descended to the other spheres.

It is, therefore, in the Primum Mobile that the whole system of nature has its origin: here, too, time has its origin; for time is the measure of motion — the movement of the spheres; the movement of sands in an hourglass, of the shadow on the sundial, of the hands of a clock. Motion, in scholastic usage, included every kind of change, intellectual as well as physical. Everything in nature is seeking a final goal in which to rest, the Source from which it came, God (*Banq.* II, iv, 1). This is the explanation for Dante's insistence on the importance of time to man: in it and through it man participates in the vast movement of Love and Light flowing from God as their source; and in the countermovement of all nature to be united with its Source, which is also its final End (*Par.* XXVII:106–120).

But God himself, the giver of every perfect gift, the Father of lights, is above time and motion. He is the Serene One (*Par.* XIX:64) in whom there is no change or shadow of alteration (*James* 1:17), dwelling beyond space and time in the Empyrean where "every where is here and every when is now" (*Par.* XXIX:12), where the living Light is always as it was before (*Par.* XXXIII:111).

Since God is timeless, he is *eternal* (*Par.* XXIX:16, 17; *Summa* I, q. 10). He had no beginning; he can have no end. He exists now, has always existed, and always will exist in that timeless present which is eternity. All things are, therefore, eternally present to him (*Par.* XVII:37–38): he has no past and can have no future, concepts which belong to time. Looking into that eternal present, Cacciaguida sees Dante's future exile (*Par.* XVII:44, 45). However as Cacciaguida points out, the fact that God knows in his eternal present, that which is, to us, the future affects its "contingency" no more than does the eye of a man who watches a boat moving with the current affect the movement of the boat (40–42). "He is where he always was" (*Par.* XXII:66); he lives, not as we do, moment by moment, but instantaneously in complete all-at-once-ness. In that sense Boethius in his *On the Consolation of Philosophy* defines eternity as the "perfect and simultaneous possession of everlasting life."

Dante's deep meditation on the *unity* of God lies behind his passion to bring unity out of multiplicity in his disordered world, one of the basic ideas of the *Divine Comedy*. The two poetic images already alluded to as portrayals of the simplicity of God, namely, the Point of Light in the Primum Mobile upon which the heavens and all nature depend (*Par.* XXVIII:41–45) and the Light which shines upon the blessed in the white rose are also symbols of God's unity. The Point of Light is, as Dante says, the revelation of the First Light, which shines on all and is received by all in as many ways there are splendors with which it unites, remaining itself One. In the depths of the Beatific Vision, which is symbolized also by light, he sees the whole universe bound into one volume by love. This unity within creation, and of creation with God its Cause, bespeaks the unity of God, the sole Deity, alone and eternal, the One Essence (*Par.* XXIV:130, 131, 140; *Summa* I, q. 11, a. 3), the great *I am* (*Par.* XXIX:15).

*O the depth of the riches of the wisdom and
of the knowledge of God!
How incomprehensible are his judgments,
and how unsearchable his ways!*

*For who hath known the mind of the Lord?
Or who hath been his counsellor?
Or who hath given to him and recompense
shall be made him?*

*For of him, and by him, and in him, are all
things:
To him be glory forever. Amen.*

— Rom. 11:33–36

The literature of the world is filled with the attempts of human beings to probe the mind and will of the Deity to discover not only his nature and attributes but his activities, both within himself and as they relate to other beings, particularly man. The Hebrews and Christians, believing God to be an intelligent Being, a *Person*, held that such a God must know and love infinitely: that, therefore, his knowledge of himself and of other beings is infinite; and that his will, which is the generator of all his activities and which is founded on his supreme intelligence is all-powerful, all-just, and all-merciful. The activity of the mind and the will of God in the awful solitude of his self-sufficiency and eternity, expressing itself in a vast universe called out of nothingness and sustained in being, challenged the intelligence and the love of men like Aquinas and Dante.

Pondering the activity of the divine intellect in relation to God himself, Dante and Saint Thomas agree first, that since God is the great *I am*, he understands and comprehends through himself, in that perfect eternal life which is the innermost life of the Blessed Trinity, that overwhelming Reality which is himself (*Par.* XXXIII: 124–126; *Summa* I, q. 14, a. 2; 18, a. 3); and second, that this innermost life of God is a profound secret, for though God knows all things as they are, none can know him perfectly (*Purg.* III:35; *Summa* I, q. 12, a. 7), since the finite cannot possibly comprehend the infinite. They agree, too, that he whose understanding transcends all (*Inf.* VII:73) knows intimately — much better than they can know themselves — all the creatures that are the result of his creative power (Hebr. 4:13); that he is aware in his eternal present of their innermost acts and thoughts and desires — past, present, and future (*Summa* I, q. 14, a. 13).

The two theologians are also agreed that according to their capacities and their merits (*Par.* I:106–114; *Summa* I, q. 12, a. 6) the angels and saints participate in this transcendent knowledge of God; those who attain to the Beatific Vision behold not only the Essence of God but see all things in God (*Par.* XXXIII:85–93; *Summa* I, q. 12, a. 8). The light intellectual of which Dante speaks in *Paradiso* XXX:40 is the immediate vision of things in the pure light of God. It is in this light that the angels of the Earthly Paradise know (*Purg.* XXX:103–145) how gifted Dante is and how great is his need of repentance; it is in this light that in the Heaven of the Sun Saint Thomas learns the occasion of Dante's thoughts and his wish for an explanation (*Par.* XI:19–25). "God sees all, and your vision is in him so that no desire can hide itself from you," Dante says to Folquet (*Par.* IX:73–75): "by the light which shines through all heaven we are enlightened; and if you wish to draw light from us, satisfy yourself," says Justinian (*Par.* V:118–120). In many other places in the *Divine Comedy,* Dante speaks of the knowledge men and angels have by perceiving what is mirrored in the Divine Mind.

> As the potter's clay is in his hand to fashion and order it:
> All his ways are according to his ordering.
>
> So man is in the hand of him who made him:
> And he will render to him according to his judgment.
>
> — Ecclus. 33:13, 14

Dante pondered the divine will in all its activities: in its eternal love of the Godhead and in its relationship to all creation. He pondered God, with his limitless infinite intelligence, looking upon that infinite goodness and justice which is himself, and loving himself with that primal will which in itself is good (*Par.* XIX: 85–87) and which never departs from himself; he pondered the divine will as the source of all things, bringing into existence a vast chain of being, each separate entity of which might participate in his glory and realize its own destiny by reflecting back to him — by whose will everything becomes what it is (*Par.* XX:76–78) — the splendor of the creative rays. He pondered the Godhead as Divine Providence (*Par.* VIII:97–109) caring for the minutiae of his vast creation, governing it, ordering all things lest they run counter to his purpose, which can never be hindered (*Inf.* IX:94; XXI:79–83). These last considerations led him to wrestle with the problem of the relationship of prayer to the will of God and the even more perplexing problem of predestination; to meditate deeply on God's justice and mercy in dealing with the rational creatures he has made, and his wrath when these rational creatures rise up in pride and assert their self-sufficiency.

We read in the *Book of Wisdom* (XI:25) that God loves all the things that are, all the things that he has made. It is because he loves the universe and knows in his infinite wisdom what he wants to do with it and in it that in his Providence he governs and preserves it with such infinite care and such flawless proficiency (*Par.* X:1–6). Each creature is directed to the end for which it was made as surely as a well-shot arrow is directed to its mark (*Par.* VIII:103–105; *Summa*, I, q. 23, a. 1). Not only is provision made for great diversity of natures in the universe but for their welfare; such order is maintained that the universe is a work of art (VIII:107–108). Order is the supreme law of the creation (*Par.* I:103–142); all nonrational creatures preserve this order so impeccably that man is never surprised; once he learns the laws that govern nature, he can proceed intelligently to harness its forces for his purposes. Order "draws the earth together and unites it" (117). "As the potter's clay is in his hand, to fashion and to order it: all his ways are according to his ordering. So man is in the hand of him who made him: and he will render to him according to his judgment" (Ecclus. 33:13).

Because man and the whole social order are in the hands of God, Divine Providence orders things not only for the good of individual men but of society. Men who do not understand how God orders our world are likely to attribute things to the vicissitudes of fortune (*Inf.* VII:67; *Summa* I, q. 116). But what men call fortune is really Divine Providence, which foresees, judges, and disposes all things: wealth, the rise and fall of nations, the transfer of power and glory from one family to another (*Inf.* VII, 67–96; *Par.* VIII: 103–105).

Moreover, in order that society may have among men the diversity of gifts needful for the harmonious carrying on of human affairs, Providence intervenes in the laws of heredity so that in one family there are capacities to fill a variety of social offices (*Par.* VIII:118–135). Providence sends peculiarly gifted teachers and rulers when and where they are needed as it sent Saint Francis with his remedy of poverty into avaricious Italy (*Par.* XI:28–34). These things being true, it behooves those who are responsible for the direction of the lives of other individuals to study their native gifts and refrain from forcing their charges into positions and works for which they are ill-adapted (*Par.* VIII:136–148). It is equally important that a man whom Providence has endowed by nature for a particular social function should fulfill his destiny (*Par.* XVII:77, 78). Providence forces no man to fulfill his appointed mission, but the one who endeavors to work out the divine will finds that he is supplied with all the necessary means. Dante insists that God's providence and prevision in no way affect man's freedom (*Par.* XVII:40). He points out also with equal insistence — and this all through the *Comedy* — that since the highest natural possession of man is his moral freedom, his peace and happiness here and hereafter lie in the free submission of his will to the will of God, that is, in his saying in very word and very deed, "Thy will be done."

There are, as we have noted, two aspects of God's providence in the ordering of the universe which propose difficulties to some minds, including the mind of Dante: predestination and the problem of providence and prayer. Some men, too, find it difficult to reconcile God's justice with his beneficent kindness, especially when that justice takes the form of eternal punishment and wrath or vengeance. There is the further difficulty of reconciling the justice and the mercy of God. With all these problems Dante deals.

In the *Divine Comedy* the question of predestination is discussed in relation to the justice of God in the Heaven of Jupiter, where in the Roman eagle Dante meets the just rulers. In the *Summa* (I, q. 23, a. 1), Saint Thomas had explained that predestination is a part of the universal providence of God inasmuch as it relates to the direction to their proper end of rational creatures capable of eternal life. Perhaps the simplest statement of the meaning of the term is that it is God's plan for the salvation of *some* men. The difficulty, of course, lies in what happens to those who are excluded from the *some*. The answer given by theologians (*Summa* I, q. 23, a. 3) is that God foresees that there are others who will lead evil lives and will, therefore, spend eternity in Hell; Dante holds — see Chapter IV, Note 18, pp. 120–122 — that there are still others who have natural virtue but who will have no opportunity to know the true God and his law and who will also be cut off from him for all eternity.

The only doctrine in all Christian theology which Dante represents as giving him real difficulty is this one of the damnation of virtuous pagans. Though he finds the eternal damnation of sinners a "hard saying" (*Inf.* III:12), his sense of justice tells him that men who deliberately turn against the laws of God and die unrepentant deserve to be forever separated from God. But that a man born on the "shore of the Indus" where no man speaks to him of Christ, where he has no opportunity to read of him, a man whose desires and acts are good as far as human reason can see — that such a man should be condemned because he dies unbaptized and without faith in Christ, Dante is tempted to find unjust. After he has repeatedly struggled with the doctrine, he is reprimanded by Saint Peter Damian (*Par.* XIX:70–82) for attempting to probe the mystery of the judgment of God. He then submits his intellect: first, because of the teaching of Sacred Scripture (*Par.* XIX:85); and, second, because he realizes that the finite mind cannot penetrate the inscrutable infinite will (*Par.* XX:88–90). The issues involved in predestination go so deep into the abyss of the eternal law that the solutions are cut off from every created vision (*Par.* XXI:94–96; *Summa* I, q. 23, a. 4 ff.).

The wisdom and justice of God, Dante concludes, are boundless like the ocean; and our sight, which is but a tiny ray of the light of the Divine Mind, can no more penetrate the eternal judgments than the physical eye can penetrate the depths of the sea (*Par.* XIX:49–63). It is vain to seek an answer to the problems of pre-destination except in the Serene One who is always untroubled and who, through revelation, gives man the answers which he must accept on faith (*Par.* XIX:64–69). That the question was an urgent one in the mind of Dante is evident from its recurrence not only in the *Commedia* but in his other writings. He discusses it at some length in the *Monarchy* (II, vii), closing the matter as he does here, with an act of faith (cf. Chap. IX, pp. 295–296), saying that "a hidden judgment of God is one that human reason sometimes reaches neither through the law of nature (reason) nor by way of Scripture but through a special grace."

In the *Comedy*, after his act of faith, Dante, by such a special grace, has at least a partial answer to his question. In the eyebrow of the eagle he sees Trajan, the Roman Emperor (*Par.* XX:100–117) whom he has depicted in the *Purgatorio* (X:73–93) as an example of the virtue of humility; and Rhipeus (XX:118–123), the virtuous Trojan praised three times in the *Aeneid*. Both of these rulers are represented as having been supernaturally enlightened to believe in Christ. According to an old legend, Trajan — through the prayers of Pope Saint Gregory — was resuscitated and after the reunion of his soul and body, was baptized, did penance, and upon his second death went to Paradise. His salvation was determined by the efficacy of prayer. It is probable that in introducing Rhipeus, a pagan who lived more than a millennium before Christ, Dante is presenting the teaching of Saint Thomas (II, *Sentences*, d. 28, q. 1, a. 4 ad 4):

> A man may prepare himself by what is contained in natural reason for receiving faith. Wherefore it is said that if anyone born in bar-barous nations do what lieth in him, God will reveal to him what is necessary for salvation, either by inspiration or by sending a teacher.[7]

Rhipeus was given an initial grace of righteousness with which he co-operated: that grace was followed by other graces; and because of his co-operation with each grace vouchsafed, he was blessed with the infusion of the three theological virtues, which replaced baptism. He was, therefore, supernaturally enlightened about the coming of the Redeemer; and was saved (XX:118–129).[8]

The principle implied in this passage from Saint Thomas is doubtless the one Dante had in mind in saving Cato (*Purg.* I:31–75), who was "worthy of reverence" (32) and Statius (*Purg.* XXII: 59–87). Rhipeus and Cato, it would seem, were enlightened directly by God; Statius with the further help of a teacher. Dante, therefore, presents three possible ways by which pagans may be given faith: through the prayers of those who have it, by direct revelation, and by the help of teachers — even of those who may themselves remain pagans. Realizing, however, that instances like these may be the exception and not the rule, Dante exclaims (XX:130–132), "O predestination! How remote is thy root from the vision of those who do not see the First Cause entire." His ultimate word on the subject is that the mystery lies so deep in the infinite will that it is impenetrable.

Though belief in Christ is essential for salvation (*Par.* XIX: 103–105), the mere fact that one has faith is not an assurance of salvation. Faith without good works is vain (James 2:14), and many who have been baptized will be found among the reprobate. Not everyone who cries "Christ, Christ" will be with him in glory. Dante summons before his poetic tribunal all the contemporary rulers of Christendom and assails them for their wicked lives and evident injustice (*Par.* XIX:106–148).

The question of the immutability of the divine will and the efficacy of prayer, one which theologians consider also under the general heading of God's providence, Dante touches only lightly. That he is convinced of the efficacy of prayer is evident throughout the whole of the *Commedia:* we have seen it operate in Bernard's prayer to the Virgin; we will discuss it in detail in following chapters. The problem here is kindred to the problem of the freedom of the will of man and of God's foreknowledge of his acts. Ezechias (Hezekiah) in the Empyrean, from which he has come to take his place in the eyebrow of the eagle in the heaven of Jupiter, has learned that "the eternal judgment is not violated when worthy prayer below makes tomorrow's what is today's" (XX:51–53).

Ezechias, who was "sick unto death," was told by the prophet Isaias that he would die. But his prayers prevailed, and the Lord sent Isaias to tell him that fifteen years would be added to his life (4 Kings 20:1–11; Isa. 38:1–5). What Ezechias had learned is that prayer does not change the unalterable will; for, as Saint Thomas says (*Summa* II–II, q. 83, a. 2), "our motive in praying is not that we may change the Divine disposition, but that, by our prayers, we may obtain what God has appointed." Ezechias now understands the mystery of how prayer, instead of altering the eternal judgment, harmonizes with it, God having willed from all eternity that what we ask should follow our asking — so that Ezechias should be cured of his illness, that Manfred should be snatched from the fiend, that Dismas, the good thief, should be canonized on the cross.

What shall we say then? Is there injustice with God? God forbid.

For he saith to Moses: I will have mercy on whom I will have mercy; and I will show mercy to whom I will show mercy.

Therefore he hath mercy on whom he will and whom he will he hardeneth.

— Rom. 9:14, 15, 18

Implicit in much of the discussion on the providence of God is Dante's concern with the justice of God. "Whatever is consonant with the divine will is just," he says (*Par.* XIX:90); then he concerns himself with the impenetrable mystery of the nature of the divine will. Saint Thomas declares that whatever God does he does justly, for it is impossible for him to do anything except what his wisdom approves (*Summa* I, q. 21, a. 1). Therefore, for him to give grace to some and deny it to others is just; for him to place the little children, who could not merit higher or lower places, in different grades of bliss in the mystic rose is also just (Rom. 9:11, 12; *Par.* XXXII:58–75). God gives grace in varying degrees according to his good pleasure; degrees of glory correspond to the measure of grace (*Par.* XIV:40–43). Man does justly what he does according to law, but God is a law unto himself (Rom. 9:15; *Summa* I, q. 21, a. 2). He deals justly with individuals when he gives these individuals that which the creature needs to play its part in the universe according to his eternal plan; what lies beyond is a matter of his good pleasure (*Summa* I, q. 21, a. 1).

Justice in the strict sense is giving to others what is their due; there are, therefore, three manifestations of justice: God renders to himself what is due himself; man renders to God what is due to God; he also renders to man what is due to man, as an individual and as a member of society. Throughout the *Divine Comedy* Dante is concerned with these three aspects of justice: we are concerned with them here only insofar as they relate to the justice of God or the justice due him. The fact that God renders to himself what is due himself and that man must render to God what is due him lies at the heart of the whole mystery of the Incarnation and Redemption and will be treated there. It lies, too, at the heart of the whole doctrine of eternal punishment and of purgation; and is, therefore, basic to an understanding of the *Inferno* and the *Purgatorio*.

How the justice of God operated in the fall of the angels and the creation of Hell we have already seen. Though the operation of God's justice in consigning to eternal perdition those men who rebel against God's law is to Dante a hard saying (*Inf.* III:12), he counters it, however, as he comes to realize the nature of sin (*Inf.* XX:27–30) by asking who can be more impious than one who feels sorrow at God's judgment upon such men, who have been spurred on to Hell by God's justice so that fear of Hell is changed into desire for the "new pains and torments" which the justice of God provides for them (*Inf.* III:124, 125; VII:19–21). The *Inferno* is a dramatic portrayal of the wrath and vengeance (*Inf.* XIV:16; *Par.* XXII:14) of a just God against those who refuse him the honor and obedience which the creature owes the One who brought him into being.

If the *Inferno* is a dramatization of the justice of God, the *Purgatorio* is a portrayal of his mercy. There are those who, for a variety of reasons, find it difficult to reconcile the justice and the mercy of God. Perhaps to the modern mind the gravest difficulty arises because of a concept of mercy which did not exist in the mind of Saint Paul when he wrote the epistle to the Romans or in the minds of Saint Thomas and Dante in the thirteenth century. The twentieth-century man equates mercy with what he calls humanitarianism, but which Paul and Thomas and Dante would call a sentimental leniency with violaters of the law which could brook no good to the social order, a pampering of ne'er-do-wells which encourages ineptitude and sloth. Mercy in the Christian tradition, as it came to Saint Thomas and Dante, meant "being affected with sorrow at the *misery* of another as though it were one's own," and attempting to dispel it, *misery* being some defect of goodness which could be removed only by some perfection of goodness. God acts mercifully not by going against his justice but by doing something more than justice (*Summa* I, q. 21, a. 4). Though Manfred (*Purg.* III:110–123) is saved from Hell, he will bend his back beneath the burdens of the cornice of the proud and pass through the purifying flames in Purgatory; though "God wills that his mercy shine" in Dante's soul (*Purg.* XIV:79–80) Dante, too, climbs the difficult mountain and weeps bitter tears of repentance.

There remains, however, the fundamental problem of reconciling the justice and mercy of God in the placing of emphasis on one or the other of these attributes. Certain works are attributed to justice, says Saint Thomas (*Summa*, I, q. 21, a. 4), and certain others to mercy because in some justice appears more forcibly and in others mercy:

> Even in the damnation of the reprobate, mercy is seen, which, though it does not totally remit, yet somewhat alleviates, in punishing short of what is deserved.

> In the justification of the ungodly justice is seen, when God remits sins on account of love.

Divine goodness, as we have often pointed out, tends to communicate itself; God made creatures to manifest his attributes. The souls of men bear witness to the splendor of both infinite justice and infinite mercy. "The potter," says Saint Paul (Rom. 9:21–23) "has power over the clay, of the same lump to make one vessel unto honor and another unto dishonor. What if God, to make his power known and to show his wrath, fits some vessels for destruction and prepares others to show the riches of his glory!"

Frequently in the Divine Comedy Dante makes dramatic use of this passage by saving one member of a family and damning another: Manfred "whose sins were horrible" he places in Purgatory (Purg. III:110–134), his gifted father Frederick II in Hell (Inf. X:119), and Frederick's mother in Heaven (Par. III:118–120); Piccarda Donati, Dante's old Florentine neighbor he places in Paradise (Par. III:49–123), her brother Forese in Purgatory (Purg. XXIII:40 XXIV:97), Corso, another brother, most at fault for Dante's exile, named by Forese (Purg. XXIV:82–84) as on his way to Hell; Buonconte da Montefeltro, Dante has in Purgatory (Purg. V:88–129), and his father Guido in Hell (Inf. XXVII:119–132): to name only a few of the more notable examples. Frederick, Corso, Guido show forth the justice of God; Manfred, Forese, Buonconte are vessels of his mercy; Piccarda and Constance show the riches of his glory.

What to Dante is unquestionably the most important theological discussion of the whole poem, that of the Incarnation and Redemption, he presents as a question of justice and mercy. The Divine Goodness, which puts its stamp on the world, was pleased to proceed by both these ways to lift men up, for God was so generous as to give himself to make man able to redeem himself (Par. VII: 109–116). Christ the God-man is the bridge between the infinitely holy God and fallen human nature.

NOTES

1. Henry Adams, Mont-Saint-Michel and Chartres (Boston, 1933), p. 345.
2. That Dante has always been recognized as a superb theologian is attested by innumerable scholars, from his contemporary, Giovanni del Virgilio of Bologna, who wrote his epitaph, to Pope Pius XI who in 1923 cast a medal using his figure. In the first quarter of the sixteenth century, Raphael placed Dante among the theologians in his Disputa (c. 1515) in the Vatican murals. Pope Benedict XV in his encyclical addressed "to the Teachers and Students of Liberal Arts in the Entire Catholic World at the end of the Sixth Century

from the Death of Dante Alighieri," after pointing out that Dante "chose as his preferred guide the prince of Scholastics, Saint Thomas Aquinas," calls the *Divine Comedy* "an immortal tapestry of Catholic dogma, a rich storehouse of Catholic doctrine . . . containing the distilled sweetness of Christian philosophy and theology."

Pope Pius XI in 1923, the second year of his reign and the sixth centenary of the canonization of Saint Thomas by Pope John XXII, cast a medal with his own likeness on one side and on the reverse a group looking up to Saint Thomas enthroned, each member of which had honored Saint Thomas in some distinguished way. First among them is Dante, who had acclaimed the theology of Saint Thomas by enthroning it throughout the *Divine Comedy* and his other writings before the Church spoke. Then in order follow three popes: John XXII, who canonized Thomas and to whom Dante seems to be pointing him out; Saint Pius V, who in 1567 proclaimed him a Doctor of the Church and in 1570 authorized an edition of all his writings; and Leo XIII, who in 1879 proclaimed him official teacher of the Church and patron of all Catholic institutions of learning. The text on the medal is as follows:

PIUS XI. PONT. MAX. ANNO. II" (one side of medal).

"ALIGHERIO PRAECINETE JOAN XXII A.D. MCCCXXIII SANCT ORD ASCRIPSIT PIUS V ECCL. DOCT. ANGEL SANCIV. LEO XIII SCHOL. CATH. PATR. DECLAR. ET INSTIT" (other side).

See Appendix for picture of medal and translation of inscription.

3. For a clear and simplified discussion of Saint Thomas' proofs for the existence of God and of other matters discussed in the first part of this chapter see James W. Regan, O.P., *et al.*, *A Primer of Theology*, Book One (Dubuque, 1953).

4. Dante, *Monarchy and Three Political Letters*, trans. Donald Nicholl (New York, 1954), p. 69.

5. This light, which Saint Thomas calls the *lumen gloriae* (the light of glory), has been discussed in Chapter V (p. 169) in connection with the manner in which the angels see God.

6. The question of the procession of Persons was a very live one in Dante's youth. At the Council of Lyons, in 1274, there was a temporary truce and prelates of both East and West chanted the Nicene Creed together, each in his own tongue. Afterward, however, the Schism again prevailed. Saint Thomas died on his way to Lyons to defend the *filioque* doctrine and Saint Bonaventure died during the meeting of the council.

7. This same teaching of Saint Thomas is found in $Q.Q.$ *De Verit.*, q. 14, a. 11 ad 1 and in III *Sent.*, d. 25, q. 2, a. 1, sol. 1 ad 1.

8. See the discussion of Trajan and Rhipeus in Edmund G. Gardner, *Dante's Ten Heavens* (New York, 1900), pp. 166–170; and in John S. Carroll, *en Patria* (London, 1911), pp. 308–310 and 315–322.

CHAPTER VIII

SON OF GOD AND SON OF MARY: DANTE'S CHRISTOLOGY

> There is nothing greater than for God to become incarnate.
> — Saint Thomas Aquinas

> Between the last night and the first day
> there has never been nor will be so exalted
> and so magnificent an act.
> — *Paradiso* VII:111–113

ante's profound realization of the place of the Incarnation in human history is evident throughout the *Commedia:* in the pageant of the Church and in the mystic rose of Paradise, he has dramatized his belief that it occupies the central point in time; he represents the beginning of his own conversion as taking place in an ideal year when the liturgical feast of the Incarnation (the Annunciation), March 25, is coincident with but replaced by Good Friday, the feast of the Redemption: the *Divine Comedy* is a song of Dante's own way to eternal happiness and the way of all men, a way made possible by the Incarnation.

As has already been said, it is important that a reader of Dante understand his Christology. It is essential that he grasp the scholastic concept of how the Second Person of the Trinity, born of the Father from all eternity, represents in himself all creation, because he is the living Idea, the Word, who was in the beginning with God; who made all things, visible and invisible; in whom is

231

light and life; who united himself to human nature and dwelt among men; who taught men the way to the Father; who on the cross redeemed the whole human race; who founded his Church, which is really his Mystical Body, so that when he had super-abundantly saved mankind and his mission on earth was completed, this Mystical Body would apply his work in time and space. The mystery of Christianity is twofold: it is the mystery of God giving himself to men in the union of the two natures which constitute Christ, the Head of the Mystical Body; it is the union of man with God through baptism, which elevates him to membership in the Mystical Body.

The reader who does not grasp Dante's ideas about the place of man as a real or potential member of the Mystical Body of Christ and hence of man's relationship to the Trinity and to the whole created universe can never get a clear idea of what the Beatific Vision means to Dante; he cannot understand Hell, which is eternal separation from God; or Purgatory, which is sinful man's endeavor by prayer and penance to apply to his own soul the fruits of the Redemption and perfect the life of grace within him by setting love in order.

The importance of the Incarnation is discussed in great detail by all theologians, from those of the New Testament down to the scholastics of Dante's time — and, of course, to our own day. The three writers upon whom Dante leans most heavily in his considera-tion of this mystery, the mystery of the Redemption and the mystery of "the whole Christ" — the "body of Christ" — are Saint Paul, Saint John, and Saint Thomas Aquinas, though occasionally he borrows an idea or an image from some other. These, and the theologians he does not quote, agree that it is Christ's humanity that unites the human race to the divinity, that the first principle of the whole supernatural order is the assumption of human nature by the Word, since this relationship gives to the human nature the personality of the Word and a dignity that is infinite. This union of the divinity, the Word, with the humanity of Christ gives the humanity an intrinsic holiness so abundant that it naturally tends to overflow and to "influence" us (*Summa* III, q. 8, a. 5). Christ in his human nature is the head of all mankind. As God, as the

Word, he is the Lord and Principle of all created things; but it is because as man he is of the same nature as ourselves and in contact with us that he communicates supernatural life to us.

Because Dante believed that the founding of the Roman Empire and the beginning of the Church were by God's divine plan at the same period of world history, he presents the discussion of the Incarnation and Redemption in the canto in which he eulogizes the Roman Empire. He teaches everywhere that the Empire's long centuries of triumph over world-wide opposition, the establishment of universal peace under Augustus — in whose reign and under whose jurisdiction Christ was born a Roman in the fullness of time — made the Empire a secure foundation upon which the Church could be established to embrace the entire human family, using the roads of Rome and her protection to push forward with the Gospel. For this reason, he treats in juxtaposition the justice of the Incarnation and the codification of Roman law under Justinian.

Dante begins his discussion of the mystery of the Incarnation and Redemption as a good scholastic would, with a discussion of their necessity and a definition of terms. Adam, "the man never born" (Par. VII:25) who came "mature" from the hand of God without the intervention of secondary causes (Par. XXVI:92; Summa I, q. 90 ff.), had failed to place a curb on his free will (Par. VII: 25, 26), disobeyed God in the Garden of Eden, and damned himself and all his descendants (Summa I–II, q. 81 ff.). They remained sick and in great error for many centuries (Par. VII:28, 29, 33) until it pleased the Word of God — the Second Person of the Blessed Trinity — by the sole act of his eternal love to unite himself to the nature which had estranged itself from its Maker (30–35). Since human nature was created directly by the Divine Goodness without secondary causes it was without flaw (70–72); it had received great gifts which made it resemble the Creator: immortality, freedom from subjection to changing things, the glow of divine love. All these, man enjoyed in his original state (66–76). But sin had disqualified him: he had lost his primal dignity (87); he was cut off from Paradise (37, 87). Left to himself he was utterly unable to recover what he had lost, for through his own free act he had turned from the way of truth and of life (37, 39).

Why God on the very day of the fall of man (Gen. 3:15) should have promised him a Redeemer and have willed the reinstatement of man "in this mode," that is, by the Incarnation, was of great interest to theologians, Dante among them (*Par.* VII:56–57). There were two ways, they argued (*Par.* VII:91–93; *Summa* III, q. 1, a. 2) by which man might recover his lost status: God might forgive man outright (91) or God might compel him to make satisfaction for his folly (93). For God to forgive man outright would be a less satisfactory method, because then man would have no part whatever in the atonement for his wrongdoing and the justice of God would have fallen short (118, 119).

But man had no power within his own nature to render perfect satisfaction and meet the demands of justice (*Par.* VII:97–103; *Summa* III, q. 1, a. 2): first, because the whole of human nature had been corrupted by sin and the goodness of any person or persons could not make up adequately for the harm done to the whole of the nature; second, because a sin committed against God has a kind of infinity about it since it is an offense against an infinite being. An offense takes its primary malice from the dignity of the person offended. Man, being finite, can never give infinite satisfaction. Man cannot descend so low in humility to render satisfaction as in his disobedience he had exalted himself (*Par.* VII:99–100). His sin was the sin of pride; he had sought to soar above humanity into divinity. To restore the moral balance in the universe, it would be necessary for him to humble himself below humanity. But to do so is impossible. Therefore (*Par.* VII:103) God must, in his own way, reinstate man if he is to be reinstated, and the way of the Incarnation was the perfect way. God by becoming man descended to a status below himself; the Incarnation is the most profound act of humility conceivable and therefore a perfect antidote for the pride of Adam. God could in his human nature, assumed in the person of Christ, give satisfaction as *man for man*; because Christ was God he could render satisfaction to *God as God* (*Par.* VII:106–118; *Summa* III, q. 1, a. 2). Man had aimed at becoming God; God restores the moral balance by becoming man.

Never, says Dante, has there been so exalted and magnificent an act, either of the justice of God or of his mercy, as the Incarnation, by which God gave himself to make man able to redeem himself (*Par.* VII:110–116). By taking upon himself our flesh, God greatly impressed upon us his divine goodness, revealing thereby his great love and generosity. It pertains to the conception of goodness, writes Saint Thomas (*Summa* III, q. 1, a. 1), that it communicate itself to others; and therefore to the conception of the Highest Goodness that it communicate itself in the highest mode, and the highest mode is the Incarnation in which the Divine and human are united.

To proclaim their joy and gratitude for this goodness the theologians in the Heaven of the Sun sing a paeon of the Three Persons in the divine nature, and it and the human in One Person. To these saints, as to all the blessed, the height of beatitude is to behold in the divine Essence our human nature and the divine nature joined (*Par.* II:40–45; XXXIII:130–132). To this height of joy the *Divine Comedy* moves. The condition for penetrating the mystery is perfect love, for it was the love of God for man that brought about the Incarnation.

In the *Divine Comedy* and elsewhere, Dante discusses the Atonement, the redemptive act of the crucifixion, by which "just vengeance was justly avenged" (*Par.* VII:20, 21; *Summa* III, q. 48, a. 2). He argues in the *Monarchy* (II, xi) that since, as Luke testifies (2:1–7), Christ willed to be *born as a man* under an edict of Roman rule, namely, the decree of Augustus that all men must register, he recognized the legality of the decree; for if anyone of his own free will observes an edict, he gives support to the conviction that it is just. Since a just edict cannot be issued without due jurisdiction, it follows that the person who approves an edict as just, also approves its jurisdiction. Christ, therefore, recognized Caesar's jurisdiction by willing in becoming man that he be "enrolled as a man in that unique register of the human race." Moreover (*Mon.* II, xi; *Par.* VI:82–90), Christ willed that he should *suffer and die as a man* under the decree of Pontius Pilate, a Roman who had penal jurisdiction in Palestine as the representative of Tiberius Caesar. Since it was the "whole of mankind that was to be *judicially executed* in the flesh of Christ" inasmuch as Christ had assumed the whole of human nature into his Person and had taken upon himself *all the sins of mankind, past and present and future* (*Par.* XIII:40–42) in order that he might make satisfaction for all sin, "no judge could be accounted appropriate unless he had jurisdiction over the whole of mankind" (*Mon.* II, xii).

Dante finds an apparent contradictory aspect of justice in the Crucifixion (*Par.* VII:40–51). Christ, because he was God, gave infinite satisfaction for an infinite offense; therefore the penalty of the Cross was an act of perfect satisfaction, and perfect "at-one-ment" was effected between the estranged human race and the Creator. Because mankind was redeemed, the heavens, closed for millenniums since the sin of Adam, were opened for him and his descendants (*Par.* XXIII:37–39; *Summa* III, q. 49, a. 5). On the other hand, Dante says, for unworthy reasons, the Crucifixion pleased the Jews (*Par.* VII:48), who because of their hatred of Christ had demanded his death. As a result of their malice in asking for the ignominious death of the Son of God, the earth trembled and all nature was convulsed (47); therefore afterward, through Rome (49–51), just vengeance came upon them in the destruction of their city and the dispersion of their nation.

But the Incarnation and Redemption did more for fallen human nature than restore man to his dignity, make satisfaction for him and reopen Paradise; it divinized him. When we have "put on Christ" by Baptism, when we have been "Christened" (Gal. 3:27), Christ begins to abide in our souls, we are become Christ, the body of Christ (1 Cor. 12:27). The Head and the members are one mystical Person. This important mystery so impressed Dante that by symbolism and all his imaginative power he tries to drive it home.

In his examination on love, Dante gives as his primary reason for loving God, God's own great goodness (*Par.* XXVI:28–30); he gives as his secondary reasons God's having created him, redeemed him, and placed him on the shore of right love so that he hopes to come to him in the heaven which was opened to him by the God-man (55–63). In the *Banquet* (II, ix, 6) Dante expresses his gratitude to Christ as the great Teacher who opened the Way to salvation by which we enter without hindrance upon the felicity of immortality, who taught us the Truth which suffers no error, who gives us the

Light which shines for us in the darkness of mundane ignorance so that we may not lose the way.

Throughout the *Divine Comedy*, but particularly in the *Purgatorio*, which is the canticle in which Dante points the way to peace, he indicates how man must follow the teaching of Christ as it is evident in the events of his life; in his Gospel — much of which Dante dramatizes — and in other Scriptural writings, particularly in the epistles of Saint Paul. For it is Dante's constant teaching, as it is the teaching of all the theologians whom he follows, and indeed of Christ himself, that since man has free will, the fruits of the Incarnation and Redemption are his to accept or reject. For him as an individual, they may be futile unless he sets his feet on the way pointed out and walks in the Truth and the Light, "worthy of the vocation in which he is called, not alienating himself from the life of God through ignorance or the blindness of his heart" (Eph. 4:1, 18). In one sense a man must effect his own at-one-ment, his own union with Christ.

That faith in Christ the Redeemer is essential to salvation is, as we have seen, Dante's conviction, for it is the teaching of Sacred Scripture and of the Church. All of the fourth canto of the *Inferno* is a dramatization of this belief: all those gifted souls of antiquity who were distinguished for merely natural goodness but were unenlightened by faith in the Messias, he places in Limbo, outside the kingdom of God. We have seen, too, that in both the *Monarchy* and the *Divine Comedy*, he wrestled with the problem, but believing Scripture and the Church to be the voice of infallible Truth, submitted his great mind to their teaching. Everywhere, too, he professes the necessity of good works, which have merit for eternal life when they are done in charity, that is, in sanctifying grace, which places a man in union with the Saviour of the world; a man's works then move in and through him from Christ and the Holy Spirit, who dwells within him. That faith without works is vain he teaches vigorously in the *Inferno*. He believes, too, in the necessity of the Church, the Mystical Christ; for in order to have the whole Christ, to have Christ as he is, man must accept him together with the Church, through the medium of which flow his life-giving sacraments, the channels of grace. To Dante the Church, like its Head, is at once human and divine: it is but the continuation of the life of the Head. Therefore he lives by its teaching; he immerses himself in its life of prayer.

> Our Lord Jesus Christ, like a whole and perfect man, is Head and body. . . . His body is the Church, not simply the Church that is in this particular place, but both the Church that is here and the Church which extends over the whole earth; not simply the Church that is living today, but the whole race of saints, from Abel down to all those who will ever be born and will believe in Christ until the end of the world, for all belong to one city. This city is the body of Christ. . . . This is the whole Christ: Christ united with the Church.
>
> — Saint Augustine
> (Quoted from his sermons in Mersch, *The Whole Christ*)[1]

> Jesu, who so with thee
> Hangs not in pain and loss
> Pierced on the cruel cross
> At peace shall never be.
>
> — Girolamo Beniveni
> *Lauda*
> (Translation of John Addington Symonds)

As Dante has three visions of Mary, so he has three visions of Christ, the whole Christ: in the Heaven of Mars, where Christ flashes upon the cross that spans the circle like quadrant lines; in the Stellar Heaven, where he leads the triumphant hosts of the blessed and then ascends into the Empyrean; and in the mystic rose where Dante sees him in his Mystical Body and as a part of the vision of the Trinity, the hypostatic union of the divine and human natures in the God-man.

As Dante enters the Heaven of Mars, he makes a complete holocaust of himself in thanksgiving for the new grace vouchsafed him in mounting into a higher heaven (*Par.* XIV:88–90); and before the ardor of the sacrifice has cooled, he knows it has been accepted (91–93). Then in the depths of Mars, which glows with ruddy light (94), splendors appear so bright that he praises the Sun which makes them so brilliant. These rays, variegated in size and brightness, form in the depths of Mars a huge cross as of two milky ways at right angles (97–102). On this cross in a flash Christ appears. But the figure of Christ is not the lone figure of the cross of Calvary: it is, as it were, formed of innumerable lights which from tip to tip and from top to bottom move, shining brightly as they meet and pass each other, lights as numerous as particles of dust, which straight and aslant, fast and slow, move through a ray of sunlight in a house. From the lights there issues a melodious song of lofty praise of which Dante can catch only the words "Arise and conquer." "Whoever takes up his cross and follows Christ," says Dante, "will pardon me for what I omit when (after death) he beholds Christ flashing in that glow" (106–108).

It seems clear that Dante is thinking here of the vision of Saint Paul on the road to Damascus (Acts 9:1–9). There are many things telescoped in the Heaven of Mars from the life and teachings of the great Apostle and martyr which have a direct bearing on Dante's life and mission. Paul, the dynamic, uncompromising, intellectual Apostle; a Roman citizen who stood on his political rights; who, driven by his own people from Jerusalem that he loved, hounded from city to city in peril of his life, seven times imprisoned because he stood firm in his convictions, misunderstood, hated, persecuted, but convinced that he had had a direct revelation from God to fulfill a mission peculiarly his own: all these things drew Dante to Saint Paul with a devotedness which shines in all his writings, but nowhere with such directness as it shines here in Mars.

Like Saint Paul, Dante had had a vision which determined him to write (*New Life* XLIII); in the *Divine Comedy* he reminds his readers of that vision (*Inf.* II:7; *Par.* I:4–6; XVII:128). Now the vision of Paul on the road to Damascus in which he heard from the "light that shined round about him" the voice saying, "Saul,

Saul, why persecutest thou me?" was a vision of Jesus. But it was not the man Jesus who walked the streets of the villages of Galilee whom Saul was persecuting, but the Mystical Christ, the Church. The vision of Dante seems also to have been a vision of the Church. As Saint Paul became, as a result of his vision, the Apostle of Christian unity, sending out of his prison in Rome those dynamic letters to Colossians, Ephesians, Philippians, exhorting these early Christians to unity, teaching that "who divides the Church divides Christ"; that "if one member suffer anything all the members suffer" (1 Cor. 1:10; 12:26), so Dante, imprisoned in the wide world outside his beloved Florence, urges unity among the Christians of his day who by their political feuding rend Christendom asunder. Though Paul had many visions, he goes back in all his teaching to that first vision on the road to Damascus, that vision of the Mystical Body. Dante's vision, too, is ever present to him.

Like Saint Paul, Dante realized that the union of all men in the Mystical Body was effected by the blood of Christ on the Cross and that he to whom the mystery is revealed must love the Cross since it was through the Cross that salvation was wrought and on the Cross that the Church was born. For that reason Dante receives his mission from the Cross, fittingly from Cacciaguida, that ancestor who died far from home on a crusade fighting under the standard of the Cross. Dante, like Saint Paul (2 Tim. 2:10–12) in making his oblation has expressed his willingness to suffer, to endure all things for the body of Christ which is the Church (Col. 1:24). Having made of himself a complete oblation, he learns of his exile and of the hardships it will entail; he is told by Cacciaguida to make his whole vision manifest, though those to whom he reveals it, because of darkened consciences, may resent and resist his message (*Par.* XVII:124–129).

When Paul gave himself to Christ on the road to Damascus, he knew that he was tearing himself from his own people; his affectionate heart must have anticipated some of the sufferings of which he writes the Galatians. Dante's letters in behalf of the Empire and the exiled Church riveted the chains which kept him from his beloved Florence, placed him in danger of death by fire, and sealed forever the edict of exile.

At the beginning of the *Divine Comedy* when Virgil offers to guide Dante (*Inf.* I:112–120) through the first two realms of the after world, Dante, after having accepted the offer, grows fearful. He remonstrates, telling Virgil that for him the journey may be folly: he is unworthy (*Inf.* II:31–33); he is neither Aeneas nor Paul, who returned in safety, each having an important work to do — Aeneas to go to Rome to found the Empire, Paul (with Peter) to establish the Church. Virgil persuades Dante, Virgil who loved the Empire. And so Dante goes. Throughout the *Divine Comedy* he is increasingly explicit about his mission to set things right in Church and Empire. He, too, in exile, cast out of Florence as Aeneas was cast out of Troy and Paul out of Jerusalem, must fulfill his mission. He must bring back to Rome the exiled Church, now under the thumb of a foreign prince; he must re-establish the Empire and bring the Emperor back to rightful jurisdiction; he must show the leaders of Church and Empire by whom "Christ every day is bought and sold" (*Par.* XVII:51) how they divide Christ; he must bring Christendom to the unity of the Spirit in the bond of peace which Paul preached from his Roman prison (Eph. 4:3).

The Cross in Mars answers to the Cross in the pageant of the Church in the Earthly Paradise; Dante's preparation in the Earthly Paradise leads to his acceptance of his mission on behalf of the Church. The thunder when the procession of the Church, in the masque of the Old and New Testaments, halts before Dante is a presage of the lightning here when Christ flashes on the Cross. The colors are the same, white and red: there clothed in white and crowned with flowers, white or red, the figures move majestically; here ruddy with love they flash on the white Cross. Here the unveiled face of Beatrice looks with joy upon that of Dante, there with stern reprimand she prepares him for his purgation and the seven gifts of the Holy Spirit which he needs here for his apostolate. The nine scenes of the drama there also prepare him for his mission: the portrayal of the ideal Church and the ideal union of Church and Empire, the review of the calamities which have befallen both because of the wrong relationship between the two. In Mars he is given his mission to make these relationships right.

> *Our gnosis (Wisdom) and our spiritual garden*
> *is our Savior himself. We are transplanted into*
> *him, and are thus removed from our former life*
> *unto good ground. But transplanting makes for*
> *a man more abundant harvest. Therefore, the*
> *Lord, into whom we are transplanted, is the*
> *true Light and gnosis.*
>
> — Clement of Alexandria

Dante's second vision of the Mystical Body of Christ is in the Stellar Heaven, where, as we have seen, Christ himself is symbolized by the rising sun. The Stellar Heaven, in the mystery of Christ, answers to the Garden of Eden as did the Heaven of Mars. Those who are crucified with Christ by dying to themselves and are "buried" with him in Baptism (Col. 2:12) will rise with him (1 Cor. 15), who is the resurrection and the life (Jn. 11:25). We see little of the Sun itself: it rises quickly and moves up to the Empyrean, a flash of the glory of the Risen Christ, shining on the blessed souls in the garden who are awaiting their own resurrection. The image changes very quickly from Christ, the Sun, the Conqueror at the head of a triumphal procession of lights, to Christ the Sun risen and shining upon a garden of lights which are flowers and of flowers which are lights. The sun, one and the same in the whole world, enlightens all that is in darkness (*Par.* XXIII:28–30). As the sun diffuses light which makes all things grow; so Christ the Light of the world, Christ the Head of the Church, pours life into the whole Church which blossoms under his light even when he himself is invisible. The Church has a visible and invisible side. Christ invisible makes the garden of the saints visible.[2]

Saint John's image of the Mystical Body, that of the vine and the branches, is taken from the realm of botany; Saint Paul's, of the body and its members, from that of biology. Both are images of organic life, of that living organism which is the Church animated by the life that descends from the Father to the Incarnate Word and through the Incarnation to all humankind. Dante's image comes from the arts. Individual plants in a garden are often combined to form an image of a cross or the emblems on an escutcheon or a coat of arms, where, like the pieces in a mosaic, they form a new unity. The flowers would lack life without the light of the sun; the mosaics would have no beauty.

The procession of the Church in the Stellar Heaven answers to the procession in the earthly Paradise. We see the procession there on the horizontal, the normal movement of a procession; though it ascends into the heavens we do not see it rise. Here Christ, the Sun of Justice, the Wisdom and the Power (1 Cor. 1:24; *Par.* XXIII: 19–21), who opened the road from earth to Heaven rises to the Father at the head of his triumphal army.

The procession in the Starry Heaven has many meanings: in it many images of the Mystical Body are combined. It is Christ's ascension into Heaven at the head of the triumphal procession from Limbo when he brings to his Father the souls of those believers in the Messias to come who had waited millenniums and centuries for the hour when the Redeemer would open the gates of Heaven (XXIII:39) so that they might follow him into glory (*Summa* III, q. 52, a. 1; *Inf.* IV:49–63); it is the triumph of all souls from the beginning of time, saved by the revolving of the spheres (XXIII:21); it is the glory of the risen body, the prelude to and the figure of the general resurrection. From the Empyrean Dante must go down again to earth to reveal what he has seen (*Par.* XXVII:64–66), all that he has learned about the needs of the Church and the Empire on earth. But these souls who were in the procession, whom he now sees in the mystical garden, he later sees rise through the vastness like the innumerable flakes of a supernatural snowstorm (XXVII:70–75), never to return; in the next vision of the Mystical Body he will see them in the mystic rose in the splendor of their risen bodies as they will be after the Day of Judgment (*Par.* XXX:43–45).

O company chosen for the great supper of the
Blessed Lamb!

— Paradiso XXIV:1, 2

I lift mine eyes, and all the windows blaze
With forms of saints and holy men who died,
Here martyred and hereafter glorified;
And the great Rose upon its leaves displays

Christ's Triumph, and the angelic roundelays,
With splendor upon splendor multiplied;
And Beatrice again at Dante's side
No more rebukes, but smiles her words of praise.

And then the organ sounds, and unseen choirs
Sing the old Latin hymns of peace and love
And benedictions of the Holy Ghost;
And the melodious bells among the spires
O'er all the house-tops and through heaven above
Proclaim the elevation of the Host!

— Longfellow
Sonnet V of "The *Divina Commedia*"

The third and last vision of Christ is the climax of the whole
Divine Comedy, that vision of the whole Christ in the mystic rose
of the Empyrean. It, even more than the other images, is an attempt
to put into words ineffable mysteries to which Dante adhered in
complete faith. With Saint Paul and Saint John, with all the early
Fathers of the Church, with the medieval scholastics, he believed
that in the kingdom of God which Jesus preached (Mk. 1:14; 4:26-
32; Mt. 25:31-46; etc.) the Eucharist is the great love feast; that
the Mystical Body of Christ is made up of angels as well as men
(*Summa* III, q. 8, a. 3, 4);[3] that the life of contemplation is a life
of intense activity; that the universe is bound together into an absolute oneness; that the greatest happiness for men and angels is to
participate in the Beatific Vision and to penetrate the mystery of
the Hypostatic Union — the mystery of duality within the mystery
of the Tri-unity: all these beliefs Dante tries to depict in the symbolism of the mystic rose of the Empyrean.

We have already seen how in this kingdom of Christ's glory Dante enthrones Mary as Queen and Empress and ranges saints and angels in that hierarchical order one must find in any kingdom. We have seen the innumerable thousands of rejoicing angels and saints, each distinct from the other in brightness and activity but all united in the radiant light which transfigures them and in the active joy of contemplation, each group and each individual contributing to the ineffable happiness of the other. For since Dante believed in degrees of blessedness and of union with the Trinity according to different measures of grace, he believed in degrees of brightness and activity. These things we have discussed in the chapters on the angels and the Virgin.

But there are still more mysteries to portray in the Church Triumphant, that aspect of the Communion of Saints and the Mystical Body with which Dante is concerned in the white rose as he considers the interrelationship of men with the Deity. Chief among these is the Eucharist. Dante believed that the Eucharist, which from apostolic times was called the sacrament of ecclesiastical unity, had for its object the incorporation of men in Christ and with Christ in one another. "We being many are one bread, one body," says Saint Paul (1 Cor. 10:17); "he that eateth my flesh and drinketh my blood abideth in me and I in him . . . he that cateth this bread shall live forever," writes Saint John, quoting Christ (Jn. 6:57, 59); "O company chosen for the great supper of the Blessed Lamb who feeds you so that your desire is always full," Beatrice says to the saints in the mystic garden blossoming under the Sun of Justice, "give heed to the immense longing of this man and refresh him" (*Par.* XXIV:1–9).

At the Last Supper, just before his Passion, Christ, having instituted the Sacrament of the Eucharist and given it to his Apostles, prayed to his Father not only for the Apostles "but for them also who through their word shall believe in me" (Jn. 17:20–21).

That they all may be one, even as Thou Father art in me and I in thee — that they too may be in us in order that the world may believe that thou hast sent me. . . .

The Church has taught and Dante believes that since the Son enjoys absolute unity with the Father in his divine nature, through the

Incarnation he communicates this unity to men; he believes it is a unity not only of individuals with Christ and the Father but a collective unity consisting in the union of all saints — and, on earth, of potential saints — with one another.

As the Eucharistic Bread is made of many grains of wheat, as each one who receives the bread receives the whole Christ, so here in the mystic rose each one receives the whole of the Beatific Vision according to the measure of his love. The rose is in a mysterious way the great supper of the Blessed Lamb, the *communion* of saints in the Church Triumphant, the Mystical Christ come into glory, the elevation in the spaceless, boundless realms of eternity of the white Host of the Eucharist.

In the white rose Dante is vouchsafed the Beatific Vision. In the flash in which it is given to him, he distinguishes three moments: the immediate and simultaneous knowledge of the entire created universe (*Par.* XXXIII:85–93); the vision of the Blessed Trinity, One God in Three Divine Persons, and the interrelationship of the Persons (109–126); and the Incarnation, the mystery of the Hypostatic Union (127–138).

Saint Thomas has said that the vision of the whole Christ will be the vision of the Head and body, of all humanity, and of the universe (*Summa, Sup.* III, q. 91, a. 1). Dante's dream of one world was not just a dream: in spite of apparent universal disunion, the primacy of existence does not belong to parts in isolation but to the whole. Dante sees all things in their scientific relationships, not in succession and discursively as we see them in time, but as God sees them, simultaneously. He sees the universal form, the archetypal idea of the universe, its order, as it exists in the Divine Mind — all things forming a simple light, all things "bound with love in one volume," because created things are the extension in time of the Divine Goodness (*Par.* XXXIII:85–93).

Without turning his eyes from the single light, but gazing fixedly upon it, Dante sees it transformed — though he knows the change is not in the light but in himself (*Par.* XXXIII:112–114). The light appears now as three circles of three colors and one dimension: one, the Son, seems reflected from the other, the Father, and the third seems fire emanating equally from both. The three colors are probably the primary colors: yellow or gold, blue, and red. Yellow, gold, the most exalted color of the ancients, represented Divinity itself, Infinite Power, and would here be the color for the Father; blue was the color of Wisdom and would here be the color for Divine Wisdom, the name given to the Son; red represented charity, Love, the Holy Spirit. These three colors would fuse into white light. The circle is an ancient symbol of Divinity; the fact that these three circles are of one dimension represents the equality of the Persons of the Trinity; the procession of the Persons by generation and spiration is carefully signified by the movement of the colors. Looking into the depths of the Divinity, Dante realizes that only God can understand God, that only God can adequately love God; he realizes that finite intelligence and finite love can never measure the infinite fullness of the Existence of the Triune God, the happiness of God within his own Being, the eternal Communion of Person with Person.

Dante's crowning vision, that of the Incarnation, is the greatest mystery of all. The understanding of the union of the divine and human in Christ is the crown of eternal beatitude. Dante's eyes are drawn to the circle which appears as a reflected light (the Son) and sees depicted within it in its own color our image. Desiring to see how the human image conforms to the divine circle, he is illumined once more by a flash of grace, by which his desire is realized and he sees the third and most complete image of the God-man.[4]

In the *New Life* (XII) after Beatrice had refused to salute Dante, Love appeared to him weeping. When Dante asked why he wept, Love answered that he was "as the center of a circle but with Dante it was not so." At the end of the *Divine Comedy*, when his desire and his will move in perfect stability, Dante has moved to that center, equidistant from all parts of the circumference. "Already," he says (*Par.* XXXIII:143–145), "my desire and will (in harmony) were turning like a wheel moved evenly by the love which turns the sun and the other stars."

Love is the final word. Love, in Dante, literally makes the world go around. The doctrine of the creation, Divine Goodness expressing itself in finite beings is a mystery of love; the mysteries of the

Incarnation and Redemption, of the Eucharist, of the Mystical Body are mysteries of love. At the close of his discourse at the Last Supper (Jn. 17:26) where the God-man brings all these mysteries into focus, he speaks of the absolute love that binds the Trinity into unity; he asks his Father

> That the love wherewith thou lovest me
> may be in them
> and I in them.

Love is the center of unity (*Par.* XXVI:55–63); love is the sum total of all the virtues (1 Cor. 13) as white is the fusion of all colors; love is the passport to the white rose; it is the key to the Kingdom of God (*Par.* XXVI:31–36).

NOTES

1. Emile Mersch, S.J., *The Whole Christ, The Historical Development of the Doctrine of the Mystical Body in Scripture and Tradition,* trans. from the French by John R. Kelly, S.J. (Milwaukee, 1938). For a recent presentation of the doctrine, see the encyclical letter, *The Mystical Body of Christ,* issued on June 29, 1943, by Pope Pius XII; also John L. Murphy, *The Living Christ* (Milwaukee, 1952). Father Murphy's book is very readable; it is in one sense an extended commentary on the encyclical of Pius XII.
2. For further discussion see Mersch, *op. cit.,* Part III, Chap. VII, pp. 472–485.
3. For further discussion of the matter of membership in the Mystical Body, see Mersch, *op. cit.,* Chap. VIII, pp. 486–498.
4. The other two were in the Earthly Paradise and Mars.

PART THREE

The Road to Peace

CHAPTER IX

PURGATION FOR PERFECTION

Two loves have built two cities: the earthly by the love of
self, even to the contempt of God; the heavenly by the love
of God, even to the contempt of self. The former, in a word,
glories in itself; the latter in the Lord. For the one seeks
glory from men; but the greatest glory of the other is God,
the witness of conscience. The one lifts up its head in its
own glory; the other says to God, "Thou art my glory, and
the lifter up of mine head." . . . The one delights in its
own strength, represented in the persons of its rulers; the
other says to its God, "I will love thee, O Lord, my strength."
. . . the wise men of one city, living according to man . . .
worshipped and served the creature more than the Creator,
who is blessed forever. But in the other city there is no
human wisdom, but only godliness, which offers due worship to the true God, and looks for its reward in the society
of the saints, of holy angels as well as holy men, "that
God may be all in all."

— Saint Augustine
The City of God XIV:28

Be ye therefore perfect even as also your
heavenly Father is perfect.

— Mt. 5:48

ll of Dante's writings bear abundant witness to his belief
in sin — original and actual — and to his conviction
that the essence of sin in men and angels lies in a free
act of the will (*Purg.* XVIII:61–73) by which the
creature turns from the expressed will of the Creator. As we have seen
in the chapter on the angels, he held that (p. 142) for them the
turning from God was irrevocable. We saw in the last chapter that
he believed, that with man, God was merciful; though he cast

251

him out of the Garden of Eden, he promised him a Saviour who would reclaim the world which belongs to God by right of Creation but which had been claimed by Satan because of his conquest over Adam and Eve. He held, too, that by the right of victory over the first conqueror, Christ by the Incarnation and Redemption won for man a "new life," the supernatural life of grace, which puts him in another order of existence from that in which he was before and that it is the task of the individual who by baptism has been elevated to this supernatural order, who has been Christened, to "walk in the newness of life" (Rom. 6:4), seeking "the things that are above."

When Adam, the father of the human race fell from grace, he lost primal innocence for all his progeny as well — Dante says, "by not enduring a curb on his will he damned himself and all his descendants" (Par. VII:25-27); and though in the Christian dispensation the waters of baptism remove from each individual soul the original sin inherited from Adam, the wounds of original sin remain. Before the fall, man had all the physical appetites that he has now; the delight of the untainted senses was keener than sensory delight is now. But all the desires and appetites were in perfect harmony, all subject to reason. No passion or desire could urge its own special claim without reference to the balance of all the powers of man — animal, intellectual, and volitional. The sin of Adam destroyed this balance: at once man's passions and desires began to war against each other, to clamor for gratification without reference to the whole balance of man. This lack of balance has been transmitted to all mankind. To heal these wounds and restore the balance is the work of purgation (Par. VII:82-84). The soul in whom the balance is perfectly restored has attained sanctity.

With all Christian thinkers Dante holds that man is free to accept or reject the offer of the supernatural life: he can surrender to the natural life with its principles of hedonism, utilitarianism, and pragmatism founded on the doctrine that whatever is useful or pleasureable is desirable or he can keep his eyes fixed not on natural but supernatural happiness; he can follow reason, not feeling; seek spiritual joy, not sensory pleasure; and strive through temporal means and the temporal social order to attain eternal verities in the Communion of Saints. In other words, he can strive for holiness, complete victory over sin, realizing that for him victory is possible only in virtue of Christ's victory — his birth, death, and resurrection. He can endeavor to reach that perfection described in the two great commandments: to love the Lord his God with all his heart and all his soul and all his mind and all his strength; and in loving God to love all that God loves in the way that God loves, including himself and his neighbor. The process by which a man attains this ideal of perfection belongs to what is known as ascetical and mystical theology, branches of the divine science in which Dante was as proficient as he was in the moral and dogmatic branches.

That all men have been haunted by the ideal of perfection is clear from any even cursory study of civilization. A study of Greco-Roman culture and many of the Oriental pagan cultures, notably the Hindu, shows advanced aspects of renunciation and consecration motivated by this ideal. The books of the Old Testament reveal an ascetic and mystic theology in Judaism born of the consciousness of a personal God who created the universe and to whom everything he had made, including man, belonged by divine right. From the beginning of the Christian Era, there has always been knowledge and experience of asceticism and mysticism, as the writings of Saint John and Saint Paul testify, and as do the works of the early Fathers, notably Saint Augustine.

The men of the Middle Ages — among them Saint Bernard, Hugh and Richard of St. Victor, Saint Bonaventure, and Saint Thomas, with all of whom Dante was familiar, and upon all of whom he draws — wrote much on the subject; but perhaps the fullest development is to be found in the works of the sixteenth-century Spanish mystic, Saint John of the Cross, who without altering in any way the teaching of the earlier theologians clarifies their teaching on several points and therefore can shed much light on Dante's presentation of asceticism and mysticism in the *Divine Comedy*.[1]

Inasmuch as ascetical and mystical theology are concerned with perfection, it may be useful to define perfection in the context of the theologian. According to the scholastics, a thing is said to be perfect insofar as it attains the purpose of its existence; for example, a watch when it keeps exact time, a paper knife when it cuts paper well. Man who even *naturally* was made to the image and likeness of God, attains *natural* perfection when he attains to uncreated Good, that is to say God, who alone is able, by his infinite goodness, completely to satisfy the human will. Man who has been revitalized by the life of Christ and is a real or potential member of the Mystical Body of Christ, attains to *supernatural* perfection — which includes and elevates natural perfection — by an ever growing likeness to God; for the more a man grows like God, the more perfect he is as a man. *Moral* theology is the theology for salvation, dealing as it does with the meaning and observance of the law of God. *Ascetical* theology deals with what a man must himself do that he may attain spiritual perfection: it is the theology which teaches a man how to make the best of himself in the eyes of God, how to do with himself the best of which he is capable. *Mystical* theology deals with the higher stages of what is called contemplation. Ascetical and mystical theology are engaged on quite different planes: ascetical theology deals with what *man himself* with the help of grace and the right use of his intelligence and free will must do to attain perfection; mystical theology deals with perfection as it depends entirely upon the leadership of God.[2] Generally speaking, the *Inferno* is concerned with moral theology; the *Purgatorio* primarily with ascetical theology; the *Paradiso* with mystical theology.

> The end of the purgative way is purity of heart;
> that of the illuminative way, truth; that of the
> unitive way, love. . . . In the purgative way
> man understands himself; in the illuminative,
> he understands God; in the unitive, he strives
> to be united and transformed in God.
>
> — John G. Arintero, O.P.
> The Mystical Evolution in the Develop-
> ment and Vitality of the Church

Dionysius, sometimes called the Areopagite but now usually referred to as pseudo-Dionysius (see Chapter V above, Note 3), brought into the Western Church not only the description of the three angelic hierarchies but also the familiar threefold division of the way of perfection: the purgative, illuminative, and unitive. He associates the two concepts in his *Celestial Hierarchy* (III:2). The general function of every angelic hierarchy and the effect of the divine light which it communicates is threefold: to purify, to illuminate, and to render perfect. "God," he says, "first purifies the souls in which he dwells, then he illumines them, and finally leads them to divine union."[3] The aim of the soul differs in each of the three ways. In the purgative way the soul is concerned with clearing the ground by removing and avoiding what may hinder perfection, thereby disposing itself for true wisdom; in the illuminative way it consistently strives to gain virtues, graces, and powers which develop sacrifice and kindle love; in the unitive way there is perfect reciprocal love, for the intellect and will are directed upward to God alone.[4]

Since, as was said at the outset, the objective is perfect love, the perfection of the Christian life — according to Saint Thomas and other medieval theologians, especially Saint Bernard — consists first and foremost in the love of God and then as a sequent in the love of neighbor. The threefold way of perfection Saint Thomas formulates as follows (*Summa* II–II, q. 24, a. 9):

> At first it is incumbent on man to occupy himself chiefly with avoiding sin and resisting his concupiscences, which move him in opposition to charity: this concerns beginners, in whom charity has to be fed or fostered lest it be destroyed; in the second place man's chief pursuit is to aim at progress in good, and this is the pursuit of the proficient, whose chief aim is to strengthen their charity by adding to it; while man's third pursuit is to aim chiefly at union with and enjoyment of God: this belongs to the perfect who *desire to be dissolved and to be with Christ.*

Upon this basis, formulated by Dionysius and developed by the mystics and scholastics of the twelfth and thirteenth centuries, the ascetical and mystical theology came down to Dante and by him was transformed into poetry, as indeed it was in a later period by Saint John of the Cross.

In Dante as in Saint John of the Cross, as indeed in Saint Paul and Saint Augustine, there is a step preliminary to the beginning of the purgative way which is known as the conversion, a step always marked by an arresting grace.[5] In the *Divine Comedy* that transforming period in the life of the soul is represented by the passage through Hell. Through the intercession of the Virgin Mary there has come to Dante a signal grace by which he will be led to understand in the "dark valley" the heinousness of sin (*Inf.* XII:86, 87) and to make reverent his knees and brow (*Purg.* I:49–51), in other words, learn how to pray. The laborious ascent of the mountain of Purgatory is quite obviously the purgative way: the clearing of the ground of the soul by uprooting the seven capital sins and planting the seed of the opposing virtues; the purifying of the exterior and interior senses; and, by prayer and penance, regaining primal innocence.

The illuminative way begins in the Earthly Paradise where Dante who has been drawn by Matilda through the waters of Lethe is taken "bathed" to the dance of the four nymphs (the cardinal virtues), each of whom covers him with her arms (*Purg.* XXXI:103–105) to signify that he has attained perfection in prudence, justice, fortitude, and temperance, "for all the other virtues" which he has acquired on the cornices and in the Ante-Purgatory "are reducible to the above four" (*Summa* I–II, q. 61, a. 3). These virtues lead him to the eyes of Beatrice, Divine Revelation. They have quieted the tumult of human passions and established a state of inward peace in which the theological virtues can bring him to the contemplation of God, which is the final happiness of man. The way of illumination continues during Dante's ascent through the Heavens of the seven planets, the Stellar Heaven, and the Primum Mobile. In the Primum Mobile he is prepared for the unitive way and the consummation of his desires in the Empyrean where he enjoys the Beatific Vision.

For this threefold way of attaining perfection as for the threefold way of arriving at the knowledge of God, Dante uses three guides and three modes of movement. Along the purgative way, where a man must do all that lies in his power to attain spiritual perfection by the discipline and penance required by ascetical theology, Virgil, reason, is his guide. The ordinary mode of progress is the laborious climbing of a spiral path, requiring great personal effort. Along the illuminative way the soul is in the hands of God and ascends by the power of God in a straight upward movement as by a spiritual elevator which carries it with the rapidity of light. The guide along this way is Beatrice, Divine Revelation. Progress in the Empyrean or quiet heaven is of another sort. It is not forward or upward but inward, for the soul is, as it were, caught up in contemplative prayer. Such movement, if it can be called movement, is circular; to describe it Dante uses the image of the wheel. The guide here is the contemplative Bernard, who wrote much on the perfection of charity, the virtue which unites the soul with God.

When Dante in his dedicatory letter to Can Grande is justifying himself for his claim that he beheld in a vision wonderful things which words cannot adequately express, he refers in some detail to the vision of Saint Paul (2 Cor. 12:1–7) and names three works outside of Sacred Scripture which deal with supernatural experiences: Of Contemplation by Richard of St. Victor, Of Consideration by Saint Bernard, and Of the Magnitude of the Soul by Saint Augustine.[6] A study of the work of Saint Augustine shows an analogy to the organization of the Divine Comedy. In Chapter 33 of the dialogue, Augustine describes seven steps or levels of the soul's power. After considering the stage of animation which man has in common with plants; that of the senses which he has in common with beasts; and the rational life, a knowledge of arts and sciences which is proper to man, he studies the degrees of the spiritual life.

These degrees which Augustine discusses beginning with the fourth level of the soul's power fall into the pattern of the three ways with which we have been concerned in this discussion. The fourth stage is that in which the soul withdraws from all base things and "makes itself spotless and stainless," in this difficult endeavor entrusting itself with complete filial devotion to the help of supreme Justice. In the fifth stage the purified soul possesses itself in all joy and is disturbed by nothing: its state is one of tranquillity in which it comes to an awareness of its own greatness. The sixth stage marks the entrance into light, which is possible only to a soul that has been made clean and whose thoughts are withdrawn from all mundane attachment and defilement. The seventh and last stage is the vision and contemplation of truth. "What shall I say," writes Augustine, "are the delights, what the enjoyment, of the supreme and true God; what breath of undisturbed peace and eternity? These are the wonders that great souls have declared, so far as they brought themselves to speak of these realities, great souls of incomparable greatness, who, we believe, beheld and now behold these things."[7]

That Dante had studied *Of the Magnitude of the Soul* intently is apparent from the use he makes of it in all of his works. That he should lean upon it in his ascetical and mystical theology is to be expected, for Augustine is recognized as the founder of mysticism in the Western Church. It is clear that the last four stages of his *Of the Magnitude of the Soul* fit perfectly into Dante's pattern in his *Divine Comedy*; the fourth into the Purgatory, especially the cornices of the seven capital sins; the fifth, the Earthly Paradise; the sixth, the nine moving spheres of the Paradise; the seventh, the Empyrean. It is possible, too, to see in the third stage the *Inferno*, where Virgil, representing reason, comes to Dante's aid in the dark wood and shows him in the nine circles the need of a virtuous life.

> *Unless a man be born again of water and the Holy Ghost, he cannot enter into the kingdom of God.*
>
> — Jn. 3:5
>
> *By Baptism a man dies to the old life of sin and begins a certain newness of life according to* Romans 6:4: *We are buried together with Christ by Baptism unto death; that, as Christ is risen from the dead . . . so we also may walk in newness of life.*
>
> — Saint Thomas Aquinas

In the divine economy of salvation the first step the soul must take is to rid itself of original sin. When Dante and Virgil emerge from Hell, which is under the dominion of Satan, they take that first step in the "second realm, where the human spirit is cleansed" to become "worthy to rise to Heaven" (*Purg.* I:5, 6). Though the "heavens rejoice" in the light of the four stars of the natural cardinal virtues (*Purg.* I:23, 25, 37), which brighten the face of Cato, these natural virtues are not sufficient to admit a man to the kingdom of heaven (*Inf.* IV:35, 36; *Purg.* VII:7–9). A man's soul must be radiant with the supernatural or theological virtues (*Purg.* VII:34–36), and the first of these is faith, which is the beginning of the way of salvation (*Inf.* II:29, 30). Natural goodness is not enough: there must be baptism of water or blood or desire; for baptism is the sacrament which removes the stains of original sin; which breaks the bonds of Satan; which elevates man to the plane of the supernatural, and by making him conformable to the Passion and Resurrection of Christ makes him a member of his Mystical Body.

This whole doctrine is presented in symbolism in the first canto of the *Purgatorio*. "Go," says Cato to Virgil, "and gird this man with a slender reed (the symbol of humility) and bathe his face so that all stains are washed from it and afterwards do not return here; the sun will show you the easiest way to climb the mountain" (*Purg.* I:94–108). Virgil softly spreads both hands on the wet grass; Dante raises toward him his tear-stained cheeks: the hue which Hell had hidden is revealed (*Purg* I:121–128). Humility and obedience counteract the lack of both in Adam. The washing away of original sin, the restoration of primal innocence which Hell had hidden, the new illumination of grace for the new way are all here in allegory.

In the Middle Ages there was among theologians a universal practice of explaining much in the New Law by showing how it was prefigured in the Old, thus emphasizing the continuity of God's way with man. One of the most popular of these Old Testament symbols for baptism was the passage of the Israelites through the Red Sea. Saint Thomas, quoting Saint John Damascene, presents the matter in the *Summa* III, q. 66, a. 11:

Damascene enumerates certain figurative Baptisms: for instance, the Deluge was a figure of our Baptism in respect of the salvation of the faithful in the Church; since then a few . . . souls were saved in the ark (*Vulg.* by water) according to I *Peter* 3:20. He also mentions the crossing of the Red Sea, which was a figure of our Baptism in respect of our delivery from the bondage of sin; hence the Apostle says (I *Cor.* 10:2) that all . . . were baptized in the cloud and in the sea.

Immediately after Virgil has washed the stains from Dante's cheeks, as they stand meditatively watching the sun rise, they see the angel of faith piloting the hundred souls from the Tiber's mouth to Purgatory's shore and hear coming over the water the plain chant *In Exitu Israel de Aegypto*. Since these souls are entering Purgatory, they are baptized souls; they are also the souls of sinners in need of penance. Is Dante the soul baptized in the cloud and have those in the boat been baptized in the sea? And was this baptism for all of them a baptism unto penance because with all of them God was not well pleased (1 Cor. 10:5)?

The point should be pursued further. Saint Thomas (*Summa* III, q. 39, a. 3), commenting on the baptism conferred by Saint John the Baptist called in *Mark* (1:4) and in *Matthew* (3:2) *a baptism of penance*, says that it is so called "by reason of its inducing men to do penance, and of its being a kind of protestation by which men avowed their purpose of doing penance." For Dante personally, the baptism at the very opening of the way of purgation is an indication of the penitential spirit which characterizes him at Saint Peter's gate (*Purg.* IX) and during the whole ascent to the Earthly Paradise.

In the passage in *Matthew* already cited Saint John says,

> I indeed baptize you in water unto penance but he
> that shall come after me, is mightier than I.
> . . . he shall baptize you in the Holy Ghost and fire.

Dante has two baptisms of fire: the imagined fire of the dream when the eagle, terrible as a thunderbolt, snatches him, and carries him to the gate of Purgatory to begin his penitential climb (*Purg.* IX: 28–33); and the fire of his purification on the seventh cornice (*Purg.* XXVII:46–51) from which he emerges ready to enter the Garden of Eden. Under the symbolism of water he is given his final absolution in the waters of Lethe, a mystical representation of the cleansing from all actual sins by the sacrament of penance. Freed from original and actual sin, as well as the consequences of sin, he is ready to mount to the stars (*Purg.* XXXII:143–145).

> *Every creature, since it is good, can be loved both well and badly: well, that is, when order is preserved; badly, when order is disturbed. If the Creator be truly loved, that is if He Himself, not aught else instead of Him which is not He, be loved, He cannot be loved badly. For even Love itself is to be loved in orderly wise, whereby what is to be loved is loved well that the virtue may be in us by which one lives well. Therefore, it seems to me that a brief and true definition of virtue is the* Order of Love, *on account of which in the holy canticle the Bride of Christ, the City of God, sings:* Set love in order in me.

> — Saint Augustine
> *The City of God* XV:22

But we have run ahead of ourselves. Though by baptism the stain of original sin is removed from the soul, though "he who is baptized is freed from the debt of all punishment" due to original sin just as if "he himself had offered sufficient satisfaction" (*Summa* III, q. 69, a. 2) the *penalties* of original sin, such as fatigue, disease, death, remain in the physical nature of man, and the *wounds* of original sin, in the intellect and will. As the first man came forth from his Maker's hand clothed with original justice, his body, free from all disordered movement, was not a heavy fetter on his soul but its docile instrument. He possessed a clear knowledge of God, of the world around him, and of himself. Now, though he is redeemed, man because of the wound of ignorance in his intellect finds it difficult to attain to truth, especially to supreme Truth. He no longer sees things in the light of first principles (*Summa* II–II, q. 166) but has a tendency to error. He has a vain intellectual curiosity about the things of this world and, through spiritual sloth, a lack of intentness on the things of God. Through spiritual pride he is prone to place too much confidence in his own reason, is loath to consult others, and is frequently stubborn in his own judgment. Spiritual blindness often gives him a false set of values so that he prefers temporal to spiritual goods and, like the ancient Pharisees, does not recognize Christ or hear his voice.

The wound in the will Saint Thomas calls the *wound of malice.* Before the fall, man's will had strength to command the passions; now it is inclined to egoism (*Summa* I–II, q. 85, a. 3; 109, a. 3). Self-love takes possession of man's will and he forgets the love due to God and to his neighbor. This self-love is the source of all sin (*Summa* I–II, q. 77, a. 4). From it are born concupiscence of the flesh, which leads to gluttony and lust; concupiscence of the eyes, which leads to avarice; and pride of life, which in regard to self leads to vainglory and/or sloth; and in regard to one's neighbor leads to envy and anger. Those sins are called *capital* sins because they are root sins, which give rise to others (*Summa*, I–II, q. 84, a. 4).[8]

In an organization which differs somewhat from that of Saint Thomas, Dante shows how all of the capital sins rise from disordered love (*Purg.* XVII: 91–139). Distorted love, the desire to inflict some manner of injury on one's neighbor, leads to pride, envy, and anger; defective love, a weak, indolent desire for good, which is sloth or a "don't-care attitude," leads to acedia, a form of sloth; excessive love, an immoderate desire for things not wrong in themselves, gives rise to avarice, gluttony, and sensuality. Any concessions made to these weaknesses in the intellect and the will may lead to actual sin.

As was pointed out in Chapter IV, p. 111, every one of the actual sins presented and punished in the *Inferno* had its root in one of the seven capital sins. What every physician knows in the physical order and every psychiatrist in the mental order, the moral theologian knows in the spiritual order: if a cure is to be effected, the root of the difficulty must be discovered and eradicated. Therefore, whether a man is guilty of deliberate sin or not (some saints like Saint Thérèse of Lisieux could affirm that they had never willfully refused God anything), he must strive valiantly to set love in order by practicing the virtues opposed to the seven capital sins, thereby uprooting the sins themselves. What these virtues are we have examined above in the chapter on the Virgin.

> Now what wisdom is, and what was her origin I will declare: and I will not hide from you the mysteries of God.
>
> For the beginning of her is the most true desire of discipline: and the care of discipline is love and love is the keeping of her laws.
>
> And if a man love justice, her labors have great virtues: for she teacheth temperance, and prudence, and justice, and fortitude, which are such things as men can have nothing more profitable in life.
>
> — Wisd. 6:24, 18, 19; 8:7

Among the devices Dante uses in the *Purgatorio* and *Paradiso* to show progress in perfection and in the *Inferno* to show the lack of it is his presentation of the cardinal and theological virtues at different stages of his journey. Since the cardinal or moral virtues are both natural and supernatural, his use of them is particularly interesting. Saint Thomas discusses them at various times and in various ways. He distinguishes as different in kind natural prudence, justice, fortitude, and temperance which can be acquired by human effort and the supernatural virtues of the same names which are infused by divine grace. The natural virtues are always social (*Summa* I–II, q. 61, a. 5) — they are so presented by Plato and Aristotle; the supernatural virtues are social, perfecting, and perfect in a Christian context. In presenting the supernatural virtues especially,

Saint Thomas notes an initial stage, an ultimate perfecting, and an extensive evolution in habitually divine living.

Since the cardinal virtues are first of all *natural* virtues, Dante presents them before the symbolic rite of baptism. Immediately upon emerging from Hell he sees in the sapphire sky the four stars which symbolize these virtues; later he observes that their rays brighten the face of Cato as though the sun were shining on him (*Purg.* I:23–25; 37–39). Cato as a virtuous pagan had acquired the natural cardinal virtues. The infused cardinal virtues like the theological virtues are given to the soul by baptism and increase in the soul as it grows in the supernatural life.

Just as the theological virtues are essential to the life of grace — faith marking the beginning of the climb to perfection; hope motivating the effort; and love spurring the soul to put forth all its strength (*Purg.* IX:48) — so do the infused cardinal virtues aid in its advancement in the way of perfection. Prudence gives counsel about all matters regarding man's activities and, contemplating the things of God, counts as nothing all the things of this world; temperance helps to establish the mean in the concupiscible appetite and to this end, so far as nature allows, mortifies the body; justice points out the way to the right relationship between man and God, man and himself, and man and his neighbor, and induces the soul to give wholehearted consent to following the way to attain this goal; fortitude helps to establish the proper balance between fear and daring in the irascible passions and to rise to heavenly things (*Summa* I–II, q. 61, a. 5).

Inasmuch as the whole business of purification is concerned ultimately with restoring in the soul the "Likeness of God," which has been lost because of sin,[9] both the theological and cardinal virtues may be considered as *perfecting* virtues, that is, "virtues of men who are on their way and tending to Divine similitude" (*Summa* I–II, q. 61, a. 5). In the *Divine Comedy* the work of the cardinal virtues is completed in the *Purgatorio;* that of the theological virtues continues into the *Paradiso.* In the Earthly Paradise, where the cardinal virtues are presented as nymphs dancing at the left wheel of the Chariot, they embrace Dante when Matilda brings him to them after she has bathed him in the cleansing waters of

Lethe, to indicate that he has successfully surmounted all difficulties and possesses these virtues in their perfection. The theological virtues, however — the nymphs dancing at the right wheel — ask Beatrice to unveil her beauty for Dante; but he, not yet ready to sustain it, is blinded by it. He does not attain perfection in the theological virtues until he has reached the Stellar Heaven and passed the examination administered by Peter, James, and John.

From one point of view, that of Saint Thomas (*Summa* I–II, q. 61, a. 3), all of the virtues acquired in the Ante-Purgatory and on the cornices may be considered as growth in the cardinal virtues; from another point of view, that of Saint Bernard, and Saint Paul, they represent growth in the theological virtue of love. In the first view, patience, the virtue so prominent in the Ante-Purgatory, is a facet of fortitude; the virtues of humility, chastity, meekness, sobriety, opposed to the capital sins of pride, anger, gluttony, and lust are matters of temperance; that of liberality opposed to avarice and prodigality is a matter of justice. All are related to prudence, which gives good counsel. In the second view, these same virtues of the Ante-Purgatory and the cornices represent a dramatization of the definition of charity given by Saint Paul, who in *1 Corinthians* 13 analyzes charity into its components and consequences as the prism refracts white light. Patience and kindness, with which Saint Paul begins, are the virtues of the Ante-Purgatory; the other virtues are found on the cornices. The total is love. Dante must have had the epistle of the great Apostle, the "Great Vessel of the Holy Spirit" as he calls him (*Par.* XXI:128), in the forefront of his mind.

Saint Bernard in his theology of purgation, emphasizes only the attaining of humility, which is the root of charity, and charity itself: the soul seeking perfection moving from knowledge of itself in increasing depths of humility to compassion for its neighbor. Then in the illuminative way he moves to consideration of the Incarnation and the Redemption, which show God's compassion for fallen man; and ultimately in the mystical reaches of the unitive way through the person of Christ to the Trinity.[10]

The purification of the intellect and the will in order to restore the soul to the image and likeness of God involves exercise in the theological virtues. The intellect must be purified by faith and the will by love; sustained hope must provide the impetus. The meditations along the cornices strengthen the soul in faith, for many of them present revealed truths; the self-abnegation required in the practice of the virtues opposed to the seven capital sins involves a growing spirit of sacrifice as evidenced by willingness to accept whatever corrective discipline of body and soul may be required for moral regeneration. So essential is this purification of the will to the setting of love in order, so close is the relationship between love and free will, which Dante proclaims the acme of human dignity (*Par.* V:19–24), that he discusses these matters central to his thought in the very heart of his poem (*Purg.* XVI, XVII, XVIII).

The converse of all these aspects of the theological and cardinal virtues is to be found in the *Inferno*. In Limbo, the first circle of Hell, Dante presents those souls who had acquired the cardinal virtues in their natural aspect insofar as they could be attained by reason, but who are cut off from God because they lacked the theological virtues. This first circle of Hell — the fringe of the abyss — stands in sharp contrast to the first terrace of the Ante-Purgatory — the fringe of the supernatural mountain — where the souls see in the sky the four stars of the cardinal virtues but almost immediately afterward are given baptism and are motivated by the theological virtues. In Limbo there is that twilight which reason can offer; in the Ante-Purgatory, the twilight of faith; in the one Virgil says the souls were blameless but are cut off because they were unbaptized (*Inf.* IV:34–36) and lacked the portal to faith; in the other the baptism of water and penance are dramatized; in the one the souls are punished only by longing without hope (*Inf.* IV:42); in the other they are filled with hope. And because we cannot love what we do not know, the souls in Limbo are cut off from love; whereas the souls in Purgatory are setting out to perfect that love which they have received with the waters of baptism.

Throughout the *Inferno* there are numerous instances of the lack of both the cardinal and theological virtues, the lack becoming increasingly evident as the descent progresses. The contrasting images by which Dante presents the outcome of the growth in virtue and in vice are the most dramatic in the *Commedia*: the white rose of the Empyrean into which the soul is caught up by love, where faith has become vision, where hope is fulfilled, and where angels and saints participate in the activity of perfect charity in the contemplation of the three Divine Persons; the frozen depths of Cocytus, where souls who have repudiated charity and are confirmed in malice are gnawed by hatred forever.

> *Temporary punishments are suffered by some in this life only, by others after death, by others both now and then; but all of them before that last and strictest judgment. But of those who suffer temporary punishments after death, all are not doomed to those everlasting pains which are to follow that judgment; for to some, as we have already said, what is not remitted in this world is remitted in the next, that is, they are not punished with the eternal punishment of the world to come.*

— Saint Augustine
The City of God XXI:13

All that has been said to this point about purification suggests activity of men in time, in this present life. To some readers of Dante, therefore, the discussion may seem irrelevant inasmuch as the *Purgatorio* obviously deals with an aspect of life after death. A major consideration about the doctrine of Purgatory is its relationship to time: Hell and Heaven are eternal; but Purgatory is a place or state of temporal discipline or suffering, which will, therefore, cease to exist when our world and time cease to exist. The whole point about this business of setting love in order, of making one's will conform to the divine will is that it *must be accomplished in time* and that if it has not been accomplished at the end of this life it can — if a man dies with his will attuned to the will of

God — be completed in the next. The price of innocence is the putting off of the old man and the putting on of the new (Rom. 6).

Perfection can be attained in this life by those who, living the life of faith fully, persevere generously in doing all that the love of God requires; in fact, it is to such perfection that every Christian should aspire. The Church has always taught that generous souls ought normally to suffer their purgatory on earth and that those who do not, have neglected graces and opportunities which were held out to them. Purgatory after death is not the normal order for the full development of the Christian life; the normal, though probably not the usual, order is for the soul to attain at the moment of death to the Beatific Vision. For that reason all spiritual writers present as the greatest suffering in Purgatory the privation of the sight of God.

But because the healing of the wounds caused in the intellect and the will by original sin entail such violence to fallen human nature, the majority of those who progress along the rugged path of Christian perfection probably do not reach their goal of perfection here. To achieve perfect union with Christ a man must take up his cross and follow him along the painful path to Calvary, making up in his own flesh what is lacking to the sufferings of Christ (Col. 1:24). Many find this a hard saying and falter in the way. Such as do must complete their purification after death.

In the *Purgatorio* Dante combines the two concepts, all of his images suggesting that he has in mind purification in this life and in the life to come. He pictures all the souls he meets as separated souls; he himself is in the flesh. He pictures the mountain of Purgatory as in our world and yet out of it, a mountain rising to the giddy height of a possible 3250 or 5000 *miles!* If he follows the data of the *Sphere* of Sacrobosco, the manual of astronomy most widely used in the thirteenth century — and indeed down to the seventeenth — the diameter of the earth was computed to be "80,181 stades and a half and third of one stade,"[11] *stade* being obsolete for *furlong*, which is an eighth of a mile. The diameter of the earth would then be 10,022 miles and the distance from the surface to the center, 5011 miles. If he follows the data he quotes from Alfergano (Alfraganus) in his discussion of the diameter of Mercury (*Banq.* II, xiv, 8) the diameter of the earth would be 6500 miles and the distance from the center to the surface 3250 miles.

Since the mountain of Purgatory was formed from the land which fled from Satan when he fell headlong from Heaven and which rose in the hemisphere of water (*Inf.* XXXIV:121–126) leaving the pit of Hell, the height of the mountain approximates the depth of the pit. Though some of the displaced land may not have risen above the water, the height of the mountain is staggering to contemplate. Since the *Sphere* was commented upon freely in all universities as well as Franciscan and Dominican studia, it was surely known to Dante; with the astronomical works of Alfraganus, which he cites and upon which Sacrobosco leans, it formed the basis of his concepts of our earth and of outer space.

Set as it is in the then unexplored southern sea, the mountain of Purgatory is so removed from the turmoil of mundane affairs that nothing disturbs it; lifting its exalted summit into that rarified atmosphere where it is untouched by even atmospheric changes (*Purg.* XXVIII:101, 102), it is symbolic of the interior solitude of the soul to which Saint Bernard exhorted his brethren in those cloistral schools of charity, which he reared in the wildernesses of France, in its isolation and separateness it has the austerity and stark beauty of the Cistercian houses of prayer and penance which Bernard founded and over which he ruled, where in "the air and light of supernatural fecundity" men gave themselves to the "common will" and advanced in wisdom and love. Dante understood, as every mystic understands, that something equivalent to the solitude of the wilderness is essential to mystical education. At the top of the mountain of Purgatory as about the monasteries of Clairvaux and Citeau flow the waters of peace.[12]

Throughout the *Purgatorio* by word and image, Dante emphasizes the fact that theologically Purgatory belongs to time. Whereas the whole journey through Hell is made in darkness and that through the heavens in the light of the eternal day, the journey in Purgatory comprises four days and three nights, with all the natural lights of sun and moon in all the hours of the day and night. Repeatedly in this canticle Dante emphasizes the importance of time: in this way he suggests that purification should be a continual preoccupation during this life (*Purg.* II:121). Those who do not complete their purification in this world have in a very real sense wasted time. As Saint Catherine of Genoa teaches, and as Dante would agree, union of the soul with God, the "one Center" is achieved "at any one and at every moment, by the whole-hearted willing and doing, by the full endorsing of some one thing — some unique state and duty offered to the soul in that one unique moment."[13] Other spiritual writers speak of the "sacrament of the present moment." The failure to seize the moment rightly is to squander the opportunity and the moment: to waste time.

Another indication that Dante is convinced that purification should take place in this life is his treatment of the sacraments of baptism and penance. He believes, of course, as the Church teaches, in the acceptability of last-minute repentance for any sin at any time of a man's earthly life: this belief he dramatizes in numerous episodes. Some of them like the story of Buonconte de Montefeltro rank among the most moving scenes of the whole poem. But the emphasis he places in the Ante-Purgatory on the baptism of penance preached by John the Baptist, the systematic working out in his own case of complete facing up to his own shortcomings, both before he enters St. Peter's gate and in the Earthly Paradise, the rigorous stressing of soul-searching satisfaction and penance and the deferral of absolution until the Earthly Paradise when the satisfaction is complete suggest strongly that man should submit himself *on earth* to the disciplines necessary to attain the perfection of his nature.

This point of view, to be sure, was essential to Dante's whole purpose in writing the *Commedia,* which was to remove those *living in this life* from a state of misery and guide them to a state of happiness. Such an aim could be accomplished, he believed, by moral agents only. The regeneration of society depends upon the regeneration of the men who make up that society. From one point of view, the *Purgatorio* is a parable of the discipline on earth of moral agents, of the highhearted courage which must sustain men as they set about eliminating the seven deadly sins, which if not vanquished spell ruin for the temporal social order. Those men who have accepted the challenge have become dynamic forces in the regeneration not only of themselves but of other men.

It has been well said that all records of mystics in the West are records of prodigious activity. Notable among these are the mystics to whom Dante was attracted and whose teaching he follows: Saint Paul, Saint Augustine, Saint Bernard, Saint Francis of Assisi, Saint Bonaventure, Saint Thomas Aquinas. Having gone up into the mountain, having set love in order, these men became ambassadors to the whole world. From the Earthly Paradise Beatrice sends Dante to deliver to "those who live the life which is a race to death" all that she has taught him (*Purg.* XXXIII:52–54); from the Heaven of Mars, Cacciaguida commands him to make manifest his whole vision (*Par.* XVII:127–128). Mystics, more often than not, when called into the arena of public life demonstrate a practical genius which astounds their contemporaries.

> *The work of the Church in this world is not to teach the mysteries of life, so much as to persuade the soul to that arduous degree of purity at which God himself becomes her teacher.*
>
> — Coventry Patmore

All spiritual writers agree that there are four requisites for the setting of love in order: the grace of God, prayer, personal effort, and pain. Nothing can be accomplished without the grace of God. The initial impulse is a gift of grace; grace is needed all along the way, for it is grace that moves the will to good. Since light is everywhere Dante's symbol for God and the things of God, light is a symbol of grace, sanctifying or actual, without which the soul is powerless to accomplish anything good. For this reason Dante and Virgil climb only in daylight (*Purg.* VII:49–57). There are instances where penitents they meet on the cornices move upward in moonlight, notably the souls of the slothful, now utilizing every possible moment in their desire to make up for lost time

(*Purg.* XVIII:76–108). One must not toy with grace but lay hold of it, for it may not return (*Purg.* IX:132); one must pray for its continuance, since without it, he goes backward who struggles most to advance (*Purg.* XI:15). Grace follows grace; so the loving soul is ever alert to its prompting (*Par.* X:79–86) and faithful in following where it leads.

Purgatory Dante presents as a sanctuary of humble prayer, prayer being the second essential for progress in the way of perfection. The kingdom of Heaven suffers violence (Mt. 11:12; *Par.* XX:94–99) and the violent bear it away; therefore throughout the whole of the *Purgatorio* there is unceasing prayer, vocal and mental. Since man is composed of body and soul, Dante represents men in all the attitudes of prayer. Since the Mass is the prayer of Christ, the renewal of the sacrificial redemptive act, it is the most efficacious prayer for the living and the dead and is the principal prayer of those climbing the mountain. Since the Divine Office, as the official prayer of the Church, the Spouse of Christ, everywhere from the rising to the setting of the sun surrounds the Mass, Dante has the souls pray the Mass and the canonical hours of the Breviary.

The third essential is personal effort. The soul which has been awakened to the life of grace, which has glimpsed the divine Reality in that moment of conversion, aware that it has had a false conception of the values of life, experiences an inner reversal. In humility and obedience it will take vigorous action to tear out the roots of self-love and will climb untiringly the austere mountian of self-abnegation. So determined will it be, that it will continue in spite of fatigue, pain, and bitterness of soul. It will concentrate all the energy of its nature on freeing itself from the fetters of sensuality and putting order into its life so that it may identify itself with the Absolute. Of this intentness of purpose the *Purgatorio* and the *Paradiso* are a parable.

Because living the life which aspires to perfection is living the life of Christ, who is the Way, and because the Way leads to Calvary, the fourth essential is pain. The path of Eternal Wisdom, the Second Person of the Blessed Trinity, the Incarnate Word, is the Way of the Cross. All spiritual as well as physical birth is painful. The birth of the "new man" is painful.

O great Key-bearer and Keeper
Of the treasuries of God!
Wisdom's gifts are buried deeper
Than the arm of man can go
Save thou show
First the way, and turn the sod,

cries Francis Thompson in his ode *Laus Amara Doloris*. Infinite Wisdom, Infinite Love, decrees that those who would be fashioned in his likeness and by virtue of his Passion soar to great heights, repay his free love by their free love; to their great benefit he sends them such suffering, physical and mental, as they may need in order to put off the old man and give birth to the new. The pain at the beginning of the way may be uncertainty, weariness, loneliness of soul (*Purg.* X:19–21); there will be bodily pain and spiritual suffering. But inasmuch as the pain is accepted willingly and with love, it will be curative; its whole function is to heal the wounds of the soul. For this reason it brings joy; the souls bear it eagerly, with delight (*Purg.* XXIII:70–75), calling it not pain but solace since they desire it. It differs greatly, therefore, from the pains of Hell which are penal, imposed from without.

> Be adored among men
> God, three-numbered form:
> Wring thy rebel, dogged in den,
> Man's malice, with wrecking and storm.
> Beyond saying sweet, past telling of tongue,
> Thou art lightning and love, I found it, a winter and warm;
> Father and fondler of heart thou hast wrung:
> Hast thy dark descending and most art merciful then.
>
> — Gerard Manley Hopkins
> "The Wreck of the Deutschland"*

Since the whole operation of the *Purgatorio* is directed to the healing of the wounds of original sin by purifying the exterior and interior senses and the intellect and the will so that they may be

---

* (New York: Oxford University Press, 1918.)

restored to their pristine integrity, everything in this section of the *Commedia* is designed to that end. As an Aristotelian and Thomist, Dante held that the exterior senses are the doorway to the intellect, the channel through which man arrives at a knowledge of reality, that without them he would know nothing, that by them he can attain to Infinite Wisdom. Since, however, undisciplined senses can monopolize the field of perception and quicken desires which activate the capital sins, sensuality itself must be mortified in them so that they may cease to war against the spirit.

For man to discipline his interior senses is equally important: the *common sense* to which all apprehensions of the exterior senses are referred, that sense which enables us to bring several sensations together and by a single perceptual act to recognize their simultaneous existence in one and the same subject; the *imagination*, which is a storehouse of all that is received through the exterior senses; the *estimative power*, which is given man to apprehend the harmful or beneficial and to grasp intentions not perceived by the bodily senses, for example, whether there is time and space to pass this speeding car; and the *memorative power*, that storehouse from which all matters perceived by the senses can be revived specifically as past (*Summa* I, q. 78, a. 3, 4). Both the exterior and interior senses must be made subject to reason — as reason must be made subject to faith — so that man may reach that infinite elevation for which he is destined, body and soul, the seeing of God as God sees himself.

It is important to emphasize that Dante's whole philosophy in regard to the purification of the senses is one of control; he is concerned with conserving the powers for right use, never in their destruction. Everywhere he teaches that the senses are man's friends if he will control and direct them to make them organic elements in a unified personality. This point of view is crystal clear in the *Paradiso*, where all the interior senses are brought into magnificent play and where sight and hearing, the most spiritual of the exterior senses are sources of deep joy. It is the purified sense of hearing that is so ravished by the singing of the *Regina Coeli* (*Par.* XXIII:127–129) that Dante says the joy has never left him; it is the purified sense of sight that is enraptured by the colors and figures he encounters in the heavenly spheres. Without the sense of sight he could not delight in the multicolored garden of the Starry Heaven, the circling choirs of angels in the Primum Mobile, the pacific oriflamme and interplay of angels and saints in the Mystic Rose. It is with his bodily eyes that he participates in the three visions of Mary and Christ and in that of the Triune God. It is essential, then, that there be specific disciplines for the purification of all the senses — but of the exterior senses, sight and hearing in particular.

In Purgatory proper Dante also provides in a variety of ways for the purification of the intellect. Sometimes this is done in conjunction with the purification of the senses; sometimes in a distinctly rational way. On the cornices by means of discussions, references to Sacred Scripture, liturgical prayer, and the arts, he presents subjects for meditation on the beauty of the virtue the soul is striving to acquire and the heinousness of the vice it is endeavoring to eradicate. He supplements these subjects for meditation by philosophic discussions of such matters as love and free will, central, he believes, to the understanding of what gives life proper direction; he introduces, too, discussion of problems of aesthetics, for by harboring false principles of aesthetics men sometime lose their moral bearings. He teaches the necessity of submitting one's intellect to that of another, implying the need of spiritual direction through the rather obvious device of having Virgil (Reason) ask souls whom the pilgrims meet (e.g., *Purg.* III:102) to point out the path; he has Dante and Virgil give respectful attention to the subsidiary guides as they proffer assistance, supply information, or give needed advice (e.g., *Purg.* VII:37–63; VIII:37–45).

For the purification of the will there are the remedial disciplines, designed not only to give practice in the virtue but to curb the vice: in governing the passions as in driving a horse, one needs a whip and a bit if one would progress in the right direction. Besides the exacting demands of the disciplines themselves, there are subsidiary disciplines: obedience to guides and unfailing courtesy to companions, humble submission to all the vicissitudes of time and place, perseverance in humble communal prayer. All these borne with love and equanimity eradicate self-will.

There are, and this is clearly part of Dante's plan, in all these purifications, elements which brighten the way and alleviate the weariness and pain: the disciplined beauty of the arts which through the senses present the subjects for meditation; the stimulating quality of the philosophic and aesthetic discussions; the dramatic life stories of those the pilgrims meet on the way; the mutual good will of companions; the echoing harmonies of plain chant throbbing through austere silences; the glowing example of Mary; and the ministrations and benedictions of angels. Always there is light, the symbol of the grace of God, sunlight or starlight or moonlight on mountain and sea. And always there is peace.

The disciplines begin at the very beginning of the *Purgatorio*. The Ante-Purgatory, Dante's own invention, is, as the word suggests, primarily a place of waiting; the disciplines there develop those homely virtues demanded of all who are eager to begin a work but are constrained to stand in line, to sit in outer offices to wait their turn or their time: obedience, mutual good will, courtesy, and patience — that form of fortitude which Saint Paul names at the beginning of the roll call of the virtues which constitute perfect love.

There is sound psychology in Dante's demanding the exercise of these virtues of the souls whom he places in the Ante-Purgatory, the excommunicated and the negligent. All of these he represents as having received the grace of repentance at the moment of death — *in articulo mortis*. For various reasons, for a long portion of their lives they had denied to God the service due him. They had let God wait; Dante represents reciprocal waiting here: the excommunicate for thirty times the period of their contumacy; the negligent of the three groups — the indolent, those who had died a violent death and were unshriven, and those who were too occupied with mundane affairs to have time for those of the spirit — for as long a time as they had been remiss in their religious duties.

It is, of course, on the cornices, in Purgatory proper that Dante presents in its fullness his design for purification. What some of the elements are we have noted above in the chapters on the angels and the Virgin. On each of the seven cornices there are eight interwoven elements by which the vice is eradicated, the contrary virtue established, the senses and intellect and will purified. There is first the *discipline* to which the soul subjects itself; this like the second element, the *meditation* which accompanies the discipline, involving the call to the virtue and the curb to the vice. Dante maintains on each of the cornices a balance between the instances cited for the call and the curb; these instances which he draws from both sacred and profane history are presented directly or indirectly through one of the *arts*, Dante's third device. As we noted above, the first example of the virtue the soul is striving to acquire on each cornice is taken from the life of the Virgin, the fourth element being *to set the Virgin before the penitents as their model*. The fifth parallel element is *prayer*, mental and vocal; the sixth, the *active purification of the senses*, which is always contingent upon the discipline; the seventh, the *benediction* pronounced by the angel guardian of the cornice in terms of one of the *Beatitudes*, which constitutes the eighth element.

Within this general parallel design there are many other parallels, particularly in the presentation of the examples for the virtues and vices. At the end of Canto XIV of the *Purgatorio*, Dante says that the heavens call us to virtue: we should by reason of the attraction to heaven and all it means be eager to prepare ourselves for beatitude. Since we do not, God provides a whip. For this reason on each cornice examples of the virtues come first. Between the instances of the virtues and the vices Dante places the penitents themselves. A study of the lives of those named in each of the three groups reveals that, taken as a whole, they represent all aspects of both the virtue and the sin, providing an impetus to acquire all facets of the virtue and eradicate all facets of the vice.

The fifth cornice serves as an excellent example. The souls on this cornice are expiating either miserliness or prodigality; accordingly, Dante places before them for the opposing virtues Caius Fabricius, the Roman consul (*Aeneid* VI:843), who gave an heroic example of *voluntary poverty* by scorning the "weight of gold" which the Samnites offered him as a bribe; and Saint Nicholas, prominent for his *liberality* in using his wealth in behalf of others. He suggests in this way the need in State and Church of the proper attitude toward wealth. Hugh Capet, chief spokesman among the penitents on this cornice tells not only of the sins to which avarice led those of his dynasty, but lists stories which those on the cornice declaim during the penitential nights. A study of these stories reveals that the characters he names from sacred and profane history and literature are guilty of crimes rooted in the seven daughters of avarice (*Summa* II–II, q. 118, a. 8): Pygmalion of treachery, Midas of insatiability (restlessness), Achon of fraud, Ananias and Sapphira of perjury, Heliodorus of trickery (falsehood), Polymnestor of Thrace of insensibility to mercy, and Crassus of violence (*Purg.* XX:99–123).

On several of the cornices (2, 3, 4, 7) the number of instances of the virtue parallels that of the vice; on 1 and 5 the individual instances of the vice outnumber those of the virtue, for pride and avarice are prolific in offspring. However, even here Dante effects groupings of the sins which reduce the over-all numbers so that they parallel the virtues. The cornice of the slothful has no numerical parallelism; however, it does maintain parallelism between instances from sacred and profane history.

> *Every work of art is an open window onto the invisible.*
>
> — Charles Damian Boulogne, O.P.

Through all the Christian centuries the Church has used the arts to teach the way to God and to enhance the worship of God. That in the *Purgatorio* Dante should so employ them is, therefore, not surprising. Beauty has always been loved by man, who was made for order: all art is order, for all art is achieved by discipline. "Art is right reason about certain works to be made," says Aquinas (*Summa* I–II, q. 51, a. 3). "Moreover, art is an operative habit which has the nature of a virtue in the same way as the speculative habits. . . . Just as science has always a relation to good, so it is with art: and it is for this reason that it is called a virtue." On this premise the scholastics based their conviction that the arts have a direct relation to morality and in them can be found allegorical, moral, and anagogical as well as literal meanings.[14] By their very nature the arts appeal to the senses and through them to the intellect; Dante's idea in using them as "a solace on the way" (*Purg.* XII:14) is that what the human understanding finds beautiful and significant the will will strive to attain. Therefore, on the mountain of purgation Dante utilizes the arts in a threefold way: to purify the senses, to present stimulating subjects for meditation, and to fire the will. In these days of audio-visual emphasis in education and in every other sphere of human endeavor, it is interesting to reflect on the audio-visual devices in the *Commedia.*

On the first cornice, that of the proud, there are all aspects of sculpture: statuary, graffiti and bas-relief, and corbels; on the second and fifth, those of envy and avarice, one finds various types of story telling; on the sixth, that of gluttony, there is the art of poetry. On the seventh cornice, that of the lustful, poets and musicians go singing through the fire. In the Earthly Paradise, Dante's own instruction and purification involve abundant use of drama and the dance. Is it not possible, too, to conceive of the landscapes and seascapes, the portraits of individuals and the graphic presentation of groups as painting, and of the mountain with its gates and steps and spiral road cut into the rock as an extraordinary architectural achievement?

Through the instrumentality of the disciplines and the arts which accompany them and through the other parallel elements which have been indicated, the purification of the exterior and interior senses is brought about, the interrelationship being so close that it is difficult to segregate the elements. Certain of them can be discussed on each cornice; then to show these interrelationships and the effectiveness of Dante's scheme the whole plan will be presented as it operates on the first cornice. The purgation of all exterior senses and the beginning of two of the interior senses, imagination and common sense, takes place on the cornices; the remaining interior senses are purified in the Earthly Paradise, where the purification of the imagination and common sense are completed. Since of the exterior senses sight, hearing, and touch are the most important, Dante gives them most attention. Though he emphasizes the purification of each of these on one cornice in particular, there are aspects of purification of each of them on every cornice. In fact, the purification of the sense of sight is not completed until Dante has attained to perfect love and is ready for the Beatific Vision.

Since pride is the root of all sin and sight is the most important of the exterior senses, Dante purifies them together on the first cornice. The souls of the proud, bent under the heavy weight of stone which they bear on their backs and shoulders so that they resemble figures which support a corbel (*Purg.* X:130–135), climb the carrara marble mountain in the glare of the southern sun throughout the late hours of Easter Monday morning, never able to close their suffering eyes, lest lacking vigilance they approach the edge of the precipice and plunge into the sea. On the next cornice the eyes, now purified by the white light, are strangely rested by being "seamed" with the iron wire used in falconry to tame a hawk, a process which does not injure the falcon but which cures her fear. Hawklike eyes have extraordinary perceptive power; purified eyes have clear discernment. Moreover, perfect use of the sense of sight lies in knowing when to look intently and when to keep from seeing. In one manner of speaking, the discerning judgment or common sense is a matter of seeing too, of seeing what right relationships are; therefore, it, too, is purified on the first cornice by much meditation on the Lord's Prayer. Man here sets his values right and learns where he fits in God's scheme of things.

The purification of the sense of hearing begins on the second cornice and is continued on the fourth and fifth. On the cornice of the envious, through dramatic stories of brotherly love and of its opposite, which angel voices present in the charity-filled air, the souls leaning against one another in blind helplessness learn how to practice the three kinds of charity which militate against envy: to give to those who lack, to expose oneself to danger and even death, and to return good for evil. On the purely literal level, the meaning is that one listens best when he closes his eyes to shut out all distractions; on the moral level, these souls must purify sight and hearing and do penance for all the times they had opened their eyes and their ears to things which made them desire the ill success of their neighbor.

On the fourth cornice, that of the slothful, the penitents, who are eager now to overcome their culpable repugnance to effort, purify the will by following the admonitions, which come to them through the midnight air, to run quickly to do good and renew grace so that no time be lost through insufficient love (*Purg.* XVIII:103–108). The eyes here know no strain in the gentle moonlight, but the ears are intent upon the admonitions. To emphasize the point that quiet sitting is often connected with fruitful activity, Dante represents himself sitting with Virgil on the stairway leading to the cornice, discoursing intently on love and free will. At the end of the discourse, the throng of penitents led by the two who are urging them to strenuous activity, sweep past them. The active fruitful listening of Dante in quiet and peace and the strained listening of the penitents rushing up the mountain stand in sharp opposition. The sense of hearing, like the sense of sight, needs to be trained to be alert when the occasion demands and unconcerned on other occasions. On the cornice of the envious and that of the avaricious, the sense of hearing is purified from that too great attention to things which lead to sins against charity and liberality; here, on the fourth cornice, there is purgation of that indolent listening which makes admonitions to virtuous activity go in one ear and out the other. It is interesting that one of the penitents is an abbot of San Zeno, who was perhaps slothful about taking and giving admonitions and who may just have sat and dozed when he should have engaged the "luminous eyes of his mind" in contemplative prayer (*Purg.* XVIII:12).

On the cornice of the avaricious, the fifth — face downward, fettered to the edge of the pavement — are those who in life had turned their backs to heaven to concern themselves with earthly things. With eyes fixed upon the dust, the symbol of the temporality of all earthly goods, they listen to one another through the day as they tell stories of men distinguished for liberality and through the night as they rehearse dark crimes to which avarice has led. Both sight and hearing are further purified on this cornice, for through these senses avarice and prodigality make inroads upon the soul.

On the third cornice, meditations on the call and the curb come by way of the imagination, which suggests visions in the mind. The interior sense which most frequently leads to sin is the imagination, and that precisely by visions in the mind against which the soul must put up a valiant fight. That the imagination should be purified on the cornice of the angry is psychologically sound. That the penitents should be disciplined by walking through a fog is symbolically sound. The anger of men is often aroused by some misinterpretation of sense impressions and the consequent forming of false judgments, for which Dante presents the physical analogy of the false sensory perceptions received in a fog. In either event reason must check the fallacious image. The whole scholastic morality and psychology of the imagination is here involved. The imagination like just anger is undeniably very useful, but both must always be directed by right reason. The soul united to the body cannot think without images, but the uncontrolled imagination can lead to vain, inconsistent, and forbidden things or to daydreaming and sentimentality.

As one would expect, taste and smell are purified on the cornice of gluttony, the sixth. Dante's use of a supernatural tree whose branches grow contrariwise from that of a fir, the widest branches being near the top, seems to have been suggested by the tree of the knowledge of good and evil from which Eve picked the traditional apple. The mortification of the two senses comes from the voluntary circling of the tree, which is filled with luscious fruit made fragrant by a spray of clear water falling from a rock and sprinkling the leaves. The craving to eat and drink is joyously overcome by uniting it with the thirst of the suffering Christ, the union turning pain into solace (*Purg.* XXIII:71–75). All mystics pay much attention not only to the necessity of fasting but to the need of overcoming fussiness about what one eats and drinks. The lives of the saints abound in stories of the extremes to which some saints went in this regard. Dante's emphasis here is on the fast only.

Though the sense of touch is purified to some extent on all the cornices in the measure in which it is involved in the vices purged on each — for example, the pressure of the rocks on the backs and shoulders of the penitents and the discomfort from the heat on the first; the hair shirts on the second; the binding of the chains on the fifth — the ultimate purification comes on the seventh, where the souls do penance for their sins of lust. High on the mountain which reaches into the rarefied air, flames the fire of charity, which burns so much more intensely than the lusts of the flesh that it destroys them utterly. Since according to Dante's philosophy every sin is basically a sin by love (*Purg.* XVII:103–105), the purgation of love itself in this fire of charity must be a part of man's penitence. By it virginal souls are conformed to the purity of the personal Christ, and those who are married, to the purity of the mystical Christ. "I could have cast me into molten glass to cool me," Dante says (*Purg.* XXVII:49–51) when he has plunged into the flames, but he emerges free and upright, complete master of himself (*Purg.* XXVII:140).

Actually the ascent of the mountain brings about not only the purification of the senses, the purging of the seven capital sins, and the establishment of the virtues opposed to them, it brings also the perfection of the evangelical counsels: the stripping of the self from all material and immaterial things, which is the perfection of *Poverty*; the mortification of the will by humble submission to all the disciplines, accidents, and commands of life, which is the self-abnegation of *Obedience*; and that triumph of detachment, that limpid purity of soul "cleansed from personal desire and virgin to all but God," which is the perfection of *Chastity*.[15]

Reader . . . *contemplate the art of the Master.*
— *Paradiso* X:7, 10

In order to see how deftly Dante weaves the eight elements of purification and to study their interrelationships it is necessary to study one cornice in detail; and since he initiates his method on the cornice of the proud, that cornice lends itself best to this analysis. The *art* is sculpture, the *sense to be purified* is sight; the *discipline,* the carrying of heavy burdens to bend the necks stiff with pride. The *call and curb* are presented through the art. The

Virgin is the Virgin of the Annunciation; the *prayer*, the "Our
Father." The angel of humility pronounces the *benediction*, in the
words of the first *beatitude*, "Blessed are the poor in spirit."

The art of sculpture, as we have already observed, is presented
in three forms: statuary, graffiti or bas-relief, and corbels. As the
penitent souls climb the carrara marble mountain (*Purg.* X:31),
they find the encircling bank adorned with groups of statuary,
presenting in "visible speech" (X:95) "stories" of those in high
places who practiced the virtue of humility. Since the penitents
are moving uphill, they can see the sculptured "stories" whenever
they raise their eyes, and by meditating upon the beauty of humility
experience the call to the virtue. Dante comments on three of these
"images of humility," the Annunciation group, suggesting the humility
of Mary and the greater humility of Christ in becoming man; David
girt and dancing before the ark, while the seven choirs sing —
probably Psalm XXIII (Douay numbering), the hymn he had written
for the occasion of carrying the ark to the temple; and Trajan, the
Roman emperor, stooping from his saddle to grant the plea of the
poor widow while above him the golden eagles of Rome strain in
the wind. The three instances represent the twofold aspect of
humility which man must learn, humility before God and man. They
are drawn, as is Dante's method on all the cornices, from sacred
and profane history and literature.

The penitents themselves are the corbels (*Purg.* X:132). The
three who speak to acknowledge their sinful pride represent the major
sources of pride: Omberto Aldobrandesco, pride of birth or family
pride; Oderisi of Gubbio, an illuminator of manuscripts, excessive
pride of achievement; and Provenzano Salvani, pride of position
or power.

Instances of pride which goes before a fall, the curb to the
vice, are represented in the graffiti which the penitents are trampling
underfoot (*Purg.* XII:13–63). The pride of the first group of four —
Lucifer, Briareus, the Giants, and Nimrod — stands in contrast to
the virtue of humility as represented in the Annunciation statuary
group. There God had stooped in the Incarnation to become man;
these in their arrogance attempted to rise to become like God. The
four in the second group — Niobe, Saul, Arachne, Rehoboam — are

contrasted with David in his humble reverence for God and the things of God, their stories showing how in each case in boasting or self-will they set themselves above or against God. The four characters cited in the third group — Eriphyle, Sennacherib, Cyrus, and Holifernes — portray man acting in pride against his fellow man and in retaliation slain by human hands. Obviously they are contrasted with Trajan, who is an example of man exercising humility to man. In the terzina which follows those citing the twelve just named, Dante indicates that all three forms of pride were the cause of the fall of Troy. A more detailed study shows great refinement in his reasons for the choice of these instances in that they represent detailed subdivisions of the roots of pride and indicate what man must watch closely if he would free himself from its insidious grip upon the soul.

Though the major discipline is the carrying of the heavy loads of rock, every aspect of the uphill climb is disciplinary and instrumental in purging the senses, the intellect, and the will. We have observed how the white light on the pavement helps to purify the eyes and the constant meditation on the "Our Father," the first of the interior senses. Meditations on the beauty of humility, suggested to the intellect by groups of statuary; on the malice of pride, made evident by the overthrow of the proud whose images the penitents trample underfoot, effect in the intellect a right set of values whereby man learns his place in relation to God and his fellow man and move the will to free itself from the shackles of self-love. The unmurmuring willingness to carry the heavy burdens in the heat of the day in whatever company the situation provides, the humble avowal of personal sins, the participation in plain chant on an uphill road when singing demands sustained effort: all these purify the will. In the chapter on the angels (above) we have seen how, when the purification of the vice has been accomplished, the angel of humility opens his arms and his wings (*Purg.* XII:91) and erases the *P* of pride and how the angel choirs chant the Benediction (XII:109–111) in terms of the Beatitude.

Suffering is the ancient law of love.

— Saint John of the Cross

The scene between Dante and Beatrice in the Earthly Paradise, the central scene of the *Commedia*, is so important in the process of Dante's purgation that it should be interpreted on all four levels of meaning: the literal, moral, allegorical, and anagogical. The moral and allegorical aspects may well be telescoped for discussion since the moral significance is everywhere presented in connection with allegorical meanings of activities, personages, rivers, etc. On all levels the scene provides for further purgation of both the interior and exterior senses and some new aspects of purgation of the intellect and the will. And because the scene is the transition scene between the purgative and illuminative ways, it provides important flashes of illumination also.

On the literal level the meaning is twofold. In the first place, Dante, who has been unfaithful to Beatrice, must humbly make his peace with her before he is ready to move under her guidance through the Earthly Paradise and the heavenly spheres so that she may open before him ever widening vistas of divine truth. In the second place, Beatrice, because she loves Dante, eager that he be given the grace of perfect contrition, must make him realize the seriousness of his infidelity and so be moved to proper sorrow. She knows that not until he had done bitter penance and recovered the state of innocence, not until he had encountered one who has come direct from the vision of God could he apprehend sin as it appears in the eyes of God and see how deep-rooted and extensive is the evil which has penetrated to the depths of his nature. To ensure this perfect sorrow she subjects him to the humiliation of public rebuke.

The discipline of this rebuke of Beatrice brings about the purgation of the estimative sense in the soul of Dante. With a clarity he has never before experienced, he apprehends all that in his life was beneficial as well as all that was harmful and made the rich soil of his soul rank with weeds (*Purg.* XXX:115–120). Now that Beatrice has revivified the idealism of his youth, those things in his life which took him from her, seen for the first time in their true light, bring him the full realization of how his infidelities have deterred him from fulfilling all that he was destined to achieve and cause him greater suffering than the combined pain and fatigue of all the seven cornices.

Reason (Virgil) had done all he could from a rational point of view and had pronounced Dante whole and upright. Revelation (Beatrice) now shows him how much remains to be done. The gull which appears white above the dark of the sea looks black against the cumulous cloud. It is not surprising that Dante, who has seen his own bruised and wounded soul mirrored in Lethe (*Purg.* XXX: 76–78), which flows between him and Beatrice, falls fainting to the ground, when at her command he lifts his eyes and encounters the radiant beauty of her unveiled face (XXXI:64–90).

The major moral and allegorical aspects of the purgation in the Earthly Paradise are associated with the rivers Lethe and Eunoë and with the figure of Matilda. When Dante meets Matilda as he enters the Earthly Paradise, she describes for him the source and function of the two streams, which, she says, flow inexhaustibly from one fountain by the will of God, who in his mercy provides Lethe, the river of forgetfulness to remove from the soul the last vestiges of sin as they remain in the senses; and Eunoë, the "river of good remembrance," to sharpen all the good. On recovering from the swoon into which his remorse had plunged him, Dante finds Matilda leaning over him, drawing him through the water up to his throat; then while the angelic choir sings the *Asperges me* she immerses his head, directing him to swallow the water, a perfect symbol (XXXI:97–102) of the cleansing of the interior senses: the completion of the purification of the estimative sense, the cleansing of the memorative faculties, and the final purification of the imagination and common sense.

Saint John of the Cross discusses at length the need of purging the sensible as well as the intellectual memory.[16] In the first place the sensible memory is filled with useless and sometimes dangerous impressions which must be erased. Then, too, memory is immersed in time and the things of time, a defect which must be remedied so that one can grasp all things in their relationship to eternity. The intellectual memory is prone to be cluttered with unimportant things, even uncharitable things about our neighbor, which crowd out God and his immense benefits. In the scene in the Earthly Paradise Dante is concerned with both the sensible and intellectual memory and does not separate them in the purgation. The passage through Lethe and Eunoë is a dramatic purging of these defects: Lethe erases from the memorative faculties what should be erased (*Purg.* XXXIII:91-96); Eunoë sharpens all that should be retained (XXXIII:121-129).

Though the purification of the imagination was begun on the third cornice, that of the angry, it is completed here in the purification of the memorative or reminiscent faculty so that the imaginative powers may be placed at the service of the intellect illumined by faith. That Dante's imagination henceforward function purely and clearly is exceedingly important in order that he may see and interpret aright all the images Beatrice will present in the Earthly Paradise and in the Paradise itself.

There is in the Earthly Paradise a further purification of the exterior senses on a new level: the sense of sight by the vision of Beatrice and the Griffin and the whole supernatural pageant; of the sense of hearing in the rebuke of Beatrice, on the one hand, and the angelic roundelays, on the other; of the sense of smell by the fragrance of the unearthly lilies and roses; of the sense of taste by swallowing the water of Lethe; of the sense of touch by the complete immersion in its waters. This new purgation is necessary because of the experimental knowledge of the presence of God, which the purified soul experiences by spiritual sensations analogous to sensations in the natural order. Dante will see God; he will see angels and saints. He will converse with saints and will hear angel choirs. The mystic *hears* the voice of the beloved in the depths of his soul. Mystics agree that there is a spiritual touch, a spiritual embrace by which the presence of God is felt in the innermost center of the soul, a substantial touch which is a unique kind of union of substance with substance as opposed to a simple moral touch as when God touches the heart of a sinner. They agree, too, that since the senses of taste and smell are only special kinds of touch (*Summa* I, q. 78, a. 3), there are spiritual taste and spiritual smell also.[17]

On the anagogical or mystical level there is a deeply significant reason for the intensity of Dante's suffering in the Earthly Paradise, when he has completed his active purgation and is on the threshold of the illuminative way. All writers on the purgative way discuss a passive as well as an active purification, teaching that our own effort at mortification and penance, no matter how earnest and seemingly complete, cannot suffice to root out all our evil inclinations and re-establish in us rectitude and purity. Left to ourselves, we are unable to realize the enormity of our evil, and for that reason we are unable to discover a remedy for it.

> All the mortifications and active purgation which we practice would serve us poorly indeed if God did not perfect and complete them with the passive purgations to which, in His mercy He subjects us. These passive purgations reach down into the very depth of our soul and there they discover and correct innumerable faults and imperfections which we ourselves would never notice, much less remedy.[18]

Some of what has already been discussed relative to the cleansing of the interior senses and the spiritual senses is part of the passive purification. But the mystics, when speaking of the passive purification, refer always to the intensity of the suffering which accompanies what they call the dark night of the senses symbolized in the *Divine Comedy* in the greeting which Beatrice gives Dante.

In this first dark night (there is a second dark night called the dark night of the soul, which Dante portrays later) the self receives a new and dreadful kind of lucidity, in which the vision of ultimate Good brings to it an abrupt sense of helpless imperfection, a bleak conviction of sin far more bitter than that endured in the way of active purgation. In the *Divine Comedy* the rebuke of Beatrice which penetrates into the depths of his soul is Dante's symbol of this passive purgation; his fainting, a symbol of the soul's helplessness in the dark night. We would never discover our thousand inadvertent imperfections without some superior light; in the Earthly Paradise Beatrice is the medium of this light. Much less are we able to correct them unless some superior power come to our aid; Matilda, the symbol of this superior power, begins to draw Dante through Lethe while he is still unconscious.

Before the soul can arrive at perfect union and divine perfection, it is necessary that God Himself have a hand in the work of its purification and rehabilitation; Matilda before she drew Dante through Lethe and Eunoë had explained that the two rivers have their origin in one spring, the will of God. By drawing him through the one she completes the passive purgation in the dark night of the senses; by drawing him through the other, she opens to him the illuminative way along which Beatrice will guide him. He has crossed the rivers into a new mystical state. Beatrice stands unveiled before him.

> *Not what thou art, nor what thou hast been*
> *beholdeth God with his merciful eyes;*
> *but that thou wouldst be.*
>
> — *The Cloud* of *Unknowing*

Let us look back over the way we have gone. In the dawn of Easter Sunday at the beginning of the purgative way (*Purg.* I:24), Dante saw in the heavens the four stars representing the four cardinal virtues; at this point, the *natural* virtues of prudence, justice, fortitude, and temperance. In the evening of that day (VIII:85–93), in the same place where these stars had gone down, he saw the heavens all aflame with the lights of the Christian virtues of faith, hope, and charity. In the Earthly Paradise Matilda brought him "bathed" to the dance of these same cardinal virtues under a new aspect, the infused perfecting virtues, now represented as nymphs at the left wheel of the chariot, who covered him with their arms to signify that he had attained to perfection in matters under their control and had reached the end of the purgative way. They led him to the eyes of Beatrice, the symbol of illumination, the while they sang of the three theological virtues who would, they said, sharpen his eyes for the light in those of Beatrice (XXXI: 109–111). He had attained that state of inward peace in which the three theological virtues could lead him to divine contemplation. But when the three theological virtues beg Beatrice to unveil

her face for Dante and she turns upon him the splendor of her
holy eyes and the gladness of her smile, he finds that though her
beauty "walls him in and makes him indifferent to everything else"
(*Purg.* XXXII:4–6), he is not yet ready for the superb graces of
higher contemplation. He is at first blinded by the light in her
face (12) and though eventually he gains strength to look upon
it, he is unable to contemplate the unity of the divine and human
natures in the Griffin, the symbolic figure of Christ. For the vision
of the Hypostatic Union he needs still further purification; four
times more the increasing brilliance of supernal light will blind
him before he is prepared for the vision of the Incarnate God.

At this point it may be well to comment on a double aspect
of Dante's symbolism in the *Paradiso*, particularly the lower heavens,
since both aspects are important for the instruction of the pilgrim
on his way to God. The first and more obvious has been dealt
with indirectly in preceding chapters, where we have noted that
all souls who have attained beatitude are actually in the Empyrean
(*Par.* IV:28–42), which is the only true Heaven, the seat of the
Deity, though by word and dramatic action Dante shows them in
the first eight heavens or moving to or from them, his object being
to clarify degrees and aspects of beatitude. We have observed that
those in the spheres of the unshadowed planets, having fallen short
of their spiritual potentialities, though they are perfectly happy,
have not attained the degree of happiness which was possible for
them; that those in the heavens of honor, having attained beatitude
through the exercise of their talents in specified activities of the
social order experience joy in ways related to these talents and good
works; that in the Starry Heaven — which answers to the Earthly
Paradise — all those whom we have seen in the lower heavens and
the whole Communion of Saints spread out before us in the garden
of the blessed in the variegated colors and designs of innumerable
flowers of sanctity. It is the second aspect of the symbolism which
concerns us at this point of our discussion of the way of perfection;
and though an observation concerning it was made at the beginning
of this chapter (p. 256), it seems wise to re-emphasize the matter here.

From the point of view of purgation these eight Heavens and
the Primum Mobile represent in the *Divine Comedy* the illumina-

tive way, the second division of the way of perfection which is proper to what Saint Thomas calls *proficients* (p. 255), as the purgative way is proper to *beginners* and the unitive way to the *perfect*. Though Dante's exterior and interior senses have been purified, though his will is now utterly conformed to the Divine Will, he is in need of further purification before he is ready for Divine Union. There will be no climbing now; God lifts the soul of the proficient from grace to grace, from light to light (*Par.* X:34-39), symbolized here in the rapid movement from star to star in ever increasing brilliance of light. Dante's human way of action under Virgil has been transformed; through penance and illuminating grace he has become a "new man" (Eph. 4:24). In the Starry Heaven as in the Earthly Paradise he will be tested: as the procession of the saints follows Christ and Mary into the Empyrean, the three examiners, Peter, James, and John, remain behind to conduct the examination in the three theological virtues.

This purification in the lower Heavens is a continuation of the passive purification begun in the Earthly Paradise: the parallelism is significant. As Beatrice after the procession of the Church had ascended remained behind to complete the purification of the exterior and interior senses, so the three Apostles remain behind to complete the purification of the theological virtues. As mystical writers speak of the first purification as the dark night of the senses, they speak of the purification in the illuminative way as the dark night of the soul. In this dark night Dante experiences the cleansing of the three powers of the soul: the understanding, the memory, and the will. According to Saint John of the Cross these three powers "must be rendered empty by the three theological virtues, each in its own power: faith in the understanding, hope in the memory, and charity in the will."[19]

Five times on the illuminative way Dante passes through blindness into greater light (*Purg.* XXXII:12; *Par.* XIV:76-81; XXV:27; XXV:122; XXX:52) to signify his passing through the spiritual night. The first, the one in the Earthly Paradise marks the beginning of the way; the second, in the Heaven of Mars, signifies the great grace he receives to make a holocaust of himself; each of the last three symbolizes his attainment of perfection in one of the theological virtues. When he has reached the perfection of charity, he is at the end of the illuminative way, ready to enter upon the unitive way of contemplation; therefore Beatrice leaves him and Bernard becomes his guide.

> *Do Thou . . . in the diligent exercise of mystical contemplation, leave behind the senses and the operations of the intellect, and all things sensible and intellectual, and all things in the world of being and non-being, that thou mayest arise by unknowing towards the union, as far as it is attainable, with him who transcends all being and all knowledge. For by the unceasing and absolute renunciation of thyself and of all things, thou mayest be borne on high, through pure and entire self-abnegation, into the superessential Radiance of the Divine Darkness.*
>
> — Dionysius
> *What Is the Divine Darkness*

Having taken this preliminary overview of the illuminative way in the nine heavens we can now go back to its beginning in the Earthly Paradise. When Dante and Beatrice begin their ascension into Heaven, it is high noon. The sun (the symbol of God or possibly here of the grace of God) is shining on Dante on its best course (*Par.* I:37–42) through the conjunction of the four cardinal and the three theological virtues. Starting as he does from the Garden of Eden, he is moving from that place and that state from which Adam would have advanced had he not fallen. Keeping his eyes fixed upon Beatrice, following her lead, he is elevated above the mere state of innocence which Adam had known and experiences an exaltation of the natural into the supernatural, "a transhumanizing" (*Par.* I:70) which is effected by the light of grace (75). Freed from the weight of sin, borne by the bowstring of the Divine Will, which always aims its shafts at a joyful mark (I:125–126), he is on his way to the Empyrean to *see* what here on earth man accepts

by faith — the Divine Essence in which he can *observe* the Hypostatic Union and understand it as clearly as one understands an
axiom (*Par.* II:41–45). To know through vision the Trinity and the
Incarnation is to reach the ultimate in beatitude.

Under the direction of the Holy Spirit, of whom Beatrice as
Divine Revelation is a quasi symbol, he moves with the rapidity of
light from star to star, from truth to truth so that he may be
sanctified in truth (Jn. 17:17). Progress through these spheres is
made through the seven Gifts of the Holy Ghost, which perfect
the soul for divine union. These seven Gifts have their unity in
love as have the virtues on the seven cornices of Purgatory, and
through their operation Dante progresses toward perfect love in his
own soul and to the vision of its manifestation in the life of the
Triune God.

Inasmuch as the seven Gifts of the Holy Ghost, are a means of
perfecting the soul in truth and are inseparable from perfect love,
they are essential for salvation and would necessarily be included in
Dante's scheme of perfection. Saint Thomas discussed them in conjunction with the theological and cardinal virtues: *understanding*
(*Summa* II–II, q. 8) and *knowledge* (II–II, q. 9) as aspects of
faith; *fear of the Lord* (II–II, q. 19) under hope; *wisdom* (II–II, q.
45) under charity; *counsel* (II–II, q. 52) as an aspect of prudence;
piety (II–II, q. 121) under justice; and *fortitude* (II–II, q. 139)
under the cardinal virtue of the same name.

Though he does not expressly say so, there are indications that
in the distribution of the Gifts through the seven spheres Dante
follows the scheme of Saint Thomas as far as the cardinal virtues
are concerned, placing counsel with prudence in the Heaven of
the Sun; fortitude with fortitude in Mars; piety with justice in
Jupiter. The Gift of wisdom, the highest of the intellectual Gifts,
Dante puts in the Heaven of Saturn, the "temperate star" where
the contemplatives are shown him. Doubtless he puts it last because
it is in a sense the culmination of the Gifts, making of the soul
"the unspotted mirror of God's majesty and the image of his goodness"
(Wisd. 7:26).

Where Dante places the three remaining Gifts it is less easy to
determine, for in the three shadowed planets he does not deal

directly with the theological virtues under which Saint Thomas discusses these Gifts. The imperfections which characterized the souls while on earth and which diminish their merit in these lower Heavens seem, however, to suggest these Gifts in a negative way, through revealing their lack. Since the fear of the Lord is the Gift residing in the concupiscible appetite, it would according to Dante's plan elsewhere in the *Divine Comedy* be in the lowest sphere, that of the moon, where are the souls who broke their vows through fear of man. In Mercury and Venus we might expect to find the lesser Gifts of the intellect, understanding and knowledge. The ambitious souls in Mercury lacked understanding of proper motives for their work; a knowledge of the meaning of love and of themselves and of God would have helped the ardent souls in Venus to direct their love aright.

The Gifts of the Holy Ghost are related to, but differ from, the infused virtues, both cardinal and theological. The theological virtue of faith sets the boundary of the activity of the Gifts; the virtue of charity is their bond of perfection. The soul itself can do nothing of itself to ensure the possession of the Gifts; it is in relation to them completely passive.[20] Though the Gifts help the soul under the guidance of faith to reach truth, the purification of faith itself frequently involves active conscious wrestling with problems instead of the passive possession which is characteristic of the Gifts. The same activity is demanded for the possession of perfect hope and perfect charity.

Dante's purification of faith is represented in the *Divine Comedy* through his discussions with Beatrice and the saints whom he encounters in the nine moving spheres. His questioning about problems in moral and dogmatic theology involves for the most part no real difficulty of acceptance of the truths of faith. But with Dante as with most souls, according to the masters of mystical theology, the chief test of faith comes in his submission to the teaching of the Church on the problem of predestination (*Par.* XIX:32; XX:70–90; XXI:94–102), which throughout the history of Western Christianity has proved a stumbling block to many. Dante's victorious rising above his own inferior way of perceiving the divine attributes of justice and mercy and his perfect sacrifice of reason to the order of grace have been grossly misunderstood by those commentators who do not comprehend his purpose in presenting the struggle and who blame the Church for requiring the submission to its teaching of an intelligence as keen as Dante's.

As a matter of fact, after his humble acknowledgment that a resolution of the seeming contradiction between the justice and mercy of God in the mystery of predestination is beyond his powers, Dante — who finds the pagan emperor Trajan and the Trojan Rhipeus among the saved — is overwhelmed by the greater mystery of the movement of divine grace which on occasion extends beyond all ordinary means of salvation. The recognition among the blessed of these two pagans kindles in Dante a lively hope that among the saved there may be a vast number from all times and nations and races who would seem to have been cut off from hope.

From what has just been said it is apparent that temptations against the justice and mercy of God as implied in the mystery of predestination involve not only the passive purification of faith but of the virtue of hope as well. In presenting the matter finally as a mystery of grace which quickens hope, Dante follows Saint Thomas (Par. XX:130–138; Summa II–II, q. 18, a. 4), who discusses under hope the sweet and terrible mystery of predestination.

Dante, however, represents himself as passing through other purifications of the virtue of hope. "To purify our hope," says Father Garrigou-Lagrange, possibly the most renowned contemporary interpreter of Thomistic theology, "to give us a better understanding of its true object and pure motive, the good God may take away from us all temporal goods that are dear to us: position, apparently deserved honors, influence, and the human help that we can expect of friends."[21] Dante's exposition of this aspect of the purification of hope comes in the Heaven of Mars.

Under the higher illumination of the Gift of understanding — which keeps him from the selfish ambitions of the souls who because of this shadow over their works were revealed to him in diminished glory in Mercury — and sustained by the Gift of fortitude, Dante represents himself (Par. XVII:46–99) as learning through Cacciaguida of his exile and the loss of all his temporal goods, precisely those goods outlined in the passage quoted above. Against this background Cacciaguida gives him his mission, which he desires ardently to fulfill and for the fulfillment of which he has already been given the grace of complete abandonment to the divine will (*Par.* XIV:88–93), knowing well that it is only by the Cross (106) and all that it connotes of darkness and of pain that any good for eternity can be accomplished and any hope be realized. "To suffer darkness is the way to great light," says Saint John of the Cross. It is noteworthy that as in the Earthly Paradise before he receives from Beatrice the prophecy about the future of Church and Empire he is blinded (*Purg.* XXXII:12), so now under the glow of the Holy Spirit and the radiance of the smile of Beatrice he has again been blinded as he enters the Heaven of Mars, where (*Par.* XIV: 76–81) Cacciaguida will give him his mission. This blindness is the prelude to his act of perfect abandonment, the complete oblation of his will.

The ultimate purification of charity takes place in even greater darkness than the purification of faith and hope. The purification of love has many phases, with all of which Dante concerns himself. On the human level there is that aspect in which the Christian schools and in particular the Cistercian schools confronted the schools of profane love and proclaimed the rights of the sole Master of love, the Holy Spirit. Of those who speak eloquently of the place of divine love, Saint Bernard is the most eloquent.[22] For that reason chiefly — though there are other reasons, among them Bernard's devotion to the Virgin — Dante makes Bernard lead him to union with God. Explicitly and implicitly, however, on the literal, allegorical, and moral levels it is Beatrice who serves as his guide in the purification of love through the *New Life* and through the *Divine Comedy*, both of which were written in her honor. Dante's preoccupation with love in all its human and divine aspects is evident throughout the whole of the *Commedia*, ranging from the episode of Paolo and Francesca reading the romantic tale of Lancelot and Guinevere in the early part of the *Inferno* to the vision of Love Incarnate in the Empyrean.

The passive purgation of faith and hope and the active acceptance of the trials of the purgation are bound up with the purification of charity and the perfecting of the will. The knowledge Dante acquires in the purification of the understanding he does not desire for its own sake but to feed and increase love (*Par.* XXVI:28–30), since Dante holds with Saint Thomas that knowledge foreruns love, that one cannot love what one does not know (*Par.* XXVIII:109–111). His desire for sacrifice and the Cross, his complete oblation in the Heaven of Mars, his ready acceptance of his arduous mission stem from eagerness to manifest love of the personal and mystical Christ.

Along the whole of the illuminative way the soul, according to the mystics, is drawn to think less about itself and more about God. The whole of the *Paradiso* bears witness to this new orientation in the soul of Dante. In the Earthly Paradise, Beatrice by her stern rebuke had helped him to cleanse his soul of all self-pity; after the passage through Lethe and Eunoë his interest is centered little on himself and is absorbed more and more in the Trinity and the Incarnation. Even the prayers of the illuminative way indicate this new outlook. They are primarily hymns of praise of God: the recurrent *Sanctus* and *Gloria Patri* and unnamed hymns to the Trinity. Though the *Ave Maria* is intoned twice, it is probable that Dante includes in his thinking only the first part which alone is included in the Mass; if so, there are among liturgical prayers of petition in the *Paradiso* only certain phrases of the *Regina Coeli*.

The theological virtues, says Saint Thomas (*Summa* I–II, q. 62) are a gift of God, involving a certain participation in the Deity, to put man on the way to happiness which exceeds his nature, but for which it is made. In both the *Banquet* (III, xiv) and the *Monarchy* (III, xvi) Dante writes of faith, hope, and charity, maintaining that by them we ascend to the blessedness of eternal life. For that reason his examination on these virtues in the Stellar Heaven is an essential part of his mystical system. The examination on charity comes last, for love harmonizes the three powers of the soul and binds them together.

When Dante has completed his examination on hope and looks upon the face of Saint John who is to examine him in charity he is again struck blind (*Par.* XXV:122, 136–139). This fourth blindness, which is the most intense and the most enduring, marks the prelude to the unitive way. In this dark night, says Saint John of the Cross, God secretly teaches the soul and instructs it in the perfection of love. Out of his darkness, Dante speaks of the object of love, of what led him to abandon love of the world and seek true love, of the reason for his love, of the nature of true love, and of the measure of love which is his. He professes the all-inclusiveness of divine love, which makes him love all other creatures in and for the sake of God and which makes him love God for bringing them and him into being, for redeeming him and giving him the hope of life with him forever. After this darkness he again experiences a greater influx of light in which he sees the hierarchies of angels and the relation of time to eternity.

Nothing remains now but the vision of God in the Empyrean, the True Heaven. Dante's exterior and interior senses purified on the mountain of Purgatory, his understanding, memory, and will purified by the possession of the theological virtues, his spiritual senses recovered: spiritual hearing and sight by faith; spiritual smell by hope; spiritual taste and touch by charity, Dante is ready to attain to the bliss of the last degree of contemplation, that hidden manna which God gives "to him that overcometh" (Apoc. 2:17). He has attained the summit of the long steep ladder of perfection. He is ready for divine union. He enters upon the unitive way. As a final preparation for this divine union Dante is blinded for the last time (Par. XXX:46–51). Out of the darkness of the divine light that shines around him he hears the instructing voice (Par. XXX:52–54) say,

> Ever the Love which quieteth this heaven
> Welcomes into itself with such salute
> To make the candle ready for the flame.

No light is now too bright for his eyes to withstand (XXX:58–60). With new sharpened vision he sees the river of grace, from which he "drinks with his eyelid's rim" — the image of a river (61) or torrent (68) being the one employed by the mystics to represent the first apprehension of the divine in the stage of union. The image is taken from Isaias (66:12): Behold, I will bring upon her as it were a river of peace and as an overflowing torrent the glory of the Gentiles, which you shall suck.

As the drinking of Lethe in the Earthly Paradise prepared Dante for the illuminative way, so this drink of light at the end of the way of illumination prepares him for the unitive way. The whole scene (*Par.* XXX:52–99) shows the awakened spiritual senses: the voice out of the blindness, the angels inebriated by the fragrance of the flowers, the drinking of the river with his eyelid's rim to exalt his vision to "the lofty height of the true kingdom." Beatrice, his mentor in truth, leads him into the heart of the mystic rose; Bernard, his mentor in love, now leads him to the vision of the Trinity. So purified is his vision now that as he gazes into the Eternal Light he believes he would be dazed if he were to turn away from it (XXXIII:76–78), a most suggestive way of saying how intimately the Divine Magnet has drawn him to union with himself. As he fixes the eyes of his soul upon the image of Christ in the vision of the Trinity, a new flash of grace illumines him so that he penetrates the mystery of the Incarnation, the goal of all his striving. Then his desire and his will in harmony are, he finds, turning like a wheel moved evenly by love.

The image of the wheel from *Ezechiel* (1:15–21) represents the prophet's vision of the four living creatures, who symbolize — as the Church teaches and as Dante reminds us (*Purg.* XXIX:100–103) — the four Gospels. From the early Christian centuries the wheel has been used to symbolize true lovers of Christ, "rounded in virtue" because freed from the defects of self-love and "circling lightly" because of readiness of will to co-operate with the faintest stirring of grace.

"The spirit of God was in the wheels," says Ezechiel. From the time of his conversion in the first canto of the *Inferno* when Virgil came to help him in the dark wood to this summit of glory in the Empyrean, Dante has been faithful to all the promptings of grace and, following humbly the leaders the Holy Spirit has sent him, has pressed forward along the difficult way of perfection. He has now attained that spiritual equilibrium attained when all the powers of the soul are in perfect harmony with the workings of divine grace, that equilibrium symbolized by the wheel. The closing statement of the *Divine Comedy* that "his desire and will were turning like a wheel moved evenly by the Love that turns the sun and other stars" means that now when he has put love in order, all the powers of his soul are perfectly accordant with the Divine Will. In the Stellar Heaven he had seen the blessed souls make spheres of themselves on poles flaming like comets and turn with varying speeds like wheels in a clock; then dance some fast, some slow (*Par.* XXIV:10–18), those revolving most swiftly having the greatest merit and therefore the greatest joy. Since Dante must come back to earth, he does not know and cannot say how great the measure of his eternal joy will be nor how rapid the revolution of the wheel. Temporarily, however, he has attained that perfect peace in perfect activity that perfect balance between his own individuality and membership in the Mystical Christ, that vision and penetration of the Hypostatic Union which is the height of beatitude. His life has come to perfect fulfillment.

NOTES

1. Saint John of the Cross, *Ascent of Mount Carmel*, trans. and ed. by E. Allison Peers, 3rd ed. (Westminster, Md., 1957).
2. For descriptive definitions given here consult Alban Goodier, S.J., *An Introduction to the Study of Ascetical and Mystical Theology* (Milwaukee, n.d.), Lecture I, pp. 1–7.
3. Reginald Garrigou-Lagrange, O.P., *Christian Perfection and Contemplation*, trans. Sister M. Timothea Doyle, O.P. (Saint Louis, 1942), p. 171.
4. For an excellent summary of the differences in the three ways of the spiritual life see John G. Arintero, *The Mystical Evolution in the Development and Vitality of the Church*, trans. Jordan Aumann, O.P. (Saint Louis, 1951), Vol. II, p. 49.
5. See Evelyn Underhill, *Mysticism* (New York, 1955), Meridian Books, p. 169, for a modern analysis of the road to perfection.
6. *The Epistle of Dante to Can Grande*, trans. Katharine Hillard, in Appendix to *The Banquet of Dante Alighieri* (London, 1889), p. 404.
7. *Fathers of the Church*, Rudolph Arbesmann, O.S.A., *et al.*, Vol. II, *Writings of Saint Augustine* (New York, 1942). "The Magnitude of the Soul," trans. John J. McMahon, S.J., pp. 136–149.
8. Reginald Garrigou-Lagrange, O.P., *The Three Ages of the Interior Life*, trans. Sister M. Timothea Doyle, O.P. (Saint Louis, 1948), Vol. II, pp. 365, 366. These pages present graphically how the seven capital sins are rooted in egoism and the cardinal and theological virtues in humility.
9. Etienne Gilson, *The Mystical Theology of Saint Bernard*, trans. A. H. C. Downes (New York, 1955), Chap. II, "Regio Dissimilitudinis," pp. 33–59. Saint Bernard discusses the point of restoring the Divine Likeness by substituting for the "proper will" or self-will, the "common will" or the will of God.
10. *Ibid.*, Chap. III, "Schola Caritatis," pp. 60–84.
11. Lynn Thorndike, *The* SPHERE *of Sacrabosco and Its Commentators* (Chicago, 1948), p. 123.
12. Thomas Merton, *The Waters of Siloe* (New York, 1949). Part Two gives a

stimulating glimpse of the ideals of the Cistercian vocation and the spirit of Saint Bernard.

13. Baron F. Von Hugel, *The Mystical Element of Religion* (New York, 1927), Vol. I, p. 233.
14. In his *Concerning Eloquence* II, 4 Dante does suggest, however, that a poem can be enjoyed as a work of art without reference to its allegorical or moral implications.
15. For an interesting observation on the evangelical counsels in relation to this aspect of purgation see Underhill, *op. cit.*, p. 205.
16. Saint John of the Cross, *op. cit.*, Vol. I, Bk. III, Chaps. 1–15.
17. A. Poulain, S.J., *The Graces of Interior Prayer, A Treatise on Mystical Theology*, trans. from 6 ed., Leonora L. Yorke Smith (Saint Louis, 1910), Chaps. V and VI, pp. 64–113. The discussion on the five spiritual senses includes writings of various mystics who detail their experiences in the area.

    In the *Confessions* X, vi, Saint Augustine speaks of how the spiritual senses carried over into his spiritual life all of the exterior senses.
18. Arintero, *op. cit.*, Vol. II, p. 64. Much of the material in the paragraphs following the quotation leans on this text.
19. Saint John of the Cross, *op. cit.*, Vol. I, pp. 79–82.
20. Walter Farrell, O.P., and Dominic Hughes, O.P., *Swift Victory, Essays on the Gifts of the Holy Spirit* (New York, 1955), p. 17.
21. Reginald Garrigou-Lagrange, O.P., *The Love of God and the Cross of Jesus,* trans. Sister Jeanne Marie, O.P. (Saint Louis, 1951), p. 145. See Chapters VII, VIII, and IX for a discussion of the passive purification of the virtues of faith, hope, and charity.
22. Gilson, *op. cit.*, Appendix IV, "St. Bernard and Courtly Love," pp. 170–197.

CHAPTER X

ALL DAY WITH GOD

> The Liturgy and attendance at the Offices of the
> Church will teach you more than books. Take a
> plunge into that immense reservoir of glory, of
> certitude and of poetry. . . . Your darkness will
> disperse little by little. . . . And who will say that
> these prayers, so many times repeated by saintly
> lips, have not by this time acquired a virtue of
> their own — *ex opere operato.*
>
> — Paul Claudel
> *A Letter to a Doubter*

n the mystic rose of Paradise, when Dante has reached
the goal toward which he has been moving through
the hundred cantos, he presents all those who have
come into the possession of the Beatific Vision engaged
in contemplative prayer, the greatest achievement of angels and
men. Along the way that leads to this ultimate goal, he shows souls
learning to pray and growing in the knowledge of prayer; he deals
with the kinds of prayer, the methods of prayer, the need of
prayer. All that the Hebrew and Christian centuries had taught
about prayer — as well as the best loved and most approved prayers
— is explicit or implicit in the *Divine Comedy*. Men, recognizing
God as the Creator and Goal of all the universe, adore and praise
him for what he is in himself and submit themselves to his sovereign dominion. Realizing their sinfulness, aware of their inability to
progress without his help, they offer prayers of propitiation and
petition. Their prayer is vocal and mental: vocal prayer recited or
sung; meditation and contemplation. They are engaged in the *Purga-*

torio and *Paradiso* in following through prayer the command which in the beginning God had given to Abraham (Gen. 17:1): "I am the Almighty God: walk before me and be perfect!"

In his choice of specific prayers, as in other matters, Dante is austere. The prayers he uses are the most simple and most ancient, prayers taken from the Breviary and the Missal. Nowhere until he reaches the Empyrean does he represent any soul as offering any prayer of his own composition; the prayers of the *Commedia* are the corporate prayers of the Church.

The prayers of the Breviary, known as the prayers of the Divine Office or the Canonical Hours, include the Psalms, sanctified by centuries of use by saints of the Old and New Law and by Christ himself; canticles from the Old and New Testaments; appropriate hymns, antiphons, and sequences; passages from various books of the Bible; data from the life of the saint whose feast is being celebrated; various carefully selected prayers; and homilies from the Church Fathers on matters relevant to the feast or season of the liturgical year. The Missal is, of course, the Mass book. It contains the prayers for the Mass: those known as the *Ordinary* and the *Canon*, which vary but little throughout the year; and those prayers and readings from Scripture which are proper to the liturgical season or the feast of the day and are therefore called the *Proper*. The Breviary also has its Ordinary and Proper: the Missal and Breviary go together; each complements the other. The Office is at once a preparation for the Mass and a prolongation of it: the Mass is the center of the liturgy; the Office a radiation from this divine center.

In the Middle Ages the time of each day was spaced out by liturgical hours. Man in those days did not keep track of the hours by a watch on his wrist; in Dante's Florence, according to Villani, the bells of the Badia (the Abbey of the Benedictine monks, established in 978) rang out the hours from midnight to midnight, for it was ordered that the bells should ring to the honor of God the hours of the day and night. In the *Paradiso* (XV:97–99) Cacciaguida speaks of these bells of the Badia from which Florence received *tierce* and *none*. In a sense, the hours were a civil as well as a religious institution: their ringing regulated the manifold affairs of the city. They marked the time for rising and going to bed; by them artisans knew when to begin and cease work. Nor was this strange, for the canonical hours were based upon the greater divisions of the Roman day.

The Romans divided the day from sunrise to sunset into twelve equal parts called hours; they again divided the day into four *greater* hours and the night into four watches. Upon these four greater hours and four watches, the Church fixed the times for the recitation of the canonical hours, retaining the Roman names for the day hours.[1] The Romans called their greater hours of PRIME, TIERCE, SEXT, and NONE temporal because, following the course of the sun, they varied with the seasons, except SEXT which marked the middle of the day or night. The Church retained the flexibility of the temporal aspect of the hours. The following tables adapted from Britt, *The Hymns of the Breviary and Missal*[2] will clarify the matter by showing the contemporary time equivalents.

TABLE A.   THE GREATER HOURS OF THE ROMAN DAY

The Roman first hour	*Prime*	from 6:00 A.M. to 9:00 A.M. our time
The Roman third hour	*Tierce*	from 9:00 A.M. to 12:00 M.
The Roman sixth hour	*Sext*	from 12:00 M. to 3:00 P.M.
The Roman ninth hour	*None*	from 3:00 P.M. to 6:00 P.M.

TABLE B.   THE ROMAN DIVISIONS OF THE NIGHT

The first watch	*evening*	from 6:00 P.M. to 9:00 P.M.
The second watch	*midnight*	from 9:00 P.M. to 12:00 A.M.
The third watch	*cock-crowing*	from 12:00 A.M. to 3:00 A.M.
The fourth watch	*morning*	from 3:00 A.M. to 6:00 A.M.

TABLE C.   WHEN THE CANONICAL HOURS WERE FORMERLY SAID

(Now, even in monastic orders like the Trappists and Trappistines, the monks and nuns telescope the last nocturns of Matins with Lauds, rising at 2:00 A.M.)

Matins:	First nocturn 9:00 P.M.; second, 12:00 A.M.; third, 3:00 A.M.
Lauds	at daybreak
Prime	at 6:00 A.M.
Tierce	at 9:00 A.M.
Sext	at 12:00 M.
None	at 3:00 P.M.
Vespers	at 6:00 P.M.
Compline	at nightfall

Today, roughly, MATINS is the time from midnight to dawn; LAUDS, from dawn to sunup; PRIME, from sunup to midmorning;

TIERCE (now usually spelled TERCE) from nine to twelve; SEXT, from noon to midafternoon; NONE, from three to six; VESPERS, from six (sundown) to nine; COMPLINE, from nine to midnight. Like all medieval men, Dante speaks of events as occurring at the hour of Prime or of Vespers or Matins. Sometimes to indicate time more precisely, he used such terms as *middle-tierce, middle-sext.*[3]

The last seven of these canonical hours became known as the Day Hours. In this daily order, the principal Mass of the day (individual priests in the monastery or cathedral might offer Masses privately) was usually celebrated after Tierce. Thus in the liturgy, the Mass is surrounded by the Office as a precious gem is surrounded by the gold or silver or ivory of its setting, the rays of its glory radiating over all the hours of the day.

In the thirteenth century and in subsequent centuries, the Day Hours were often bound separately in the volume known as the Book of Hours. In the Romanesque period — in fact, from the time of Pope Gregory I to the early thirteenth century — several books were used in the recitation of the Office: the Psalter for the Psalms; the Antiphonary and Responsory for the choral prayers; the Bible and homilies of the Fathers for the readings or lessons. But in the early Middle Ages, for the convenience of the officials of the Roman Curia, who were often engaged in travel, and later for the convenience of the friars, whose active work for the Church kept them on the road also, a single book known as the *Breviary* (the word means a *summary*) was compiled. The Breviary of Dante's time contains all the prayers and readings for Matins and Lauds: the other Hours are not included, possibly because the clerics, for whom these books were intended, would have memorized the psalms, hymns, prayers, and antiphons for these Hours.

The contemporary Breviary has the psalms distributed throughout the eight Hours; in the course of the week, however, the one hundred and fifty psalms are said. It would seem that in Dante's time as in our day the Day Hours were bound separately, largely for the convenience of the laity who did not rise for the prayer hours of the night. Today, lest the Breviary prove too bulky for either clergy or laity, it is frequently bound in four small volumes, one for each of the seasons. The contemporary Books of Day Hours contain all the Hours except Matins.

I will declare thy name to my brethren:
in the midst of the Church will I praise thee.
— Ps. 21:23

There are many reasons for Dante's predilection for and use of liturgical prayer. First of all, he was familiar with it; its words and its spirit were part of his daily life and would be part of the daily life of his readers who would readily understand his liturgical references. There is abundant evidence from the records of the time that the Book of Hours was in the hands of most men who could read, and that even those who could not read were in such regular attendance at the Divine Office and the Mass of the day that the words of the liturgy were very familiar to them. Old stories such as Wolfram von Eschenbach's *Parzival* tell of knights and ladies, kings and queens, as well as monks and nuns assisting at Prime or Vespers or Compline. In the *Nibelungenlied* it is as she is leaving the castle in the gray of the dawn to attend Matins that Kriemhild stumbles over the body of the murdered Siegfried.[4]

Biographies, too, bring evidence. From Joinville's *Life of Saint Louis IX*, we learn that the good King made his sons read the Day Hours in his presence so that they would form the habit of assisting at the Hours and be prepared to do so in future days when they ruled their own territories.[5] It is said that Saint Frances of Rome, a busy matron of the next century, was interrupted repeatedly in the chapel of her palace while reciting the Office privately, always at the same phrase in the psalm, and found on her return from the fifth or sixth interruption, her guardian angel pointing to the words, now glowing in letters of gold.[6] "A wife is bound to leave her devotions at the altar to find God in household work," she once had said. Saint Elizabeth of Hungary is pictured by her biographer as a little girl in the chapel of the castle, reading from a big Breviary.⁷ Many of the Books of Hours used by laymen, books beautifully illuminated, have come down to us.

Popular literature of the Middle Ages is filled with incidents which show that men and women participated in daily Mass. In the collection of Gaultier de Coincy known as *Miracles of the Virgin*, there is a charming story of a knight who, on his way to the tournament, stopped for Mass and then stayed for a second and a third and arrived at the lists to find that the tournament in which he was to have participated was over. However, he received congratulations from everyone he met, and discovered that the Virgin, in whose honor the Masses had been offered, had taken his place in the lists and had won all the jousts for him. In the *Nibelungenlied*, Kriemhild and Brunhild have their famous quarrel at the door of the cathedral as each queen is about to enter with her entourage for a weekday Mass.

Beyond the fact that Dante, like every other man of his time, was familiar with liturgical prayer, there are profound religious, social, and poetical reasons why he would love it and build it into the poem in which he is showing man the way to God. Of these the most fundamental is religious. Saint Paul in the first chapter of his epistle to the Ephesians had said that the Father of our Lord Jesus Christ had *predestined us unto himself . . . unto the praise of the glory of his grace . . . in his beloved Son in whom we have Redemption.* God made man — as indeed he made all creation — to praise him. But because when God made man he foresaw the Incarnation and Redemption, he *predestined man unto the praise of the glory of his grace in his beloved Son* in whom man was redeemed and through whom, by virtue of his incorporation into the Mystical Body, the prayers of man have immeasurable value. For this reason part of the prayer with which the faithful begin the Office runs: *O Lord, in union with that divine intention wherewith thou didst offer praises on earth to God, I offer these Hours to thee.* The two facets of liturgical prayer are therefore the praise of the glory of God and of the grace of the Redemption.

Dante, who saw clearly how all nature praises the glory of God by reflecting his attributes and adhering to his law, was deeply aware that man — because of his elevation to the supernatural order of grace — must, by all that he is and does, praise God's glory into which it is his high destiny to enter at the end of his life. And since of all earthly creatures he is the pinnacle in the hierarchy of being, since he alone has the gift of words and can therefore serve as the mouthpiece of the terrestrial universe, he is under obligation to sing to the Lord of creation hymns in praise of his glory, echoing the praise of the angels above him and giving words to the silent praise of irrational creatures below him. This portion of man's duty to God the Old Testament saints had understood and joyously fulfilled.

But Saint Paul emphasizes man's duty to praise the glory of God's grace *in his beloved Son*, whom the Old Testament did not know, and in the Redemption which had not yet come. In this injunction of Saint Paul, Dante, in whose soul appreciation of the twin doctrines of the Redemption and the Mystical Body burned with a bright flame, finds an even deeper incentive for urging liturgical prayer. We have seen that Dante and the other scholastics saw the creation as an expression of ideas which had originated in the Divine Mind; all created things were, therefore, expressions of the Divine Wisdom, the Word. All the marvels of the created universe served only to lead up to the manifestation of the Word itself in the Incarnation, and on to the social incarnation of the Word in the Mystical Body of Christ.

The Mystical Body was born on the Cross; and in that Sacrifice of praise and atonement which is continued from the rising to the setting of the sun in the Eucharistic Sacrifice called the Mass, the Incarnate Word and all the members of his Mystical Body continue to offer praise and satisfaction to God. The closing words of the Canon of the Mass, the culminating point of the Sacrifice, express the concept very clearly:

It is ever through him (Christ our Lord) that all these good gifts created by thee, Lord, are by thee sanctified, endowed with life, blessed, and bestowed upon us.

Through him, and with him, and in him, thou, God, almighty Father, in the unity of the Holy Spirit, hast all honor and glory.

World without end. Amen.

For man, silent praise is not enough. All members of the Mystical Body of Christ should praise the Father and the Holy Spirit in and through and with their Head in the sanctified words of liturgical prayer in the hallowed words of the Mass. In the Mass the praise and adoration and satisfaction of Christ and Christians rise together to the Father, and the prayer and sacrifice of Christians, who are truly incorporated with the God-Man, acquire inestimable value.

> *Every other man is a piece of myself, for I am a part and a member of mankind. Every Christian is part of my own body, because we are members of Christ. . . . Nothing at all makes sense, unless we admit, with John Donne, that: "No man is an island, entire of itself; every man is a piece of the continent, a part of the main."*
>
> — Thomas Merton
> *No Man is an Island*

In Dante's *social* philosophy there is a fundamental reason for his preference for liturgical prayer. Everywhere in the *Divine Comedy* he pictures man in society. Only twice, at the beginning of his journey when he is lost in the dark wood and at the end when he has reached his goal, is Dante alone. Since man is social, he must worship socially. The liturgy — the very word *liturgy* means a work by the people or for the people — emphasizes the social aspect of Christian life: it is essentially collective action, an undertaking that has a definite social relationship; therefore it stresses the social solidarity so characteristic of Dante's thought. Its program is the perfect union of all men in Christ with the Father and the Holy Ghost. Its philosophy is that priests and people, those in the cloister and those outside, should — with the Supreme Pontiff and civil rulers — be united throughout the day the world over in a unity of prayer to raise, as it were, one voice to God. Prayers of the liturgy unite the prayers of all men; and since liturgical prayer is the prayer of the whole Church, Dante makes it the prayer of the Church suffering in Purgatory and the Church triumphant in Heaven. The sinners struggling up the mountain of expiation have their prayers reinforced by the prayers of the faithful on earth and of the saints in heaven; the feeble individual voice helps to swell the great chorus of praise and adoration and thanksgiving; the private petition becomes the petition of the whole Church. The living and the dead in magnificent plain chant raise one voice to God.

There is another reason, *partly social and partly religious* (Dante does not separate the two), which is perhaps even more fundamental. Dante sees the Church as the medium by which the fruits of the Redemption are poured out upon the souls of individual men. All through the *Divine Comedy*, the reader is aware of Dante's deep love of the Church: of her theology, her mission, her external and internal life. The whole of his devotion is bound up with the concept of the Church as the Spouse of Christ, a concept familiar to the thirteenth-century man but somewhat foreign to the thinking of many contemporary Christians. Dante sees the liturgy as the prayer of the "Spouse and Secretary of Christ" (*Banq.* II, vi, 2), the movement of the Bride to her Spouse. In *Paradiso* X:139–144 in speaking of the hour of Matins he says,

> Then, as a horologe that calleth us
> What time *the Bride of God is rising up*
> *With Matins to her Spouse that he may love her*
>
> *Wherein one part the other draws and urges*
> Ting! ting! resounding with so sweet a note,
> That swells with love the spirit well disposed. . . .

The antiphonal chanting of the psalms in choir, the give and take of the choirs, suggest to him the reciprocal love of Christ and the Church in that marriage in which Christ returns love for love and showers his graces upon those who thus pray to him. As the bridegroom listens to the voice of the bride, Christ listens to the voice of the Church; for it is the voice of her whom he loves. He who prays with the Church is of one voice with the Bridegroom and the Bride.

Dante was not only a theologian and liturgist and social re-

former, he was above all a poet. His love of poetic symbolism alone
would make him a lover of the canonical hours with their historical-
redemptive background. Not only on certain days but also at certain
hours of each day, the Church recalls some event in the history
of the Redemption which is associated with the hour; she offers
some special thought associated with the need of the hour.[8] A
brief look at the selection of psalms, hymns, antiphons, and readings
for each of the hours will suggest the richness of the symbolic
meaning. Later, by making an analysis of two of the hours, we
shall see how Dante employs the symbolism in the *Commedia*.

With MATINS, sung during the darkness of the night watches,
the Church brings before her children the thought of the *Parousia*,
the second coming of the Lord, which, it was widely believed, would
occur at midnight; she reminds them, too, of the nocturnal vigils
of Christ in the gardens and on the mountain slopes of Galilee,
and of the early Christians who spent the night watches in prayer
in the catacombs: she teaches that night is a time for prayer as
well as for sleep. Then, too, the three nocturns of Matins may be
likened to a three-act drama in honor of the feast being celebrated:
at the beginning, two heralds in a sort of reveille "step to the
middle of the choir and proclaim the liturgical character of the feast."

LAUDS, the Hour sung when dawn is breaking, represents the
joyous hour of the Resurrection, the hour when the Redeemer broke
the bonds of death. It is the hour when all men should awaken not
only physically but spiritually, cast off the bondage of sin, and
rise to the new day of Redemption which God has granted them to
spend in his service. Though Lauds is the real morning prayer of
the Church, PRIME, introduced later, is a second morning prayer.
It is the first of the so-called small hours, all of which are short,
because they begin, break into, and close the day's work. The prayers
of Prime prepare us for the struggles of the day; pledge fidelity
in the service of God; beg him to give us patience and charity; and
to preserve us from sin. "May Almighty God direct our actions
and our days in his grace," says the Father Abbot at the close of
Prime as the monks make ready to disperse to perform the tasks
of the day.

According to tradition, the Holy Spirit descended upon the

Apostles about the third hour; therefore in the Office of TIERCE the Church reminds us that we are temples of the Holy Spirit and that we should be characterized by love of God and love of neighbor, gifts of the Spirit of Love. The hours from SEXT to NONE (noon to three) are the hours when Christ hung on the cross and Hell unleashed its might against him. During these hours the day's struggle is at its height; the heat of our passions is at its strongest. "Lead us not into temptation" is the meaning of the prayers of SEXT. The theme of NONE is perseverance. Three o'clock was the hour of Christ's death on the cross, which None is intended to commemorate; it hurries to six o'clock, the end of the day's work, and leads to thoughts of the end of life and prayers for a happy death.

VESPERS is the ancient evening prayer of the Church. As Lauds is the morning tribute of praise for the gift of the new day, Vespers is a prayer of praise and thanksgiving for the favors and graces the day has brought. The greatest Vesper prayer is the MAGNIFICAT: the Church thanks God in the words of the Blessed Mother of the Saviour. Vespers is the candlelight service, sung at that hour when Christ sat down to the Last Supper with his Apostles; therefore many of the Vesper psalms are Eucharistic psalms sung at the Last Supper, or gradual psalms sung on the way to the temple. Sung now at the end of the day as the shadows lengthen, they are symbolic of the finality of things: of the last journey to the heavenly Jerusalem and of the great Eucharistic Banquet of the Beatific Vision.

The Office of COMPLINE, the liturgical night prayer, is filled with exquisite symbolism, of the setting sun, of the darkness which is creeping over the earth and that spiritual darkness which can come to the souls of men should they lose the light of the grace of God, symbolized by the sun. Compline recalls the death of Christ, his commending of his spirit to his Father; it recalls the NUNC DIMITTIS of Simeon. It asks for the protection of God and the Mother of God. We shall see how beautifully Dante weaves the symbolism of Lauds and of Vespers and Compline into the poetry of the cantos recounting the activity at the beginning and the end of the first day on the mountain of Purgatory. Poetry and music and symbolism fuse with prayer in the heart of the liturgy.[9]

We praise thee,
We bless thee,
We adore thee,
We glorify thee,
We give thee thanks for thy great glory.

　　　　　　　　　　　　　　　　— *Gloria* of the Mass

Give us this day our daily bread,
Forgive us our trespasses as we forgive
　　　those who trespass against us,
Lead us not into temptation,
Deliver us from evil.

　　　　　　　　　　　　　　　　— *Our Father*

Since in the prayers of the Breviary and Missal, the four motives of prayer converge as do the three methods of prayer — vocal prayer, meditation, and contemplation — Dante chooses in the *Divine Comedy* prayers of adoration, praise, thanksgiving, and petition for his vocal prayer, and shows by his penetration of the inner meaning of the prayers and hymns how they lend themselves to meditation and contemplation. And since the rubrics of the liturgy (the detailed directives for the conduct of divine services) are so designed as to make the whole man pray, body and soul — the words, melodies, and gestures being the external expressions of internal devotion — he carries over into the *Commedia* not only the prayers themselves with their chants and melodies, but the bodily attitudes as well. In the Valley of the Princes, the garden of the elect in the Starry Heaven, and even in the Empyrean the souls sit together before, after, and during prayer as the brethren sit in choir. In the Ante-Purgatory, the Earthly Paradise, and even in the Starry Heaven where they are shown on their way to the white rose of the Empyrean, they participate in processions. In the Purgatory there are the bent knees and folded hands before the majestic angel messengers; the prostrate forms of the avaricious; the bowed bodies of the proud; the leaning toward each other of the envious in a suggestion of the kiss of peace. Even in the highest Heaven the saints fold their hands when they join in Bernard's prayer to Mary.

Since in the medieval abbey, cathedral, and nobleman's chapel there were innumerable helps for meditation in the frescoes, stained-glass windows, groups of statuary, and passages read from Sacred Scripture and homilies of the Fathers, Dante transplants these helps into his poem. We find them in sculptures made by angels, in the stories they tell, and in their apt quotations from Scripture and other literature. By these means the minds of those who make their way up the steep mountain are filled with fruitful thought.

In using the prayers of the Breviary and Missal, Dante does not take them in the order in which they appear in the liturgy. His point of view seems to be that somewhere in the Church, any prayer is being said or sung at any moment and that the Christian who has been present at the canonical hours or at the Mass can pick up during the day the prayer that meets his need and unite himself with that segment of the Church engaged at that moment in offering that prayer to God. For every portion of the official prayer of the Church is being offered somewhere in the world at any given moment. A study of the prayers used in the *Divine Comedy* demonstrates clearly Dante's plan to use segments of all the canonical hours and to suggest by prayer and action all the parts of the Mass. Within the compass of this chapter it is impossible to present in detail all of the liturgical materials to which Dante directs attention or which he uses dramatically. There is the problem of selecting a sufficient number to show how complete his coverage is and the further problem of discussing some of the matter in sufficient detail to indicate how admirably he enters into the spirit.

In an attempt to meet both demands I have used in the five sections which follow a combination of approaches to the problem. The first section presents the use in Dante and the liturgy of the four prayers which are most basic in the life of the Christian; the second, a group of other prayers used very frequently. The third section shows how Dante enters into the symbolic spirit of the Divine Office by analyzing his dramatic presentation of Lauds and Compline, the morning and evening prayer hours of the Church; the fourth examines briefly the position in the liturgy of a sampling of hymns and readings which Dante utilizes in memorable ways. The last section is an attempt to clarify by summary and some detailed

analysis how the prayers and actions of the Mass, the heart of the
liturgy, are also at the heart of the action of the *Divine Comedy*.
Pope Pius XII has instigated revisions in both the Breviary and the
Missal which are still under way. The material given here is based
on usage current in 1955. On March 23 of that year the Sacred
Congregation of Rites issued a decree for the reducing of the rubrics
to a simpler form and the omitting of many of these prayers. None
of the revisions are considered here.

The four basic prayers learned before all others and said most
frequently, which are found in all the canonical hours and in whole
or in part in the Mass are the *Pater Noster, Ave Maria, Gloria
Patri,* and *Credo.* The first of these, the Lord's Prayer and the
Angelic Salutation, are said inaudibly before all the Hours except Compline — when they are said later, also inaudibly; the
Our Father closes all the Nocturns of Matins and is sung in the
Mass just before the Communion. The *Apostles' Creed* is always said
before Matins and Prime and when Compline is finished; the
Athanasian Creed is recited on most Sundays throughout the year.
The *Gloria Patri* is chanted immediately upon the conclusion of
the seventeenth verse of Psalm 50, "Thou, O Lord, wilt open my
lips; and my tongue shall announce thy praise," which is the audible
opening of each of the Hours. Since praise of the Trinity is the
whole purpose of the Hours, the *Gloria Patri* (Glory be to the Father
and to the Son and to the Holy Ghost) is the conclusion of every
psalm.

In the *Divine Comedy* the Lord's Prayer is said on the cornice
of the proud, the first step of the purgative way. The basic evil
in the universe is pride: it caused the fall of the angels; it brought
about the fall of man in the garden of Eden; it is at the root of
all sin whatsoever. The man who would be united with God must
learn his place in the universe; he must learn to put first things
first. And so he repeats again and again — in the company of those
who climb with him, their heads and backs bent with the burdens
they are carrying to teach them to bend their too-stiff necks — the
words of the *Our Father.* The proud man has concentrated on his
ego: in the Lord's Prayer there is no *I;* the pronouns are *our* and *us.*
Dante distinguishes on this cornice three kinds of pride: inordinate

national pride, inordinate family pride, inordinate personal pride in one's work or achievement or position. The prayer taught by Christ to the Apostles is an antidote for all of these.

The *Our Father* emphasizes the basic precepts of the Christian life: *Thou shalt love the Lord thy God with thy whole heart and with thy whole soul and with thy whole strength.* This is the first commandment. And the second is like to it: *Thou shalt love thy neighbor as thyself.* "Our Father who art in heaven," penitent souls repeat again and again, here, where, at last, men have learned that in the brotherhood of man, predicated by the fatherhood of God, all men have but one fatherland. "Hallowed be thy name," they say, realizing that all men should be eager not for the honor of their own names but for the honor of the name of God. "Thy kingdom come" is the prayer of men who had been interested in seeking position or personal honor for achievement. The proud man is imperious — he wants what he wants, when he wants it; now he prays, "Thy will be done on earth as it is in heaven," that is, by men as it is done by saints and angels. He has been egocentric, interested in his own desires, concerned only with his own needs, real or imaginary; now he prays for the needs of all mankind, including himself as just one of the many children of God, asking for bread, material and spiritual, for the whole human family. For the proud man forgiving an injury is difficult; now he asks for forgiveness for himself and all others in the measure in which they forgive. And for all men he asks deliverance from temptation and from evil.

In the liturgy of the Divine Office, except in Compline, the AVE MARIA follows the *Pater Noster*. Eight times a day Mary is greeted in the Office with Gabriel's salutation and with that of Elizabeth. Devoutly in the second part of the *Hail Mary* the Church today asks her to pray for sinful men at the two important moments of their lives, *now* and the *hour of death*. Though the section of the *Ave Maria* which the Church added seems to have originated in the twelfth century and is found in a hymn which must have been widely diffused since it appears in a number of manuscripts, it was probably not a part of the Office; it did not then nor does it now appear in the Mass.[10] That section taken from Holy Scripture, the greeting of Gabriel and that of Elizabeth, occurs frequently as an Offertory or Tract (the Tract being those Scriptural verses sung just before the Gospel throughout the Lenten season and on certain other occasions); as Offertory in all Saturday Masses sung in honor of the Virgin; as Tract on the feast of the Archangel Gabriel, March 24; and as both Offertory and Tract on the feast of the Annunciation, March 25, and on some other feasts of the Virgin. Elizabeth's greeting, "Blessed art thou among women," is sung by the four and twenty elders in the Earthly Paradise (*Purg.* XXIX:85–87); the *Ave Maria*, Gabriel's greeting only, is sung twice in the *Paradiso:* once by Piccarda (III:121) and once by Gabriel (XXXII:94–96). It is fitting that Piccarda, who has just told her story of being torn from the cloister by her brother Corso to enter into a marriage to which he had pledged her, should — after she has attained that peace of which she so beautifully speaks — sing as she fades from Dante's sight, the best-loved canticle to the Virgin ever faithful. Why Gabriel sings it, when and where he does, we have seen (p. 171).

In the liturgy there are three phrasings of the basic tenets of Christian doctrine known as the CREED: the Apostles' Creed, the Athanasian Creed, and the Nicene Creed. Of these the Apostles' Creed is the most familiar to contemporary Christians; though in Europe and French Canada it is not unusual to hear men and women and quite small children chant the Nicene Creed in processions and during visits to basilicas such as Saint Peter's in Rome, Notre Dame at Lourdes, or Saint Anne at Beaupré. All of the Creeds have important places in the liturgy: the Apostles' Creed, as already noted, is said before Matins and Prime and after Compline; the Athanasian Creed is part of Prime on Trinity Sunday and on lesser Sundays during some liturgical seasons; the Nicene Creed is sung at High Mass on all Sundays and principal feasts and during the octaves of these feasts and recited at Low Masses at these times. In the *Divine Comedy* (*Par.* XXIV:130) while Saint Peter is examining him on faith, Dante says the Creed, though from the portion quoted, the reader is not quite clear which one.[11] In any single day the *Gloria Patri* is prayed more frequently than any other of the four basic prayers because of its being the close of every psalm and being used in other ways already indicated. At the opening of *Paradiso*

XXVII it is sung so sweetly that Dante is intoxicated with joy as
he listens, and the whole universe seems to smile.

> To the most holy and undivided Trinity,
> to the crucified humanity of our Lord Jesus Christ,
> to the fruitful purity of the most blessed and glorious
>   Virgin Mary,
> and to the multitude of all the saints,
> may everlasting praise, honor, power, and glory,
> be given by every creature;
> and to us may there be granted the pardon of all sins,
> for infinite ages,
> world without end.
> Amen.
>
>   — Saint Bonaventure
>   (Closing prayer of the Divine Office)

Among other prayers used variously in the liturgy and included
in the *Divine Comedy* are the CONFITEOR; the TE DEUM, which
includes the SANCTUS; the LITANY OF THE SAINTS; and a number
of psalms, from which two — Psalm 50, known in the liturgy as the
MISERERE, and Psalm 118 have been selected for discussion here.
Often significant psalms are commented on elsewhere. It may be well
to observe at this point that Dante includes by name or implication
the four antiphons of the Virgin, introduced into the Office in the
thirteenth century, used today to conclude the canonical hours during
the different seasons of the Church year, and used variously in the
liturgy of Dante's day. Dante dramatizes all of them: the ALMA RE-
DEMPTORIS MATER (O Loving Mother of the Redeemer), the REGINA
COELI (O Queen of Heaven), and the AVE REGINA COELORUM
(Hail, Queen of Heaven Enthroned) in the *Paradiso;* and the SALVE
REGINA (Hail, Holy Queen) in the *Purgatorio.*

The CONFITEOR, a profound acknowledgment of sin, is said
often. It is frequently recited at Prime and regularly at Compline;
it is said at the foot of the altar before every Mass: at the beginning

and close of the day, man bows his head before God and the whole
court of heaven — as well as before his brethren here on earth —
strikes his breast, and humbly accuses himself of his sins of thought,
word, deed, and omission. Dante on the topmost step before he
enters the gate of Purgatory kneels and repeats the prayer; the
priest before he mounts the altar steps pauses and repeats it, after
which the congregation says it also.

> I confess to almighty God, to blessed Mary ever a virgin, to blessed
> Michael the archangel, to blessed John the Baptist, to the holy apostles
> Peter and Paul, to all the saints, and to you (father or brethren) that
> I have sinned exceedingly in thought, word, and deed: through my
> fault, through my fault, through my most grievous fault. Therefore
> I beseech the blessed Mary ever a virgin, blessed Michael the arch-
> angel, blessed John the Baptist, the holy apostles Peter and Paul, all
> the saints, and you (father or brethren) to pray to the Lord our God
> for me.

Since every sin injects poison into the whole organism of the Church
it demands public confession and expiation. Dante, like every other
medieval Christian, shows himself mindful of his need for penance
and of the intercessory prayer of others as he humbly asks forgiveness
of his sins.

In the *Purgatorio* hard upon the *Confiteor* comes the TE DEUM
(IX:140) intoned by an angel as Dante, the contrite sinner, begins
his ascent of the mountain of expiation. Probably Dante had in
mind the Scriptural saying that there shall be more joy in heaven
upon one sinner doing penance than upon ninety-nine just who
need not penance (Lk. 15:7). He may also have had in mind the
legend about the composition of this Ambrosian hymn, sung, so
the story runs, antiphonally by Saint Ambrose and his neophyte,
Saint Augustine, as they left the font after the baptism of Augustine,
who according to his own account was a great sinner. There is
further reason for associating the *Te Deum* with Saint Augustine. In
his examination on faith (*Par.* XXIV:113) Dante again hears the
opening verse of the *Te Deum* after he cites as the greatest miracle
in proof of the divine origin of Christianity the fact that an unlearned
man of such humble birth as that of Peter, his examiner, should
have been chosen to preach the Gospel and that through such poor

instruments the faith should have been spread — an argument which he borrows from Saint Augustine.

Included in the *Te Deum* is the SANCTUS, the "Holy, holy, holy" that Isaias heard sung by the seraphim in his vision of the heavenly court (Isa. 6:3). No doubt Dante uses the *Te Deum* as the angels' chief hymn of praise in the *Commedia* because of its identification with the angelic choirs in the court of the Most High. The nine choirs sing the *Sanctus* as they circle around the Point of Light in the Empyrean (*Par.* XXVIII:94); they sing it when Dante has passed his examination on love and is ready for the vision of God (*Par.* XXVI:69).

The *Te Deum* and the *Sanctus*, separated from it, have many uses in the liturgy. The *Te Deum* is sung at Matins except on certain days, for example, the ferial Offices of Lent) as the early morning canticle of praise; it is used on all occasions which call for special praise or thanksgiving within the parish or the community or Christendom, two of the most important being the consecration of a bishop or the election of a pope. The *Sanctus*, as such, closes the Eucharistic prayer of the Mass known as the Preface, which varies with the season and the feast. A study of the fifteen Prefaces reveals that in them eight of the nine choirs of angels are named and that in a variety of ways the Church asks that men be permitted to join their voices with those of the angelic choirs in giving unceasing praise to the Triune God.

The union of men with angels and of men with each other is brought out in many ways in liturgical prayer. Man needs the help of the angels in praising God; he needs their help in keeping the commandments; he needs their protection. For all these things he needs also the help of the saints. On the cornice of the envious where souls are learning brotherly love, they meditate on the great charity that exists in the Communion of Saints, where all are interested in each and each in all and all in God. "Mary, pray for us," they cry; "Michael and Peter, and all ye saints" (*Purg.* XIII: 49–51). Once again in the Stellar Heaven, this time in dramatic form, we are reminded of the Litany, when in the mystical garden we see the saints grouped in the tableau in the categories of the liturgical prayer. This Litany, like all others, closes with a form of the *Agnus Dei,* a cry for mercy to the meek Lamb of God. Dante uses the *Agnus Dei* on the cornice of the angry; since it is a cry for peace as well as mercy, it is the AGNUS DEI of the Mass.

There are many liturgical uses of the LITANY OF THE SAINTS: for the intercession of the saints is asked on numerous occasions, one of the chief being Holy Saturday after the blessing of the new fire and the font and, in Dante's day, the subsequent baptism of the catechumens and infants. It is a part of the ritual of processions held for the blessing of fields, of new churches, of cemeteries; it is chanted in processions of petition for rain, for calm weather, or in time of plague.[12] An antiphon in the Office of Lauds for the Easter season implores the suffrage of the saints in words which are almost paraphrased in Saint Bernard's prayer to the Virgin in the last canto of the *Commedia* (34–39). In fact, the cornerstone of the whole *Divine Comedy* is this belief in the interest of the saints in men who are struggling on their way to God. Dante's prayer to Beatrice, his own special saint (*Par.* XXXI:79–90), is quite within the pale of Catholic theology.

Everywhere in the life of prayer in the liturgy of the Church there is this brotherhood of prayer. All through the Ante-Purgatory souls ask Dante to pray for them and to beg prayers for them when he returns to earth. Dante, surprised to find that Forese Donati, one of his Florentine friends, has moved so rapidly up the mountain, learns that his good wife Nella by her prayers, her flood of tears, and her sighs has won advancement for him (*Purg.* XXIII:85–90). When Cacciaguida meets Dante in the Heaven of Mars he urges him to pray for his great-great-grandfather from whom he has his name, who for a hundred years has been suffering on the cornice of the proud (*Par.* XV:91–96). The Divine Office includes many prayers for the faithful departed; there is a special Office for the dead. In every Mass there is a Memento for the Dead; there is a special group of Masses for deceased brethren. All Catholics down the centuries — as the prayers of the Breviary and the Missal give evidence — have believed in the efficacy of prayers for the dead and of the efficacy of the prayers of the saints for the living. Dante (*Purg.* XI:22–24) also asserts his belief that the prayers of the souls in Purgatory can assist the living.[13]

David's act of deep sorrow for sin, Psalm 50, known as the MISERERE is used widely in the liturgy. The Divine Office, as we have already noted, begins with the seventeenth verse: "Thou, O Lord, wilt open my lips and my tongue shall announce thy praise." There is a touch of whimsy in Dante's placing the verse on the lips of the gluttons (*Purg.* XXIII:10–12), who chant it in tears in such manner that it causes both joy and grief, a sly suggestion that when gluttons open their lips it is not — usually — to praise God. The ninth verse of the psalm is chanted by the angels in the Earthly Paradise as Matilda draws the penitent Dante through the river Lethe after he has made his confession. That verse, known as the *Asperges me,* is sung by the choir on Sundays before High Mass as the priest sprinkles the congregation with holy water while the choir chants, "Thou shalt sprinkle me with hyssop, and I shall be cleansed: thou shalt wash me and I shall be made whiter than snow." Having climbed the mountain of expiation, having been purified by a sincere confession, Dante is made ready for the illumination of spirit he receives through the teaching of Beatrice and the other saints and for his sacrifice in offering himself for the mission to which he is called and ultimately for the Beatific Vision.

The entire *Miserere* has many uses in the liturgy. In the *Divine Comedy* Dante represents the souls of the late repentant chanting it antiphonally (*Purg.* V:22–24) as they make their slow way across the plateau on the second level of the Ante-Purgatory. Since most of these souls met death by violence, the psalm is peculiarly fitting here, for it is known as the prayer of the unshriven. The psalm is part of the Office of Lauds on the Sundays of Lent, known as "Miserere Sundays"; it is used in Matins on Wednesday; it is part of Lauds in the Office of the Dead. It is chanted in the liturgy of Maundy Thursday, Good Friday, and Holy Saturday; it is chanted as a corpse is borne into a church for the Requiem Mass; where there is a cemetery joining the church it is chanted also when the body is being carried to the grave. In some monasteries and convents, monks and nuns chant it in procession as they pass from the refectory to the chapel at noon and at night, possibly because when monastic customs were being formed the way often led across the crypt where the brethren were buried.

In Psalm 118 BEATI IMMACULATI, man asks for help in keeping the Commandments. The psalm is the longest in the Psalter and structurally one of the most interesting: in it each of the twenty-four letters of the Hebrew alphabet is made to praise the Commandments of God and to ask for grace to keep them. In translation, the full beauty of the acrostic is lost because the verses cannot begin with the letters which are announced as headings of the twenty-four parts. Today, the one hundred seventy-six verses are divided and sections of the psalm are sung at Prime, Tierce, Sext, and None on Sunday; in Dante's day the psalm was found also in Matins and Lauds. Selected verses are used as Introits, Communion verses, and Offertories, as they doubtless were in the thirteenth century, for they occur in Masses celebrated then; for example, verses 75 and 120 as the Introit of the Mass *Cognovi*, designated for such feasts as that of Saint Monica, the mother of Saint Augustine, May 4; verses 161 and 162 assigned as Communion verses for the feast of Saint Lucy, December 13; and some twenty verses used as Offertories for Masses of the season of Lent.

The verse to which Dante makes reference is 25 under Daleth, found today in Prime. Souls chained to the pavement on the cornice of the avaricious and the prodigal, expiating in this way the sins of their earth-bound lives keep repeating, "My soul hath cleaved to the pavement: quicken thou me according to thy word." That avarice was the root of many of the evils of his day and led to the breaking of many of the Commandments was one of Dante's strong convictions. When the avaricious have learned the poverty of spirit which characterized the Holy Family at Bethlehem, they hear in a jubilant chorus all around them the GLORIA IN EXCELSIS DEO which filled the air about the lowly shepherds at Bethlehem, and which is a part of the Ordinary of the Mass.

*Open, O Lord, my mouth to bless thy Holy
Name: cleanse also my heart from all vain,
perverse and distracting thoughts; enlighten
my understanding, inflame my will, that
I may worthily, attentively, and devoutly
recite this Office, and deserve to be heard
in the presence of thy Divine Majesty.
Through Christ, our Lord, Amen.*

*O Lord, in union with that divine intention
wherewith thou didst offer praises on earth
to God, I offer these Hours to thee.*
— Prayer said before the Office

The cantos of the Ante-Purgatory, which present the activities
of the beginning and the close of the first day on the mountain
(*Purg.* I and II; VII and VIII) give a clear picture of how intimately Dante enters into the complete spirit of the sequence of
prayers in the liturgy. He and Virgil have reached the strand of
the island on which the mountain rears its majestic height while
the dawn stars still shine in the clear sky in which the "oriental
sapphire" of morning is forming. All the heavens smile in the
radiant light of Venus, the morning star. This is the Hour of
Lauds, the joyous Hour of morning praise, the Resurrection Hour,
an Hour doubly joyous this Easter dawn because, like Christ, the
pilgrims have risen from the bowels of the earth, victorious over
sin and Hell. Literally and figuratively they are on the threshold
of a new day.

In the pregnant silence of the dawn from which the unknown
activities of a new day and a new way and a new life will emerge,
they stand deep in meditation as the monks of the monasteries in
the heart of the wildernesses of Europe stood steeped in the quiet
of their houses of prayer. The liturgy of Lauds forms here the
symbolic background of Dante's thought and of his poetic expression. Since the time is Easter Sunday and the place the shore of
that uncharted Western sea whose waves break against the foot of
the mountain of Purgatory, Psalm 92, the first psalm of Lauds for

Paschaltide, must have sung its rhythm into the pensive soul of the poet:

> The Lord hath reigned, he is clothed with beauty:
> the Lord is clothed with strength and hath girded himself.
> ....
> The floods have lifted up, O Lord:
> the floods have lifted up their voice.
> ....
> Wonderful are the surges of the sea;
> wonderful is the Lord on high
> ....
> Holiness becometh thy house.
> ....
> Alleluia, alleluia.

Psalm 92 slips into Psalm 99 with its urgent, "Sing joyfully to God all the earth . . . praise ye his name"; and into 62, "O God, my God, to thee do I watch at break of day . . . for thee my soul hath thirsted . . . in a desert land. . . ."

But the most significant basis for his meditation — for he dramatized it — was the BENEDICTUS, that splendid canticle of praise in *Luke* (1:68–79), and the thoughts it awakened of the work of John the Baptist. The Church has placed this canticle of Zachary in Lauds because Saint John was the precursor of Christ, as the dawn is of the sunrise, an idea dear to the heart of Dante.[14] John, crying in the wilderness, preached the baptism of penance (Mt. 3:8, 11; Mk. 1:1–4; Lk. 3:2–8) to make men return to the road they had lost (*Purg.* I:119), to urge them to break the bondage of sin and make the crooked ways straight. This baptism of penance is symbolized in the Ante-Purgatory by the washing of Dante's tear-stained cheeks with dew from the wet grass of the deserted shore. The purification is accomplished just as the sea trembles under the brightness of the still unrisen sun which lightens the horizon. The significance of the baptism of penance is clear. Dante has lost the road; now he is about to enter upon his penitential journey to make straight the crooked ways of his soul, to fill the valleys with the fruits of good works and level the mountain of pride. In ways like this does Dante indicate how liturgical prayer, though the prayer of the whole Church, is fruitful for the needs of individuals who unite in raising the prayer to God.

All of the hymns of Lauds have images of the dawn sky and the rising sun. In Paschaltide, the hymn for Sunday morning is AURORA COELUM PURPURAT ("The morn has spread her crimson rays"), which doubtless inspired the second and third tercets of Canto II, descriptive of the opalescent sky changing from purple to crimson to orange just before the boat bearing the hundred singing souls from Tiber's mouth appears on the horizon. Psalm 113, IN EXITU ISRAEL (When Israel went out of Egypt), which they are chanting was in the thirteenth century a part of Lauds, though today it is a Vesper psalm. Dante uses it here because of the way in which it ties into the whole spirit of the opening of the *Purgatorio*, the baptism unto penance of the Israelites in the cloud and in the sea (1 Cor. 10:2). These souls, who like Dante, though by another route, have come out of the dawn into the sunrise, will with him begin a new life *unto penance*, he having been baptized in the dew, signifying the cloud, and they having been baptized in the sea.

There are two additional uses of this psalm in the liturgy — one of them only semiliturgical — which Dante may have had in mind, for both signify the entrance upon a new life. Formerly when the body of the dead Christian was borne into the church, it was the custom in some places to sing Psalm 113 as well as the *Miserere;* in some religious houses it is still the custom for the newly received novices to be covered with the pall when they prostrate themselves before the altar after having put off their bridal gowns and clothed themselves in religious habits, the choir the while chanting the *In exitu Israel de Egypto*. The significance of the ceremony is, of course, that these novices are dead to the world and are at the dawn of a new life of penance and abnegation.

As Dante began the dramatization of Lauds just before dawn had really broken — to give, as it were, a prelude to his tone poem of the Liturgical Hour; so he begins his dramatic presentation of the Hour of Compline not at nightfall but at the sunset hour, the close of Vespers, "the hour that melts the heart and penetrates the pilgrim with love if, from afar, he hears a bell that seems to deplore the dying day" (*Purg.* VIII:1–6). The "Ave Maria bell," in our day called the Angelus, has just rung; the SALVE REGINA sung by the spirits in the Valley of the Princes still hidden from Dante and Virgil by the shelving rock has floated to them on the evening air. Sordello will not guide the pilgrims to the valley until the last rim of the sun has gone to rest in the sea. Thus Dante closes the day which opened when the sun first showed above the horizon in Lauds. The Compline Hour begins with the falling of darkness.

There is a tenderness and pathos in this prelude to Compline which makes the reader mindful of incidents in the life of the exiled Dante and fills the words of the SALVE in this setting with peculiar significance. Liturgically, it is somewhat strange that Dante should have it sung here *before* Compline, for in the Middle Ages it was sung after Compline when it was sung at all as a part of the Divine Office.[15] In Dominican houses it was and still is recited daily in procession.[16] In the contemporary Roman Breviary, it is assigned to First Vespers of the period between Trinity Sunday and the Saturday before the first Sunday of Advent. Poetically, the antiphon belongs just where Dante has put it, in the nostalgic sunset hour.

> Hail, holy Queen, Mother of Mercy, hail, our life, our sweetness, and our hope, to thee do we cry, poor banished children of Eve; to thee do we send up our sighs, mourning and weeping in this valley of tears. Turn then, most gracious advocate, thine eyes of mercy toward us; and after this our exile, show unto us the blessed fruit of thy womb, Jesus. O clement, O loving, O sweet Virgin Mary!

All the circumstances of the first sunset in Purgatory suggest the words of this favorite prayer to the Virgin: the valley, the waiting in exile, the hope in the souls eager to begin the climb which will lead them to Christ.

One who is familiar with the beautiful Casentino Valley which lies between Florence and Arezzo, where — as we saw in Chapter II — Dante is known to have been at different periods of his exile, reads into many of the lines connected with the Purgatorial Valley of the Princes the homesickness in the heart of the exiled Dante, for the Casentino was in a very real sense a valley of princes. From the chapels of the castles of the Conti Guidi topping every hill, from the belfries of the forty stately Romanesque churches built by Matilda of Tuscany in the little villages of the valley, from the Badia in Poppi or the church of the hermitage at Camaldoli where Saint Romuald had had his vision of the ladder reaching to heaven (*Par.* XXI:28–30), or from the basilica at La Verna where his loved Saint Francis received the stigmata (*Par.* XI:106–108),[17] he had often heard the "Ave Maria bell" as his weary feet walked the paths of Romena or Porciano, whose scarred towers still rear themselves above the lush fields and vineyards of the valley.

Nor was he safe there from his enemies, for in the valley men still tell the story of his meeting armed men who had heard of his being at Porciano and who were coming up the rugged hill to apprehend him and their asking of the vagrant whom they met on the way down, "Is Dante there?" and of his ready answer, "When I was there, he was." The *Salve* would seem to be peculiarly Dante's prayer in the valley. No wonder that the Compline prayer in the Valley of the Princes is made so dramatic a prayer for safety; no wonder that in presenting the prayers of Compline Dante emphasizes the notes of hope and divine protection.

When the sun has set, Sordello brings Dante and Virgil into full view of the valley where the princes are now ready to begin the night prayer of the Church. The Hour of Compline opens with the blessing, "May the Lord almighty grant us a quiet night and a perfect end"; the blessing is followed immediately by a short lesson from *1 Peter* (5:8 and 9):

> Brethren: Be sober and watch because your adversary the devil, as a roaring lion, goeth about seeking whom he may devour, whom resist ye, strong in faith. But thou, O Lord, have mercy on us.

After the lesson come the *Our Father*, the *Confiteor*, and three psalms: 4, 90, and 133. Though Dante makes no direct reference to any of these, the spirit expressed in them hovers over the valley which has echoed to the chant of verses like these:

> The light of Thy countenance, O Lord is signed upon us.

> In peace in the self-same I will sleep and I will rest: for thou, O Lord, hast established me in hope.

He shall overshadow thee with his shoulders:
and under his wings thou shalt trust.

. . . .

For he hath given his angels charge over thee:
to keep thee in all thy ways.

. . . .

Lift up your hands by night to the holy places,
and bless the Lord.

As if in response to this last verse, one of the princes looks to the east, joins his hands and lifts them up, and devoutly intones the Compline hymn TE LUCIS ANTE TERMINUM ("Before the closing of the day"). In Caswell's translation, which is usually used in English versions of the canonical hours, it runs as follows:

Now with the fast departing light
Maker of all, we ask of thee,
Of thy great mercy, through the night
Our guardian and defence to be.

Far off let idle visions fly;
No phantom of the night molest;
Curb thou our raging enemy,
That we in chaste repose may rest.

Following the hymn is the short responsory, "Into thy hands, O Lord, I commend my spirit" with its answering versicle, "Thou hast redeemed us, O Lord, the God of truth"; and the versicle, "Keep us, O Lord, as the apple of thine eye" with its responsory, "Protect us under the shadow of thy wings." The antiphon for Eastertide; the canticle of Simeon when he saw the Christ Child at the time of his presentation in the temple; the Apostles' Creed; and various brief versicles and responsories lead to the concluding prayer. Both the antiphon and the concluding prayer are filled with the spirit which Dante catches and holds in Canto VIII:

Save us, O Lord, when we are awake and keep us while we sleep that we may watch with Christ and rest in peace. Alleluia.

Visit, we beseech thee, O Lord, this dwelling, and drive far from it all snares of the enemy: let thy holy angels dwell herein, who may keep us in peace: and let thy blessing be always upon us. . . .

Having finished their prayer, the princes in the valley slumber.

But the watchful pilgrims witness the dramatic literal answer to all the petitions. As we have seen elsewhere (pp. 149, 183), the vigilant angels of hope with glowing faces like searchlights and with flaming swords take their places on the heights overlooking the valley and when the devil of Peter's lesson (a serpent, not a lion) slinks in, expel him, while the souls slumber in peace without ever knowing he has come and gone. The angels came from Mary's bosom, Sordello explains, in answer to the *Salve.* Then as the moon rises over the valley, Dante, too, falls asleep. The whole valley is at peace, flooded with light, a symbol of the protection of God, which rests upon it in answer to the Compline prayers.

> *Come and let us go up to the mountain*
> *of the Lord,*
> *and to the house of the God of Jacob,*
> *and he will teach us his ways,*
> *and we will walk in his paths.*
>
> — Isa. 2:3
> Ordinary of Lauds

A further brief word should be said about Dante's use of the choral parts of the liturgy — the hymns, canticles, and antiphons of the Divine Office — and of the readings from the Bible and the Fathers of the Church. Attention has already been drawn to two hymns, the *Te Lucis ante Terminum* or Compline hymn and the *Aurora Coelum Purpurat* of Paschaltide; to the three canticles of the New Testament, those of Zachary, Simeon, and the Virgin Mary; and to the dramatic use of the four antiphons to the Virgin. Since Dante builds in the poem upon many other hymns from various seasons of the ecclesiastical year — all of them in significant ways — and suggests some of the Old Testament canticles, it would be profitable to discuss them. Space, however, allows for only two, both of them ancient, the VEXILLA REGIS ("Abroad the regal banners fly") of Fortunatus (530–609) and the SPLENDOR PATERNAE GLORIAE of Saint Ambrose (340–397). They have been chosen for discussion here because they are set, so to speak, in apposition — one being presented at the court of Lucifer; the other, in the mystic rose of the Empyrean.

Dante's use of the *Vexilla Regis* is ironic, daring. To the majestic first line of the hymn, sung in the Ordinary of Vespers in Passiontide and during the procession from the altar of repose on Good Friday, Dante adds the word *inferni* so that the line becomes "The banners of the king *of Hell* go forth." Used at the opening of the last canto of the *Inferno* to introduce Lucifer, it brings the shuddering reader to the scene of infernal adoration in the lowest pit of Hell, where the souls of traitors, eternal votaries of the Prince of Darkness, fast frozen in the ice which binds him forever, are bent in obeisance before him, cut off for all eternity from the glories won for men by Christ the King under the victorious standard of his Cross. The whole scene is in direct antithesis to that in the great white rose of the *Paradiso*: the triple-faced Lucifer is a travesty on the Blessed Trinity; the field of ice at the center of physical gravity, on the boundless rose to which men were drawn upward by the magnet of Divine Love; the immobility under the black skies of the abyss, of the activity of saints and angels in the luminous white of the Empyrean. Nothing could introduce more vividly a meditation on the two kingdoms than this presentation of the two standards.

The Ambrosian hymn *Splendor Paternae Gloriae,* sung on Monday at Lauds, offers a liturgical background for Dante's description of light in the Empyrean, the river of light and the ocean of light, the roseate oriflamme, the vision of the Word. Though Dante does not actually sing the hymn, he calls upon the Splendor of God (*Par.* XXX:97) to give him power to describe the light; here as at the opening of the *Purgatorio* when he uses the Sunday hymn of Lauds, he builds his images on the words and images of the hymn, in this instance, particularly upon those in the first, second, and eighth stanzas.

> O Splendor of the Father's glory,
> O thou that bringest light from light,
> O Light of light, and Source of Light,
> Day illuminating day!

O thou, true Sun, descend,
Shining with everlasting brightness
And infuse into our hearts
The radiance of the Holy Spirit.

The aurora leads on the light:
With the light may there appear to us
The whole Son in the Father
And the whole Father in the Word.

Splendor in Dante is always a *reflected ray* (*Banq*. III, xiv, 3). From the Eternal Light, God the Father, flows a ray, which is the Light of all men, the Word, which penetrates from sphere to sphere down to earth, forming Dante's river of grace by which men are saved. Saint Paul calls Christ the Splendor of the Father's glory (Hebr. 1:3); he is the Orient from on High (Lk. 1:78); who illumines by his grace every man that comes into the world (Jn. 1:9). The aurora which foreruns the light brings us to Mary and the pacific oriflamme; the light to which she leads us is the Beatific Vision, where in Dante's image of the interflow of the triple light the whole Son — God and man — is seen in the Father and the Father in the Word.

The readings from the Bible and the Fathers of the Church have a variety of liturgical uses and of poetic uses in the *Divine Comedy*. To these should be added readings from the acts of the martyrs and accounts from the lives of the saints which Dante also utilizes. In the Middle Ages, the whole of the Bible was read in the canonical hours and the Mass in the course of the ecclesiastical year: as lessons in the Divine Office; as Introits, Graduals, Offertories, Communion verses; as Epistles of the Mass; and (sections from the Evangelists) as the Gospels of the Mass. In the *Divine Comedy* Dante makes hundreds of references to the Vulgate: there are quotations from about half of the books of the Old and New Testaments, some of them like *Psalms, Acts,* the *Apocalypse,* the epistles of Saint Paul, and all the Evangelists recurring again and again. Many of these parts of Sacred Scripture are utilized in a dramatic way; for example, much of the *Apocalypse,* in the Earthly Paradise, as has already been shown in Chapter IV.

In Dante's presentation of the saints in the *Purgatorio* and the

Paradiso the reader finds both the letter and the spirit of the lessons assigned for their feasts or related feasts in the common of the Divine Office. A good example of how the *Divine Comedy* incorporates such a reading is found in an excerpt from a sermon of Saint Bernard on the *Apocalypse* assigned as the third lesson for Matins on Saturdays during October, Saturday being the day of the week dedicated to Mary. This, of course, is but one sermon in which Bernard presents his belief in the intercessory power of the Virgin.

> Let us cling to Mary's footsteps, my brethren, and cast ourselves at her blessed feet with earnest supplication. Let us hold her and not let her go, until she bless us; for she is mighty. For as the fleece is between the dew and the threshing-floor and the woman is between the sun and the moon: so is Mary set between Christ and the Church. . . .

As an example of how bits of biography included in the nocturns have been absorbed in the *Commedia* one might cite Lesson VI of the second nocturn on the feast of Saint Romuald, February 7. Since the Camoldolese monks, whose congregation he founded, had their hermitage near the Casentino, the legend told in the Lesson would have a peculiar appeal for Dante.

> . . . Like the patriarch Jacob, he saw in a vision a ladder that reached from earth to heaven, on which men in white robes ascended and descended. He interpreted this miraculous vision as signifying the Camoldolese monks, whose founder he was. . . .

In the *Paradiso* (XXI:28) Dante pictures this ladder, down the golden rungs of which come Peter Damian, who had lived at the hermitage for a time, Saint Romuald himself, and Saint Benedict; for the Camoldolese monks were a branch of the great Benedictine Order.

Throughout the *Paradiso* numerous saints whose feasts were celebrated in the liturgy of Dante's era are presented so vividly to the reader that he understands how Dante, when asking their help in resolving his doubts or in clarifying theological questions, may well have in mind their powers of intercessory prayer strongly suggested in the Collects of both the Mass and Divine Office of their feasts and reiterated in the Postcommunion. An example of such a Collect is one taken from the Office and Mass of Saint

Peter's Chair at Rome and at Antioch, the first celebrated on January 18 and the second on February 22. With slight changes in the phrasing it recurs in the commemoration of Saint Peter on the feast of Saint Paul, June 30:

O God, who in delivering to the blessed Apostle Peter the keys of the kingdom of heaven, didst confer on him the pontifical power of binding and loosing: grant that by the help of his intercession we may be loosed from the bonds of our sins.

This Collect, of course, is based on the Scriptural narrative of the conferring of the power (Mt. 16:13–19) which is the Gospel of the feasts of Saint Peter — the Tract, Offertory, and Communion all being parts of the Scriptural narrative also. The whole episode at Peter's gate (*Purg*. IX:115–129) is flavored with the prayer.

In the *Divine Comedy* angels frequently chant portions of the Scriptural readings which in the liturgy are chanted by the choir as Introits, Graduals, Tracts, Offertories, and Communion verses on Sundays, feasts, or ferials to which they are assigned. These two instances will clarify the matter by showing how Dante's use of the passages is in the spirit of the liturgy. On the feast of All Saints, verses 8, 9, 10 of *Matthew* 5 are sung as the Communion of the Mass. In the *Commedia*, verse 9, "Blessed are the peacemakers, for they shall be called the children of God," is chanted on the third cornice as the souls purified from wrath are leaving the cornice; verse 8, "Blessed are the clean of heart, for they shall see God," is sung on the last cornice. Verses of Psalm 30 (*Purg*. XXX:82–84), chanted by the hundred angel witnesses to strengthen Dante's hope when in the Earthly Paradise he suffers the rebuke of Beatrice for his infidelity to grace, are used as Introits in the penitential season of Lent — verses 7 and 8 on Wednesday of the third week and verses 10, 16, and 18 on Saturday in Passion week.

I will go in to the altar of God.

— Mass of the Catechumens

O God, who in creating man didst exalt his nature very wonderfully and yet more wonderfully didst establish it anew; by the mystery signified in the mingling of this water and wine, grant us to have part in the Godhead of him who hast vouchsafed to share our manhood, Jesus Christ, thy Son, our Lord . . .

— Offertory of the Mass

We therefore humbly pray and beseech thee, most merciful Father, through Jesus Christ thy Son, our Lord, that thou wouldst accept and bless these gifts, these offerings, these holy and unspotted sacrifices which we offer thee. . . .

— Canon of the Mass

May the Body of our Lord Jesus Christ keep my soul unto life everlasting. Amen.

— Communion of the Mass

In the *Divine Comedy,* implicitly or explicitly, Dante includes the complete liturgy of the Mass. Since the Mass is the core of the Christian day around which all the Hours and the activities of the day revolve, he makes the Mass the core of his poem. It is not possible in brief space except in barest outline and by suggestion to show how he includes, actually or by implication, the most important prayers and actions of the four major divisions: the Mass of the Catechumens (which in a sense is introductory to the Sacrifice), and the three parts of the Sacrifice itself — the Offertory, Consecration, and Communion.

The ASPERGES, the prelude to the Sunday High Mass, Dante presents in the Earthly Paradise, rightly so, for it is a symbolic cleansing from sin. From the prayers at the foot of the altar, he has chosen the most important, the CONFITEOR. As we have already noted, many of the verses which he quotes from various psalms are used as INTROITS; the KYRIE is a part of the *Litany of the Saints;* the GLORIA is sung by the angels on the cornice of the avaricious and the prodigal; GRADUALS and TRACTS are found in readings he quotes from Scripture. There are dozens of passages from the epistles of Saint Paul and those of the other Apostles; there are selections from *Acts,* and the *Apocalypse* and from such books of the Old Testament as *Isaias, Wisdom,* and the *Canticle of Canticles* (they are identified in other chapters), which signify the EPISTLE. The words of the GOSPEL are quoted frequently, notably in the *Purgatorio,* where some of them are presented graphically. The Gospel concludes the Mass of the Catechumens; between it and the Offertory lies the Creed. When the Christian has heard the word of God in Epistle and Gospel, he joyously answers CREDO as Dante does in his examination on faith.

The Mass is often called a drama; Dante so presents it, particularly the three principal parts. To the accompaniment of the music and movement of their dance, the theologians in the Heaven of the Sun, which Dante is about to leave, chant three times the OFFERTORY VERSE for Trinity Sunday. The verse, which changes with the feast sets the key for what is to follow, as indeed this verse does for the whole of the *Commedia:*

> Blessed be God the Father
> And the Only-begotten Son of God
> And the Holy Spirit

is the chant of the caroling saints (*Par.* XIV:28–33) as Dante and Beatrice ascend to the Heaven of Mars, where the scenes of the Offertory and Elevation take place.

Saint Paul to whom Dante holds fast in this scene (see pp. 239–241) had said (Rom. 12:1), *"I beseech you, therefore, brethren, by the mercy of God that you present your bodies a living sacrifice, holy, pleasing unto God, your reasonable service.* From the time of the Apostles, therefore, the Church marches down through history as a sacrificial society. The early Christians, mindful of the bloody sacrifice of Calvary, living in the awareness of imminent martyrdom, joined in the liturgical procession at the Offertory to offer their gifts and themselves that they might receive the grace of heroic death; in later centuries, the crusaders, of which Cacciaguida was one, marched to the Holy Sepulcher in that spirit; in that spirit Cacciaguida, according to his own declaration (*Par.* XV:148), died there.

Dante, having come the long way up the mountain of purgation, realizes that the life of every conscientious Christian is a constant martyrdom, that victory over the world, the flesh, and the devil is the result of complete victory over self, possible only under the standard of the Cross. Having purified his ego so that his will is whole and upright (*Purg.* XXVII:140) and operating in complete harmony with the divine will, now in a silent prayer (*Par.* XIV:88), which surely signifies the SECRET — so-called because it is said inaudibly by the priest — he presents himself as a holocaust, offering to the service of God all the powers of his body and soul and knows immediately (91) that his holocaust has been accepted.

In the Mass, following the Offertory of priest and people, the words of CONSECRATION are pronounced over their gifts of bread and wine; then, above the altar as above the hill of Calvary, the ELEVATION takes place, the elevation of the Body and Blood of Christ; for every medieval Christian believed that the consecrated Bread and Wine had become in very truth the Body and Blood of the Saviour. Here in the Heaven of Mars, on a white cross which is lifted up in the reachless spaces — a cross "which the joining of quadrants in a circle makes," the circle emblematic of the round Eucharistic Host — Dante sees the elevation of the Living Christ, the Mystical Christ (*Par.* XIV:97–104). Through this image he presents the further liturgical concept that Christ's Sacrifice in the Mass is the crowning of man's sacrifice, man's sacrifice in union with Christ's being his chief duty as a member of the Mystical Body.[18]

That this Body is made up of many members is as we have seen (pp. 239–241) actively depicted by the movement of the lights which make up the figure of Christ on this cross. We have seen how Dante observes them move from tip to tip and from top to bottom of the cross (*Par.* XIV:109–111) and how, as he watches, one of the lights moves to the bottom of the cross and identifies himself as Caccia-guida. Taking up the words Dante had heard in the Offertory Verse chanted by the saints in the Heaven of the Sun, "Blessed be thou, Three and One," and addressing Dante, he becomes, as it were, the mouthpiece of the Mystical Christ to whom Dante had pledged him-self (*Par.* XV:28–48). He gives Dante his mission in the Church, the mission of making his whole vision for the peace of Christendom manifest, to labor to bring about the fulfillment of the prayer at the opening of the Canon of the Mass for peace and unity through-out the Christian world. With outstretched hands the priest says in the prayer known as the TE IGITUR:

> Wherefore, O most merciful Father, we thy suppliants do pray and beseech thee, through Jesus Christ, thy Son our Lord, to receive and bless these gifts and offerings, this holy and unblemished sacrifice. We offer them up to thee first for thy holy catholic church, that it may please thee to grant her peace, to watch over her, to bring her to unity, and guide her throughout the world; likewise for thy Servant N. (insert name) our pope, and N. our bishop, and for all true be-lievers, who keep the catholic and apostolic faith.

Other parts of the Canon of the Mass are telescoped here: the PREFACE and SANCTUS, which lead into it; the MEMENTO OF THE LIVING; the MEMENTO OF THE DEAD; the COMMUNICANTES, those parts which are like jewels in a crown encircling the Consecration, bringing together the whole Church. That this should be so is fitting, for the *Paradiso* brings the reader into God's eternal present. One senses the prayers of the saints on the Cross for the living Dante just as one hears the hundred witnessing angels praying for him in the Earthly Paradise and sees all the blessed clasp their hands in prayer for him in the mystic rose. One remembers here just before the representation of the COMMUNION how those souls praying the *Our Father* on the cornice of the proud pray for those who will come after them; how Cacciaguida in his MEMENTO OF THE DEAD urges Dante to pray for his great-great-grandfather. They are all bound together in the heart of the Mass: the faithful struggling on earth; the faithful suffering in Purgatory; the blessed in Heaven.

The prayers of the liturgy of the Mass cite the mysteries beyond the "blessed passion": the mysteries of the Resurrection and Ascension, which form a unit with the Sacrifice of the Cross and crown the work of Redemption. How Dante presents these mysteries in dramatic form in the Stellar Heaven and how he activates the fourth part of the Mass, the *Communion*, in the Empyrean we have already seen. We have observed, too, how he presents in vivid drama the teaching of the Church that Communion is not only the union of man with Christ and the Blessed Trinity but with the angels and saints. The Mass, essentially a social act of worship, the full meaning of which Dante clearly grasps and vividly presents, ends with the Communion of saints as well as union with God. At the Last Supper, the first Mass, Christ offered this prayer for his Church (Jn. 17:21–23).

> That they all may be one, as thou, Father, in me and I in thee; that they also may be one in us . . .
>
> And the glory which thou hast given me, I have given to them; that they may be one as we also are one;
>
> I in them, and thou in me; that they may be made perfect in one: and the world may know that thou hast sent me, and hast loved them, as thou hast also loved me.

The purpose of Sacrifice and Consecration and Communion is fraternal union of all the children of God in Christ in union with the Father, here and hereafter. For that reason one of the Communion prayers is the *Our Father*.

As the liturgy just before the Communion, aware of impending danger, prays for the grace of final perseverance and life everlasting, so does Saint Bernard pray for Dante just before he is admitted to the Beatific Vision, lest when he returns to the daily life of earth to fulfill his mission he weaken and falter. ITE MISSA EST, usually translated "Go; the Mass is finished," permits of the translation, "Go forth! the hour of your mission is come."

At the end of the Mass, the Church places before the faithful the first fourteen verses of the Gospel according to Saint John. Before they disperse to perform their assigned tasks in the service of God, she carries their thoughts back to the beginning, back to Infinite Absolute Being — the Source of all being, back to God and the Word. She reminds them that the Word was made Flesh and dwelt among men and redeemed them, that the Sacrifice of the Mass in which they have just participated is the renewal of that Redemption. She points out that in the Mass they have seen his glory, the glory of the only begotten of the Father, seen it with the eyes of faith. It is with the actual vision of that glory vouchsafed to Dante that the *Divine Comedy* closes, the vision of the universe bound together by love, the vision of the God-Man in the glory of the Father and the Holy Spirit.

Though the Church in her liturgy displays a passion for unity, she never loses sight of the individual man. What is true of the Church is true also of Dante — in his use of prayer as well as in his whole program for political, religious, and social solidarity. The prayers throughout the *Divine Comedy* stress this solidarity; nevertheless, Dante makes it quite clear that he believes also in prayer which wells from the heart of the individual man to meet his peculiar individual needs. In fact, many of the liturgical prayers which he uses — as, for example, the *Miserere* — were originally intensely personal. Three of the prayers in the Empyrean, among the most beautiful in the whole *Commedia* and in the whole realm of literature, are the outpourings of Dante's own heart: his prayer to Beatrice (XXXI:79–90); Saint Bernard's prayer to the Virgin (XXXIII:1–39); and the rhapsody to the Trinity (XXXIII:124–125), which may well be called a prayer. Indeed, all through the poem, Dante shows how, by meditation and contemplation, all liturgical prayer can and does have a highly individual flavor even when there is one sound of many voices indistinguishable lifted with one fire of charity to praise one God.

NOTES

1. Among the Jews and in Apostolic times, as is evident from *Acts* (3:1 and 10:9), some of these hours which later became canonical hours designated by the Church for the recitation of the Office were held as hours of prayer. For further information on this point, consult Pius Parsch, *The Breviary Explained,* trans. by William Nayden, C.Ss.R., and Carl Hoegerl, C.Ss.R. (Saint Louis, 1952), Chapter II, "Some Historical Notes on the Breviary," pp. 10–28.
2. Matthew Britt, O.S.B., *The Hymns of the Breviary and Missal,* rev. ed. (New York, 1924), p. 31.
3. See the *Banquet* III, vi, 1 and IV, xxiii, 8 for Dante's discussion of these hours.
4. *Nibelungenlied,* 17th Adventure, stanza 1004.

5. John of Joinville, *The Life of St. Louis*, trans. René Hague from the text ed. by Natalis de Wailley (New York, 1955), p. 202. John of Joinville has more to say of the King's own devotion to the Office and the Mass. Evidently the love of liturgical prayer was inculcated by his mother Blanche of Castile, as John writes on page 41:

"His soul was watched over by the teachings of his mother who taught him to believe in God and to love him, and chose for him the company only of men of religion. Child though he was, she made him hear all the hours of the Office and listen to the sermons on feast days."

John of Joinville wrote also of the liturgical ordering of the days of Louis when he was king of France, p. 36:

"He so arranged the business of governing his country that every day he heard the Hours of the Office sung, and a Requiem Mass without chant, and then a sung Mass of the day or the feast if there was one. Every day after dinner he rested on his bed, and when he had slept and rested he said the Office of the Dead privately in his room with one of his chaplains, before hearing Vespers. In the evening he heard Compline."

6. *Book of Saints* compiled by Benedictine Monks of St. Augustine's Abbey, Ramsgate, 3 ed. (New York, 1942). See also Joan Windham, *More Saints for Six O'Clock* (New York, 1937), pp. 92–97.

7. Elizabeth von Schmidt-Pauli, *Saint Elizabeth*, trans. Olga Marx (New York, 1932), p. 20.

8. Much of this material on the historical-redemptive background of the canonical hours is adapted from Parsch, *op. cit.*, pp. 31–41.

9. For a classic appreciation of the prayers of the Breviary see Newman, *Tracts for the Times* (Oxford, 1840), No. 75. For a modern appreciation see E. I. Watkin, *The Praise of Glory, A Commentary on Lauds and Vespers* (New York, 1942).

10. Herbert Thurston, S.J., *Familiar Prayers, Their Origin and History*, ed. Philip Caraman, S.J. (Westminster, Maryland, 1953), "The Origins of the Hail Mary," Chap. VI, pp. 90–114.

11. There are at least seven phrasings of the Creed, all of which are a faithful summary of the truths taught in the Church. Some of them, for example, the long form of the Creed of Epiphanius (c. 374) and that of the Council of Trent (1564) were prompted by controversies and were phrased to refute the errors of unbelievers or heretics; others served merely as a profession of faith. The three which are part of the liturgy of the Western Church and are named here for that reason date from early Christian centuries. The *Apostles' Creed*, though not written by the Apostles, is an official summary of faith. The title *Apostles' Creed* is found for the first time in a letter sent by the Synod of Milan (390) to Pope Siricius (384–398). The creed known as the *Nicene Creed* stems from the creed promulgated at the Council of Nicaea (325), the first ecumenical council. The form which is used in the Western Church and is familiar to all Catholics as the creed used in the Mass was called the Nicene-Constantinopolitan Creed (381), which made its way into the liturgy of the Eastern Church after the Councils of Ephesus (431) and Chalcedon (451). It was introduced into the liturgy of the Western Church toward the end of the eighth century. The exact date of the *Athanasian Creed* is not certain nor is its author, who almost certainly was not Athanasius. It was probably written in the fifth or sixth century.

The material on the creeds is adapted from John F. Clarkson, S.J., *et al.*, *The Church Teaches: Documents of the Church in English Translation* (St. Louis, 1955), pp. 1–9.

12. *The Roman Ritual in Latin and English,* trans. and ed. by Philip T. Weller (Milwaukee, 1942), Vol. III, pp. 444–461.
13. Not all theologians, among them Saint Thomas, believe that the souls in Purgatory can and do pray for the living. Dante echoes the popular belief, popular in the thirteenth century as it is in the twentieth, that the souls in Purgatory can and do help living, struggling men. Frequently in the *Purgatorio,* Dante and Virgil have difficulty in finding their way from one cornice to another and ask souls to direct them. Dante could have chosen other means of solving their difficulties, but he chooses to have the souls direct him. In an article in the *Ecclesiastical Review* Albert R. Bandini, says, "Dante's point of view should have weight because he has always been esteemed the greatest of lay theologians; in fact he is called 'Theologus Dantes.' " Albert R. Bandini, "Orthodoxy of Dante's Purgatory," *Ecclesiastical Review,* November, 1930, Vol. 83, pp. 463–473.
14. The image of Saint John the Baptist as the precursor of Christ is a favorite in the works of Dante. In the *New Life* XXIV, there is another striking use of the image. See the discussion of this point in Chapter III, p. 67.
15. "In the chapel of St. Louis IX, it was the almost invariable custom to sing the antiphon *Salve Regina* at the end of Compline. In 1239 Gregory IX decreed that the *Salve Regina* be sung after Compline on Fridays." Parsch, *op. cit.,* p. 174.
16. There is a charming story told of the origin of the so-called *Salve* procession. Blessed Jordan of Saxony, the second Master General of the Dominicans, in his *Lives of the Brothers* (the Dominican counterpart of the *Fioretti,* which tells stories of the early members of the Franciscan Order) writes of how one of the Brothers — tradition says he was Blessed Jordan himself — in a dream saw the Virgin Mary blessing the brethren in the dormitory as they slept. Straightway Blessed Jordan ordered that the *Salve* be sung in procession as part of the Office. It is quite possible that Dante knew this story; be that as it may, he makes the safety of the princes in the valley hinge on the intercessory prayer of the Virgin who has sent the protecting angels in answer to the *Salve.* It is significant also that Mary's queenship and her role as the Mediatrix of all graces are presented to Dante on the first rung of the ladder that leads to God; a sort of prelude to his presentation of her in both of these roles in the Empyrean. See *Lives of the Brethren of the Order of Preachers 1206–1259* in the translation of Placid Conway, O.P. (New York, 1924), p. 44; or (London: Blackfriars, 1955), p. 108.
17. At La Verna in the chapel built over the spot where Saint Francis received the stigmata there is a reference to *Paradiso* XI:41–117, where Dante eulogizes Saint Francis and refers to his receiving the stigmata. In the wood of the back of each choir stall is the effigy of one who vouched for the sanctity of Saint Francis, among them Dante Alighieri.
18. For an excellent discussion of the participation of the laity in the Sacrifice of the Mass, consult Dom Boeser, O.S.B., *The Mass Liturgy,* trans. Charles Cannon, O.S.B. (Milwaukee, 1932).

EPILOGUE

DANTE SPEAKS TO US

This way he goes who goes in quest of peace.
Purgatorio XXIV:141

ante speaks to contemporary Americans on subjects which are of grave importance to them in this era of anxiety and perplexity about peace and freedom, unity among nations, and ways of making love and justice prevail. Since Dante's objectives in writing the *Divine Comedy* — and for that matter the *Monarchy* and the *Eloquence* also, which he wrote as interludes during the period when he was working on the *Commedia* — express his concern with the same problems and his suggestions for their solution, it is not surprising that men are turning to all these works with renewed interest. Nor is it surprising that since Dante wrote the greatest of these works in the vernacular in order to reach the learned and unlearned citizens of his Italy, we, too, should be making his message available to all the people of our day by translating his books into our language. For what Dante has to say about politics, righteousness, and love, which in the *Eloquence* he calls the three fit subjects for poetry, has, even in a translation of his vivid and impassioned verse, power to stir the minds and wills of men beyond the possibilities of the most lucid prose.

Dante wrote his poem at the beginning of the rise of nationalism in Europe. Alarmed at the disunity in the human family, convinced that increasing disunity would prevail if nationalism developed, he raised his voice in protest against the dog-eat-dog attitude in the political world of the early fourteenth century. Between that century and the heyday of nationalism which lies immediately behind our

344

generation, that statism in religion and politics which developed seemed altogether acceptable to the vast majority of the people of the Western World. But the "rugged individualism" which gave nationalist states complete autonomy in colonization and other governmental activities, including the exploiting of "inferior" peoples and the whole theory of progress which was concomitant with it exploded in the second quarter of the twentieth century with the rise of totalitarianism. Men, especially in the democracies, began to re-examine the ideals of political unity expounded by the master poet of the Middle Ages to see what they might hold for modern man.

Thoughtful men in the democracies faced up to the fact that totalitarianism was the bitter fruit of the long growth of anthropocentric humanism which characterized the Renaissance and post-Renaissance centuries, that each branch of the vicious tree represented an ideology which was the development of a false ideal of individualism and of the place of the individual in the social order, that each branch threw the individual man out of his proper relationship to God and his fellow men. These men were appalled at the superman and superrace ideology of the National Socialists with its utter disregard of all individuals except the supermen of the superrace and its reduction of the God of the universe to a deity interested in one nation only; they were even more appalled at the collectivist ideology of the Communists, who swallowed the individual completely and who denied the very existence of God; they were terrified by the ruthless inhumanity displayed by both totalitarian groups and by their declaration of intent to subjugate the world.

It was then that men interested as Dante was in politics, righteousness, and love realized with an awakened surety that the inalienable rights of man — of every man — have their soundest foundation in religion and the historic Christian values, that without these it is impossible to establish international good faith. Some of these men rediscovered the political, philosophical, social, and religious outlook of thinkers like Dante, whose ideas, at the height of liberal theology and nationalist autonomy, had seemed hopelessly obsolete. Having experienced two global wars and a disquieting cold war and finding totalitarianism still rampant, they read with quickened understanding statements from Dante's treatise on government: "peace is the best of all those things which are ordained for our blessedness"; "freedom is the greatest gift conferred by God on human nature, for through it we have our felicity as men here and hereafter"; "peace is impossible unless there is right legislation by a justly ordained government operating under the concept that men exist for their own sakes and that government exists to insure justice and freedom to individual men."

Dante saw that man is possessed of a wondrous yet frightening freedom. More and more, our generation is turning from the behavioristic and mechanistic psychology of recent decades to renewed faith in the freedom of man to act, an arresting realization that man is free to do evil as well as good, free to destroy as well as to build. In a technological age this renewed faith breeds a sense of insecurity and danger as well as a sense of confidence. The man of yesterday engaged in the labor of technological research on the basis that technology promoted the well-being of man; it gave him leisure for cultural pursuits; it harnessed nature and made it man's servant. The man of today realizes that the major objective of technology is to promote power, which *may* be used for creative purposes; but which, in the hands of the autonomous state, can be used for ruthless destruction, even — and perhaps one can say especially — for the destruction of humanity itself. More and more, thoughtful men realize that what happens to power and to mankind depends upon the use man makes of power. They realize, too, that our times demand with an urgency which is immediate even for temporal safety, a universal standard of ethics, a divine standard of righteousness such as prevailed in Dante's day, and an authorized teaching body to expound and enforce it. Much of the derangement in our modern world rises from the confusion of tongues in this moral crisis.

Dante taught and practiced the ethical principle that where there is freedom there is responsibility, individual responsibility; for freedom of the will is a gift to individual men. Contemporary students in this age of technology and the machine, which has produced the "mass man," who is inclined to live according to the laws of standardization and conformity, who in the name of democracy frequently dodges individual responsibility behind committee decisions, who frequently claims that society or environment is at fault when criminals violate the moral law, are curiously interested in a poet who every-where declares unequivocally that justice is and must be meted out to individuals for what individuals do or fail to do, who brings before them with unforgettable vividness the lives of the damned, the repentant, and the blessed, who makes them see evil for what it is and turn from it, who makes them desire that truth and light which make the Empyrean radiant and shows them how to climb toward that radiance.

Nowhere in literature do personalities represent so powerfully what they are as in the *Divine Comedy*. All through Hell, though sinners are categorized according to the sins they have committed — adultery, violence, fraud, or treachery — they are distinct persons accepting their changeless punishment according to their unique characteristics: Francesca, Pier delle Vigne, Ulysses, Bocca. In Purgatory it is the same. To set love in order there is a mountain to climb, at the top of which there is peace. But each climber attacks the problem in his own way and as a result of what he is and what he has done; the personalities are distinct and unforgettable: Pia and Buonconte in the Ante-Purgatory, Forese and Statius and Marco on the cornices. And who could forget Saint Thomas dancing the carol in the Heaven of the Sun, Cacciaguida moving with meteoric swiftness to greet Dante in Mars, or Bernard praying to the Virgin? Here is a thirteenth-century poet who presents graphically the principle of individual differences on which American education is presumably built and the Christian philosophic concept of the indestructibility of the entire human personality.

The *Divine Comedy* is a study of what man through the exercise of his free will can make of himself and of the society of which he is a part. Dante believes that man is a rational social animal who lives in ever widening circles of the temporal social order: as a member of a family, a community, a state, and a world-state, which he called empire. He believes, moreover, that these social groups are not mere aggregates of individuals like a heap of kernels of wheat but that among men there is organic unity because all men are actual or potential members of the Mystical Body of Christ and that there-fore there can be no such thing as a private sin or a private virtue. Every act of every individual man has social repercussions. Dante believes that since justice is a virtue involving other persons, peace can exist only among disciplined persons dedicated to maintaining the harmony of the universe. Those in Hell are there because they have destroyed the peace; those in Purgatory, who have made mistakes and are now learning how to correct them, are in quest of peace; those in Heaven have attained peace. In order to describe the fullness of life, Dante needs the canvas of eternity, for the ultimate answers to the solutions of the problems of this life are not — for a man of faith — to be found in time.

"Peace," wrote Saint Thomas Aquinas, "is the work of justice indirectly, insofar as justice removes the obstacles to peace: but it is the work of charity directly since charity according to its very nature, causes peace. For love is a unitive force." Dante believes quite literally that it is love that makes the world go round. Everyone who has heard of Dante has heard of Beatrice. But not everyone knows that it is Beatrice who leads Dante to perfect peace and perfect love. This poem written to honor Beatrice is the world's greatest love poem. The romance of Dante and Beatrice has always had a singular appeal and is not the least important factor in the contemporary interest in the *Divine Comedy*. In our world, where love and its mutual responsibilities are taken lightly, Beatrician love has become a symbol of spiritual love as opposed to animality. In a philosophic and theological as well as a romantic way, the *Divine Comedy* is an exposition of the abuse or right use of love as well as of freedom. Hell is disordered love; Purgatory is the setting of love in order; Heaven is perfect love.

Since Dante wrote the *Divine Comedy* in the language of the people because he wanted to reach the ordinary citizen, throughout the poem he is addressing in a particular way the individual man. He says to us of the twentieth century in our efforts to attain world peace what he said to his contemporaries of the thirteenth and early fourteenth centuries, that we must begin to build at the foundation and not at the pinnacle. The foundation is the individual man, not the United Nations. World peace is every man's responsibility. The individual man must cast out the seven capital sins of pride and envy and anger and sloth and avarice and gluttony and lust. These destroy the peace in a man's own soul, in the family, in the nation, in the world.

There are other facets of Dante's thought in relation to peace and love and social solidarity which are extremely significant and which have been emphasized in the past decade. One of these is the matter of the spirit world of angels and devils. The early twentieth-century man was inclined to identify the real with the seen, with what can be weighed or measured in a laboratory. A certain type of technician of the early decades of the century, who like his predecessor of the nineteenth, made a religion of science had no place in his scheme of things for an angel, fallen or faithful. What he could not understand he was prone to deny. In these mid-century days, however, the metaphysicians and scientists have been coming to terms: some of the best of the contemporary scientists are moving back to the synthesis of physics and metaphysics, characteristic of the work of Plato and Aristotle and of the schoolmen of Dante's time. In our universities there are today scientists who are also philosophers, who, like Dante, have professed their belief in the spiritual nature of the universe.

This change in point of view is not surprising in the face of the findings of modern science. Today our physical universe seems almost limitless: astronomers have discovered whole galaxies of stars and uncounted Milky Ways spreading out into space, geologists point out that our world existed for millions of years before man came into it. All of this scientific evidence serves to push human history into its proper place in the history of the physical cosmos and to lead thoughtful men to a revaluation of that immense spiritual universe of the philosophers and theologians, made up of spiritual worlds of which the world of man is but one. Men who today have become conscious of the immensity of the physical universe find themselves not unwilling to conceive the possibility of a spiritual universe even more mighty, that spiritual cosmos involved in the theology of the angels — intelligences not bound by the laws of time nor by those of space. Such a universe was familiar to the thought of Dante.

Scholars in other fields (to say nothing of men whose avocation is letters) are displaying an interest in another aspect of the spirit world which to Dante was extremely important, namely, the power of Satan. Santayana in one of his last books *Dominations and Powers* discusses the demoniac lure of power; a recent book called *German History: Some New German Views* edited by Hans Kohn, professor of history in the College of the City of New York, presents essays by ten leading contemporary German historians, several of whom speak of the demoniac lure of power among their leaders. One of them quotes Bismarck as saying he believed he was possessed by a Teutonic devil; another speaks of the daemon in Hitler; Romano Guardini in his *The End of the Modern World* warns that demons may take possession of the faculties of man if he does not answer for them with his conscience. The reader of these books is mindful of Saint Paul (Eph. 6:11–17) that our wrestling is not against flesh and blood but against principalities and powers.

There is another important way in which Dante speaks to the man of the present time, not to the academicians but to all those God-hungry men and women who make up the rank and file of the nations, especially it would seem in America, where religion today makes a strong appeal. There is no doubt that in these past decades there has been a quickening of interest in the supernatural. Church attendance has increased; books of all kinds with a religious emphasis are best sellers; popular magazines carry long articles on religious subjects. Broadway and Hollywood have "tried God" and profited. To all of these Dante has a vital message in many areas, one of which is his firm belief that men should manifest their social solidarity by praying together, the whole of mankind raising their voices in chanting the psalms and by engaging in other communal prayer. Today we have slogans which Dante would approve, for example, "The family that prays together stays together." The cult of self, of the individual going out to commune with nature and nature's God without ever turning to worship with his fellow man, is fading. Today men of all creeds gather for prayer in parks and theaters and football stadia. There has been in many religious groups a return to Gregorian chant and a revival of interest in ancient liturgical prayers. But there is a concerted effort to accommodate liturgical prayer and other prayer to the needs of the people moving on the close schedule of the machine age, to shorten the ritual, to bring out its dramatic quality, to encourage communal participation. Everywhere there is evidence of the restoration of communal worship.

The living Dante in his strife-torn world had so powerful an appreciation of the rights and responsibilities of the individual in the social order that throughout his life he dedicated all his resources to achieving the values he treasured. In his early political life in Florence and in the difficult years of his exile even when he was under penalty of death by fire for his fearless pronouncements, he used his towering talents in his labor for peace and freedom. Out of these years chastened by suffering came the "poem in which heaven and earth had a part," the poem which had made him "lean for many years." Though its political message and the message of the other writings of the exiled years are important, it is possible that in the countries of the free world his message is a more personal message to individual citizens for whom in the beginnings of American history there is a splendid example set by the signers of the Constitution, and in contemporary history by the revolt of the Hungarians, both of which exemplify the spirit of sacrifice, high courage, and persistent hope which characterize Dante.

Perhaps Dante's primary message to us of fewer gifts is an ethical message completely within our powers of fulfillment. To each of us in the countries of the free world he says today as he said in the fourteenth century to the individual men and women of his own Italy that while there is still time we must shake ourselves out of our lethargy; by self-discipline set love in order in ourselves, our families, and our immediate social groups, using all our powers to make righteousness prevail. From us, if every individual man of us will make an earnest effort and call upon God for help, love and righteousness can and will spread throughout our troubled world.

APPENDIX

"Dante pointed the way; John XXII in 1323 enrolled him (Saint Thomas) in the ranks of the saints; Pius V proclaimed him a doctor of the Church, calling him the Angelic Doctor; Leo XIII declared and appointed him patron of the Catholic schools."

The column erected at Compaldino in 1921 to commemorate Dante who fought there in the cavalry of Florence on June 11, 1289

The chapel of St. Dominic at Santa Maria Novella in Florence. On the pillar at the visitor's left is the plaque commemorating Dante